Concepts and Issues in
Health Care Computing

COMPUTERS IN HEALTH CARE   VOLUME I

Concepts and Issues in Health Care Computing

H. Dominic Covvey
Clinicom Computing Services International, Inc.
Winnipeg, Manitoba, Canada

Nancy H. Craven, M.D.
Clinicom Computing Services International, Inc.
Winnipeg, Manitoba, Canada

Neil H. McAlister, M.D.
Clinicom Computing Services International, Inc.
Toronto, Ontario, Canada

Illustrated

The C. V. Mosby Company
ST. LOUIS · TORONTO · PRINCETON   1985

362.1028
C873 C

A TRADITION OF PUBLISHING EXCELLENCE

Editor: Nancy Mullins
Assistant editor: Maureen Slaten
Manuscript editor: Dale Woolery
Book design: Jeanne Genz
Cover design: Kathleen A. Johnson
Production: Barbara Merritt

Cover photograph by Four By Five, Inc.

This is a revised and updated edition of books previously published by Addison-Wesley Publishing Company, Inc., entitled *Computers in the Practice of Medicine,* Volumes I and II.

Copyright © 1985 by The C.V. Mosby Company

All rights reserved. No part of this publication may be reproduced, stored in a retrieval system, or transmitted, in any form or by any means, electronic, mechanical, photocopying, recording, or otherwise, without prior written permission from the publisher.

Printed in the United States of America

The C.V. Mosby Company
11830 Westline Industrial Drive, St. Louis, Missouri 63146

Library of Congress Cataloging in Publication Data

Covvey, H. Dominic.
  Concepts and issues in health care computing.

  (Computers in health care ; v. 1)
  Bibliography: p.
  Includes index.
  1. Medicine—Data processing. 2. Medical care—
Data processing. I. Craven, Nancy H.
II. McAlister, Neil Harding, 1952-   . III. Title. IV. Series.
[DNLM: 1. Computers. 2. Delivery of Health Care.
3. Medicine. 4. Information Systems. W1 CO457XY v. 1 /
W 26.5 C873c]
R858.C683   1985   362.1′028′54   84-14908
ISBN 0-8016-3196-3

VT/VH/VH 9 8 7 6 5 4 3 2 1   03/D/330

TO
Dr. William Cass,
Dr. R. M. Cherniack,
and **Dr. John Toogood,**
who helped us bring computers
and medicine together

PREFACE

The computer is becoming increasingly more commonplace in the practice of health care. We find desktop computers in many hospital departments and physicians' offices, and we see the number of hospital information systems growing. In the last decade the health care field has begun to realize the potential benefits of computerization that business and industry were the first to discover.

Unfortunately, health care professionals often have not had the training to use computers effectively or to make decisions on how computers might aid them. The books in this series will try to provide this necessary information. They will be useful for physicians, dentists, nurses, hospital administrators, laboratory personnel, and students who expect to use computers in their health care careers. The goals are to make readers comfortable with this new technology and to address some of the important issues in health care computing.

Perhaps the most cogent reason for health care professionals to become at ease and competent with computer systems is to retain control. If control over the employment of computers is in the hands of the health care professional, then there is good reason to believe the computers will be applied in the right areas and in the most productive ways. Alternatively, the technology will be in the hands of the technocrat and the nonmedical expert, resulting in what we believe will be a deleterious effect on both personnel and health care itself.

This book, the first in the series, describes computing machinery and concepts of programming, along with considerations in implementing computer systems in the health care environment. Lists of people and current books and journals in health care computing, as well as magazines and journals reviewing computer systems, appear in the appendices. A glossary is also included.

The reader will notice that each chapter is preceded by a schematic diagram of a computer system. In some chapters these areas are shaded to indicate topics covered in those chapters. We hope that use of this block diagram will help the reader see computers from a systems viewpoint (i.e., an integrated whole composed of many parts).

We hope this book will also be useful to computer specialists, although the technical details will be familiar to them. The special problems faced by health care professionals and the unique features of health care systems will give computer scientists a clearer picture of health care computing as a separate academic field and perhaps stimulate students' interest in this exciting career area.

We wish to acknowledge the assistance of Bill Gruener in helping to make this book possible, Nancy Mullins for her advice and encouragement, Maureen Slaten for her suggestions, and Pat Miller for her efforts above and beyond the call of secretarial duty.

H. Dominic Covvey
Nancy H. Craven
Neil H. McAlister

CONTENTS

Introduction, 1

1 Computer systems, 3
Objectives, 4
The computer configuration, 7
  Hardware, 7
  Software, 8

2 Computer hardware, 9
The central processing unit, 10
Internal memory, 11
Input devices, 14
Output devices, 19
Storage devices, 23
Small, medium, and large computers, 26
The computer in context, 30
What's next? 30

3 Communications, 33
Asynchronous method, 35
Synchronous method, 36
  Full duplex mode, 37
  Half duplex mode, 37
Branches of the family tree, 37
Networks, 41
Other communications structures, 41
A forgotten alternative, 42
Trade-offs, 42

4 Hardware in summary, 45
Going shopping, 46
First things first, 47
Buy, lease, rent, 47
Choosing a supplier, 49
Warnings, 52
The fight against extinction, 52
Resistance to change, 53
What's missing? 54

5 Computer software, 55
An analogy, 56
What is a program? 56
Hard-wired programming, 57
The stored program, 58
Assemblers, 58
Beyond assemblers, 59
The programming process, 60
When to program, 61
Not so soft, 62

6 Operating systems, 63
Time-driven operating systems, 67
Event-driven operating systems, 68
Limitations, 70
Other functions of operating systems, 70
Problems with operating systems, 71
Doing the impossible, 72

7 Programming languages and applications packages, 73
Taking shortcuts: the macro assembler, 74
Higher-level languages, 75
  Compilers, 76
  Interpreters, 77
  Beyond high-level languages, 78
  Extensions to high-level languages, 78
Applications programs and packages, 79
The language hierarchy, 80
  Very high-level languages, 80
Choosing your tools, 81

8 The system in situ, 83
People and their roles, 84
The well-tempered system, 84
The software specification, 85

The functional specification, 85
The contract, 86
Turnkey systems, 87
Do-it-yourself systems, 87
Selecting a supplier, 88
Computer personnel, 89
   Development staff, 90
   Operational staff, 91
Getting going, 92
Monitoring progress, 93

9 Limitations of technology, 97

The unreality of computer memory, 98
Limitations of the input process, 99
How output limits us, 103
Software and its limits, 104
Communications: design versus reality, 105
The human factor, 105
On creativity, 107
A series of hurdles, 107

10 What are the issues? 109

Funding health care computing, 110
Technical issues, 110
   Software engineering, 110
   Human engineering, 111
   Privacy and security, 111
   Economics, 112
   Functional specifications and contracts, 112
Management issues, 113
   Managing systems development, 113
   Organizing for automation, 113
Educational issues, 113
   Training health care–computing specialists, 113
   Conspicuous computing and consumer education, 113
The future of health care computing, 114
Who cares? 114

11 A story of failure, 117

12 Software engineering, 123

Why engineer software? 124
The design phase, 126
   Documentation, 127
The coding phase, 128
The testing phase: exterminating bugs, 128
Software maintenance, 130
Project management, 131
The bottom line, 131

13 Human engineering, 135

Humanizing technology, 136
   Human engineering, 136
   The input process, 137
   The output process, 139
   Privacy and security, 140
   Reliability, 141
Computerizing people, 142
Beasts of burden, 142

14 Privacy and security, 145

Privacy, 146
Security, 147
Security of computer-based health care data, 147
Threats, 148
   The magnitude of the threats, 149
   Protective measures, 150
      Backup, 150
      Physical security, 151
      Fire protection, 151
      Computer defenses, 151
      Procedures, 153
   Conceptual security, 153
Thinking the unthinkable, 153

15 Economics of health care computing, 157

Cost-effectiveness, 160
Costs: think of everything, 162
   Hardware, 163
   Software, 164
   Hardware maintenance, 165
   Software maintenance, 166

Staff, 167
Supplies, 167
Environmental costs, 168
Miscellaneous, 168
Savings, 169
  Reducing personnel costs, 169
  Increasing productivity, 170
  Reducing staff turnover, 170
  Saving supplies, 170
  Collecting more money, 170
  Decreasing reliance on more expensive methods, 171
  Discounts and tax savings, 171
Adding it up, 171

16 Functional specifications and contracts, 173

Why a functional specification? 174
  Reality versus dreams, 174
  Peer review, 174
  Guidance to developers, 175
  Contracts, 177
The format, 177
  The introduction, 177
  The external specification, 178
  Software tools, 179
  Hardware, 179
  Applications software, 180
  Documentation, 180
  The schedule, 180
  General terms of acquisition, 181

17 Managing health care–computing projects, 183

Attributes of the health care–computing manager, 184
Feasibility study, 184
The proposal, 185
The development/acquisition period, 186
  The overseer, 186
  The interpreter, 186
  The quality control officer, 187
Turnkey systems, 187
The most important job, 188

18 Organizing for automation, 191

The impact of computer systems, 193
Evolution versus revolution, 194
Politics of computing, 195
  Administrative computing versus patient-care and medical research computing, 196
  Patient-care computing versus medical research computing, 197
Avoiding conflicts, 197
  Management's role, 197
  The computer advisory committee, 200
  The user's role, 201
Realities in health care computing, 201

19 Training health care–computing specialists, 203

Skills of the health care–computing specialist, 205
  Computer science background, 206
  Health care background, 206
  Special training, 207
Universities meet the challenge, 208
  Degree programs, 208
  Supplementary courses, 209
Continuing education: keeping up, 210
  Specialist journals, 210
  Books, 211
  Medical/nursing/allied health journals, 211
  Other technical journals, 211
  Symposia and conferences, 211
  Human interaction, 212
Getting started, 212
The health care–computing specialist, 213

20 Conspicuous computing, 215

Consumer education, 216

21 Funding health care computing, 219

Applying for money, 220
A plan for a formal proposal, 221
  Summary, 221
  Introduction to the problem, 222
  Functional specification, 222
  Previous work, 222
  Critical analysis and comparison, 223
  Selection or plan, 223
  Economic analysis, 224
  Schedule, 224
  Operational detail, 224
  Appraisal of system, 224
  Appendices, 225

22 The future of health care computing, 227

Why use a computer system in health care? 228
  Personnel augmentation, 228
  Management augmentation, 229
  Brain augmentation, 230
  When a computer system is inappropriate in health care, 230
  Robot health care providers, 230
  Self-aggrandizement, 231
  Supporting obsolute methods, 231
  Robbing people of work, 231
  Enshrining the theoretical, 232
A promising future, 232
  Hardware advances, 232
  Software advances, 233
  Advances in our attitudes, 234
A positive influence, 235

Glossary, 237

Appendices

I People active in health care computing, 247
II Books and journals in health care computing, 261
III Journals and magazines reviewing computer hardware/software, 277

**Concepts and Issues in
Health Care Computing**

INTRODUCTION

Health care computing has changed dramatically over the last 15 years, partly because of changes in the capabilities of computer hardware, and partly because of an increasing understanding by the health care community of the potential benefits of computerization for health care.

In the 1960s computers first appeared in hospital business offices and research laboratories. These large machines were used mainly for "number crunching" purposes and were largely isolated from the patient care areas. Gradually an awareness

---

FIGURE I-1
The communication gap.

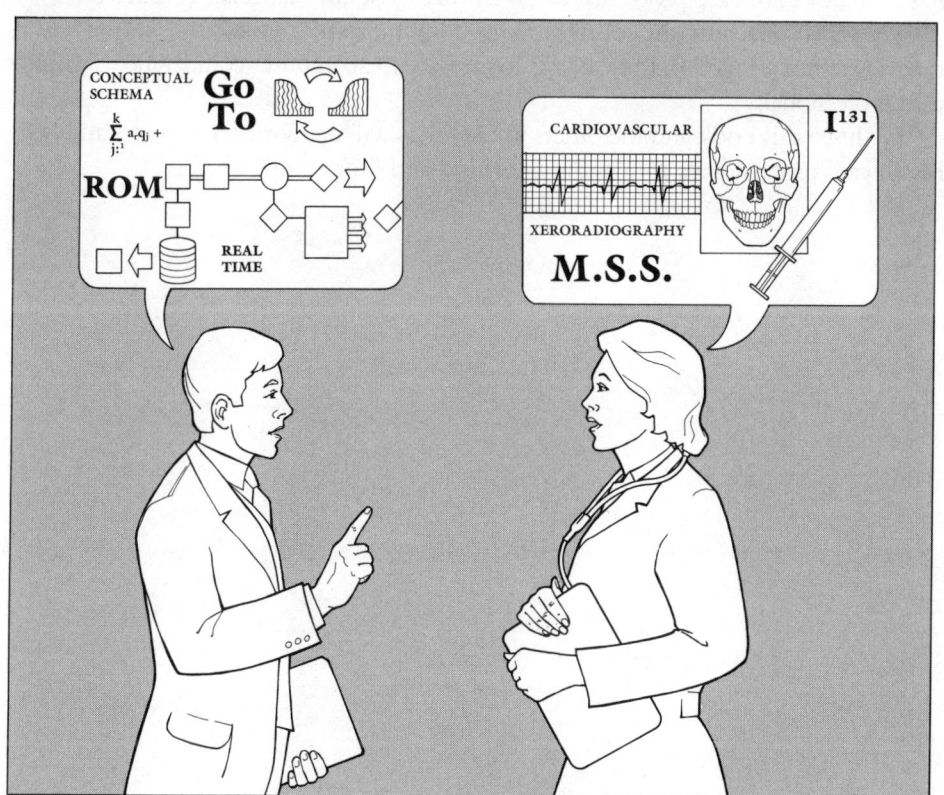

1

developed that computers might also be useful in other areas, and we began to see a few examples of this new technology in admitting departments, intensive care units, and clinical laboratories in the early 1970s.

It was unfortunate, in a sense, that computers were becoming a status symbol in the world outside the hospital, because this attitude also became predominant in the hospital. Thus, a large number of computers were brought into health care areas without serious consideration of their impact.

Now it seems that the health care community is becoming more realistic in its expectations of computers. As computers have become commonplace in our everyday lives, we realize they are simply a tool to make certain tedious tasks easier to do. And we are beginning to understand that a computer is not the solution to every problem.

A communication gap now exists between health care and computer science. On the one side are the physicians, nurses, and other health care professionals who feel that computers may somehow help them in their work, but who do not understand enough about these machines to approach them intelligently. On the other side are the computer professionals who fully understand computers, but who find health care so inscrutable that they do not know how their computing skills might assist in solving current health care problems, or even what these problems are (Figure I-1).

We are approaching the solution to the communication problem from the health care side, attempting with these books to increase the computer competence of health care professionals.

We hope this book and the others in the series will demystify computers and help health care professionals to identify their uses and limitations.

CHAPTER 1
COMPUTER SYSTEMS

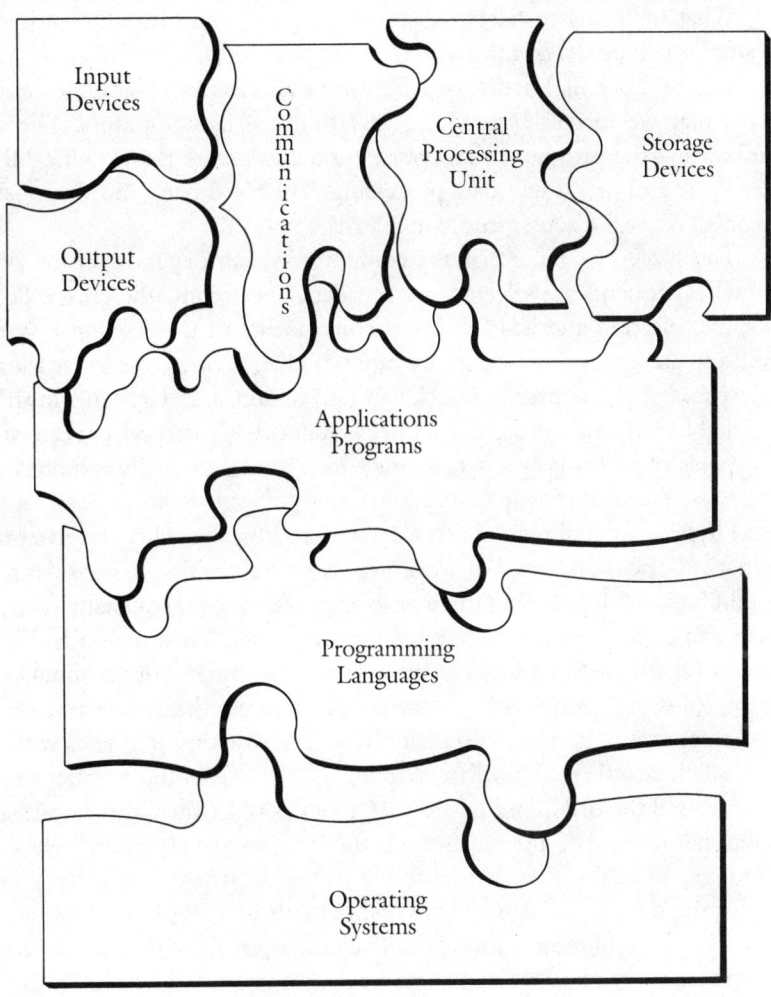

CHAPTER 1

OBJECTIVES

Prerequisite to effectively using computers to solve problems in the health care environment is establishing appropriate **computer systems** in that environment. Using the term "system" is important, for it implies a rational mixture of integrated parts working synergistically to form a useful whole. To gain a basic understanding of the "gross anatomy" of computer systems, it is helpful to separate these systems, somewhat artificially, into components. We will do this in the current section.

What are the parts that make up a computer system? Broadly speaking, a computer system is composed of three parts.

The first part is **hardware**—the physical, electronic, and electromechanical devices that we instantly recognize and think of as computers. The second part is **software**—the programs that control and coordinate the activities of the computer hardware and that direct data processing. The third part, and the most important, is people. We will discuss people in later chapters.

The success or failure of any computer system depends on the skill with which these components are selected and blended. Too frequently, critical decisions regarding the selection and acquisition of components of the computer system for health care use are determined either by random chance or by the persuasion of computer salespersons. Some users are lucky and do obtain useful systems in this manner, but inevitably many others are not so lucky. A poorly chosen system can be a monstrosity incapable of performing the tasks for which it was originally acquired. The danger of such a system is not only failure but also significant financial loss.

Physicians, nurses, administrators, and technicians who perceive problems, either in patient care or in health care research, are often the first to consider that a computer might be helpful in solving these problems. How, then, is a health care professional to plan and direct a computer project that he or she has initiated and help bring it to successful completion? Part of the answer is learning enough about computer hardware, software, and the roles of the people who use these systems to feel comfortable and competent with the jargon and the way of thinking that goes with these systems. We will discuss these in the first chapters. In fact, we would be truer to our concerns if we reversed the order and talked first about people, then about software, and finally about hardware, because hardware is the least important component of the solution. We must, however, first demystify the technical parts of the system.

In the discussion of hardware components and types of software, a rather loose metaphor of evolution is followed. The development of the various components of a computer system has been in some ways a story of the survival of the fittest. At any particular time, the "fittest" component is the one that provides the best performance at the lowest cost. Over the decades that computers have been in existence, advancing technology and automation theory have rendered obsolete a number of devices or concepts. On the other hand, machines and theories that have been able to respond to "evolutionary pressures" have proliferated and given rise to numerous more sophisticated descendents.

Whether evolving computer science theory (which often precedes reality by many years) has actually provided the impetus for new developments in hardware and software, or whether computer scientists have mainly figured out what to do with technology after it has been made available, is a matter of debate—perhaps never to be resolved. One can only observe that the technological imperative often leads to remarkable technical developments in the absence of any justifiable need.

Undeniably, computers are subject to possible abuse. They can make possible a delivery system for nuclear weapons, or they can be used to violate our right to privacy. On the other hand, in the health care field, computers can potentially provide one of the most productive applications of technology for the betterment of humankind.

The evolutionary pressures at work in the health care environment today seem to be concerned mainly with money. Therefore, in the long run the role of computers in health care may be dictated by the degree to which they can demonstrably reduce costs (as opposed to improve the quality of patient care). So far they have not been particularly successful in this regard. However, evolution is at work, and only time will yield the final verdict.

The health care–computer user must know some computer system theory and also where and how these systems can be obtained. Therefore we shall give some attention to the practical considerations of selecting, pricing, and obtaining hardware and software. We may be in a fairly stable period in total computer system cost. Although the cost of hardware has been declining in the past several years, labor costs—and consequently, the cost of software development—have been increasing at the same time. Therefore, the total cost of the complete computer system (both hardware and software) has leveled out and probably will not decline much further (Figure 1-1).

A computer system does not exist in a vacuum. It is always a part of a larger human "system"—less easily defined, but no less real than computer hardware and software components. For instance, some computer systems serve as part of an instrument, such as in a computerized tomography (CT) scanner. To be useful, such computers are carefully interfaced with the instrument, appropriately programmed, and expected to work in synergy with the other parts of the instrument. Other computers are integrated into departments or institutions such as hospitals. These computers must function in this large milieu in ways analogous to how they function in an instrument. In the largest applications, a computer system may be only one component of a very large network. In short, a computer system should never be considered in isolation. Its success or failure is measured by its success in the situation in which it is used.

Therefore, if computer systems are to serve health care needs they must be carefully integrated into the human and procedural domain they are intended to improve.

The computer system cannot do all the adapting, though. The human milieu must also be groomed to accept the computer system. People's fears, concerns, and even anger must be faced and rationalized. A delicate balance will be struck between the human engineering of computer systems and educating potential users to make realistic, attainable demands on such systems.

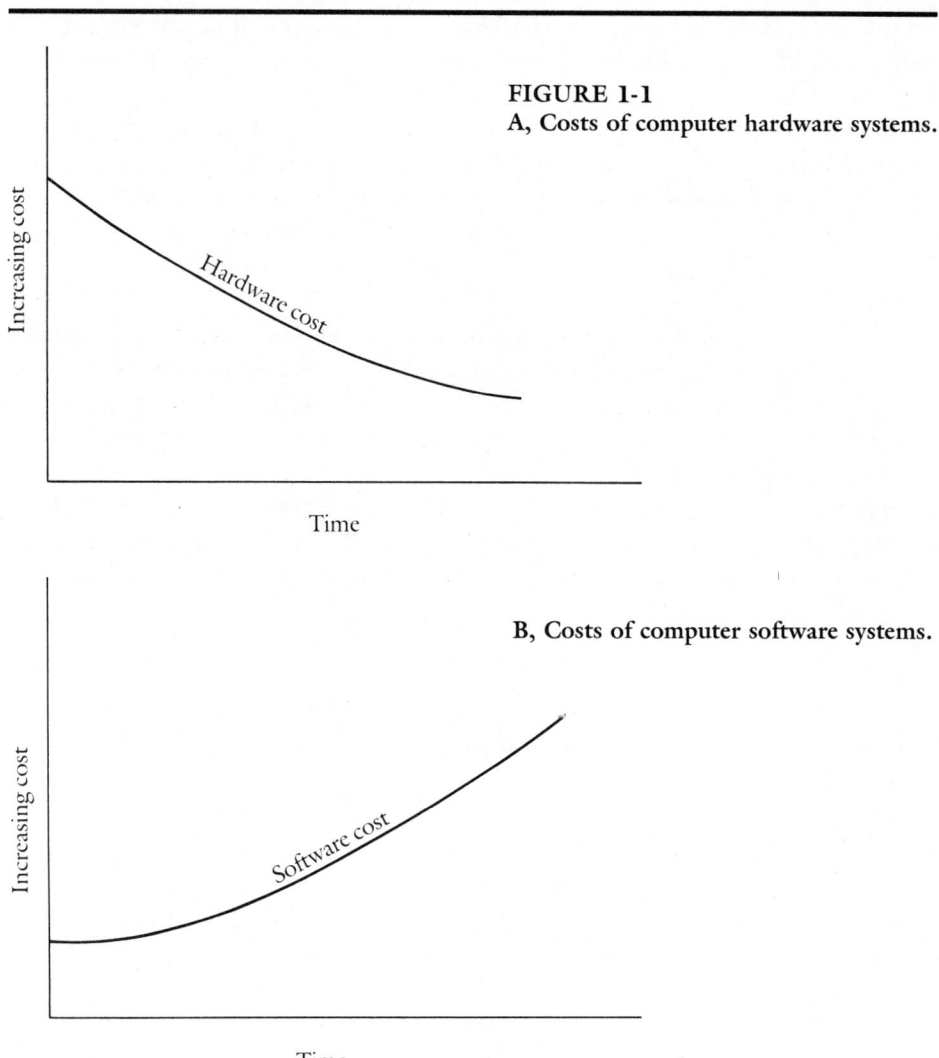

FIGURE 1-1
A, Costs of computer hardware systems.

B, Costs of computer software systems.

THE COMPUTER CONFIGURATION
HARDWARE

Figure 1-2 shows schematically the fundamental components of computer hardware joined together in a computer system. The centerpiece is variously called the **computer,** the **processor,** or usually the **central processing unit (CPU).** We use the term "CPU" to include those parts of the hardware in which calculations and other data manipulations are performed (the **arithmetic logic unit**) and those parts that control the sequence of instructions (the **control unit**). Associated with the CPU is an **internal memory,** in which data and instructions are stored during the actual execution of programs. These components are normally housed in the same enclosure; it makes sense to think of them together. Attached to the CPU are the various **peripheral devices. Input devices** are used to enter data or programs into the computer for processing. Punched-card readers and keyboards are two common examples of input devices. After processing data, the computer gives its answers back to us through **output devices;** printers and videoscreens are two examples. When data or programs must be saved for long periods of time, they are stored on various **secondary memory devices** (or **storage devices**)—magnetic tape or magnetic disk, for instance.

Peripheral devices are usually electromechanical, and as such their rate of performance is many orders of magnitude slower than the purely electronic circuits of the computer itself. Because of this reason, input, output, and storage operations are often the rate-limiting operations in computer data processing. In a personal com-

FIGURE 1-2
Hardware components of a basic computer system.

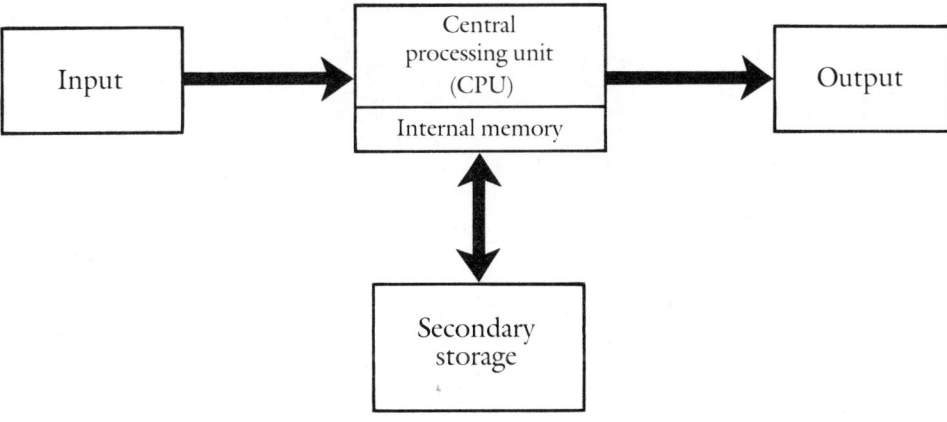

puter the CPU is often idle, waiting for the electromechanical peripheral devices to catch up with it. Because the CPU often has the potential to work much faster than any one task demands of it, in some kinds of systems this feature is exploited so that many users can employ the same computer without mutual interference.

SOFTWARE

Computer software can be divided into two very broad categories—systems software and applications software. Applications software is often simply referred to as **programs.**

Systems software is further divided into two general types: **operating systems** and **programming languages.** Operating systems are the master programs that coordinate the activities of all hardware and software resources in a computer system. In a multiuser environment, operating systems also coordinate the activities of all systems users, so that they do not interfere with each other while sharing the system. Normally, computer programmers write their applications programs conveniently in a human-readable programming language. Programs written in a programming language must be translated from human-understandable statements to the machine instructions the computer system can understand. The systems software that does this, depending on its design, is called a **compiler** or an **interpreter.**

Applications programs, when brought into internal memory, direct the computer to perform particular tasks for users. They may be provided along with the hardware by a systems supplier as part of a computer product designed to answer a specific need in some areas. These complete hardware and software products are called **turnkey systems. Software packages** (groups of applications programs) for general application categories such as statistics or word processing may be purchased, leased, or rented by users, who select the packages that most closely correspond to their individual needs. For many applications, unique programs are written, either by an outside developer or by the user's own inhouse computer group.

• • •

With this brief orientation we may now look more closely at the constituent parts of computer systems. In the following chapters, we shall deal in far greater detail with the topics mentioned only briefly here.

CHAPTER 2
COMPUTER HARDWARE

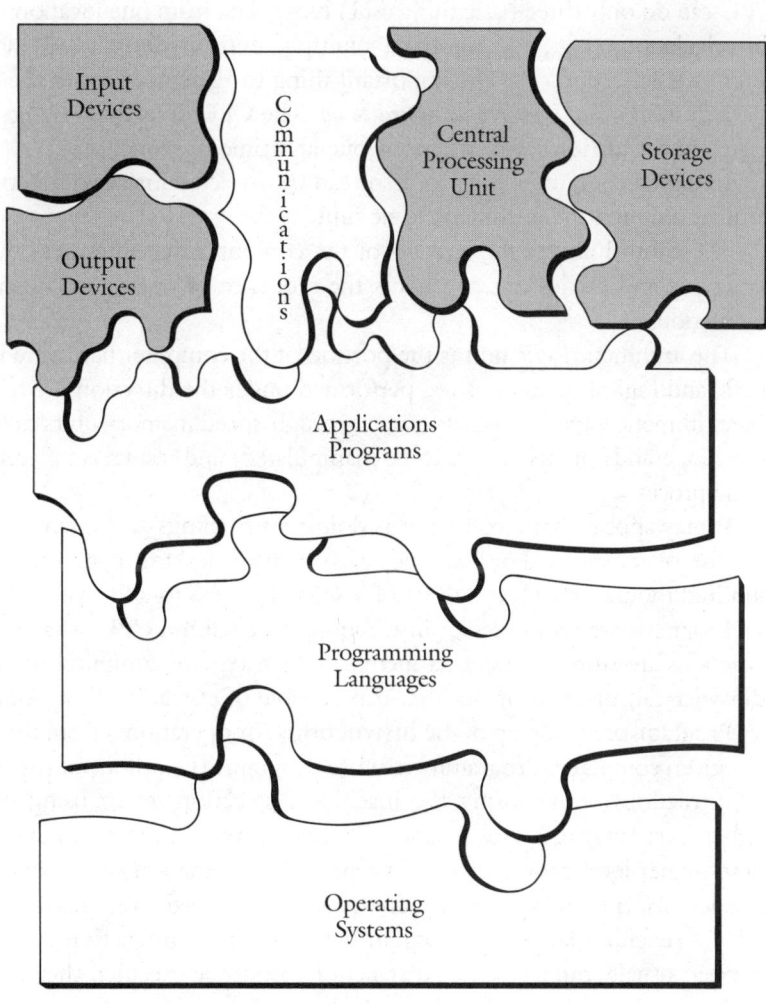

CHAPTER 2

The easiest way to learn about computer hardware is to examine each of the various components and their functions. In doing this, it is important to note that all computers contain common elements, regardless of whether the machine is a mainframe that fills a room or a simple desktop machine.

THE CENTRAL PROCESSING UNIT

The part of every computer that does the "computing" is the central processing unit (CPU), sometimes called "the processor." In today's systems, physically it may be simply a semiconductor "chip" (microcircuit) or a collection of chips on a board. The CPU can do only three basic things: (1) move data from one location to another, (2) do calculations (e.g., add, subtract, multiply, and divide), and (3) do comparisons (e.g., true-false, and/or). The important thing to remember about the CPU is that *it does only what it has been programmed to do*. The CPU does these things at a very high speed, but it carries out instructions one at a time in sequence.

In digital computers the processor can be dissected into two functional units: the control unit and the arithmetic logic unit.

The control unit is the portion of the computer that interprets the program instructions and carries out or directs the sequence of operations determined by the instructions.

The arithmetic logic unit is the portion of the computer hardware in which arithmetic and logical operations are performed under the directions of the control unit. The arithmetic logic unit has its own very high-speed memory units called **registers** in which operands (items of data to be manipulated) and results are placed during arithmetic processing.

It may appear that a computer is doing many things at the same time, but this is because of its speed. For example, even a small desktop computer takes only one hundred thousandth (1/100,000) of a second or less to add two numbers.

Programs are sequences of instructions that tell the CPU what to do. These instructions are stored in internal memory. Each type of computer has its own (often idiosyncratic) **instruction set** that it is capable of executing (i.e., doing).

Programs are made up of the **instructions** (or operations) from the instruction set of a given computer. Programmers write programs (i.e., they put together sequences of instructions) either using the machine instruction set or using what are called higher-level languages (see Chapter 7). Special translating programs exist that turn these higher-level programs into the proper combination of the machine's internal instructions. A sequence of instructions written using the machine's instruction set is called a **machine language** program. Each machine instruction is represented by a number, usually **binary**. When instructions are to be executed they are put into successive internal memory locations. A detailed discussion of programs is found in Chapter 7.

At this point it is reasonable to explain the terms **"bit," "word,"** and **"byte"** and how they relate to the binary number system. As you probably know, the system of numbers we use every day (the decimal system) is structured on a base of 10, probably because we have 10 fingers. In this system there are 10 values a digit can take—0, 1, 2, 3, 4, 5, 6, 7, 8, and 9. In a number with two or more digits (e.g., 35) the number in the rightmost column contains the number of *ones* and the next column contains the number of *tens* (e.g., in 35, there are five ones and three tens). The successive columns contain powers of 10 (e.g., 100s (10^2), 1000s (10^3)).

A computer, however, functions on a much simpler number system. Its number system is formulated on a base of 2, called the binary system, because of the two positions of an electrical switch—on and off. Therefore at the machine level digits only have two possible values—0 and 1. Each digit in such a number is called a *bi*nary *digit* (bit). To write numbers using this system we use powers of 2 instead of powers of 10. The box on pp. 12-13 compares numbers in the decimal and binary number systems. Thus 1011 means (from left to right) 1×2^3, 0×2^2, 1×2^1, 1×2^0 and is equivalent to the number 11 in base 10.

When we hear the term "8-bit machine" or "16-bit machine," this refers to the number of digits used to represent numbers (often called a "word"). Thus it tells us the largest number that a computer can store in a single memory location. For an 8-bit computer the largest number is 11111111 (base 2), or 255 in base 10. For a 16-bit computer the number is much larger 1111111111111111 or 131,071 (base 10). This points out that a clear advantage of range of the larger word computers is quicker arithmetic. It is, of course, possible to store large numbers in even an 8-bit machine, but they must be broken up into pieces, which makes them more difficult to handle quickly. The term "byte" refers to a group of 8 bits that are all (in the case of an 8-bit word) or part (in the case of a 16- or greater bit word) of a word. Usually a byte holds the code for one **alphanumeric** character, whereas the term "bit" refers to the component binary units. Obviously a machine that could contain single numbers in 32-bit words or bytes would be potentially more powerful.

The configuration of bits in every computer not only allows for storing integer numbers, but also for storing alphabetic letters, numeric characters, punctuation characters, and the codes for instructions to the machine. In today's computers the data and the programs are stored in exactly the same way in the memory. This means that programs can be written to change themselves. This facility sometimes turns to a disadvantage, however, when through an error the computer is programmed to pick up data and treat it as instructions.

INTERNAL MEMORY

Closely associated with every CPU is an internal memory. This is a set of temporary storage locations holding the program being run and that the CPU uses to store the results of a calculation or comparison, for example. The memory is physically merely another collection of electronic circuits that provide these storage locations.

DECIMAL AND BINARY NUMBER SYSTEMS

BASE 10 (DECIMAL)

2 9 6 4 (properly written as 2964_{10}, and read as "two nine six four base ten") is a number in base 10.

2964_{10} means (from left to right):

2 thousands	($10 \times 10 \times 10 = 10^3$)	or	2000_{10}
9 hundreds	($10 \times 10 = 10^2$)	or	900_{10}
6 tens	($10 = 10^1$)	or	60_{10}
4 units	($1 = 10^0$)	or	$+\ \ \ 4_{10}$
			2964_{10}

NB: Any number to the zero power is defined as being equal to 1 (e.g., $1^0 = 1$; $10^0 = 1$, etc.).

We can write it this way:

10^3 (1000s)	10^2 (100s)	10^1 (10s)	10^0 (1s)
2	9	6	4

In base 10, the number system we have all learned to work with, there are 10 possible values each digit can take: 0, 1, 2, 3, 4, 5, 6, 7, 8, and 9. Thus numbers can go from:

As many digits as desired to the left of the decimal point	...00000.00000...	As many digits as desired to the right of the decimal point
	to	
As many digits as desired to the left of the decimal point	...99999.99999...	As many digits as desired to the right of the decimal point

BASE 2 (BINARY)

1 0 1 1 (properly written as 1011_2, and read as "one zero one one base two") is a number in base 2.

1011_2 means (from left to right):

1 eight	($2 \times 2 \times 2 = 2^3$)	or	1000_2
0 fours	($2 \times 2 = 2^2$)	or	0000_2
1 two	($2 = 2^1$)	or	0010_2
1 one	($1 = 2^0$)	or	$+0001_2$
			1011_2

NB: Any number to the zero power is defined as being equal to 1 (e.g., $1^0 = 1$; $2^0 = 1$, etc.).

We can write it this way:

2^3 (8s)	2^2 (4s)	2^1 (2s)	2^0 (1s)
1	0	1	1

In base 2, the number system used in digital computers, there are only 2 possible values each digit can take: 0 and 1. Thus numbers can go from:

As many digits as desired   ...00000.00000...   As many digits as desired
to the left of the point   to the right of the point

                                      to

As many digits as desired   ...11111.11111...   As many digits as desired
to the left of the point   to the right of the point

The good news about base 2 is that (for example) addition tables are simpler (there are only 4 rules):

$0 + 0 = 0$
$0 + 1 = 1$
$1 + 0 = 1$
$1 + 1 = 0$ carry 1 or 10_2

To add 1011_2
       0010_2
       $\overline{1101_2}$

          $1 + 0 = 1$
          $1 + 1 = 0$ carry 1
          $0 + 1$ (carried) $= 1$
          $1 + 0 = 1$

(NOTE: $1011_2 = 11_{10}$; $0010_2 = 2_{10}$; and $11_{10} + 2_{10} = 13_{10}$; finally 1101_2, the result of our base 2 addition, $= 13_{10}$.)

In base 10 we would have to remember many more rules (and that would lead to complex circuitry to do addition in a computer).

$1 + 0 = 1$ $2 + 0 = 2$ $8 + 9 = 7$ carry 1, etc.
$1 + 1 = 2$ $2 + 1 = 3$ etc.
$1 + 2 = 3$ $2 + 2 = 4$
$1 + 3 = 4$ etc.
etc.

Thus the binary number system is simply an easier system to design computers to use.

The memory size is commonly measured in bytes. One byte can store one alphabetic or numeric character. A computer with 1024 bytes (or 1 **kilobyte**) can store 1024 (1024 is 2^{10} or 10000000000 base 2) characters. Often this is abbreviated simply as "1K" (and usually called "1000" bytes, although 1K is really equal to 1024 but 1000 is close enough). So, if you are told a particular machine has 64K, this means there is room in the internal memory to store about 64,000 characters.

A memory location will hold one number of the appropriate bit length for the machine. This number might be either one machine language instruction or a data item, depending only on the context in which it is used. Each memory location has an **address,** a unique number associated with each memory location in the computer. The memory location can be thought of as an empty house, its address identifies it, and its contents are a binary number. This number can represent an instruction, a letter, or other information.

To execute a program, the control unit must be told where the first instruction is. Then the CPU performs the sequence of operations that the first instruction represents. The control unit then gets the next instruction from each successive memory location. It may get an instruction telling it to execute an instruction from a nonsequential memory location, but otherwise it will continue getting instructions from one location after the next, in order. An analogy would be of going down a street, stopping at each house, doing what the person at home told you, and then going to the next house in sequence until you were told to skip the next five houses or to go to another street.

When an instruction is encountered involving an arithmetic or logical operation, the arithmetic logic unit will be put to work, the same way a person might use a hand calculator in solving a mathematical problem. When the calculation is complete, the result is stored in a memory location for later use. The program then continues as directed by the control unit.

The CPU and internal memory are the heart of the computer, but they are useless without certain **peripheral devices,** which will be discussed next.

INPUT DEVICES

To put instructions or data into the CPU so that useful work can be done, it is necessary to have a device for "inputting" the instructions or data. Many types of input devices can be connected to the CPU, and we will discuss a few of them here.

One of the most common input devices is a keyboard (Figure 2-1). This usually has the appearance of a typewriter keyboard. It may, however, have additional keys for entering exclusively numerical data (a keypad) and special function keys that take the place of a whole sequence of key strokes. Keyboards may stand alone and communicate with the CPU by wires or infrared beam. Some keyboards are housed with the CPU in a single unit that may contain other peripheral devices such as a display

FIGURE 2-1
Keyboard.

screen. When a keyboard is put together with a screen or other output device, it is usually called a **terminal** (Figure 2-2).

Data or instructions are typed on the keyboard and are internally changed to a sequence of electronic signals (representing 0s and 1s), which are then transmitted to the CPU. Some terminals transmit one character at a time, as typed. These are called **dumb terminals.** Other terminals transmit information to the CPU in blocks (or groups of **characters**). The advantage of these is that data can be prepared and temporarily stored in a buffer (a small memory) in the terminal and transmitted to the computer when the user and the computer are ready. This can significantly reduce the communications costs when the computer is remote, and can also reduce the load on the computer because the terminal itself handles data acquisition. These keyboard-based devices are often called **smart terminals.** Some of them even permit editing and correcting data before it is sent to the CPU. Because of the greater power of these devices, they are usually more costly than the dumb terminals mentioned above.

One of the older but also very common methods of inputting data or instructions into the CPU involves using **punched cards** (Figure 2-3). A machine called a **keypunch** (Figure 2-4) is very much like a typewriter, except that it produces the cards with patterns of holes that represent letters and numbers. The prepared cards are then fed into an input device called a **card reader** that sends electronic representations

16 *Concepts and issues in health care computing*

FIGURE 2-2
Hard copy terminal.

FIGURE 2-3
Punched card.

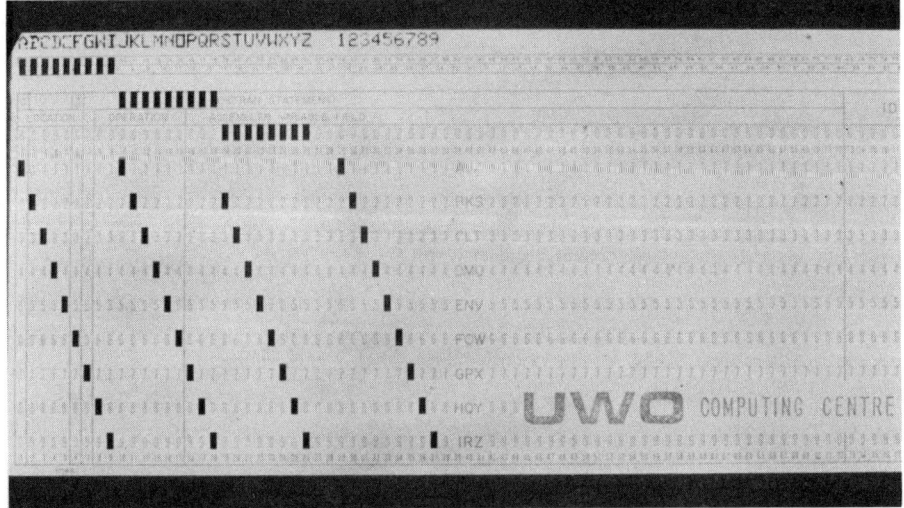

FIGURE 2-4
Keypunch.

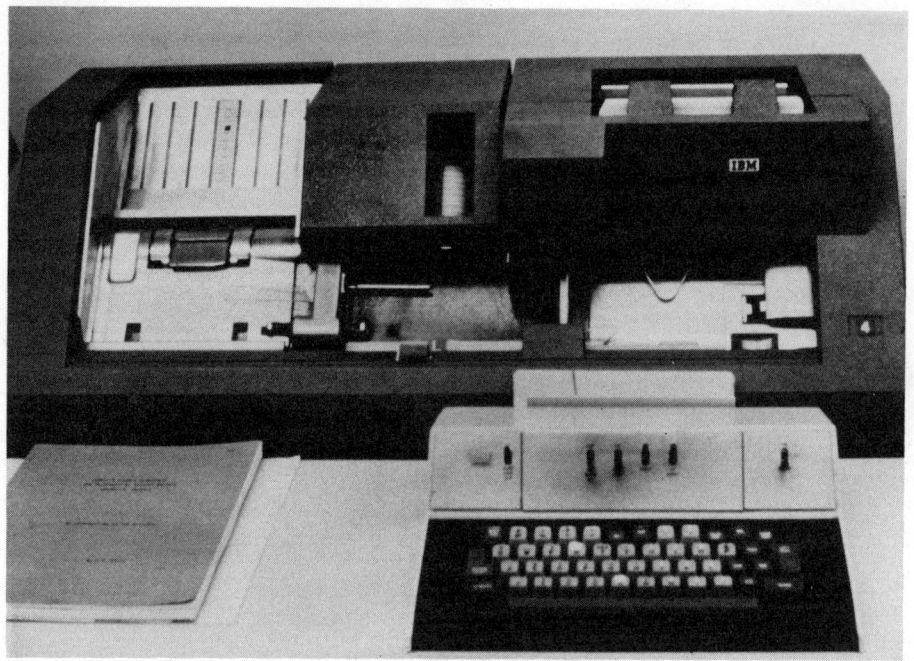

of the data on the cards to the CPU. Each card can hold up to 80 characters of information, and the card reader will input these characters at a rate of about 400 characters per second (approximately 300 cards per minute).

Obviously the card reader can input information much faster than a person could type on a keyboard device. Therefore card input is useful for large volumes of information because one card reader can serve as an input device for many clerks producing punched cards on keypunch machines.

After punched cards had been around for awhile, a method was developed to input data from cards using pencil marks to indicate patterns representing numbers and letters. The medium devised is called **optical mark recognition (OMR)** cards. Cards are marked by hand (instead of being punched) and then read into a device called an OMR reader, which is connected to the CPU. The pencil marks on the cards are treated just like the holes on cards and are transformed by the card reader into electrical signals that are sent to the computer.

A modification of the OMR card is the OMR form, which is a piece of $8^{1}/_{2} \times 11$ inch paper on which descriptive material and boxes for the pencil marks are printed. An early use for this medium was in testing, because the student could simply mark

FIGURE 2-5
Bar code.

the answers to questions in the appropriate boxes, the sheets of paper were fed into an OMR reader, and the information transmitted directly to the computer for scoring.

A dramatic adaptation of the OMR concept was the development of devices that can read characters printed on paper. Characters in special fonts can be produced by a typewriter. These stylized characters are readable by machines called **optical character recognition (OCR)** readers, again connected to the CPU. The advantage of this method is that the OCR characters are readable by both machines and people. Today devices exist that can read many different fonts (even the one in this book) and handprinted characters.

Some of the newer input devices include **bar code** (Figure 2-5) readers—usually using a device called a **wand** (Figure 2-6). These are commonplace in department stores and supermarkets. Information is coded on packages or tags in the form of thick and thin lines representing letters and numbers. When the bar code is passed over a scanner or a wand is passed over the label the pattern is converted into characters that are inputted into the computer.

In combination with video display terminals (to be discussed in further sections) a **light pen** can be used as an input device. This pen is pointed at a spot on the screen to select one of a list of choices, from a "menu," for example. A further elaboration of this technology is using a "mouse" that causes a cursor (cross-hair) to move around the screen as one moves the mouse around on a table surface. With **touch screens** a person's finger serves as the pointer. Using these devices one can point at a position on the screen containing a desired response. The pointing device gives the computer the coordinates of what one is pointing at, and a program knows where on the screen the various responses are.

The future holds promise for a much easier to use type of input to the computer—the human voice. Already some computers have a "vocabulary" of approximately 100 words that can be understood as commands to the terminal. The input

FIGURE 2-6
Bar code reader (*wand*).

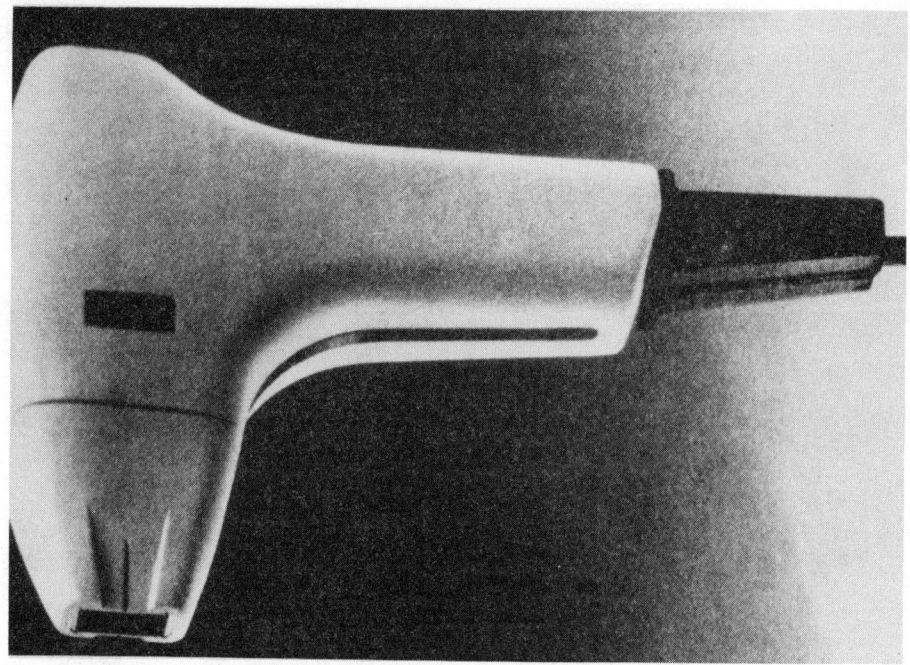

device is a microphone, built into a special terminal, into which a person speaks. The terminal recognizes the spoken command or number and sends a code to the CPU as if it had been typed. This probably will never replace mechanical forms of input because of speed limitations. However, simple and repetitive tasks not requiring inputting numerical data may use the human voice as the standard input mechanism in the near future.

OUTPUT DEVICES

Just as it is necessary to have a way of entering instructions or data to the CPU through input devices, it is also necessary to have ways of getting information out of the computer. The devices used to do this are called output devices. These machines have changed greatly over the years because of changes in technology and because of the varying needs in environments where computers are used.

The first output device was a simple display of lights on the front panel of the CPU. A group of lights indicated the on and off condition of the various bits in a certain memory location. The display was thus in binary form. As one might imagine,

FIGURE 2-7
Dot matrix character printer.

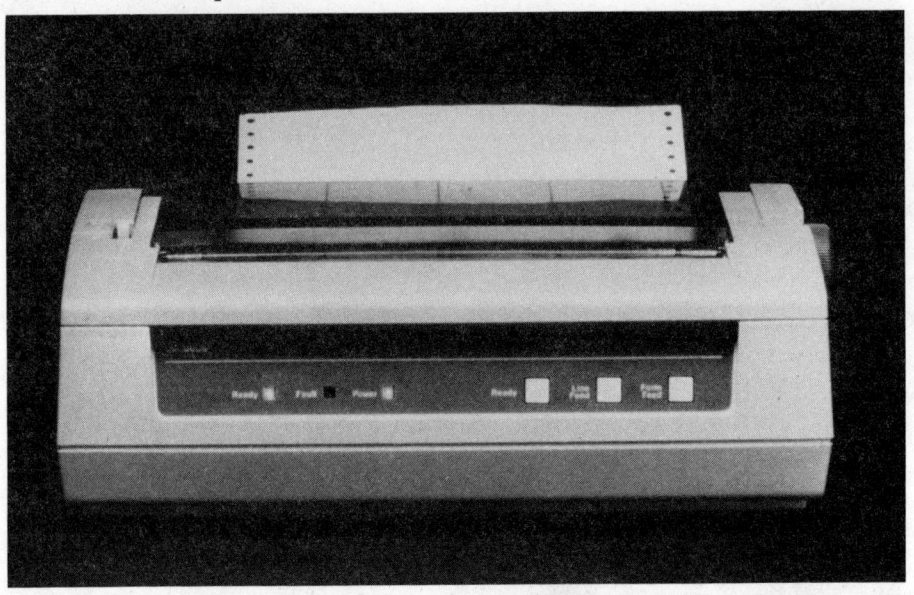

deciphering what these combinations of on and off lights meant was very tedious. It became clear that a form of output more easily readable by humans was needed.

The character **printer** was the first output device that made information coming from the CPU easily readable by people. The first printers were much like typewriters or **teletype** machines we still use today. Because they printed one character at a time with a hammer striking the paper they were called impact printers. The speed of these machines was 10 to 15 characters per second (CPS). The output speed was adequate for small jobs, but it became necessary to vastly increase the speed for applications with a large amount of output.

Thus the **line printer** was developed. This machine used multiple hammers and rapidly moving multiple sets of characters on a belt (chain). It still worked on the impact method, but now a whole line of information could be typed in about the same time it took the character printer to print one character.

Modern character printers still use the impact method, but a different way of producing print was devised using a set of solenoid driven wires instead of a printhead. Printers using this technology are called **dot matrix** printers (Figure 2-7). The output produced from these machines appears as a bunch of dots that form the various alphabetic and numeric characters. The dots are printed by a column of little wires in a printhead that moves horizontally to scan out each character on a line. Some dot

FIGURE 2-8
CRT (or VDT) unit.

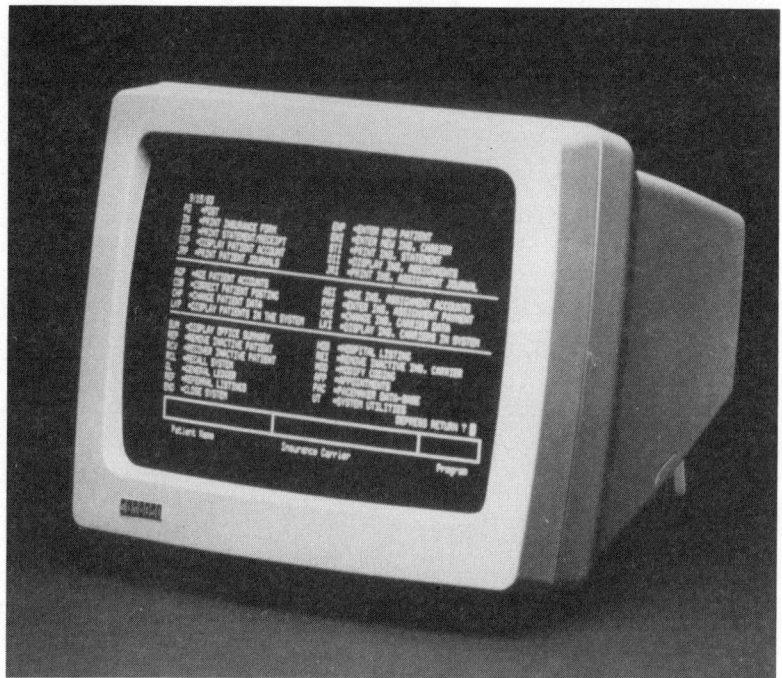

matrix printers today are quite sophisticated because they alter the position of the type head slightly and overlap the dots so the spaces between the dots will not be so obvious. However, the broken style of dot matrix printing is never quite as pleasing as solid-type printing produced by solid-type face (letter-quality) printers.

Two new printers we will briefly mention are ink-jet and laser printers. At present they produce the best print, but are also the most costly.

Printers are useful when one wants to carry a **hard copy** of the output away from the computer. However, hard copy is not always needed. Often one wants simply to look at some information and does not need a permanent copy of it. **Cathode ray tube (CRT)** or **video display terminal (VDT)** devices were developed to provide such "soft" copy.

CRTs or VDTs look like and electronically are very much like television screens (Figure 2-8). They display information quickly and silently on the screen, eliminating paper and working at much higher speeds than printers. Many types of display are available, from the simple white-on-black print in upper case only to sophisticated color graphics and everything in between. Some screens have the capability to split the

FIGURE 2-9
A single graph may represent a huge amount of numerical output.

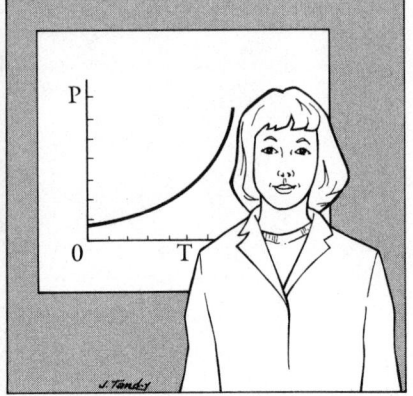

image so text is displayed on one part of the screen and graphs on another part (windowing). Some of these output devices also have hard copy devices built in so that if a hard copy of the screen output is required, this can be produced with the press of a button. These VDTs also produce dot matrix output, but the dots are bright points on the screen.

Because of the usefulness of graphic output (Figure 2-9), devices called **pen-plotters** were developed. The first plotters used a pen that traveled back and forth across paper attached to a rotating drum. Other plotters feature a pen that moves in two dimensions on a flat sheet of paper. Pen-plotters are relatively slow because they can usually draw only one curve or line at a time. Complicated patterns can take a long time to produce. More modern electrostatic plotters can achieve slightly less artistic results in a short time because they do not depend on a moving pen. Rather, they electrostatically place patterns of dots on paper to make up a graph. The process they use is very similar to that employed in photocopiers. Some electrostatic **printer-plotters** can produce both print and graphic displays with equal facility. These machines offer advantages over regular printers because they are fast (no hammers need move) and it is possible to change the style and size of the letters electronically.

There are devices that also allow output onto film (microfilm or microfiche). Computer output microfilm (COM) devices are used by large institutions producing vast quantities of output, but not wanting to use paper because of its expense and storage requirements.

The latest form of output device is one the speaks. Voice output synthesizers today produce word sounds from groups of characters sent to them. These are understandable and can even be adjusted for a normal intonation produced by the human voice. These devices are used now in supermarkets in conjunction with the bar code readers to let one know the price of purchases. (Bar code printers are another output device, used to produce package codes and labels in laboratories.)

STORAGE DEVICES

Earlier we discussed the internal memory associated with the CPU. Here programs are temporarily stored and made immediately available for processing. This type of memory is called **random access memory (RAM)**, which means any part of the memory may be accessed equally quickly. Most internal memory is used transiently. For example, information is kept in the machine only while a program is running and is then overwritten by the next program. Also, when the power to the machine is switched off the contents of these internal memory locations are not saved. Therefore, to avoid having to input a program by hand every time it is to be run, it is necessary to have a more permanent type of storage. These are called **secondary memory devices** or **mass storage devices.** For simplicity we will divide these devices into two types: **sequential access memory** and random access memory.

The earliest type of mass storage was magnetic tape similar to that used today in reel-to-reel tape recorders and videotape cassettes. Information in the form of magnetic "0s and 1s"—the analog of the punched card hole is a magnetic field in some direction—is stored in blocks sequentially. A machine called a **tape drive** senses these magnetic fields and translates them into the electronic signals that are sent to the internal memory (Figure 2-10). The tape drive can also write information onto the tapes by the inverse process of translating signals coming from the internal memory into magnetic fields for storage.

Tapes are normally kept **off-line** (not mounted on the tape drive) in tape libraries. They are loaded by an **operator** onto the drive when the data or programs they contain are needed. Tape reels are usually 2400 feet long and can contain variable amounts of data depending on the tape drive used. Although drives commonly record information at a density of 800 or 1600 bits per inch (BPI), the newer units can record at 6250 BPI. At that density, a reel can hold approximately 125 million characters. Most tape drives today store data in nine parallel tracks running lengthwise down the tape. Each character is written by a set of magnetic recording heads across the tape, one bit per track. Some older drives used a seven-track format.

The **read–write** speed of tape drives varies considerably. Some units are as slow as 25 inches per second (IPS), whereas others reach speeds of 200 IPS or more. Magnetic tape is the slowest storage **medium** in terms of access to data. At 25 IPS it would take $12 \times 2400/25 = 1152$ seconds or 19.2 minutes simply to read a 2400-foot tape from end to end. Magnetic tape is therefore best suited to storing information that is organized sequentially and accessed only occasionally. Because magnetic tape is such an inexpensive medium, it is an attractive choice for archival storage of large quantities

FIGURE 2-10
Magnetic recording devices. A, Magnetic recording head. B, How digital data is recorded on 9-track magnetic tape; storing a 1 is indicated by black marks. C, Magnetic disk, top view. D, Magnetic disk, side view. E, Disk pack of five platters with ganged moving heads.

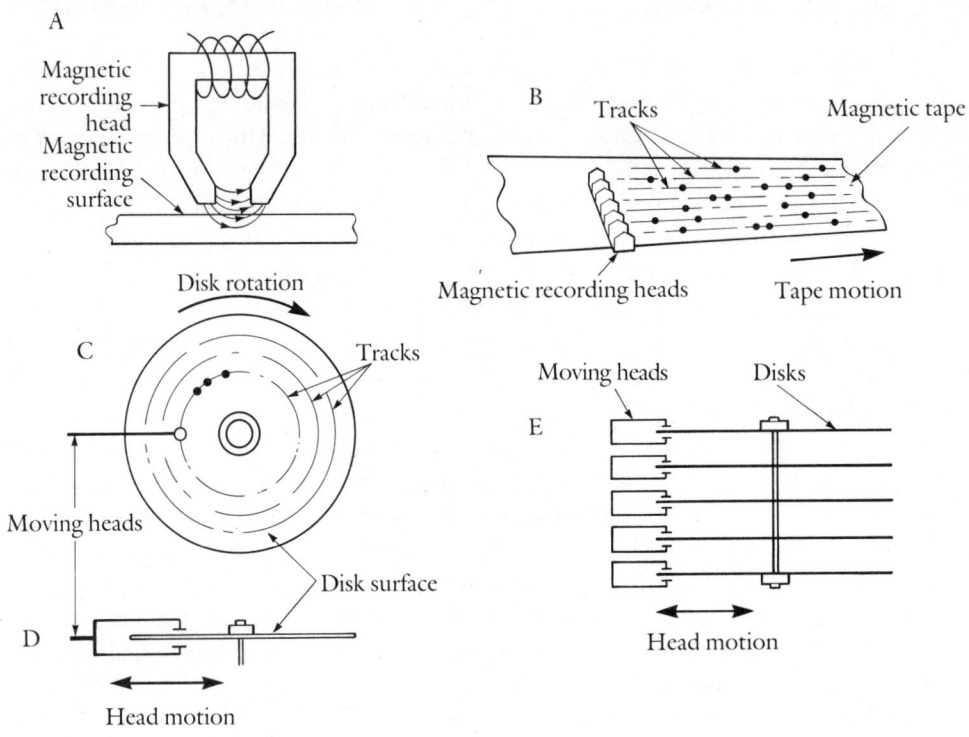

of information. When data manipulation has been completed in the computer, results can be dumped onto a tape. The next time a program user needs the data on the tape, it may be read directly or transferred onto high-speed devices such as disks.

Tape format is highly standardized and is probably the medium most transportable between different systems, although incompatibilities exist that sometimes frustrate such attempts. When transportability is essential, equipment and software compatibility must be checked.

With today's smaller computers it is possible to use cassette tapes and videotapes as well as the large standard tapes. These are an inexpensive and portable form of storage.

Magnetic disk storage was developed to accommodate the need for a fast, near random-access type of storage. Disks (the storage medium) come in many capacities and types. The two main types are flexible or **floppy disks** and hard disks. The way information is saved and retrieved on disks is the same for both types.

The disk surface is magnetizable and has **tracks** similar to the tracks on a phonograph record, except the tracks are concentric instead of spiral. The disk is spun at a high speed in the disk drive. A special read-write head positioned above the track can either read or write information in the track and can be moved from track to track. By this we mean that the head can access any track of the disk quickly, only having to wait for the disk to rotate to get the information of interest on the selected track. For this reason disks are called **pseudorandom-access memory** devices—they are faster than tape but slower than memory.

The simplest arrangement is a 5¼-inch floppy disk with information stored on one side (single-sided: SS), which is read in a disk drive with a single head that passes over the disk surface. Floppy disks also exist with data on both sides and disk drives with heads on both sides to read the data (double-sided: DS).

The storage capacity of disks depends on the recording density. Manufacturers abbreviate disk densities as SD for single density and DD for double density. Other floppy disk sizes include 7-inch and 3½-inch types. This is measured in terms of both the number of tracks per inch of disk surface and the number of bits in each track. It is common to see floppy disks that can hold 1 **megabyte (Mb,** 1 million characters). Most floppies have a slower access time, even up to 500 milliseconds.

Many **microcomputers** today have hard disks. They are simply rigid versions of floppies that can hold more data (10 to 20 Mb is typical), but usually are sealed in a container in the computer housing and not removable. Rigid disks on some microcomputers and on larger computer systems are often removable from the disk drives and can be stored off-line in a library. Just as one tape drive can be loaded with many different tapes, so a single disk drive can be loaded with many **disk packs.** The smallest capacity removable disks are called disk cartridges and they contain one **disk platter** in a protective plastic cover. A more complex arrangement is the type used in large computer systems where a number of disk platters are connected together in a disk pack, and where each platter's data can be read simultaneously by heads interdigitated between the platters. Disk cartridge and disk pack drives (Figure 2-11) typically allow information to be accessed in about 20 milliseconds.

Floppy disks, or **diskettes,** have become extremely popular in the microcomputer markets because of their low cost and convenient size. A double-sided, double density (DSDD) diskette can typically hold about 360,000 or more characters of information. There are also micro-disks that hold only about 90,000 bytes.

Diskettes are very manageable media. They are relatively durable and they can be sent through the mail or filed in ordinary folders. They are thus attractive for health care applications in which data is collected from several remote locations and sent to a central computer, or where data files are small (typical of smaller clinical research projects).

FIGURE 2-11
Disk pack and disk drives.

Another type of disk technology now being introduced is the optical disk or laser disk. In them information is stored as little pits burned into a special surface. The presence or absence of pits (like holes in the old punched card) can be sensed by a reading laser. These disks have enormous capacity, in some cases 5 to 10 times greater (or more) than the largest magnetic disk drives. They are real hope for the future for storing images such as radiographics where over 1 Mb may be needed per image.

Disk technology thus comes in a wide range of capacities, speeds, and costs. There are disks to serve all types of users, from the computer hobbyist to the largest corporation.

SMALL, MEDIUM, AND LARGE COMPUTERS

Most of today's computers are more sophisticated than any of those of 20 years ago. Computers are also available today that have a wide range of capabilities and prices. Therefore, a computer must be carefully chosen to meet particular needs and to fit within a budget.

It is convenient to classify today's computers into general categories. One commonly thinks of micro-, mini-, midi-, maxi-, and super computers. As technology progresses, today's "large" computer (powerful, expensive, and often physically big) becomes tomorrow's "smaller" computer (powerful, cheaper, and physically small). The machines of tomorrow will have capabilities far beyond yesterday's best.

The most exciting development of recent years has been the **microprocessor.** In retrospect one can discern what has been a gradual but predictable evolution toward microprocessors over many years. The trend toward modularization (the use of relatively few kinds of boards interconnected to form complete subsystems), came to commercial fruition in the late 1960s. At that time, computers made up of multiple modules, each module holding many transistors, became commonplace. A significant advance quietly took place in the early 1970s when it became possible to construct a whole central processing unit with the use of integrated circuits (ICs) called "chips" after the tiny chip of silicon or other semiconductor on which the circuits are constructed. Each IC was equivalent to about 100 transistors and they were put on a single, rather large, module or card. Finally, the step of placing a whole processor on a single semiconductor chip—not much larger than the earliest transistors—was taken in the early-to-mid 1970s. The microprocessor had arrived. Each such microprocessor chip contains the equivalent of several thousand to upwards of 500,000 transistors.

Each day, yesterday's marvel is outdone as greater and greater miniaturization packs more powerful processors and more memory into the same space, thereby greatly reducing manufacturing costs. Today, whole processors can be soldered into place on a board in the amount of time and space formerly dedicated to a lone transistor, and the process itself is automated so that people control and supervise but do not assemble the circuits. Mass production allows larger numbers of computers to be produced more reliably and less expensively than ever before.

The implication of physically small, inexpensive, yet powerful computers is evident. Instruments of all kinds, including health care tools, can now contain a computer, and can benefit from this revolution. This means that instruments can be more adept at manipulating and transforming data, and can quickly give us final results instead of partial data that we must then turn into useful information. Adapting instruments becomes far more reasonable, because expensive rewiring or complete redesign is replaced by reprogramming.

With microprocessors we have new alternatives. For example, instead of expensive central facilities, individual ICU and CCU monitoring units can be placed at the patient's bedside. This reduces the cost per bed monitored in smaller CCUs. Moreover, using single processors for individual patients assures that the failure of one piece of equipment will not affect the data of more than one patient. Also, it is possible to keep spare units to quickly replace one needing repair. The modularity derived from small, less expensive instruments means that growth can be accommodated by adding units rather than by trading in a whole system for a more powerful one. This also means that one adds power when one adds load—such systems can grow without saturating, a problem with older central-type systems. Furthermore, today's microprocessors cost only tens or hundreds of dollars. Complete, usable microcomputer systems (CPU, memory, disks, printer) can cost about $3000, and they are getting cheaper every day.

Although microcomputers are very limited in terms of sophisticated numerical computation ("number crunching"), they are often adequate for the type of calculation and data management functions important in health care applications. The concept of the computer-aided physician's office may have been introduced prematurely, but the economic environment in general practice may soon warrant or even demand computer support for common business functions such as accounting and word processing. Small microprocessor-based computer systems are becoming comprehensive enough that they can fill this need, and their cost is beginning to be easier to justify. The important factor is that computer hardware itself is no longer such a big deal.

At the next stratum of complexity, the **minicomputer** system usually costs from $10,000 to $250,000 or more, of which the processor itself represents only a small portion (in the range of 5% to 25%) of the total cost. In return for this substantial investment, one obtains a machine with more overall power than many of the largest computers of the 1950s. Minicomputers today are suitable for simultaneous use by even dozens of users, for **database** management, for many small computer-based products, and for limited computation-oriented functions. The term "limited" should not be misinterpreted. Although minicomputers are generally unsuitable for solving complex sets of equations quickly, they can solve the sophisticated problem of reconstructing pictures from CT scans in seconds to minutes. In very specialized areas such as signal processing, they can be augmented by special processing units (Fourier or array processors) and can then solve computationally heavy problems in fractions of a second.

Information processing in the health care environment has already benefited immensely from minicomputer technology because of the relatively low cost of these machines. The first major breakthrough was the LINC processor, developed during the 1960s under the auspices of the National Institutes of Health. This prototype unit was integrated into a number of commercial computers (e.g., the LINC-8, the PC-12) and served as the stimulus for much health care–computing development. Many commercial products running the programs developed for these earlier machines are still in existence.

There are many minicomputers available commercially. A recent survey listed 38 companies selling 95 models—numbers that are definitely underestimates.

Today the power of minicomputers is being extended by using microcomputers as peripheral processors, terminals, or controllers. By "unloading" the central minicomputer of simple but time-consuming data management operations, these controllers can create a faster, more efficient computer system. Perhaps the most important advance has been to unburden the system of low-speed user-oriented interaction by using microcomputer systems as terminals (sometimes called **intelligent terminals**) for data collection and editing. In this setup, the processor in each terminal does the work of collecting data or word processing and the central computer is interrupted only when blocks of correctly formatted and validated data have been assembled.

The distinction between micro- and minicomputers has disappeared. More powerful micros are even now surpassing older minis and support dozens or even larger numbers of users. It is also possible that arrays of microprocessors may take over functions now assigned to much larger single computers. A number of systems are now available that allow one to plug in more and more microprocessor boards to expand the capacity of a shared system.

Occasionally the most powerful minicomputers and the bottom end of the line of **maxicomputers** are classed together and called **midicomputers.** One source has defined them as machines with word lengths of 24 or 32 bits. We will not deal separately with these here.

Throughout the entire spectrum from micro- to maxicomputers, more powerful computers differ from less powerful machines in several ways. More powerful machines have a larger repertoire of more complex instructions, and they can execute these instructions more quickly, some in only a few billionths of a second (nanoseconds). The longer word size of "larger" machines permits a bigger instruction set, access to more memory in a single step, and more rapid large-number arithmetical functions. Whereas "smaller" computers may take several steps to perform a given operation, a "larger" machine may accomplish the same task with one instruction. Moving upward through this spectrum one will find the increasing use of peripheral processors to unload the main computers of input–output functions, to store and retrieve data from disks, and even to carry out sosphisticated calculations.

Micro- and most minicomputers have only one **channel** connecting disk to computer (the channel is the set of wires over which data is moved), and this may be quite slow. The largest minicomputers and larger machines introduce parallelism, a method by which several channels are available for simultaneous data movement, with each channel itself able to transfer more data. The more powerful computers also use very high-speed supplementary main memories (cache memories) into which data and programs to be imminently dealt with are transferred for rapid access. Some computers can even execute parts or all of several instructions simultaneously. These internal architectural features are apparent to the user as much higher execution speeds or, to use an industry term, as higher throughput.

Maxicomputer systems (mainframes), incorporating some or all of these features, are most suitable for big, centralized health care applications such as state or provincial health insurance systems. They are also appropriate for processing immense amounts of data, such as those in large-scale epidemiological research projects. Research of many types may also benefit from maxicomputer systems—for instance, mathematical modeling of physiological systems or even of health care delivery mechanisms.

There are a few notable **supercomputers** (e.g., CRAY 1 and CYBER 204). Each of these costs millions of dollars. The goal in developing these systems is to create machines that can execute many operations in parallel, thus achieving previously impossible speeds. They will permit us to get the results of a calculation in minutes or hours when before we had to wait days or weeks. These currently have little relevance to health care, except in special research projects.

THE COMPUTER IN CONTEXT

A bare CPU is relatively inexpensive, but useless. The CPU in a $100,000 minicomputer system may cost only $5000, with the internal memory generally adding about $10,000 to $15,000 more. The remaining 80% of the cost is made up of the peripheral devices that transfigure the naked computer into a usable computer system.

A computer system does not stand alone. Just as the CPU requires peripheral devices, so a computer system must be placed in an environment tailored to its requirements. Numerous factors must be considered.

Computers generate heat. Each 6-foot-high rack develops at least a few thousand BTUs. Large computers generate so much heat that they have internal cooling systems, including refrigeration and water-cooling schemes. Almost any room intended to house something larger than a microcomputer system needs air conditioning.

Whereas microcomputer systems can plug into the standard wallpower outlet, many minicomputers require special plugs and higher currents than are usually available. Big machines often have peculiar power and voltage requirements. Uninterruptible power supplies are needed to keep essential computers operational in the face of brownouts and power failures.

Security for inexpensive computer systems holding private information includes physical measures such as locks on doors, limited access to facilities, and controlled access to terminals. There must also be protection against fire. Gas fire extinguishers must be installed in the computer area, because water is as damaging as flames to electronics and storage media.

The physical bulk of a computer system may, in some cases, dictate where it can be used. Housing very large computer systems can tie up expensive floor space.

Of course, computers are worthless without the people who maintain and program them. Personnel represents a large hidden cost in a computer operation.

WHAT'S NEXT?

Computers have progressed a long way since the days when they were all multimillion-dollar monsters. There are still huge and expensive computers, but their power was unimaginable in the early days of computer history. Today, sophisticated computer systems are available at prices nearly every enterprise can afford. Even the consumer who can afford a stereo system can purchase a computer more powerful than the legendary ENIAC of not too many years ago. The proliferation of hobby computers in the consumer domain guarantees that the computer will become even more available, easier to use, and less mysterious. Therefore, computers are moving toward becoming simply another tool—and a common one at that.

We are only beginning to exploit the computer's capabilities in health care practice and research. The CT scanner, patient-monitoring devices, radiology reporting systems, admission and discharge systems, and computers for the physician's office are but a few examples of applications in which the computer is a tool that can help to support an essential process.

We hope that physicians and other health care workers will use this tool themselves to advance health care, because creativity in applying computers in any area is increasingly dependent on the professionals in that field.

CHAPTER 3
COMMUNICATIONS

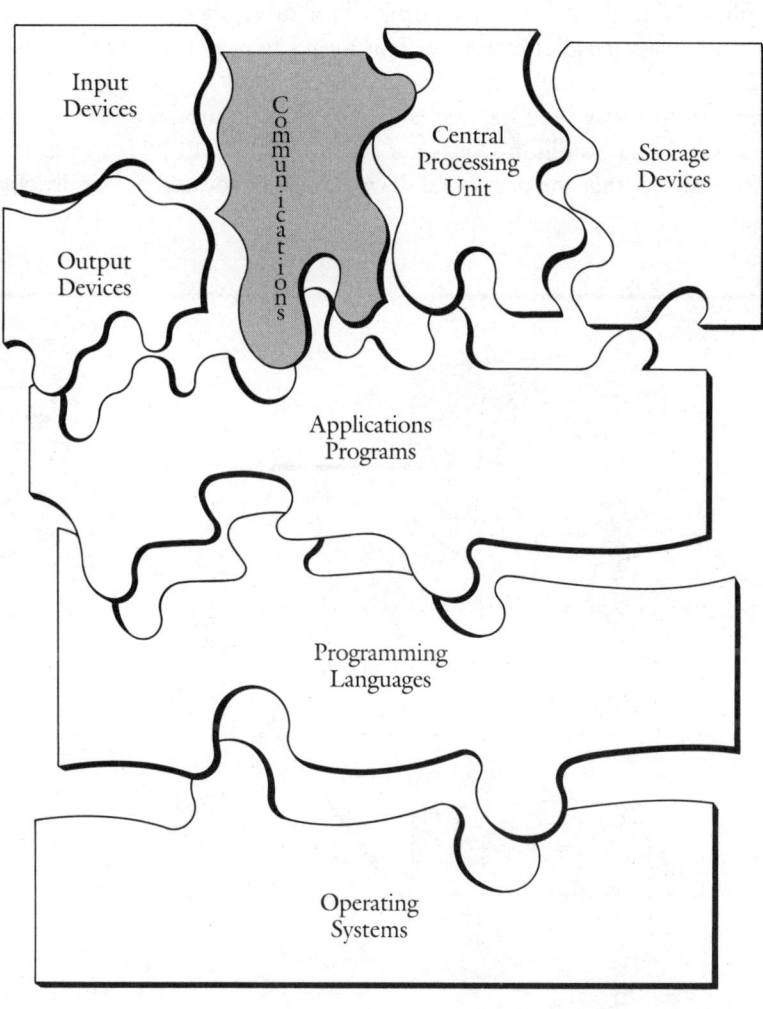

CHAPTER 3

The hardware of computer systems includes the CPU, input and output devices, and storage devices. An important area of hardware has not yet been discussed: the way that the various pieces of hardware communicate with each other.

These days there is a lot of talk about **networks** that allow virtually anyone with a computer to communicate with anyone else with a computer (Figure 3-1). To understand how this can be accomplished it is necessary to understand some of the basics first.

There are two ways of moving data from point to point: in parallel or in serial. High-speed devices such as disk drives, tape drives, and line printers are connected to the CPU via a **parallel interface.** This means that as a word of data is moved, all the component bits (usually 16 or 32) are moved simultaneously along 16 (or 32) parallel wires. In this way, very fast rates of data transfer are possible. For example, a disk drive may send 1 million words per second to the CPU. However, the limitation of this method is that the peripheral devices must be located physically close to the CPU

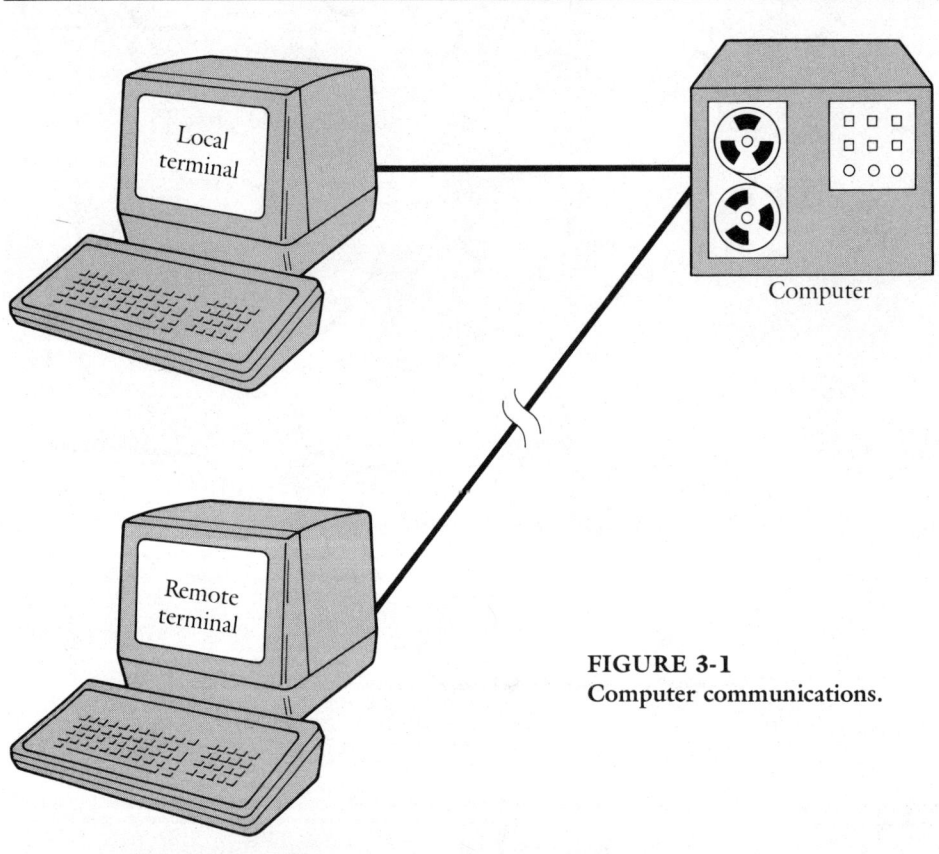

FIGURE 3-1
Computer communications.

because excessive lengths of cable could cause signal delays and distortions.

When a more remote device must gain access to the CPU, a different method is used. Here the data is transferred in serial mode (one bit at a time), usually along a single wire. The words of data are broken down at the sending end and reassembled at the receiving end. This method is considerably slower than the parallel method but allows for accuracy over long distances. Because serial communications are rather more complex than parallel communications, we will discuss serial communications methods in more detail.

To conceptualize this method, imagine that we are attempting to communicate over a wire between two points. Digital data can be represented by two voltage levels. For example, a positive voltage can represent a "1" (one) and no voltage or ground can represent a "0" (zero). Each one or zero is a bit, and combinations of ones and zeros make up the codes for characters.

ASYNCHRONOUS METHOD

In **asynchronous** communications, the one most commonly used today, characters (bytes) are transmitted (or received) with an arbitrary time between each of them. For example, one character is sent whenever a user hits a key on the keyboard of the terminal. Each transmitted character has one "start bit" and one or two "stop bits" added to the beginning and end, respectively, of its own 8-bit code, for a total of 10 (most commonly) or 11 transmitted bits per character. The start and stop bits are there precisely because of the uncertain arrival time of each character. The start bit effectively says "here comes a character," whereas the stop bit ensures adequate min-

FIGURE 3-2
Asynchronous data transmission
(also called start/stop transmission).

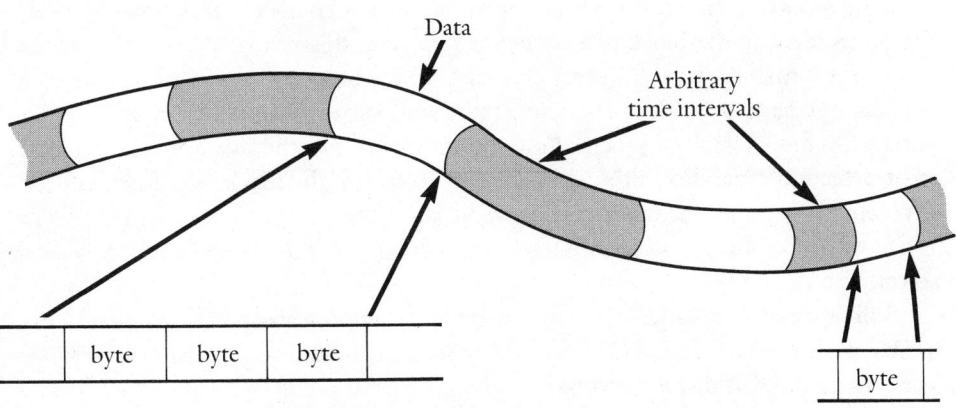

imum delay between characters. The time duration of each bit that forms a character is constant for any given transmission rate, but the time interval between characters is random (Figure 3-2).

An advantage of asynchronous communications is that relatively little circuitry is required to handle it. The device that must be attached to a central computer to receive asynchronous communications often costs only $150 to $600. However, the usual maximum rate for asynchronous transmission over telephone lines is 1200 bits per second (BPS) or about 120 characters per second (CPS)—if one start bit and one stop bit, for a total of 10 bits, are used per character.

The term "rate" indicates the total amount of data that can be transmitted from point to point in a unit of time. It is dependent on the time we allow for the signal representing each bit. We use the term "rate" and give our rates in BPS, instead of using the older term "baud," which is ambiguous but usually the same as BPS at lower data rates.

Asynchronous communications technology is often uesd in a time-sharing environment in which users at remote terminals or micros send and receive data at relatively low speeds. Most public databases (e.g., the Source) expect async (as it is abbreviated). Because asynchronous communication is possible at much higher speeds if short runs of wire are used, it can be used for high-speed terminals (19,200 BPS at least) near a computer.

SYNCHRONOUS METHOD

To achieve higher data transmission rates and automatic error detection, **synchronous** communications technology is invoked. In synchronous communications, the communications hardware at each end of the linkage is "synchronized" to send or receive data at particular instants in time, and bits of data must be "plugged into" the time slots one after another in lock-step fashion (Figure 3-3). Complex protocols for synchronous communications exist. Special synchronization characters start a transmission; blocks of characters are sent instead of one character at a time; "header" characters identify the block of data being sent; and this is all followed by a special block of information used for error checking. Many protocols for synchronous communications have been developed and these will vary from system to system. The potentially higher rate of synchronous transmission and the associated unattended error-detection capability, although necessary to realize the maximum potential from any communications medium, cost more at both the computer and terminal ends. When error-free transmission of large files is required, this is the only safe way to accomplish it.

Both asynchronous and synchronous communications can operate in either of two modes, which may be dependent on the type of communications hardware one selects. These are **full duplex** and **half duplex**.

FIGURE 3-3
Synchronous data transmission.

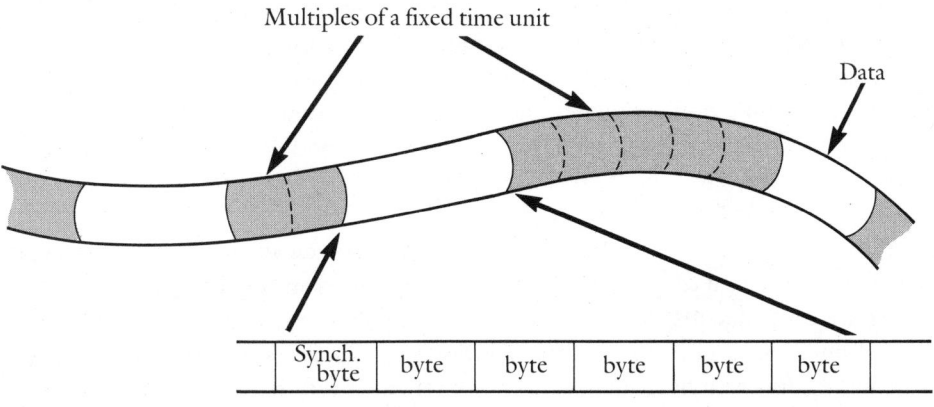

FULL DUPLEX MODE

Full duplex mode means that the two connected devices are capable of transmitting to or receiving from each other simultaneously. This feature is often exploited by asynchronous communications in a time-sharing environment. Data is transmitted from a terminal to the computer on one channel, and the computer "echoes" back to the terminal on another channel what it received, even while the terminal is sending the next character. In the case of telephone lines, for example, "send" and "receive" channels operate on different frequencies transmitted on the same line. Through full duplex operation, one can verify that the computer receives what one sends, because the characters printed by the terminal are the ones that have been received and sent back by the computer.

HALF DUPLEX MODE

In the half duplex mode, the equipment can transmit in both directions, but not simultaneously. The computer cannot echo the characters it receives, because this would interfere with characters being sent by the terminal. Therefore, characters are generated within the terminal, and thus one sees only what one types—not what the computer receives. Basically the channel can only be used one way at a time.

BRANCHES OF THE FAMILY TREE

Several types of technology have been developed for serial digital communications. Some were created to take advantage of existing communications facilities, and others were the result of research into novel areas. The purpose of the devices is to make the best possible use of communications resources, which may vary from telephone lines to microwaves. The cost and complexity of these devices are commensurate with the performance required and the limitations of the media.

The amount of data that can be transmitted over a communications channel depends on three things: the strength of the signal, the amount of signal compared to the amount of noise on the channel, and the maximum frequency that the channel can carry. Thus different "grades" of channels are available, and these will be able to carry more or less data in any unit of time. The reader should remember these points during the discussion that follows.

Today, we often wish to locate microcomputers or terminals in offices or areas remote from a central computer. For this purpose, cables strung along walls or in the ceiling are quite adequate within a department or building. Plans for today's new medical buildings and hospitals should include installing such cables and conduits. Such wiring for peripheral devices to a computer is referred to as **hard-wired** or dedicated, meaning that a dedicated cable is permanently connecting particular devices.

One encounters difficulty, however, when seeking to communicate with a computer at some distance. Creating one's own hard-wired link is expensive and difficult. Fortunately, there already exists a wiring system that goes almost everywhere on this continent and over much of the rest of the world—the telephone system. Some of the most ubiquitous devices for data communications are specifically designed to take advantage of the voice-carrying telephone systems, otherwise known as the direct-distance dialing (DDD) network.

The **acoustic coupler** is one device for transmitting digital data over telephone lines. Because the telephone was specifically designed to carry sound (voice), the acoustic coupler translates the sequence of high- and low-voltage levels representing the bits of a character into variations of an audible carrier frequency—for instance, high frequency for a "one" and low frequency for a "zero." These sounds are piped into the telephone mouthpiece at the sending end by the acoustic coupler, they travel down the line, and they are "listened to" at the receiving end by another coupler that converts the sounds back into voltage levels (bits). To make a good acoustic connection, the headset of an ordinary telephone is pressed into rubber cups in the coupler. Such devices are therefore compatible with ordinary telephones. An acoustic coupler costs as little as $150 for a 300 BPS device. The maximum transmission rate for which there exists a commercially available device is 1200 BPS, but such a unit is a bit more expensive. The usual transmission rate of these devices is probably adequate for low-speed interactive applications (human-computer dialog) in which relatively few characters are transacted and low speed is not a limitation. In health care, these devices are used for the transtelephone transmission of digitized electrocardiogram (ECG) signals to central interpretation systems.

An attractive aspect of acoustic couplers relates to the mobility they allow. A terminal with such a device can be used anywhere there is a telephone. However, using them on heavily loaded telephone systems, or on a system in which another person can pick up an extension, can lead to frustration with the number of transmission errors encountered.

A device developed along similar lines to make better use of the telephone is the **modem** (MOdulator/DEModulator), also called a **dataset.** A modem performs the same function as an acoustic coupler, except that it connects electrically, through a standard telephone jack, rather than acoustically, to the phone line, skipping the step of going through the microphone and speaker in the handset, and thus avoiding distortion. Although the lower end of the speed range of modems overlaps that of acoustic couplers, modems can achieve much higher rates of transmission; 4800 BPS and 9600 BPS are possible when good quality lines are used. Above 2000 BPS the synchronous mode is usually used. The cost of higher-speed modems reflects the complex electronics that must be employed in using voice-grade telephone facilities to carry digital communications. For very short distances, though, a less sophisticated, and therefore less costly, limited distance dataset (LDDS) can be purchased or obtained from the phone company.

Telephone lines, of course, were developed for carrying human speech, not digital information. The amount of information they can carry in a unit of time is limited. Higher-capacity, more reliable digital communications networks have been established to accommodate the ever-increasing volume of data traffic. In the United States, Arpanet is used for digital communication among researchers; in Canada the DATAPAC service is used. Digital networks are specifically designed to transmit digital data at high frequencies, and therefore the acoustic couplers and modems needed for interfacing with the telephone system are not required. Such digital resources will become more important as time goes on, and we are approaching the day when voice communications will take a back seat to more profitable digital data communications.

It would be inefficient to tie up such high-speed lines with one user who might be communicating with a computer at a very low data rate in an interactive mode. Therefore, **multiplexers** are used to collect lower data-rate communications from several users and then to send the combined data from point to point at much higher data rates. At the receiving end, a demultiplexing system separates the data of different users from one another.

For transmitting great quantities of data in short periods of time, high-capacity communications media exist or are under development. Point-to-point ground-based microwave facilities and orbiting satellites are now routinely used by commercial communications carriers to move masses of data at extremely fast rates. These are especially useful between distant points where the lack of direct lines previously necessitated communications over roundabout routes, with all the attendant problems of noise and signal distortion. High capacity electromagnetic waveguides are hollow tubes that carry data at even greater rates, although their cost limits them to relatively short runs. These latter devices can carry several billion BPS. At such rates, the entire text of the Bible could be transmitted in about one one hundredth of a second. Optical fibers using light waves to carry digital signals are now being widely installed as an alternative to thousands of copper wires.

Finally, experimentation into using the familiar TV cable as a relatively high-capacity carrier of two-way digital information has been under way for several years. Variations on it are being used in local area networks (LANs) for intrahospital communication.

FIGURE 3-4
Basic network structures.

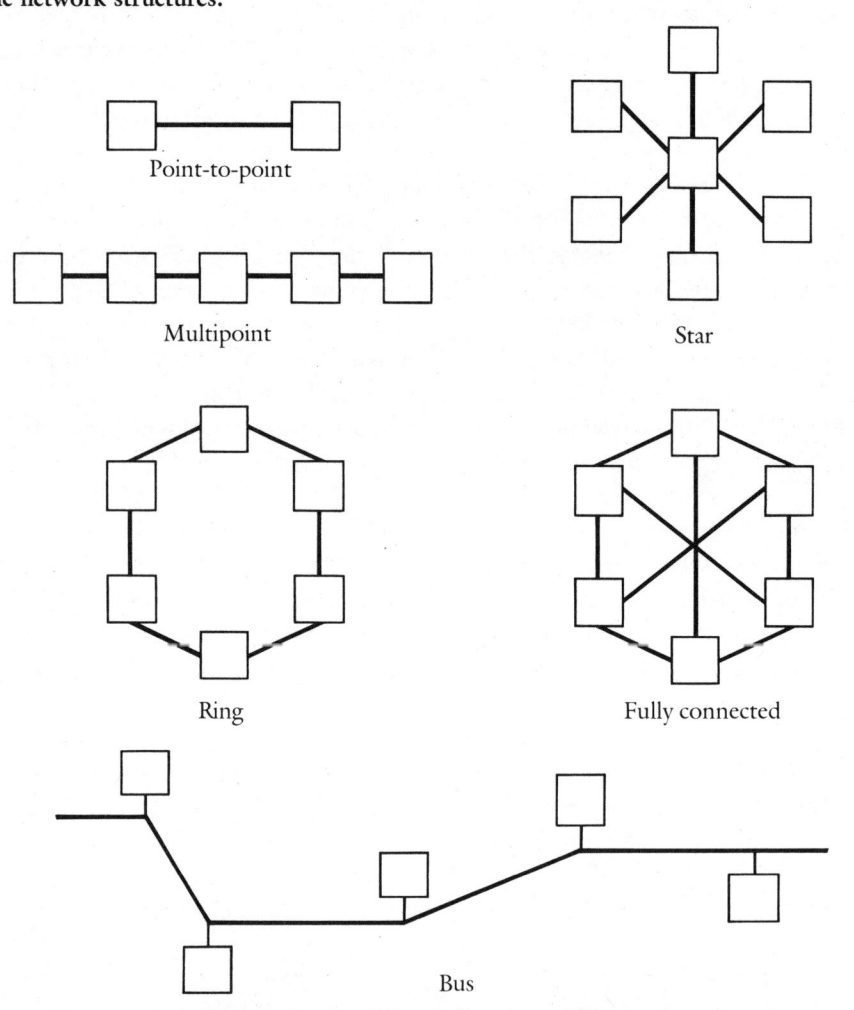

NETWORKS

It is sometimes necessary to develop an organized network of data communications pathways to link multiple computer systems. There are a number of ways of approaching this problem. Some general cases are shown in Figure 3-4. Most networks use synchronous communications between points.

The simplest networks are point-to-point and multipoint networks; each point is called a **node** and is connected at most to only two other points. Multipoint networks string several nodes serially. The drawback of these types of data networks is that a break in the chain isolates some points from each other. For somewhat enhanced reliability, a ring network is preferred, because a breakdown at any point in the ring still leaves an alternative pathway for data, back around the loop. Beyond the feature of somewhat enhanced reliability, simplicity of routing communications is probably the single greatest motivation for using the ring network approach.

A star network connects several peripheral computer systems to a central system. The most complex networks involve links from each point to every other point in the network. Such arrangements, called fully connected networks, are the most expensive kinds, because so much equipment is used to interconnect all the nodes. They are used especially in missile control systems.

Another type of network is the data bus. A bus can be compared to a pipeline of data with a number of computers tapping into it.

Computer networks and **distributed processing** are receiving a great deal of attention, and practical systems are now being delivered. It would appear that computer networking is a growing area both within and among institutions.

In considering networks of systems, it must be remembered that even the best communications links cannot help when there are fundamental incompatibilities between different computer systems and their communications software. When choosing a system it is essential to determine what kind of communication and specifically what network hardware and software a given computer supports—presuming communications are necessary.

OTHER COMMUNICATIONS STRUCTURES

Instead of creating a linkage to every remote terminal, a computer can support multiple terminals through **polled** communications. Point of sales (POS) data collection systems—increasingly seen in retail stores—often operate in this manner. The day's transactions are saved in each cash register, possibly on a cassette tape drive. At night, when telephone rates are cheaper, a central computer polls (requests the day's transactions from) each data terminal, one terminal at a time. It does this usually by automatically dialing a telephone to which the terminal is attached, but sometimes via direct wiring with all terminals on the same wire. In the health care environment, such a system can be easily used when data must be collected from several locations, but can be sent for central processing later. The advantage of polling is that many terminals can be connected to the same data communications channel without mutual interference, because the main computer permits only one terminal at a time to send data.

This is a good point to define **remote job entry (RJE).** By means of RJE technology, high-speed input and output devices (e.g., a card reader and a line printer) may be located far from a computer. The RJE station reads the input and temporarily saves it. When a block of input is ready for transmission, the RJE equipment sends it synchronously at a high data rate to the main computer. The main computer processes the program or data and similarly saves up the output. When blocks of output are ready, a controller on the computer transmits the information to the RJE station, where the output is produced on the local printer. This is an effective way of locating high-speed input devices (such as card readers) and output devices (such as line printers) remotely from the computer. The communications line is used for a minimum time, and when it is used, it is saturated with data at full capacity. Synchronous communications techniques are used, and the data received at either end is checked to detect errors caused by noise or other problems on the line. Formerly, quite expensive controllers were needed in RJE stations, but microprocessor technology has changed this situation.

A FORGOTTEN ALTERNATIVE

Some applications exist in which the charges incurred in using long-distance communications links might be considered excessive. Such applications may include either those in which instantaneous communication between points is not necessary, or those in which the volume of data to be transferred is great.

In these circumstances one should not overlook the potential of shipping such storage media as disks or tapes from one place to another. If speed is not important, high-density diskettes holding a million characters of information can be mailed. For large transfers, a courier service may be the answer. Even if it takes 2 hours to carry physically a 3 Mb disk cartridge between one computer and another, the effective data transfer rate exceeds 4000 BPS—better than the usual 2400 BPS rate in most telecommunications networks. When larger-capacity media are involved, the effective transfer rates are even higher. Therefore, as long as the reliability of the messenger can be assured, the taxi, courier, or mail services should never be overlooked as potential communications links in computer systems.

TRADE-OFFS

Deciding on the best source for the acquisition of even simple data communications facilities is not necessarily easy. Consider the modem. Some people are aware that this device is readily available from the telephone utility company, but they are probably not aware that the annual rental price for one of these sets can exceed the cost of purchasing one from a modem manufacturer. On the other hand, the telephone company is noted for speedy response when their devices fail. They may replace a defective unit the same day a problem is reported. This **mean time to repair (MTTR)** is hard to beat. It is worth noting, though, that the **mean time between failures (MTBF)** of some modems is reported in terms of tens of thousands of hours. Still another point to consider is that in some places the telephone company will want to charge a monthly rental for a **data access arrangement (DAA)**, a device that electrically insulates the external modem from their lines.

Unfortunately, in buying complex high-speed systems the trade-offs among cost, reliability, and service are not easily balanced.

• • •

An overview as brief as this cannot provide sufficient background to enable computer system users to fill in, unaided, the missing links in their systems. This job is difficult, and may involve significant expenditures that are not always considered in the initial planning of systems. For example, to interconnect three hospitals' computers in a fully connected 2400-BPS network requires six modems. If we rented the six modems for $125 a month per unit, it would cost a total of ($125 \times 6 \times 12$) $9000 a year—and we have not yet even considered the cost of synchronous computer interfaces and private telephone lines. Somewhat more economical arrangements might be obtained in some cities, but the overall cost is never negligible.

Even the average computer system consultant is not very knowledgeable in this field. Therefore, the help of communications consultants (provided by most common carriers [e.g., telephone companies]) should be sought when planning anything but the most trivial distributed systems.

CHAPTER 4
HARDWARE IN SUMMARY

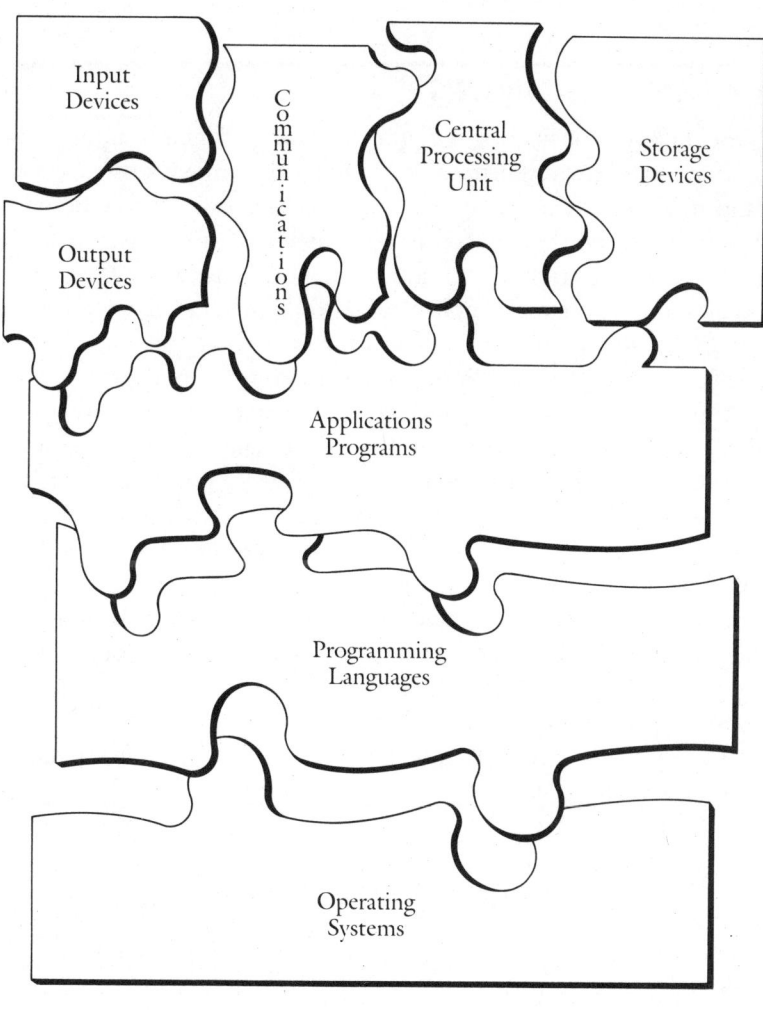

CHAPTER 4

Up to this point we have talked about the basics of computer hardware. We have separately examined devices that serve various purposes. In reality, none of these devices stands alone. In the same way that all the bones of the body go together to form the skeletal system, individual pieces of hardware combine to form a computer system.

If properly assembled, computer hardware will be a sturdy skeleton. Adding appropriate programming can transform the skeleton from lifeless bones into a useful entity that can provide valuable assistance in solving problems in the health care environment. Improper assembly of the bones can result in a ridiculous hoax—just like the Cardiff "giant" perpetrated by scientific pranksters many years ago. In the worst case, the developer might even create a monster capable of hindering progress.

GOING SHOPPING

Before even considering the problem of acquiring a computer system, one needs to study one's environment very carefully, determine those specific problems one wants to solve, and come up with what has been called a **functional specification**—that is, a detailed description of what functions the system is to perform and its general characteristics. In an ideal situation, one would present this functional specification to potential suppliers who would then indicate what they could or could not do. At this point, we will skip the important step of writing the functional specification and deal with it in greater detail in Chapter 16.

Suppose one would like to include in the functional specification a fair amount of detail about computer hardware. This will usually not be something one would do oneself, but one may hire someone to do it instead. What are the hardware capabilities one might want to consider?

When listed in detail, the hardware capabilities are known as the **hardware specification.** With this specification or "shopping list" in hand, one could "go to the store" to shop for hardware. Selecting equipment is not a small step. We recommend that one never go shopping for hardware directly, because once one commits oneself to purchase given hardware, one may find that essential software might not be available on the hardware selected.

The hardware specification would include such items as the following:
1. The kinds of hardware needed: the number and kind of input and output devices, the types and amounts of storage, the type of computer, and the amount of memory and details relating to communications
2. Detailed requirements relating to each piece of hardware in terms of speed, capacity, density (e.g., BPI, on tape), format (such as tape format), access time, and special features (such as floating-point arithmetic processors)
3. Overall considerations such as the total system **throughput** (the amount of work the system must do in a unit of time), physical size, power requirements,

heat output, and availability of and compatibility with software (operating system, languages, applications packages) one intends to run on it
4. Company-related considerations: maintenance arrangements, future development, availability of local support, delivery date, and acceptance test procedure
5. Financial arrangements: purchase, lease, or rental cost, and discounts

FIRST THINGS FIRST

Under normal circumstances, one might be able to find a complete commercially available computer system (a hardware package) that meets the hardware specification and provides the matrix on which to build a system that performs the desired functions. Of course, the sensible consumer adjusts performance requirements (to a reasonable extent) so that they are consistent with real products and are not based on wishful thinking. But suppose no packaged product exists with all the necessary hardware, or at least that none is commercially available as a unit. In this case it would be necessary to write a contract with a company that will take responsibility for modifying an existing product or creating a system from appropriate hardware components (e.g., computer, input and output devices). We believe that development and modification of hardware should be avoided and that wherever possible one company's hardware components should be used throughout.

Because very few of us know much about writing data processing contracts, we often fail to take adequate precautions at this stage, and end up bearing inordinate responsibility for the ultimate hardware package. Alternatively, we expect entirely too much of vendors—often almost precognition.

The potential user who acquires a system without a contract is performing an act of blind faith. In hardware acquisition, much is involved in writing a contract, especially when the hardware comes from several sources or may need to be specially modified.

BUY, LEASE, RENT

Once one has specified all the parts that make up the system, one can estimate its cost. When one adds up the price of all hardware items, one may discover how tentative early rough estimates can be. On the one hand, one may be pleasantly surprised by the ever-falling cost of hardware. More often, the initial enthusiasm about low-cost technology may fade after one sees the final price tag of even a basic microcomputer system. Figures in the neighborhood of $10,000 are common when one requires CRT terminals, hard-copy output, and a useful amount of secondary storage.

Whatever hardware one selects, one should obtain a written quotation from each company approached, or preferably an everything-included quotation from the company who will put the pieces together (OEM or system integrator). Such a quotation has a limited period of validity (often 30 to 90 days), but while it is valid the supplier is committed to supplying the hardware listed at the prices given.

For most micro- and minicomputer systems, the user is typically given only a purchase or lease option, because the availability of a rental arrangement is uncommon when small systems are involved. How one chooses to amortize costs to determine how the system will affect cash flow depends on the approach of one's organization. It should be remembered, however, that a used computer is worth next to nothing after only a few years. Today's hardware will soon be obsolete. Furthermore, a used system will probably be unattractive to potential buyers, compared to the hardware then available. Therefore do not count on recouping much on used computer hardware.

There are, nonetheless, companies specializing in used computers. Sometimes bargains can be found. If a machine has been maintained under a service contract by the previous owner, one must arrange to continue its maintenance contract under one's own name. If it has not been maintained, one must try to negotiate preinstallation inspection and adjustment—at a cost—if one wants to put the equipment on a maintenance contract.

When the hardware price is high (as it is especially with larger systems), there may be another way of proceeding: through rental. However, this option may not be available in all situations.

A lease is essentially an arrangement wherein the leasing company buys the equipment and lets one use it for the period of the lease, charging for the cost of the money, the payback of the money, and a profit. During the term of a lease (most often between 3 and 5½ years) the user normally will use the same equipment. But some leases include an agreement to opt out on several months' notice, after which you can take out the old equipment and bring in a new system. This escape clause may require paying some penalty for opting out or a higher monthly rate. When a lease expires, one usually has three options—extend the lease at a greatly reduced monthly rate, purchase the equipment outright for a lump sum, or allow the lease to expire and return the equipment to the lessor. Leasing arrangements for computer hardware usually demand that the lessee buy a maintenance contract, which typically costs from 10% to 12% of the total hardware price every year.

In approximate figures, on $100,000 worth of hardware, a 5½-year lease would cost the user $148,500 (based on 66 months $\times$ 2.25%—a figure used as an example). A maintenance contract (assuming a 6-month free-warranty period) would cost $60,000 (12% $\times$ $100,000 $\times$ 5 years) for a grand total of $208,500, or about $37,909 per year during the lease period.

In a rental agreement, the user pays nothing toward ownership of the hardware; consequently the monthly charge is often lower than in a lease. When the term of a rental agreement expires, the user may either renegotiate the agreement or return the equipment to its owner. Unlike a lease, the rental agreement usually includes maintenance. Although it also usually contains an opt out clause, there is a financial penalty for terminating a contract prematurely.

Most hardware is manufactured in the United States, and its price is frequently quoted in United States dollars, even in foreign countries. However, various taxes and duties substantially increase hardware cost in many countries outside of the United States. In Canada, for example, the physician in a private office would have to pay 20% to 30% more than the list price, and would also suffer the currency exchange difference. Fortunately, in Canada at least, many institutions such as hospitals qualify for special exemptions from these extra taxes. In the United States the purchase of capital equipment entitles the customer to a 10% investment tax credit.

There are alternatives to procuring one's own in-house hardware. When the cost is excessive in proportion to the projected use of the machine, it may be best to buy time on someone else's computer—for instance, one owned by a time-sharing service bureau or the laboratory down the hall.

In some situations, starting a shared facility may be attractive. A group of physicians might join together to buy a computer with appropriate software that allows multiple users. On the other hand, people who do not need to use a computer all the time might group together to buy a fairly simple machine, and then share it by scheduling its use among themselves.

CHOOSING A SUPPLIER

If one can afford computer hardware, a number of factors will influence choosing a supplier.

Interestingly, previous contact with a certain kind of machine is a strong influence. Familiarity appears to induce a sense of security in computer users. For this reason large computer manufacturers are anxious to have their computers and terminals used in universities. They compete to offer attractive deals because they know that every student is a potential future customer.

Another influence on the consumer is advertising. The general goal is to get one's attention through promotion and attractive packaging. Some small computers are deliberately styled to look like their more powerful relatives. Sometimes specifications in hardware advertising may be misleading, though not inaccurate. What one really wants to know about storage devices is their capacity in bytes (characters), but some manufacturers list their devices' capacities in bits. The wary user will divide this figure by the byte length (typically eight) to see just how much storage the vendor is talking about.

Nearly all manufacturers of computer hardware try hard to offer quality products. Their objective, however, is that one should be sold on *their* products, for once one is committed to a particular manufacturer, the chances are that one will remain with that one. The point of concern, though, is whether or not a particular product will best suit one's specification (both hardware specification and functional specification) for the application. Do not expect the sales representative to make the final decision. How many times, when one asks the grocer if the bread is fresh, does he say "no"?

Having distilled the facts out of advertising, one may have several alternative products that meet the general hardware specifications. It is then necessary to look at the price and performance characteristics of each.

One must first decide whether to take a chance on newly released products or to stick with tested ones. The choice could have great bearing on the system's survivability. A brand-new product will probably have quite a few **bugs.** On the other hand, obsolescence occurs rapidly in the computer field. Manufacturers may abandon obsolete hardware after a time, leaving users with little potential for upgrading their hardware or sometimes for even obtaining parts or service.

Not only computers but also companies become obsolete in this business. This will be true especially in the microcomputer marketplace, where fierce competition will drive many new entries into bankruptcy after a short time and thus leave users of those systems without support of any kind.

To partially insulate their users and themselves against change, some manufacturers build emulators of their previous processors into their newest offerings (or make more advanced systems capable of executing their predecessor's instruction set). In this way users can obtain more modern hardware with better performance than their old hardware, without having to rewrite all their programs. (These old systems are called upward compatible.) Fortunately, even when a new machine has made obsolete an old and very popular model, a company may continue to market the older computer because of the tremendous user inventory of software for that machine and the company's investment in its own software. Sometimes, though, neither of these things happens.

It is generally advisable to obtain state-of-the-art hardware from a company that has the promise of surviving for several years, unless one plans a project with a short lifespan and sees no need for expansion.

When the need for computer resources will predictably increase over time, some hard decisions must be made, because there are at least three initial ways to select hardware. First, one can buy a machine more powerful than what one initially requires, but of course one is paying for unused resources until actual usage increases. Second, one can purchase only the machinery needed, making sure it is capable of future expansion. Finally, one can select an adequate system that is not expandable, but later obtain a separate second system when the need arises. No one approach is always right—users should be aware of all three possibilities and consider which is best for their particular situation.

For larger acquisitions the usual practice is to request legal tenders (Request For Tender [RFT]) for equipment capable of meeting one's specifications. When only tens of thousands of dollars are at issue (as for a micro- or minicomputer system), it may be beneficial to create at least an informal competition among several possible suppliers who know that you are shopping around. Perhaps everyone should consider official tenders.

How long will it take for the hardware ordered to be installed on the premises? Sometimes new equipment is preannounced. Waiting lists for some new machines are often months long. A manufacturer who supplies a few single machines to an anxious customer-base can technically claim that the product exists. The person who is told to wait 24 months for delivery may feel differently.

Even common peripheral devices may not be as quickly available as one might hope. Usually one must wait at least 30 days after placing an order, and waits of 3 to 4 months are common. In this respect, hardware supply houses may help because they stock certain devices. Furthermore, because they buy in volume, they will often sell a particular device at a lower price than the manufacturer's list.

The user's preference for one supplier over another should be influenced by the warranty each offers. We have seen warranty periods as short as 1 month and as long as 1 year.

When the warranty on the hardware expires, it will be necessary to buy a service contract or to arrange for an in-house group to carry out maintenance (and stock spare parts) because all hardware fails sooner or later. Because the annual cost of a service contract is usually 10% to 12% of the total hardware purchase price, the advantage of a long warranty period is evident—with a 12-month free warranty on a $100,000 system one would save $12,000 on maintenance the first year. Maintenance contracts are not all the same. Sometimes there is a deductible clause, as in car insurance. The guaranteed response time to a service call (the time it takes repair personnel to get to the site once one has notified them of a problem) may not be an explicit part of the agreement unless one makes sure it is included. How long will it take to obtain spare parts? If long waits are intolerable, will the supplier contract to keep vital spares on the site or at least on the company's premises? Beware of buying from suppliers who do not have local offices. Consider these things *before* acquiring any system—not after the hardware has been **down** (a genteel term for kaput) for 1 week. Maintenance raises some particularly difficult issues when it comes to decision making.

In selecting computer hardware one faces a fundamental decision—whether to buy everything from one supplier or to take advantage of the best products of many separate manufacturers. Some companies make peripheral devices that are similar, if not functionally identical, to the offerings of the computer manufacturer. For instance, these devices may be **plug-to-plug compatible,** meaning that they simply plug into the manufacturer's computer without modification. Unfortunately, even plug-to-plug compatible devices are not always compatible with the systems software (operating system) of the main computer. Installing such devices may demand modification of the computer's operating system, sometimes by adding software supplied by the peripheral manufacturer. The interchangeable peripheral device market is confusing. One must consider carefully what one is getting into. Even substantial savings may not make it worth the risk. If one is not wary one will wind up being the mediator between different companies who blame each other for a given hardware problem. Moreover, the user gets the task of managing warranties, coordinating delivery dates, arranging repairs, and every other job that the user could avoid if one company assumed responsibility. What one saves in money, one can lose in peace! A much safer approach is to deal with one of the many companies that provide systems made up of diverse components and that also assume overall responsibility for all of the hardware.

Some companies manufacture computers designed to imitate better-known machines. For instance, Amdahl makes its own versions of the larger IBM systems. Some micro- and minicomputers are capable of imitating those of other manufacturers. Sometimes these machines offer advantages (such as speed) over the original equipment. Probably the best example is the compatibility of many new micros with the IBM units.

When possible, listen carefully to the triumphs and tribulations of other health care users of similar hardware. Remember that there has hardly ever been a computer installation without some hardware-related problems.

When the final choice is made, two more factors must be considered. Computer hardware is fragile and it is sometimes damaged during shipment. Insurance should be purchased for transit. Note also that prices quoted for hardware are usually Freight On Board (F.O.B.) at central destinations. If one deals with companies that have no local representative, one may have to pay rather high additional transportation costs. Second, there should be an acceptance test procedure (ATP) that the user and the vendor agree will be a sufficient demonstration that the computer works. Be sure to understand what the ATP is and be sure to be present during its performance.

WARNINGS

The acquisition of a computer is somewhat like getting religion; it will change one's life.

Some new users welcome their conversion for the wrong reasons. Fascination and pride can prevent corrective measures from being executed, even in those cases where a system is patently failing to serve its intended purpose. Another problem concerns those who invest their egos in their hardware. When all decisions that have been made are "perfect" ones, critical assessment of a system and its deficiencies is interpreted as a personal attack. It is a classic case of "love me, love my dog." The best medicine here is preventive; always realize there are alternative and perhaps better answers, and remain critical.

THE FIGHT AGAINST EXTINCTION

The moment computer hardware is acquired, it starts to become obsolete. In health care environments many applications of computers are exceptionally short lived. Research and patient-care priorities seldom remain static over a number of years. Priorities may be poorly specified to begin with, and may need to be altered as true needs are more clearly perceived. Needs sometimes change because of advances in health care and fluctuations in the level of financial supports. Finally, one may be asking the impossible in demanding radical adaptation in the health care environment to suit the introduction of a given system—a fact often discovered only after installation.

Computer hardware, however, is selected to address the needs that have been discerned at one point in time. Foresight should have provided some potential for expansion of the system, but inevitably the needs in a health care environment will change. By the time a computer system is installed, programmed, and functioning it may already be too late. The real world may have passed it by. It is quite possible for a computer project to fall short of its goals from the first day of operation. Even when a system initially serves its purpose, change in the environment ensures that the day will come when it will probably be either inadequate or no longer needed. Health care is a dynamic field and systems that are selected or developed with a capability of being changed will have longer lifetimes.

RESISTANCE TO CHANGE

Acquiring a given hardware system is like taking a photograph of one's operation. There is a big financial and emotional commitment in taking the picture, but the picture will have to be updated periodically if the computer is to continue to reflect the current state of affairs and be a useful tool. The effort to change an existing computer system is often painful and expensive. Once one has recognized the need for change one will have to convince others that change is necessary. At this point those who first resisted the introduction of a computer may fight even more vigorously against changing the existing computer system. Be prepared for this natural resistance to change. In a way, the ideal computer system would be a tool for continual change, but we are still far from realizing that dream.

Computer systems exhibit a great deal of inertia. They are expensive, hard to get used to, and they demand significant adaptation of the organizations that use them. For these reasons, a process that uses computers is difficult to start, hard to redirect, and sometimes nearly impossible to stop, once it is rolling.

Successful steering of a computer system is like flying a huge jet aircraft. It does no good to attempt drastic last-minute alterations in course. The inertia of the craft is so great that it responds only slowly to the controls. To steer a project one must try to anticipate where one wants the system to be at a considerable distance in the future, and then apply slow but steady pressure to achieve the necessary course adjustments.

Remember that a computer project is a complex body of people and systems. It is true that sufficient force will overcome the inertia of any body, resting or moving. However, excessive force exerted over too short a period of time will result in what aircraft designers euphemistically refer to as hull losses. If one tries to start, stop, or redirect a computer project too quickly one will probably destroy it.

WHAT'S MISSING?

A paleontologist can assemble the bones of a dinosaur into the appropriate configuration, but nobody can make the skeleton live. Similarly, once one has assembled the bits and pieces of hardware for a computer installation, one still has a lifeless object that does nothing in spite of its high cost and impressive appearance. Do not let the specification and selection process or the expense of computer hardware lure you into thinking that your problems are over once this machinery sits in the computer room. The work and financial commitment have just begun. Hardware is a vitally necessary but insufficient part of a computer solution.

Systems and user programs (software) will be necessary to breathe life into this hardware, and one will have to buy them or hire people to write them. In Chapter 5, therefore, we shall turn our attention to software.

CHAPTER 5
COMPUTER SOFTWARE

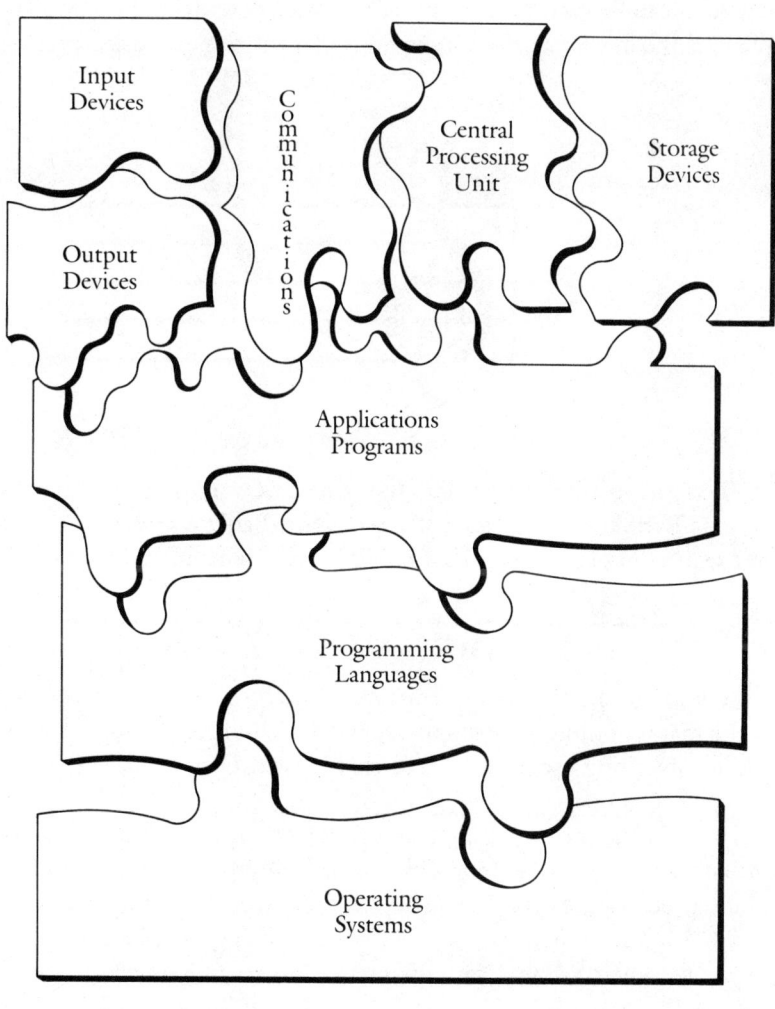

CHAPTER 5

The preceding chapters have looked in some detail at computing machinery, or hardware. We have seen that the selection of appropriate hardware for a computer system is not easy.

However, the difficult part of a computer system is developing software—the programs that tell the computer what to do.

AN ANALOGY

To understand the nature of software it might be useful to consider the software for another kind of hardware: the piano. The piano has an instruction set—the 88 keys that can be used to tell it to make certain sounds (the notes). The software for a piano is the music: a set of commands in a language (music notation).

Means make "C" sound for a certain period of time

It is this software that makes the same hardware provide a Beethoven piano concerto, a Bartok dance, or a Beatles rock tune. Badly written music makes for unpleasant sequences of sounds. The same hardware, but different software.

WHAT IS A PROGRAM?

Put most simply, a computer program is a set of commands in the form of numeric codes that is put into the computer's memory to direct its operation. Programming is the art of writing the proper sequence of instructions to make the computer do what we want it to do.

It should not be surprising that through time, programming has evolved as both an art and a science. Computer scientists have improved the methods for devising, generating, and testing programs. They have also worked on methods for insulating themselves from the tedious process of writing the appropriate numeric code sequences.

At first their job was very difficult. Early computers had to be programmed (or coded) through the use of machine language—the actual numerical instructions idiosyncratic to the given machine. Computers can perform only the most fundamental operations (called the computer instruction set) such as "add" or "store." Any particular model of computer is designed to perform a finite number of different operations (microcomputers generally have a relatively less powerful instruction set than large-scale computers). Because computers are capable of executing only a rather small number of different instructions, it is frequently necessary to combine several instructions in sequence to achieve the overall result we want. For example, to compute the result of the expression A = B + C, the following sequence of machine instructions would be required in most computers:

- Clear the result register and put the number found at memory location B into it.
- Add the number in memory location C to the result register.
- Put the result in memory location A.

In other words, the functions that we humans expect the computer to perform must be expressed at the machine level by a sequence of steps that is quite microscopic compared to our usual way of thinking. In a way one can compare programming a computer to the tedious process of telling a person how to walk. Suppose we had to say, "lift your right foot, move it 32 cm forward, put your right foot down, now lift your left foot," and so on. What we really want to say is "walk over here," but we are forced by the simplicity of the computer to tell it *how* to get here (i.e., the finite microscopic motions must be instructed).

Machine language, therefore, is only the most rudimentary kind of programming language. It is very difficult for people to use. Consequently, over the years computer scientists have created increasingly ingenious translators that take programs written in languages that humans can easily use and convert them into instructions that the machine can understand. We will discuss these translators later in the chapter.

Many different programming languages exist today, and each was developed for particular reasons or for a particular type of human program writer. Each is restricted in some regard and is therefore more suited to certain applications than to others.

HARD-WIRED PROGRAMMING

Programming techniques have come a long way since the days of the first computers. The earliest computing machines supported neither programming languages nor programs as we understand them today. The computation to be done was programmed by wires that interconnected the various circuits. Each individual circuit could perform some specific function such as "negate" or "increment." The way in which these circuits were wired together determined the overall function performed on the input data. To provide at least some flexibility, removable electrical panels called **patchboards** permitted the user to program at the desk by rearranging the pattern of wires. Obviously, the programming that could be done in this manner was not very powerful, because the physical bulk of the patchboards limited the number of instructions that could be wired by the user. Although such computing was limited to specific kinds of functions, it was sufficient for some early applications in accounting. Historical specimens of these patch-wired machines still exist.

These sorts of computers retained their programs because the programs were implemented in the actual wiring of the machine. Interestingly enough, some recent advances in calculator technology call to mind this early concept. Certain calculators now feature plug-in **read only memory (ROM)** modules (sometimes called **firmware,** a term for the no-man's land between hardware and software). By plugging in different modules—just as the earliest programmers mounted wired patchboards on their computers—the user can obtain different sets of factory-supplied programs.

THE STORED PROGRAM

Modern computers and the idea of computer programming as we know it developed with the concept of a **stored program** (as opposed to hard-wired programming). In the stored-program concept no physical difference exists between the way program instructions are stored and the way data is stored in the memory of modern computers. This type of machine is often referred to as a "Von Neumann machine." Whether a number in a memory location represents a program instruction or data depends only on how we treat that number. (When a programming error causes the computer to try to execute data as if the data was an instruction, the computer will do this but the results are unpredictable.)

Historically, entering a program into the computer's memory required significant effort. One of the earliest techniques for entering machine-language programs into the computer's main memory was through using dials and switches. For instance, if the instruction for "add" were "1101," then the programmer had to set the front panel switches to "up-up-down-up" and then press another switch to store this in memory. Some programmers became incredibly quick and accurate in programming the machine this way.

Punched cards and punched tape, invented very early in computer history, provided both a convenient way of preparing programs away from the computer and a means of saving machine-language programs for later use. In this case, the numerical instructions were represented by patterns of punched holes instead of by switch or dial positions. The availability of the typewriter like keyboard devices gave programmers a somewhat more convenient means of entering machine-language programs directly into computers.

Although these latter developments were more convenient than using dials or switches, machine-language programming both taxed the patience of programmers and provided them with many opportunities to make errors.

ASSEMBLERS

A new era in programming came with the use of **assemblers.** Each numerical computer instruction was given an alphabetic code, usually of three or more letters.

(This short form is also known as a mnemonic code.) The set of codes that could be used made up what was called the "assembly language." For example, the instruction to add a number to another number stored in an arithmetic register might have been expressed as "ADD." This made things easier for the programmer because it is easier to remember the word "ADD" than to memorize "1101"—the equivalent numeric code.

Assemblers brought another big advantage to programmers. At last they could assign symbolic values to variables. Instead of having to keep track of the actual location of data items in internal memory, a programmer could simply refer to a variable as "A," for example, and let the computer keep track of precisely where that variable was stored. The assembler would accept mnemonic instructions (in assembly language), translate them on a one-to-one basis into the corresponding machine-language instructions, and assign locations for storing variables.

Although they are relatively tedious to use, assemblers represent a significant advance over machine-language programming. They use the computer as a tool in the programming process, and thus allow programming to become at least a somewhat more human-compatible activity.

We will talk about a further advance on assemblers in Chapter 7.

BEYOND ASSEMBLERS

Although infinitely preferable to machine-language programming, assemblers had drawbacks. As we have seen, simple operations such as adding two numbers and saving the result could require several instructions. Writing programs to perform more complex **algorithms** (sequences of logical steps to perform specific tasks or operations) was even more complicated. Even the performance of input and output functions is extremely tedious when an assembly language is used. Soon, a crisis threatened. It was becoming apparent that it was extremely difficult to produce large, reliable pieces of software by using assembly language. Programmers were wasting a lot of time doing the repetitive coding required to implement their designs.

To overcome this difficulty, more and more advanced kinds of English-like programming languages were developed. These languages enable a programmer to express many machine-language instructions in a single statement. An additional advantage of high-level programming languages is that they are nearly machine-independent. This means that a program written for execution on a particular computer can often be run on a different computer with little modification. Although assembly languages are still used in some situations, such as writing high-speed specialized programs and operating systems, more programmers these days use a high-level programming language. (FORTRAN and BASIC are two common high-level languages in widespread use today. A subsequent chapter will deal with programming languages more fully.)

THE PROGRAMMING PROCESS

Encoding logical steps into a programming language is not particularly difficult. Analyzing a problem and formulating the logic to be used in solving that problem are the most difficult aspects of programming. These facts are reflected by different job descriptions for **systems analysts** (those persons who analyze the problem and formulate its solution in the outline of a program) and for **programmers** (those persons who are responsible for encoding the outline into an actual program and testing it). Today it is usually accepted that both functions are performed by senior programmers.

First the analyst must study the working environment in all its many aspects, for it is this environment that gives rise to the problems that need to be addressed by automation. For example, an accounts-receivable program for a physician's office will be different from accounts-receivable progams for other sorts of businesses. The person or persons doing the programming will need to be familiar with the level of expertise of the eventual users of the programs, so that they can human-engineer the programs. Only by knowing the individuals for whom a program is being written can one hope to design easy-to-use software that produces the kind of output desired in an understandable form.

If these studies have been performed properly, the problem or problems to be addressed should emerge clearly in the mind of the **programmer/analyst.** Possible solutions will then become apparent. Sometimes, a data processing expert will find a possible solution that has nothing to do with automation.

If automation is the appropriate approach, the next step is to organize the solution into a series of logical, step-by-step processes. The logical processes are broken down further into subprocedures and sub-subprocedures, until each small step, in sequence, can be associated with a command or a group of commands in some programming language. Such a process of stepwise refinement is one of the basic principles of **structured programming.**

Many times a programmer will formulate the logic of a program intuitively. Experienced programmers who know their environments will quickly perceive a problem, grasp the solution, and begin to write a code, starting at the beginning of a program and working through to its end. Almost subconsciously the good programmer knows what to do. Science fiction fans will appreciate the analogy to the man from Mars in Robert Heinlein's *Stranger in a Strange Land,* who could instantly understand everything about a problem by a mysterious process of comprehensive intuition that he called "groking."

Unfortunately, earthling programmers are not endowed with this faculty. When we write a program off the top of our heads, it usually contains mistakes. Either the program will not work at all or it will produce erroneous output. Remember that the computer does only what we tell it to do. It will not let us know if there is an error in logic. Therefore much additional work normally must be done to check that a program is working properly and to correct it if necessary. These processes are called **testing** and **debugging.** These processes are also error-prone, and even when done well do not guarantee the correctness of a program. Even when a program appears to be working, we cannot take its perfection for granted. Some kinds of programming errors (or bugs) can remain hidden throughout many successful executions of a program, only to emerge much later when a particular set of data triggers them and causes their effects to surface.

In addition, once a program has been in use for a while, users may think of extensions or modifications that they would like to see. Their needs may also change over time and thus necessitate revising a program that had been functioning well up to that point. Therefore, **software maintenance**—the ongoing correction of errors in and modification of working programs—is a late stage of the programming process that never ends.

In an effort to reduce the number of errors that occur in program writing, the science of **software engineering** has provided formal methods for writing and testing programs. Software engineering will be considered more extensively later in this book. It should be noted in passing, however, that the old technique of **flowcharting** after a program is written—preparing a logical diagram of the steps involved in a program—is now virtually obsolete. Flowcharting post hoc is no substitute for systematic program design and testing methods.

WHEN TO PROGRAM

Creating a computer program and making sure that it works is a difficult job: it requires considerable time and effort by skilled people. Not surprisingly, these skills cost money. The most junior programmer earns as much as many managers. A programmer with a university degree in computer science will exceed the cost of a senior technologist. A senior computer scientist with a postgraduate degree and a background in systems analysis commands a salary usually associated with senior administrators, and that increases with seniority and experience.

Therefore, in today's economic climate the cost of software development can frequently exceed all hardware-related costs in a computer installation. When the problems of ongoing software maintenance are considered, expenditures for software can easily be double those made for hardware acquisition and maintenance. Clearly, then, the effort necessary to create a program is undertaken only under certain circumstances—when the benefits will justify the work and the expense.

Occasionally a computer program is written to perform one single calculation or one specific set of data manipulations that might take literally years to do in any other way. In such cases the computer program may be used only once, but the effort is essential because of the lack of a feasible alternative.

Usually, though, the tasks that we program computers to perform are not particularly complex or, for that matter, inordinately time consuming when they are done once. However, when even a relatively simple task must be performed many times—perhaps each time on different data—then it is beneficial to write a general program that can process any legitimate data. The effort required to create the program is reimbursed because the computer repeatedly performs the tasks that cumulatively would have required a lot of human time.

Most health care–computing applications fall into this latter categorty. Tasks such as biostatistical calculations, creating laboratory reports, or even reporting ECGs are all carried out quite satisfactorily in most institutions without any computer support. However, when computers are programmed to perform these functions, they soon repay the programming effort by greatly reducing the workload on human beings who previously bore the entire burden of doing this repetitious work.

Of course, when a task is both complex and recurrent, the incentive for writing a computer program is even greater. A prime example of such a health care–computing application is the CT scanner. The calculations involved in producing a single image are so numerous and complex that it would not be practical to perform them without a computer. Furthermore, because the computer can use the same calculations with different variables, many scans can be processed every day. Thus computer programming achieves what would be impossible by any other method presently available.

NOT SO SOFT

Software is difficult to create, and because of the large amount of effort that must be expended, writing a program is justified only in particular circumstances.

Once it has been created, software can be anything but soft. On the contrary, it can be completely rigid—that is to say, inflexible. For this reason, the people who create computer programs must often balance the advantages of general-purpose repetitious programming against the disadvantages of the added time and cost involved. On the other hand, a program directed specifically to one application may be small and relatively inexpensive to develop. But if it fails to anticipate slightly different needs that may emerge later, the original economy may be wiped out by the need for extensive modifications.

Although research is continually attempting to formalize and fail-safe the programming process, the self-programming computer of science fiction does not exist. It is therefore apparent that in the health care environment, as in any other place where computers are used, hardware alone is worthless. It is naive to budget only for hardware-related expenses in a computing project. Software and the people who create it are indispensable components in the development, implementation, and continuing modification of any computer system. To achieve anything worthwhile in health care computing, be prepared to spend the greatest proportion of the investment on software.

CHAPTER 6
OPERATING SYSTEMS

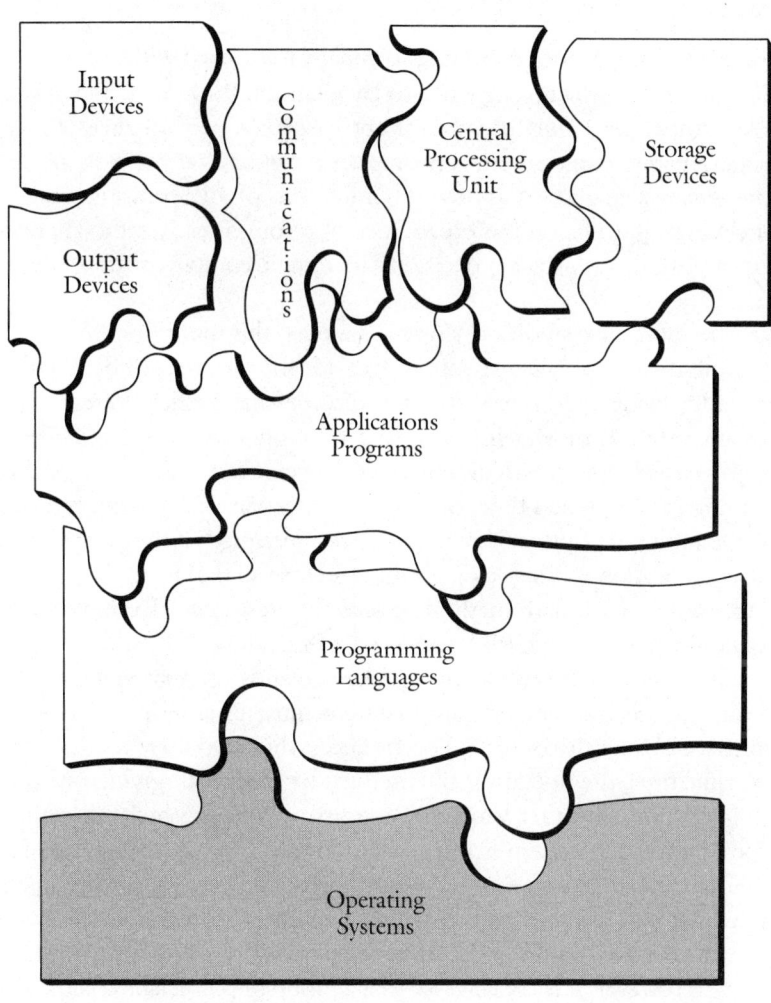

CHAPTER 6

Software (programs) brings computer machinery to life. The two major categories of software are systems programs and applications programs. When specific programs are written to carry out specific user's tasks, these programs are called applications software or applications programs, usually referred to simply as "programs." In the next chapter we will discuss some of the most general features of applications software and the programming languages in which they are written.

In this chapter we will discuss one type of systems program—the operating system.

The operating system is a level of programming users do not supply but is usually provided by the vendor or another company to be used with specific hardware. Examples common on microcomputers today include CP/M, MP/M, MS DOS, and UNIX. A key software product has critical impact on the performance of a system for all its users. The operating system is the master program that controls all the resources of a computer system. The features and limitations of an operating system have an overwhelming influence on the capabilities of a computer system. Therefore, the person responsible for approving decisions to obtain computers must be aware of a few basics.

The more one studies operating systems, the more one becomes aware that no clear-cut divisions really exist. However, for the purposes of basic understanding, it is useful to divide operating systems into somewhat artificial categories: **batch, multistream batch, time-sharing,** and **real-time operating systems.**

When a computer is dedicated to one specific task it may have to do only one thing at a time, one step at a time. Such a computer can wait for the **resources** required to do the job (e.g., input and output devices, memory) if they are busy. For such dedicated applications, a simple operating system is all that is needed; its primary function is to provide a standard method of accessing resources. Examples of these dedicated operating systems are CP/M and MS-DOS.

However, when several users make demands on a system's resources simultaneously, a more complex operating system must exist to permit shared access to resources and to settle conflicts. For instance, when two users request data from a disk at the same time, the operating system must be capable of giving one user the go-ahead while making the other wait until the first user is finished. This more sophisticated type of operating system is responsible for arbitrating who gets to be first.

There are several reasons why a group of users may want to use the same computer system. It may be the only way users can afford a computer. An individual family practitioner, for instance, might not be able to afford a dedicated computer capable of billing. However, it is conceivable that a group of physicians could economically share the cost of a computer system to handle such needs.

Although a shared system may be dictated by financial considerations, it can have other advantages. With such a system users can also share data, programs, and ideas. This cooperation is especially valuable in an interdependent medical research environment. A group of users may also be able to afford the sophisticated resources of a machine more powerful than any one of them could afford alone. Yet if users are to cooperate in using a system, they must be willing to tolerate some degree of inconvenience. The best operating systems try to minimize this inconvenience while distributing limited resources among all users equitably.

In the simplest case users can take turns, one after the other, in using a computer. This approach is called **scheduled access.** The users themselves do the scheduling. This solution is attractive because it is simple and inexpensive. For a small number of users it may be quite adequate. The operating system for such a machine will be simple, because all of the machine's resources will be dedicated to the particular user scheduled to use the computer.

At the next level of complexity, the operating system schedules access to the machine. In a batch operating system, many users submit their jobs to the computer at once—often in the form of decks (batches) of punched cards—and the computer then proceeds to execute these jobs as quickly as possible, one after the other. It usually does this by reading in the cards for the first job and doing what they say, then reading in the next batch of cards, and so on (Figure 6-1, *A*). By taking care of the scheduling, the computer minimizes the time between jobs.

Such simple **batch processing** has its limitations. When a system is designed to deal with only one job at a time, its throughput (number of jobs performed per unit of time) is very low. The amount of work the computer does will be small compared to the potential of the machine. Processors are so fast that, when dedicated to one job (assuming the job is not solving a complex numerical problem) they spend very little time actually computing. The CPU is usually idle, waiting for slow operations such as input and output to be completed. When a dedicated processor must wait for input from a terminal, the CPU is wasting time—literally doing nothing. (Remember, a user inputting data may average one character/second; a computer could execute a million instructions during a second.) In single-task computers, the percentage of **processor utilization** (the amount of time the computer spends actually executing instructions divided by the total elapsed time $\times$ 100) may be very low.

One solution to this efficiency problem is the multistream batch system (Figure 6-1, *B*), which allows multiple jobs (batches) to run apparently simultaneously by giving another job a resource as soon as a previous job is through with it. Thus one job can be using the CPU and another the disk. The resources are kept busy and for all practical purposes several jobs are getting done at once. Some microcomputers equipped with the proper hardware operating systems can do something like this. For example, output can be sent to a device attached to the printer and stored there. The CPU can return to word-processing functions while the printer is finishing printing out the portion of the text sent to it. When that is done, the printer says it is done with that batch of text and requests the next block of data, interrupting the CPU for only a short time.

FIGURE 6-1

Batch processing. **A,** In a batch processing system, a job (a batch of cards or the equivalent) is processed completely, then the next job, and so on. Each job uses whatever system resource it needs, when needed. Between the times a resource is used, the resource is idle—wasted. This idle time could be used if a proper method of assigning resources to other jobs (i.e., sharing the resources) were available. **B,** One such way of sharing is to have several jobs waiting in line and to assign a given resource to one of them when a previous job has released the resource. This will use the wasted time and it will appear that several jobs are being done at the same time. Such a system is called a multistream batch system.

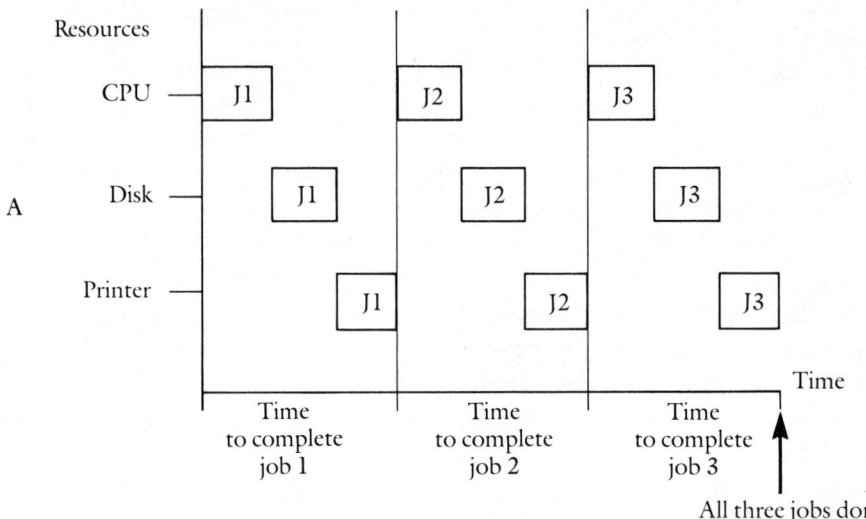

A

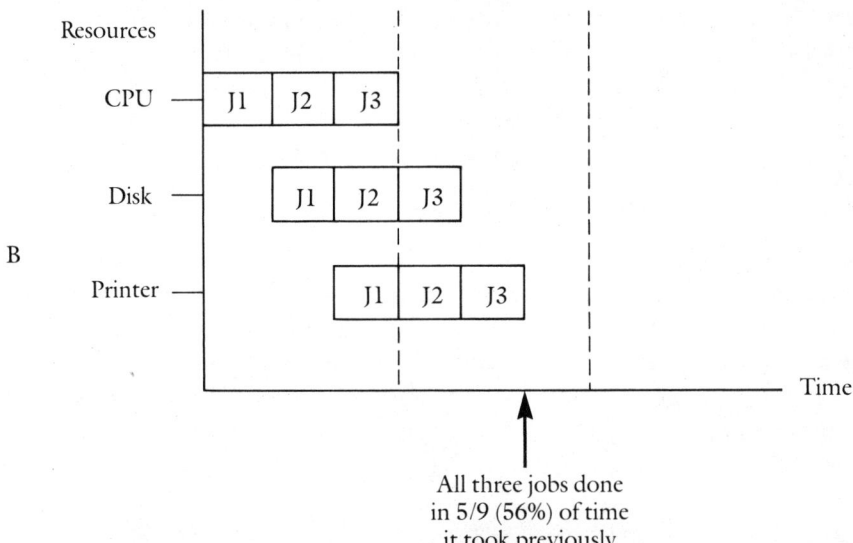

B

TIME-DRIVEN OPERATING SYSTEMS

There are several ways in which an operating system can be designed to make use of what would otherwise be idle CPU time to accommodate multiple users. In a time-sharing operating system the computer's CPU devotes a finite amount of time (a time slice) to each user's program in sequence.

There are two kinds of time-sharing. The oldest and least efficient is called **swapping**. When job A's turn (time slice) has expired, it is transferred out of main memory onto secondary storage (disk). Job B is then read from the disk into the main memory, executed for a time, and then put back onto the disk, so that the computer can turn its attention to job C. When job A's turn comes around again, it is read back into the main memory and execution is resumed. The process repeats indefinitely in a round robin fashion until each job is completed (Figure 6-2). The disadvantage of swapping is that a significant portion of the computer's time is spent in switching from job to job (taking programs and data to and from the disk). During this process no execution of the users' instructions is carried out.

A modern method of time-sharing is one in which all the jobs to be time-shared remain resident in internal memory until they are completed—whether or not they are actively being executed. With the decreasing cost of memory, this has become the more common method. In many modern systems swapping is a recourse only when the main memory is full. In the memory-resident case, the operating system executes each user's instructions for a short time, then goes to the next user, and so on, but the step of moving each user's program to and from the disk is eliminated. There is still some time wasted in switching from job to job but this is very much reduced compared to the swapping approach.

Time-sharing works amazingly well in certain health care applications. That the computer can easily cope with the (for it) light workload of apparently doing several jobs simultaneously gives each person the illusion of sole use of the machine. The computer can serve many users, making its use feasible when it would otherwise be economically impractical.

Sharing extends to resources other than the processor—such as a disk. However, using other resources is sequential, on a first-come-first-served basis. For example, when the user needs data or has some data ready to be saved or printed, the user's request for the disk or printer is **queued** and the user will be given service as soon as his or her turn comes up.

The ultimate basis for time-sharing is the assumption that users do relatively little computing (use of the CPU), and that the system quickly gets to the point of waiting for user input or for slow output terminals to type out results. During this input/output (I/O) time other users can be served. It is easy to see there are ultimate, practical limits on any system, however, because sooner or later the waiting periods in queues for various resources will become lengthy, and the system will simply take too long to complete any one job. Interestingly, a very powerful processor will not help

FIGURE 6-2
Time-sharing. The CPU is dedicated to each job (user program) for a short period of time. Even though only milliseconds are involved, the CPU can execute thousands of instructions during each time slice. The round robin rotates on the order of a hundred times per second. The general idea here is that a job should be complete in a very few rotations. If not, then the overhead (the time taken to switch from job to job—ignored in the diagram) is excessive. Special (algorithmic) procedures exist in some systems to give a larger time slice to jobs that remain in the round robin too long. Thus the jobs are finished off, and overhead is reduced.

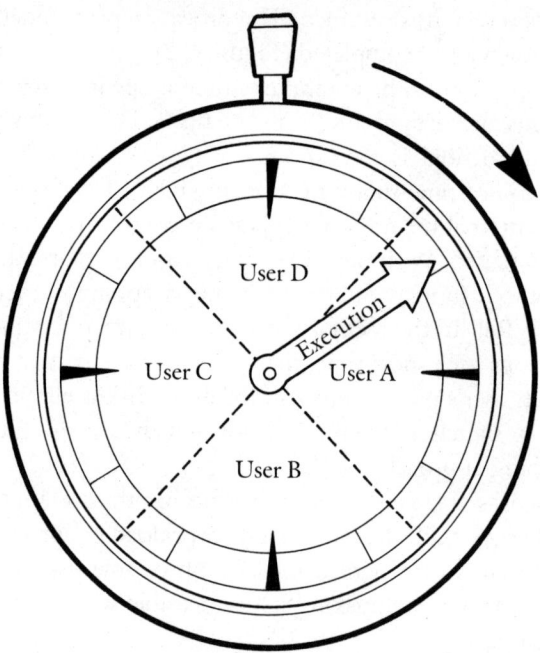

here; access to other slower resources is the rate-limiting step. A system limited by the time spent in I/O queues is called **I/O bound.**

EVENT-DRIVEN OPERATING SYSTEMS

A class of circumstances exists for which time-sharing operating systems are not suitable. If, for instance, we must detect an event or measure it in real time (that is, as it happens), the computer obviously must act when the event occurs—not when the

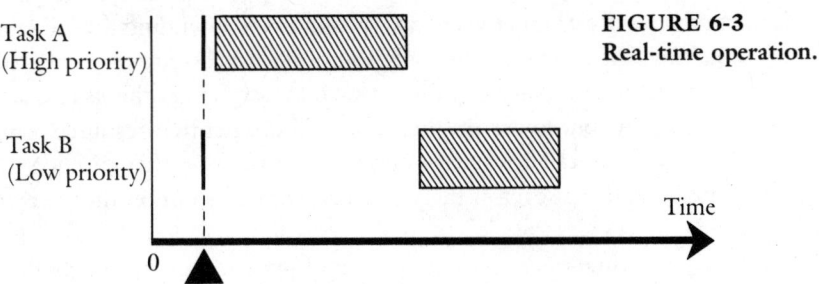

**FIGURE 6-3
Real-time operation.**

Tasks A and B request resource simultaneously.
A is served first, then B.

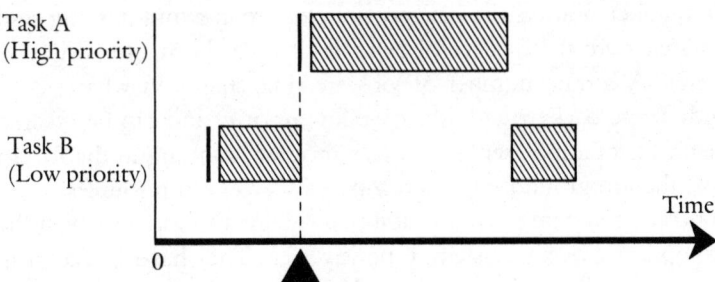

Task A requests resource while task B is using it.
Having higher priority, A interrupts B and gets resource.
B gets resource back when A is finished with it.

computer chooses to do so. An operating system that can respond to events as they happen is **event-driven** and is called a real-time operating system. A real-time operating system allows external devices to preempt the computer's attention precisely when they need it. Even time itself can be used to drive the system. In this case an electronic signal occurring at a given rate (called a **real-time clock**) is the event to which the system responds.

Another kind of real-time event is entering a sequence of items that make up a record or transaction. In this case the arrival of the collection of data stimulates the operation system into a sequence of steps to store and to file this data. Real-time operating systems come in simple and complex varieties. An event-driven system dedicated to a single **task** (job or program) simply waits for events to occur and then does what it is supposed to do (such as perform a measurement or a computation). A **multitasking** or **multiprogramming** system is one that attempts to cope with several tasks at the same time by interspersing their component computational parts and by scheduling access to systems resources. In this case, requests for resources must be coordinated because they are driven by external happenings in the real world. Sooner or later conflicts will occur between jobs (programs) contending for the same resource at the same time. At this point, the only solution is to allocate resources according to some predefined priority, favoring one task while sacrificing others. The favored job is served immediately, but lower-priority tasks will not get that resource until the other job has finished with it. The systems designer must ensure that conflicts are resolved quickly enough and that even if there are delays, the system on the average keeps up (Figure 6-3).

Ideally, a real-time operating system would inform users when conflicts occur or would at least be able to generate output indicating how conflicts had been resolved. In practice, this kind of service is rare.

Many other ingenious operating systems have been designed in an effort to give the greatest number of users the best possible service in a multitasking system. Some operating systems are hybrids, combining features of both time-driven and event-driven systems. A certain number of jobs are time-shared in what we will call the **background.** These background jobs have low priority and can be preempted when an instrument, for example, sends data to a program running in the **foreground.** In other words, the foreground job has top-priority access to resources.

Some operating systems have the ability to juggle the way in which they allocate resources to optimize overall system responsiveness. They have special programs that are able to discern what is happening and to adjust scheduling resources to needs. They differ from other operating systems in their adaptability to different demands placed on them.

LIMITATIONS

Many multitasking operating systems theoretically permit a large number of jobs to be done apparently at the same time. In practice, however, the whole process breaks down at some point in every system. For one thing, it takes time (called **overhead**), to switch from the job currently being executed to another. A certain amount of time is lost from every second. If a computer is asked to perform too many tasks or to serve too many users, at some point it will simply not get around to completing a given assignment in time or at least sufficiently quickly to satisfy a user. Some time-shared operating systems are sufficiently advanced so that when they perceive one job coming around for execution too many times (and thus generating unacceptable overhead by taking too long to finish) they will give that job a large time slice to finish it off and get it out of the way.

OTHER FUNCTIONS OF OPERATING SYSTEMS

Besides permitting resource sharing, a useful operating system will provide other services essential to operating a shared computer system. Not all operating systems provide every one of these features, but the better ones will provide most of them.

The operating system protects individual users and their data from one another and from intruders (this is called "security"). It controls access to the system by passwords, ensures that users' programs do not interfere with each other during execution, and makes certain that users cannot tamper with each other's data either accidentally or maliciously. This is called a security capability.

An operating system will provide resources to permit mundane tasks such as **backup**—copying all data and programs contained on the system's disks onto other disks or less accident-prone media such as magnetic tape. **Transaction logging,** a process that keeps a copy (usually on magnetic tape) of every user interaction with the computer, may also be provided. These kinds of programs are usually called **utilities.**

The operating system is also responsible for accounting for systems use, especially in commercial installations that sell computer time.

If desired, the operating system can provide statistics on resource use so that adjustments to its methods of allocating these resources can be made as required.

Finally, the operating system provides all users with standard methods of storing, retrieving, and transferring data—even between jobs when necessary. It can also provide **device independence.** This means that users need not be aware of the precise characteristics of the devices that are used for input, output, and storage.

PROBLEMS WITH OPERATING SYSTEMS

Operating systems are among the most intricate programs ever devised; for some of them, development time was counted in thousands of person-years. Because these programs are so complex, it is nearly impossible to get all of the bugs (errors) out of them. These programs can be executed in a nearly infinite number of ways, with the result that perfection is impossible. Every run is a test. Users therefore will note problems from time to time and report them to the company that supplied the system. This company will provide corrections (**patches**) and will periodically issue a revised version of the operating system. New versions of an operating system are usually palliative measures designed to eliminate old bugs—but sometimes they introduce new ones of their own.

The never-ending campaign against bugs necessitates that the user purchase a **software maintenance contract,** so that the old operating system will be replaced by refined versions as they become available. Updates may occur up to several times a year. An operating system is expensive, and in the case of purchased operating systems, yearly software maintenance costs to the user is up to one third of the original cost of the software. More on software maintenance will be found in Chapter 8.

Not only do operating systems contain errors, but it may also be impossible to add more disk storage to a computer simply because the operating system was not designed to handle that much secondary memory.

A couple of final observations should be made regarding the limitations imposed by operating systems. Generally, the more complex the system, the more memory it will require. Advanced operating systems for big machines can occupy large amounts of internal memory. Internal memory used by an operating system is usually not available for user programs. If a system is tailored for a specific application, its operating system will probably be reasonably small. But if the operating system is designed for a general-purpose system, it will be correspondingly larger.

Another restriction of operating systems is that in general, the bigger they are, the longer they take to perform their functions. Users who demand a sophisticated operating system may find systems performance slowed down in direct proportion to their demands for sophistication.

DOING THE IMPOSSIBLE

We make nearly impossible demands on operating systems. Time-shared operating systems are supposed to facilitate access to computer resources by many users, but they must achieve this in such a way that any individual user thinks that he or she has sole use of the computer. What is worse, operating systems are forced to do this "on the fly" because the demands on them are unknown until after those demands are actually made.

In a computer installation designed to serve more than one user at a time—as is the case even with the majority of minicomputers and some microcomputers today—the operating system is a vital consideration. If the right one is chosen, it will seem to do the impossible. But an inappropriate one will be a source of continuing frustration and perhaps ultimately of project failure. Therefore, before getting involved with any computer, carefully choose and get to know its operating systems. The operating system is the software that gives life to inanimate hardware. In many ways it is the operating system that gives a computer its characteristic personality—a fact nowhere as obvious as in those cases in which several companies supply different operating systems for the same hardware. The resulting systems can be radically different in what they can do and in the types of applications they can serve.

CHAPTER 7
PROGRAMMING LANGUAGES AND APPLICATIONS PACKAGES

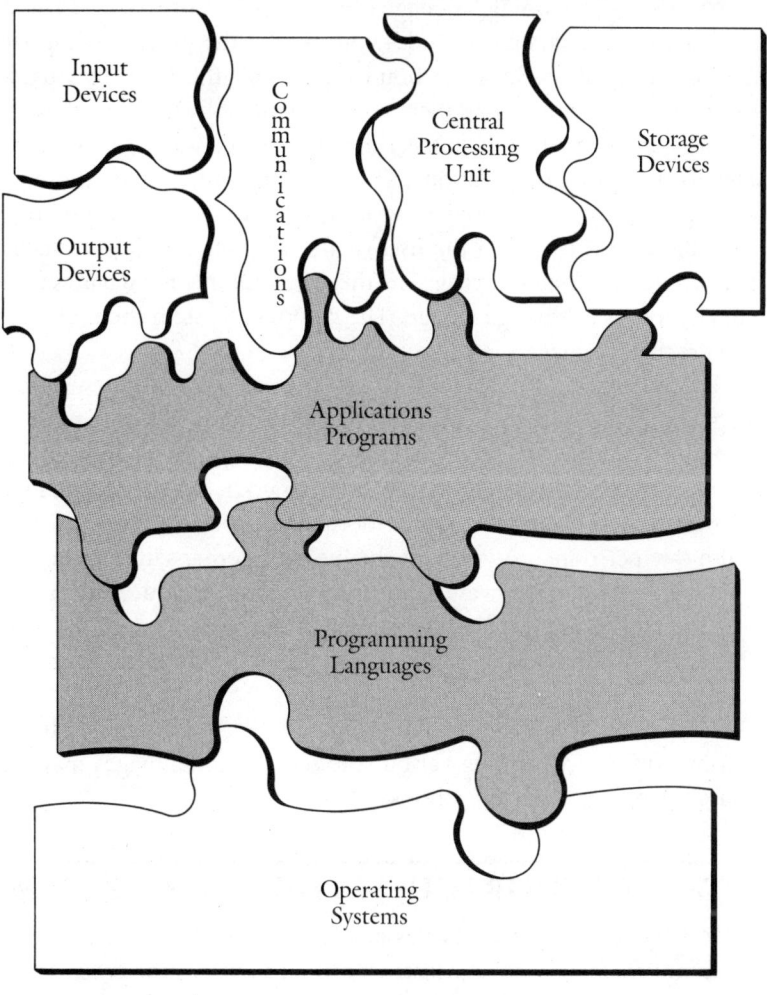

CHAPTER 7

In Chapter 5 we saw that computers are able to understand only instructions coded in machine language—the numeric codes that instruct the machine to perform its most basic, primitive functions. Machine language, however, is difficult for people to comprehend. Consequently, computer scientists have created systems software that converts applications programs written in more human-readable programming languages into the machine-language instructions that computers can carry out. There are numerous different programming languages, each developed for particular kinds of applications. Each language has individual strengths and weaknesses, depending on the purposes for which it was created.

Some programming languages are function related (i.e., they have been developed to cope with a general area of data processing such as database management or scientific calculation). Other languages have been created to serve specific target areas such as health care, business, or scientific programming.

No one programming language is ideal in all circumstances. Therefore, evaluating a given computer system includes considering the programming language(s) available on that system. In an in-house operation, the languages used may affect the productivity of the programmers and the kinds of programs they can write (e.g., a language designed to facilitate arithmetic calculations may be awkward for character-string [text] manipulation). Even in an instrument with a computer built in, the language the developer used in writing the program is important, because it may affect the ease with which the user or the supplier can modify such a system in the future. Finally, whatever programs the user acquires for whatever applications, they will be written in some language. The computer system the user intends to use *must* support that language.

The purpose of this chapter is to give the reader an overview of the general sorts of programming languages available for different kinds of programming applications. It is not our intention here to provide an exhaustive list of all programming languages or to give detailed instructions on how to program in any particular language. Computer programming is a profession that normally lies far outside the interest or skills of health care personnel. A word for the future is perhaps important at this point. Computer scientists and software companies are coming out with a new generation of programming languages that are far more user friendly than the languages of today. This development should eventually put the ability to create systems in the hands of the user.

Those who wish to study the techniques of programming and the syntactic and semantic differences among various programming languages may seek this information in computer science textbooks.

TAKING SHORTCUTS: THE MACRO ASSEMBLER

In Chapter 5 we saw that assembler languages translate mnemonic, alphabetic codes into machine-language instructions on a one-to-one basis. Although this was an improvement over machine-language programming, it was still fairly tedious.

The next enhancement of assembler-programming languages was to allow programmers to save on some secondary storage medium the **routines** (short parts of a program or a related series of program instructions) they frequently used. Programmers could associate a new mnemonic with each routine. Such a mnemonic is called a **macro.** Macro instructions could thereafter be used in programs in the place of these routines. Every time the assembler saw one of these macros, it would automatically substitute the appropriate series of assembler instructions. A library of useful macros enabled an assembler programmer to be more productive because it eliminated much repetitious coding.

Sophisticated macro assemblers are still very much in use. Assembler-language programming is generally used when programmers need to manipulate the individual locations or the bits of computer memory. Most operating systems (which are themselves programs) are written in assembler.

An assembler can be a powerful, efficient tool to produce the fastest kinds of programs that use the least memory—which may be important in certain real-time applications (an application where the computer must process data as soon as it is received and not get behind), especially in support of instrumentation. However, assembler-language programming is tricky. Assembler programs are often lengthy, and errors in them may be difficult to find or to prevent. Programmers who must modify an assembler-language program they did not themselves write may have a difficult time in simply trying to figure out how the program works before they can even consider modifying it. In fact, assembler-language software is obscure enough that companies can usually count on its acting as a form of encryption, effectively protecting their proprietary software from modification by customers.

Health care–computing applications are usually not static, and ultimately one must face updating the applications software. It is usually best if the vendor does this, preferably at a reasonable cost. If not, then updating will fall to inhouse staff personnel, who did not write the original program. This can lead to a project of uncontrolled cost and interminable length. So unless the vendor is willing to alter the program to meet changing requirements, using assembler-language programming may therefore be an especially critical problem in health care.

HIGHER-LEVEL LANGUAGES

Assembler languages are closer to machine instructions than to human language. Because developers recognized this handicap affecting human productivity, they saw the need for programming languages closer to our way of expressing logical procedures, arithmetical calculations, and textual manipulations. Today there are many higher-level programming languages: ALGOL, BASIC, COBOL, FORTRAN, Pascal, RPG, and SNOBOL, to name but a few on a very long list. Their variety attests to the diverse purposes for which they were created. However, these languages are not even close to everyday human language. They still require trained programmers to use them effectively, although an introduction to one of them is sufficient to get a neophyte started.

COMPILERS

Getting closer to the human way of expressing problems demands that the computer do more translation work for us. A compiler is a program that takes **source code** (a program) written in a higher-level language and translates it into **object code**. Object code may be machine language the computer can directly execute, or it may be an intermediate language that requires another translation step at execution time to get to machine language. A translation process much more complex than the simple one-to-one translation characteristic of the assembler is used. This allows the closer-to-the-human form of expression (Figure 7-1).

One of the earlier but most durable languages using a compiler is FORTRAN, an acronym that stands for FORmula TRANslator. As the name suggests, this language was designed for scientists. It permits them to say, for instance, "C= (A+B)*3.125/E" close to the way we would write it algebraically: "C = (A + B) × 3.125 ÷ E"—an expression that would require many machine-language or assembler instructions to program.

Other languages were developed for different purposes. COBOL is a business language. Although some consider it cumbersome and verbose, it is nevertheless fairly easy to learn and permits flexible manipulation of text strings and handling data files on secondary storage. Most high-level languages support including nonexecutable comments to assist others in understanding the programs. Still another language is ALGOL—a language that seems to be preferred by people involved in numerical analysis.

A favorite among computer hobbyists is BASIC. It is perhaps the first programming language most people learn.

FIGURE 7-1
A programmer writes a *source program* in a human-readable programming language. A compiler translates these English-like statements into instructions that the computer can execute—an *object program*. At execution, the computer usually does further processing of the object program (e.g., adding library routines), and then the program is executed and its *output* is produced.

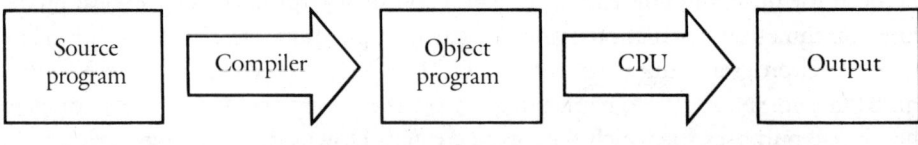

There are many other compiled languages, and each can support some kinds of applications more easily than others. Each programming language generally can be considered to have its own domain of application or a type of expert who prefers to use it.

A certain degree of **software transportability**—the ability to take a program written on one computer and run it on a different computer—has been realized through using high-level languages. Standards have been defined for a number of high-level human-readable languages. Programs following these standards will execute in exactly the same way on different computers. Adherence to these standards is, however, not universal. FORTRAN, for example, has undergone numerous revisions during the past decade, and every company seems to have its own variations, incompatible with those of other companies. Each nonstandard extension of a common language gives added flexibility to programming, but it also has the negative effect of closely binding a user to one company or even to one machine type. Often an institution will use the machines of only one manufacturer, with the hope that programs can be run on all computers in that institution without modification. This can be in vain, however, because the same manufacturer may change its versions of programming languages from model to model or even between different releases of the same operating system.

Some compilers are smarter than others. Some are **optimizing compilers** that automatically correct obvious inefficiencies in source programming. As one might expect, faster compilers with more luxury features are usually available on larger computers. Today they can sometimes be found even on microcomputers.

New languages are constantly being developed and released for use. Not many of these ever seem to achieve widespread popularity. Instead, programmers seem to prefer a few well-established programming languages—possibly because of previous training and simply because they are familiar with them.

INTERPRETERS

Another approach to implementing a high-level programming language is the interpreter. Interpreters do not produce machine-language object code for a whole program (as in the case of compilers). Instead, they accept source language and interpret it one small segment at a time, executing the user program piece by piece as each portion is encountered. When the interpreter moves on to the next part of the code, it forgets the previous part it has just executed. A large amount of overhead is involved in processing with an interpreter. Instead of compiling a source program only once and then executing machine language thereafter, each piece of source code has to be translated each time it is encountered before it can be executed.

BASIC (a simplified FORTRAN-like language), is probably the most widespread interpretive high-level language. BASIC is a common language for personal microcomputers. Other languages such as APL (a language favored by mathematicians) are also popular interpreters. In the health care environment, MUMPS is a well-known interpreter for database manipulations. (It is actually a language implemented as part of an operating system.) LISP is an interpreter used mostly by artificial-intelligence researchers.

Although interpreters are slow compared to compilers, they offer some advantages. When a user wants to debug (correct) a program, an interpreter can make the job easier because the source code can always be worked on at any point in execution. A program can be stopped and changed, and its execution can be resumed far more easily than with most compilers. Therefore, a number of high-level languages are available in both interpretive and compiled modes—the former for debugging, the latter for high-speed execution after the bugs have been corrected.

In this discussion we have (for the sake of simplicity) deliberately avoided some of the more detailed technical aspects of overlaying techniques, different structures of languages, and compiler and interpreter design. Interested readers can refer to many textbooks in a computer science library or a well-equipped book store on the topics of languages and compilers.

BEYOND HIGH-LEVEL LANGUAGES

The ultimate goal in the quest for a human-like programming language would be a computer that could understand ordinary (or natural) language and formulate its own program. Of course, only very limited examples of such ideals exist, although a goal of artificial-intelligence research is to develop such a language.

However, computer scientists are continuously striving to develop programming languages that are less and less dependent on exact syntax. Less formal languages would enable nonprogrammers to instruct computers to perform certain tasks. Some success has been realized with **query languages**—languages that allow a person to sit down at a terminal and request from a database the data that meet the criteria specified. The ultimate goal here is that users should be able to instruct the computer on *what* they want done in as normal a way as possible—they should not have to tell it *how* they want it done, as required by most of today's languages.

EXTENSIONS TO HIGH-LEVEL LANGUAGES

For specialized applications, an ordinary programming language may not have all the required features. For this reason, various sublanguages that append to a regular high-level language have been written. A **data management language (DML)** is a special sublanguage for handling data storage and retrieval in a database system. A **data definition language (DDL)** enables one to structure (organize) the storage of data on secondary-storage devices. Real-time systems must include appropriate extensions to their programming languages for such applications as **analog-to-digital conversion.**

Newer languages are just beginning to become commonly available that are high-level enough that everyday users can use them with relatively little instruction. Languages such as NOMAD and RAMIS can be used after a few days' training to do data retrieval and produce useful reports. The most important single reason for using such languages is that they can potentially reduce or eliminate the need for programmers and allow users to use the computer directly without intermediaries. The result will be short-circuiting of the usual long waits and high costs associated with programmer development of software.

These early very high-level languages are not the final word—and they are not universally successful. But they are the leading edge of a new era that will bring software finally up to speed and parallel in the software domain what very large-scale integration (VLSI) has meant in the hardware domain. Research has already led to the first example of formal descriptions of a data management environment being able to be compiled into operational programs that meet specific needs.

APPLICATIONS PROGRAMS AND PACKAGES

We usually label as programs those sets of instructions (written in some programming language) that direct the computer to perform a specific task or operation.

Certain kinds of programs are needed by many users. In health care, biostatistical support is a requirement of those involved in administration or research. People who use computers in areas such as statistics do not want to write programs; they only want the computer to supply results. To serve users such as these, various companies market software **applications packages,** designed to be easily used by many different users. In biostatistics, for example, SPSS and SAS are two well-known and time-proven packages. Detailed instruction manuals enable nonprogrammers who understand statistics to process their own data.

Many other applications packages are designed to meet widely different needs. Popular examples of these include VisiCalc, a program that allows complex calculations to be easily set up by the user, and WordStar, a word processing package.

There are advantages in using software packages. The main advantage is that the cost of purchasing such packages is enormously less than the cost of developing them. The reason is that the companies developing sophisticated programs can spread out their costs over hundreds or even thousands of users, each of whom pays a relatively small fee to use the final product. Packages are usually well tested in the field (and consequently more bug-free), thanks to scores of users who have employed them in different circumstances. Another advantage is that using a common applications package allows users to exchange data when necessary.

Some companies market specific software packages with specific hardware systems as complete, integrated products. These are called turnkey systems. This practice is common in business systems in which hardware is provided along with applications packages to deal with hospital business problems such as payroll and accounts receivable. Radiology reporting systems and admitting/discharge/transfer (ADT) systems are two other common examples of health care–oriented turnkey systems.

The main disadvantage of applications software packages is that they are often large and monolithic. One must take all or nothing. The user who needs only basic statistical analysis may be frustrated when the other 70 statistical tests that are part of a package will not fit into the memory of that organization's small computer. Another potential drawback is that most applications packages are copyrighted and cannot normally be modified to suit individual needs.

As a rule, the user is well advised to purchase, lease, or rent a software package if one exists for the kind of application needed. It does not make economic sense to reinvent the wheel.

THE LANGUAGE HIERARCHY

There has been a steady evolution of programming languages from primitive machine language to the most sophisticated optimizing compilers. The languages at each level have specific uses, and each language in the hierarchy represents a significant advance over lower levels.

Machine language	01101000	00001000
	01110000	00001001
	00010100	00001010
Assembler	CLA A	
	ADD B	
	STO C	
High-level languages	C=A+B (FORTRAN—a scientific language)	
	ADD A TO B, GIVING C. (COBOL—a business language)	

VERY HIGH-LEVEL LANGUAGES

"Print the current balance." (The system knows what "current balance" means and performs the necessary calculations, presenting the result to the user.) The particular needs of certain types of applications have spurred the evolution of new species among high-level languages. These needs can be as diverse as those associated with high-level mathematics (needs that spawned APL), or those associated with database management in a health care environment (needs that gave rise to MUMPS). Applications packages have developed in response to similar needs in many environments.

However, different computers may support different programming languages and consequently different software packages. Considering the programming languages available for a given vendor's system, therefore, is essential in setting up any health care–computer application.

In a health care environment, computing needs are likely to change frequently. A dynamic research situation may necessitate a continuous process of program writing and rewriting. Alternatively, failure to study thoroughly a problem before writing programs will automatically set the stage for software modifications. It makes sense to use a programming language that can be a powerful tool for the original programmers and that can be understood by future programmers who may have to modify programs they did not write. The installation that uses assembler-level programming or some obscure higher-level language not well known to most programmers may have difficulties. It has been shown that programmers generally produce the same number of lines of program daily, whether they are using low-level assembler language or high-level languages. High-level languages can often accomplish more in one line of code than a hundred or more assembler-language statements could. Economics dictates that a high-level language is preferable, whenever it is possible to use one.

Factors such as the speed of execution, the kind of computer, along with the amount of internal memory required to support different languages, and the availability of specific needed language features must all be considered before a systems design can be finalized.

The cost of programming languages must also be reckoned in planning any system. In any given system, the system software may come either **bundled** (its cost included with the price of the hardware) or **unbundled** (its cost figured separately). Unbundled costs make up a significant proportion of the whole systems cost. A BASIC interpreter for a microcomputer system typically costs less than $100. A data management language (e.g., dBASE II or Oracle) for the same system can cost hundreds or even a few thousand dollars. A COBOL compiler for a minicomputer can cost up to $10,000. When several different kinds of applications are contemplated that may require several languages, the cost of providing these languages cannot be ignored. Finally, there is an annual cost associated with their maintenance by the supplier.

It must also be remembered that programming languages are intimately dependent on the operating system of the computer on which they run. The operating system may therefore dictate which languages one can use.

Even an excellent computer system with an appropriate operating system and a superb high-level language may not be appropriate if a needed applications package is not available for that machine, in a language that the machine supports.

CHOOSING YOUR TOOLS

Obviously, then, these are things to think about before acquiring a system. Programming languages and applications packages are the fundamental tools that permit programmers and users to approach the particular job at hand. Select these tools carefully. An artist can use a sharp chisel to work wonders with wood, but cannot use a chisel to paint pictures.

CHAPTER 8
THE SYSTEM IN SITU

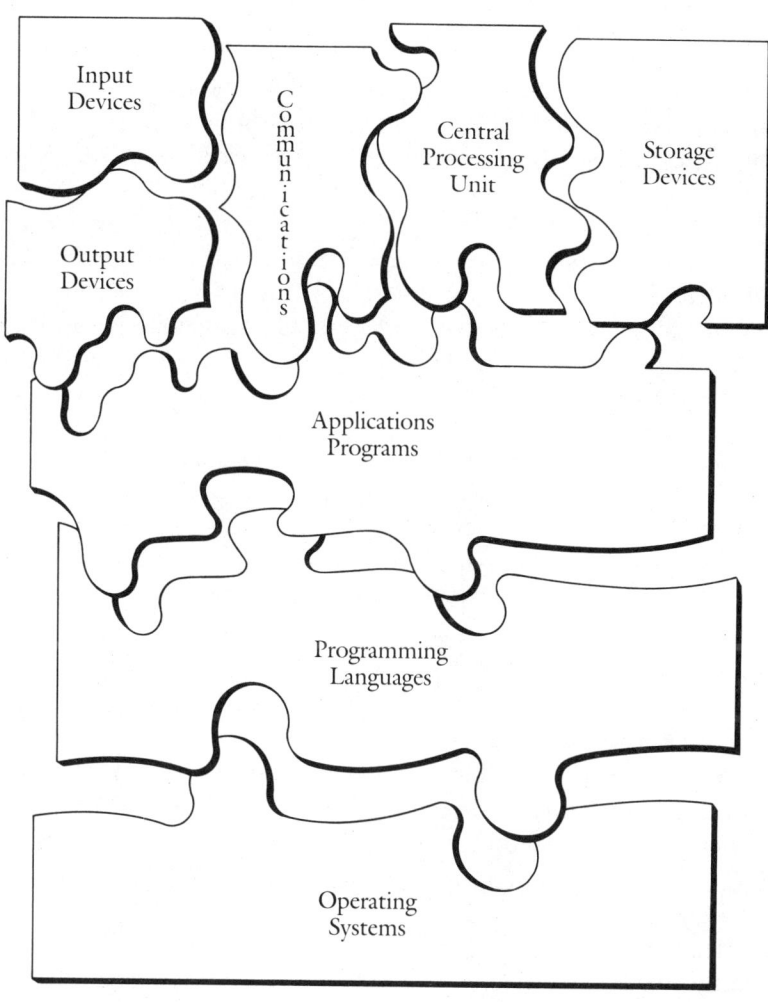

CHAPTER 8

PEOPLE AND THEIR ROLES

Computer hardware and software are the two fundamental components that, when combined, make a computer system. One more element, however, is essential to the effective application of computers in any environment—people.

Clinical and ancillary personnel must ultimately use, and are supposed to benefit from, the computer in a clinical setting. They should be involved with system-design experts from the very beginning, thereby contributing to the process of specifying and selecting any system.

In many situations computer professionals (e.g., programmers and analysts) will be needed to develop software and to modify programs from time to time. If development is going to be carried out in-house, then these individuals will be part of the on-site team. When larger-scale computer systems are used, people will be needed to run the computer or at least to change tapes and disks (computer operators), and to collect data and enter this data into the computer (**data-entry clerks**). This will necessitate a redefinition of existing office and staff roles, or in some cases, hiring additional staff personnel. Furthermore, if output from the computer is to be used to the best advantage, staff personnel must be educated in how to use output. Inevitably, there must also be an effort to overcome misconceptions about what the new tool can do. User training is essential so that the tool can become familiar enough to be usable.

It seems appropriate, then, after dealing in such detail with the characteristics of hardware and software, that we consider the computer system in situ and focus on the people who put it there, keep it working, and use it.

THE WELL-TEMPERED SYSTEM

A computer system intended to have a reasonable impact on an environment does not magically appear one day. Successful implementation of any computer application in the service of health care is the culmination of a lengthy and thoughtful process involving many individuals.

First among these people are those who perceive the need for, analyze the effects of, and plan the system—this may be the user or a systems analyst. To avoid conceiving a fiasco, they must do their homework and proceed in an organized and cautious way to document whatever area they intend to affect, what it is they want done, and how they want to do it.

Those who set out to introduce a computer system should write out a detailed functional specification (see Chapter 16) for that system. This step should be taken in conjunction with health care–computing experts, perhaps employed as consultants. With the functional specification in hand, it will be possible to request information and eventually quotations from vendors and to write more detailed hardware- and software-related specifications.

Before attacking the functional specification, we should fill in a gap we left earlier in Chapter 7: the specification of systems software. As with hardware, whatever is expected of or needed in terms of systems software should also be laid out in a document.

THE SOFTWARE SPECIFICATION

It is not possible to detail fully a systems software specification here, and developing one requires expert help. However, one should remember that at some point a customer must specify what kind of operating system is required (e.g., batch, time-shared, or real-time); what the system should provide in terms of resources (e.g., input and output terminals and access to secondary storage devices); what functions are needed (e.g., backup and security); and other considerations such as response time and method of use.

Next, the required language(s) (e.g., BASIC, Pascal, COBOL, or MUMPS) and the general speed and size characteristics of programs written in that language should be given. Whenever possible, specify a high-level language that will make future modifications to the program easier. The **documentation** expected should be stipulated. It should ideally include not only user manuals that show end-users how to employ the systems software, but also a detailed description of its design and functions. One may also want the program listing (the source code), although this may be difficult to get. There should be no problem in demanding full documentation if the systems software is written by outside developers under contract specifically for a given use. However, when manufacturers or systems houses sell standard computer-system products to many users, they usually protect their investment in systems software and refuse to supply detailed software documentation. In such circumstances there is little a user can do short of selecting another vendor who may possibly be more compliant.

It is a good idea to talk with other users to see what their experiences have been with the vendor and to learn what the vendor has previously agreed to supply.

Finally, the general kinds of applications programs the system will be required to support and as many specifics as possible about them should be detailed. If even partial examples exist, these should be made available so the vendor or development company can see what is expected of their system.

THE FUNCTIONAL SPECIFICATION

Now that we have looked at the hardware and software specifications for a system, we should note the following:
1. The hardware and software specifications can be put in their final form only by experts.
2. These specifications are completely dependent on what the system is to do (i.e., what functions it is to perform).

What we need, then, is some clear, precise statement of what the system is supposed to do for its users. This is the functional specification (see Chapter 16 for a comprehensive look at functional specifications). Functional specifications must be developed by those who intend to use the computer, perhaps with the help of someone with previous experience.

The functional-specification document should begin by describing the applications area, the input the users will bring to the system, and the output expected from the system. The maximum potential workload of the system and the maximum acceptable **turnaround time** (the time it takes between submitting input and obtaining relevant output) should be stated. Any **processing** (e.g., calculations) of data should also be specified. In addition, details on what data is to be stored, how much is to be stored, how long it is to be stored, and how quickly it must be accessible should be stipulated. In other words, the functional specification for the whole computer system provides a detailed picture of the environment and of what the user wants the system to do. As such, it is a precise statement of what is expected of the systems developer. Because the functional specification talks about what must be done and because health care personnel are the experts in the health care area, this part of the design depends more on the user than on consultants or external help. This is the user's part—and the essential part—of the process and the user must become secure about carrying it out. But more about that later.

THE CONTRACT

Because the functional specification is the user's view of the system, its terms should be written into a contract. If the system obtained is to be useful, it must be at least what the functional specification states. Therefore, if something does go wrong and the user does not get what was wanted, the user will have some recourse based on this specification. Such contracts are not covered here, but further detail can be found in Chapter 16. When the time comes to formalize the terms of a contract, legal counsel is necessary. Do not bank on the goodwill of the systems vendor. Never believe anything except what is written in a contract.

We would also suggest that mature vendors will expect to see the functional specifications and expect a contract. Be skeptical of vendors who try to sell their computer solution even before they inquire about specific requirements.

When all decisions regarding the kind of system required for a particular application have been made, and when appropriate functional specifications have been laid down, it must then be determined how best to obtain the required system. At this point the user can go to the marketplace with the functional specification to acquire a complete application system. Or, with the help of experts, the user can develop hardware and systems software specifications to buy a system on which development of the user's own applications package can be done. In terms of acquiring a complete hardware and software system, there are the same three alternatives we looked at before, for hardware:

1. One can buy a prefabricated hardware and software system and use it as is.
2. One can buy a prefabricated system and modify it.
3. One can assemble appropriate hardware and systems software and write programs from scratch.

TURNKEY SYSTEMS

In some cases (and this should be the preferable way to go), there may be a turnkey system—a hardware and software package that some manufacturer has developed to serve the user's kind of need. Turnkey systems are the quickest way of getting a computer system into operation in a health care environment. When chosen carefully from a reputable supplier, such systems are, theoretically, greatly advantageous to the user.

Unfortunately, some turnkey systems are not the working products they are advertised to be. A review of even a few of the numerous examples of turnkey systems for health care applications will show that this is a tricky and potentially treacherous path to take.

As one example, a company planning to develop a new product recently counted 300 companies producing computer-based systems for use in the physician's office. Some of these have all the features a physician might want, whereas others lack important features. Each is different from the others in significant respects. In any applications area in which several vendors compete, a survey of existing turnkey systems will show which ones, if any, correspond to one's functional specification. Probably no system will be precisely satisfactory, but some might be close enough. Choosing the right one can be very difficult.

The probability that one will be able to obtain an instant computer system from a supplier is relatively small. At the very least, one will probably require some modification to an existing turnkey system before it will suit one's individual needs. If the user arranges for the original vendor to do this, the functional specification written into a contract is all-important. If the user decides personally to modify a turnkey system, the user must make sure the original supplier (who owns the copyright on the software) will permit him or her to do so. When the user's own computer department starts modifying a vendor's product without written approval, the vendor may quite understandably void the product's warranties.

DO-IT-YOURSELF SYSTEMS

If one cannot buy a turnkey system to be used directly or modified, then it will be necessary to acquire the appropriate pieces of hardware and to get special software written for a particular application. One may arrange to have this done on a contract basis by an external developer, or one may have to use or establish one's own in-house software development group. If one decides to establish an in-house group, then one must find the money and working space for the necessary personnel. One may have to be prepared to live with systems development personnel almost indefinitely, because the development process is sometimes lengthy. Frequently, in a health care situation, in which the requirements faced by a system may begin to change even before its first development cycle is complete, "finished" may be a word seldom spoken.

SELECTING A SUPPLIER

The suppliers of computer systems (especially of the turnkey variety) work in several different ways. Some manufacture everything—hardware, systems software, and applications programs. More commonly, a **systems house** or original equipment manufacturer (OEM), such as the major computer companies, will buy hardware, an operating system, and languages from a computer manufacturer, and will supply only the applications programs as its own product. There are occasions, however, when systems houses even write their own versions of operating systems and languages.

What does the supplier's modus operandi imply for the user of the computer system? The overwhelming question the user must answer before finally becoming committed to a particular supplier is: can that supplier fully back up the system provided? The only way to answer this question is by doing one's homework.

If the company supplying the system is also furnishing the software, did its own staff members write the software? If so, are the staff members stationed at the local office? Nine times out of 10, the answer is no: the software was probably developed at a central office. The user will often be surprised to learn (except with the larger companies) that no one is capable of providing software maintenance located in the user's region, let alone in the user's city. Given this problem one should expect the vendor to have a hot line—a toll-free 800 number that one can call to explain a problem and to get help.

Is the company offering to provide hardware maintenance support? Do they have their own hardware-maintenance technicians, and do they keep spare parts on hand so they can fix your system quickly when it breaks down? Or do they get the computer manufacturer(s) to maintain the hardware? This is a critical consideration when the company is selling a system composed of parts obtained from several different hardware suppliers.

If one is dealing with a company that has a local office assuming responsibility for all the hardware, software, and maintenance of the systems it provides, one is in much safer hands. If, on the other hand, a company with a small local bureau and a head office in Timbuktu sells a "bargain" system composed of diverse hardware and software components, all provided by other companies that retain nominal responsibility for these parts, expect trouble! One may find oneself a wobbling domino that can be felled by the failure of any of several separate components in the "system" (Figure 8-1).

FIGURE 8-1
The more companies involved, the more likely a project is to fail.

COMPUTER PERSONNEL

Depending on the size and complexity of a health care–computer application, the health care user will be exposed to a varying amount of contact with the people who develop computer systems. In the simplest case, a physician will consult appropriate experts who may find a company that already makes the needed computer product. Installation and user training (in this case the user might be the physician and his or her nurse) for this new product may be straightforward and brief. In the more complex case, there may be an in-house group dedicated to developing health care–computer applications, or there may be a continuing relationship with a systems house. Either of these situations will involve new personnel and a longer time-base of interaction with the daily activities in the clinical environment. In the case of in-house development, computer personnel will be a new and expensive item in the budget.

Development Staff

Whether a computer application is developed in-house or by an outside agency, the skills of a number of people with distinct roles will have to be applied.

Before taking any definite steps in computing, a hospital or similar large institution may enlist the aid of **management consultants** or **data processing consultants** to help them discover the potential needs for data processing and its role in their environment. Once a real need and a definitive role for automation have been ascertained, any computer application will require a responsible, trained individual as a **project manager** during development. Physicians seldom will have the time or expertise to manage properly large projects even in areas over which they maintain ultimate control. The exception would be when a physician wanted a program developed for a microcomputer used in some local area—in this case the physician would likely be the responsible project manager. Usually, then, an expert in health care computing may be called in to aid in developing the system and to be the project manager. Health care data processing is still a fledgling discipline, but an increasing number of physicians have a special interest and expertise in this area. It should be noted that within the general area of health care computing there are people with subspecialist interests and abilities, and consequently finding the best health care–computing professional may take a little time.

The decision making must be done by the health care or administrative staff members who perceive problems and recognize that computers may help to solve these problems. Their decisions, however, will be guided by those who have experience with the potential and limitations of computers. A large project may in itself justify acquiring such expertise.

If users whose individual projects are small can get together, they may be able to form a critical mass large enough to justify steps toward establishing a source of computer expertise and a shared computer system. Whatever the approach, seek help. Even an excellent internist asks a radiologist's opinion when necessary. Similarly, no one expects persons in the health care field or the administrator to know enough about data processing to deal with the number and variety of problems that crop up in a real development situation.

When software development actually begins, systems analysts will be working closely with the project manager or chief systems developer. They will be responsible for the overall design strategy for attacking specific problem areas. In moderately large installations, "systems analyst" will usually be a job category in its own right. In smaller operations, the manager of the computing group may assume this role, or programmers (programmer/analysts) who are capable of doing systems analysis may be employed.

Those responsible for actually **coding** (writing) programs in a programming language and for the tactics involved in developing specific routines are computer programmers. There often is a senior or lead programmer who is responsible for immediately supervising and delegating jobs among junior programmers. Programmers often assume responsibility for documenting software so others can understand programs and change them later. Sometimes a developer will employ a professional documentation writer or a secretary for this purpose. Programming staff members often do a poor job of documentation if left to their own resources. Because adequate documentation is vital to the survivability of any health care–computer application, it is essential to make sure this job is done properly.

Some or all of these people will be required for developing health care applications in-house. All of these roles will exist, but the number of people that fill them will vary with the size of the project, department, or institution. Health care departments may wish to retain outside systems-development groups with significant experience in the project(s) they are doing, especially if these projects are large and costly. However, institutions should never fail to have at least one person on their payroll who protects the institution's interests and who has institutional responsibility.

OPERATIONAL STAFF

Even after a computer project leaves the development stage, the organization will need a creative expert to make systems-related decisions. This person will be responsible for overseeing the system on a practical level and for assisting health care personnel in formulating requests for changes to the system as necessary. The importance of the job of overseeing the development and continuing growth of computers is reflected in a recent trend in the business world. It has become common for a business institution (where data processing is already an economically important area) to make a vice presidency of data processing a part of the administrative hierarchy. The message here is clear: someone must be administratively responsible.

Given a functioning computer system, somebody must turn it on, load tapes, and so on. These people are called operators. A large installation will have an operation supervisor who manages junior operators. In small installations—often the case in health care environments using minicomputers—programmers may absorb these roles, or there may be a part-time operator. Of course, when programmers are changing tapes, loading disks, and putting paper into the printer, they are not writing programs. The workload of the operator increases with the size and busyness of an installation.

Finally, **data-entry personnel** will be required to collect data and enter it into the computer. The importance of these people is often underrated. When one considers that the success of a computer application is totally dependent on these individuals for the quality of data input into the machine, one's respect for them and their vital role in the system will be great. Sometimes it is possible to use a computer system to unburden existing secretarial or technical staff members. These people can then be trained to become excellent data-entry personnel. If, however, no job role can be augmented by the computer, one must realize that a new job category has been created. Additional help will then be required to get data into the computer.

When a health care–computer installation assumes responsibility for continuing program modification and developing new programs, the development personnel (analysts and programmers) will have permanent roles in that organization. Despite the continuing role of these individuals in applications programming, a software maintenance contract must always be arranged with the original developer. This contract will ensure that the developer continues to provide corrections for errors and the latest versions of systems software (the operating system and the programming language updates). Software-maintenance contracts are expensive, but they cannot be ignored simply because in-house applications programmers are employed. In general, for maintenance one must depend on the company that supplied the systems software.

GETTING GOING

It is not easy to implement any worthwhile computer system. A rapid and painless transition may mean only that the computer system being introduced is so unimportant that it has no discernible effect on its environment.

The best break-in procedure is to run manual and automated systems in parallel until the automated system is running smoothly enough that manual procedures can be stopped. It is difficult to be sure that a program is performing exactly as designed and that it is free of bugs. Manual procedures, therefore, should never be totally abandoned. Some alternative way of performing a task will be necessary when the computer system fails because of some obscure software error previously undetected, or because of a mechanical or electrical breakdown. It is surprising how many turnkey systems are sold without formal backup procedures being specified. When disaster eventually strikes, the need is acutely perceived but little can be done. If only the School of Hard Knocks had an extension program so that everyone could appreciate the problem without having to go through a disaster!

Put simply, backup procedures fall into two categories:
1. Manual procedures that permit an operation to continue while the computer is unavailable
2. Computer procedures that will enable the computer system to recover from any disruption that its failure might have caused

Automatic procedures for backup include periodically printing cumulative paper documents (permitting support of manual procedures and collecting data transacted during the period the system is down); regularly copying all data onto spare disk packs or tapes (preventing the complete loss of data stored on secondary-storage devices if they fail); and redundantly recording all data transactions on another magnetic medium (often tape)—a process called transaction logging or journaling. If a system fails, data can be collected on manual forms and reports can be produced manually. When the computer is again operational, the last copy of the data kept on secondary storage can be loaded onto the system (if the original was destroyed) and the transaction log can be used to play-back to the system everything that happened up to the point of destruction of the data. Then, the only data that must be entered by hand will be the data collected during down-time. These **fail-soft** procedures will eventually pay off in every installation and will enable a failed computer system to be brought back **up** with a minimum of work.

However, when a system must be available all the time, the only way to approach 100% availability is to acquire redundant hardware. This need for redundancy is a force that makes the multiple small computer approach (distributed computing) often preferred today instead of a single central system. Any given piece of computer hardware will fail sooner or later, so even the CPU itself may have to be duplicated and a tandem system may even have to be considered in some critical applications. Even a 1% down-time per year means that 20 hours might be lost per year during the day shift alone. One should also realize that beyond such unscheduled down-time, there are also normal computer housekeeping activities (such as doing backup and preventive maintenance) that will usually remove the computer from user service at least a few hours per week.

MONITORING PROGRESS

Once installed, a computer system will go through phases in its life cycle. From time to time, parts of it, such as specific items of hardware or particular programs, may need replacement or expansion to cope with increasing workloads or changing needs. Such replacement or expansion of programs has been called software maintenance, and it often represents 50% to 80% of the ultimate investment in any program package.

Certain landmarks in the life course of a system should be envisioned during the planning stages and defined courses of action should be followed when each landmark is passed. Included in these checkpoints should be the signs and symptoms indicating when a health care–computer application is no longer meeting needs and should be improved, or when it is obsolete and should be replaced. The failure to consider growth and change will eventually result in a computer system that is only an end in itself—costing everyone and serving no one.

• • •

For good or ill, a computer system will substantially alter one's way of doing business in the health care environment. Often a whole department or institution will change in the process of accommodating a computer. This is not necessarily bad if a rational approach is taken and one foresees and plans for the effects.

But one should be an agent of change before a system is installed. It is ridiculous and sometimes impossible to automate a mess, so a serious effort needs to be made to clean up procedures before introducing automation. Automation involves more than merely computerizing the status quo. Before committing any operation to a computer and facing the concomitant cost, one should take the opportunity afforded by the advent of automation to improve, adjust, and reorganize existing procedures to eliminate waste and redundancy.

Consider also the people who will make the system work, use it, and maintain it. Every person who works with a computer system, however indirectly, is part of that system and will therefore be affected by it. Each person should be aware that he or she will also, conversely, affect the system. One should ensure that staff members do not feel alienated or threatened by the new computer in their midst. Listen to people's fears. Take time to show them how they fit into the new computer-based system as surely as they fit into the old manual one. Often, in fact, their roles should be enhanced in a properly implemented system.

Obviously, then, one should study the impact of a computer system on a health care environment and be fully aware of its effects before proceeding. It is unrealistic and self-deceptive to pretend that introducing a computer system will be painless, cheap, or totally satisfactory. No system is ever fully satisfactory to all of its users. Inevitably there will be unrealistic or conflicting demands that have been or will be made on it.

One of the most frequently made and least frequently kept demands of computer systems is that they should save money. Many systems acclaimed as economically in the black are made to appear that way by people who conveniently ignore some of the costs associated with them. It is very difficult, especially in a government-run health system, to use computers to save money, especially if they are not incorporated throughout the operation and are instead merely add-ons. A more realistic hope for most computer systems is that they earn their keep in situations when the workload is expanding and when the projected increase in staff members can be eliminated or reduced. The computer can absorb additional work, thereby containing costs at a certain level. These financial facts often come as both a surprise and a disappointment to users who approach the use of computer systems full of blind faith created by sales pitches.

After the early period of enthusiasm, the naive user will often find a computer system to be significantly less capable than originally anticipated. An inevitable letdown ensues. It is a blow for the average user to realize that this new computer equipment will not fulfill every fantasy. Seasoned systems developers tend to ignore complaining clients until the clients become acquainted with the things the system can do. There is a real danger, though, that the disappointment of unprepared users may deepen into permanent disgust. At this point they may give up and radically change automation priorities for no particularly good reason. The user frustrated by a new computer system might do well to ponder the examples of the credulous child enraged at the family dog because it refuses to talk. Serious developers will prepare users early for this problem, and make sure they understand and appreciate both immediate and long-term constraints. The mature user will be able to weather the initial phase and will be able to face realistically what the computer can and cannot do.

Those unfamiliar with the potential and the limitations of systems in relation to their particular problems can seek the opinion and assistance of experts. In the United States, the American Medical Association has created a health care–computing consultation group—potentially a powerful resource for clinicians who need help with computers. Nurses too are forming special interest groups for the purpose of educating and sharing computer information.

The system chosen by amateurs frequently serves not their needs, but those of the computer supplier. Ill-considered acquisitions are often abandoned once they are perceived as useless. Alternatively, and, much worse, it is not unknown for a health care–computer system's sponsor to throw lots of good money after bad to keep his or her reputation in shape. Some sound initial advice and a few midcourse maneuvers from an expert may save one from such a fate.

Stripped of their mystery, aura, and the erroneous notion that they can solve every problem, computer systems emerge as basically a mixture of hardware, software, and people—a combination that acts as yet another useful tool for the health care community.

CHAPTER 9
LIMITATIONS OF TECHNOLOGY

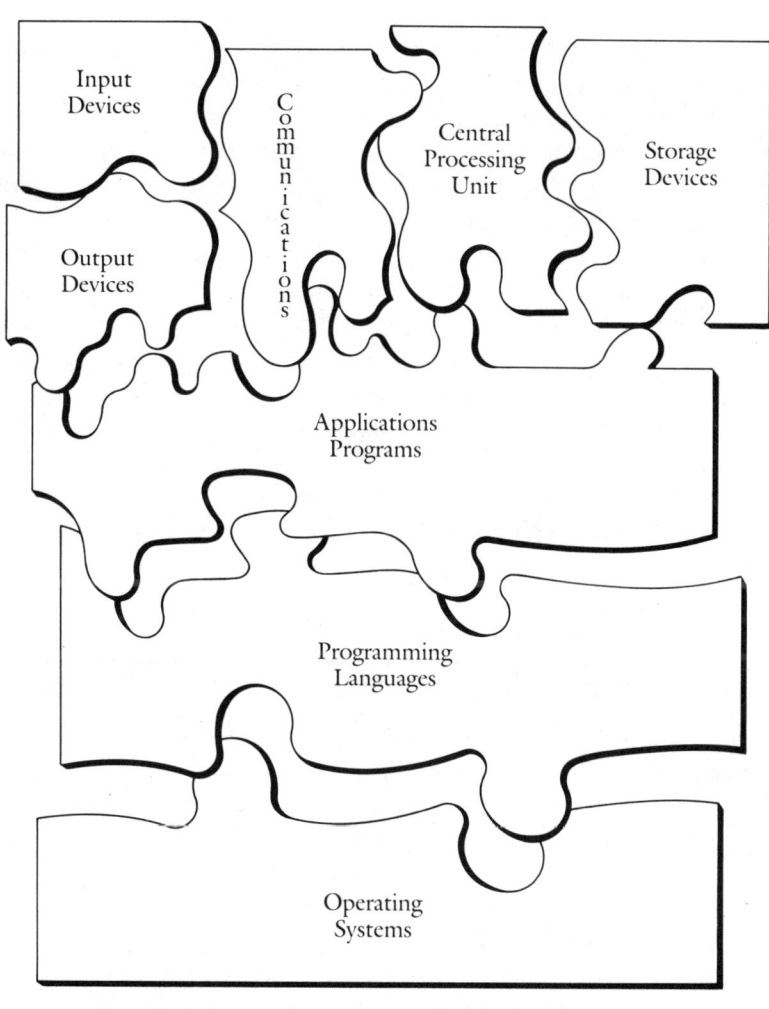

CHAPTER 9

In preceding chapters we have seen that each component in a computer system has its limitations. In the case of hardware, these limits are usually technological—sometimes the devices we would like to have do not yet exist. The limits of software are manifested in the difficulties encountered in programming computers and in implementing systems capable of dealing with humans on human terms. Health care–computer systems developers frequently come up against these limits of existing computer technology. The human mind can imagine a perfect, completed computer system ideally suited to cope with some problem. But the constraints of current technology usually stop us short of our goals. When the ideal solution does not exist, we must accept the best possible system, and that may be disappointing compared to our dream system.

When we first thought about computers, we might have imagined a magical machine that refines murky, raw data into crystal-clear information. In fact, the converse is often true. Using a computer system to process information can distort or coarsen that information. The output we obtain from computers is only an imperfect image of the reality we try to input to them. This is an important hidden problem affecting all applications of computers.

When we try to use computers in health care, the limitations of systems technology can frustrate developers and users. Because computers cannot communicate the same way people do, people must transform information to suit the computer. Humans must adopt fixed procedures, limited vocabularies, and rigid formats to input data to the computer in a form in which it can deal with the data. Similarly, when seeking information from a computer, people must accept it in the format and on the media that the machine offers.

Health care workers will be disillusioned if they approach health care computing with unrealistically high expectations and little appreciation of the boundaries of the state of the art. To prevent such disappointments, let us consider the problems posed by a computer reality that lags behind our dreams.

THE UNREALITY OF COMPUTER MEMORY

Consider the page you are reading. You can see and touch it. If the ink is new, perhaps you can even smell it. This page is part of our world. We are used to encountering information with our entire sensorium. The more senses employed, the more complete the contact, and the better we learn.

Suppose you merely scan this chapter now but want to read it in detail later. There will be a number of methods for locating it. You can be compulsive and keep a card index. It is probably more likely, however, that you will remember it as being in the book with a particular cover; or you may recall having put it in a certain place. Your idiosyncratic scheme of sensory cues would help you find the book and the chapter with a minimum of rummaging.

We have become used to handling information in tangible, physical form. But let us now consider the case of information going directly into a computer. In this process, the physical context of the data is missing. When you first look at the data on a CRT there will be none of the physical cues to help you remember where you saw it. In this case we become very dependent on the person who indexed the data. If the data is not completely or competently indexed we will not be able to find it again. The data has been put into a logical context instead of a physical one. Not only must the data be properly cross-referenced, but we must know the proper terms under which it is cross-referenced to retrieve it.

Computers are incapable of providing data on the basis of imprecise requests. They cannot find the information stored in the memory unless some human has told them exactly how to find it.

Thus, to use computers effectively, we are forced to index information thoroughly—random rummaging, cue association, and approximate locating are usually impossible. We have surrendered, in some sense, direct contact with our data.

It is therefore not surprising that health care providers might feel insecure about putting patient records in a computer. Clinical data about living patients must not be lost. Clinical research data may have taken months to gather, and one is justifiably possessive of it. Paper records are physically reassuring. It is more of an act of faith to believe that the data is secure on a spinning disk. It is possible to see the data, providing the system is available when one wants it. Even then, however, insecurity can persist. To be truly assured, one is inclined to seek printed output. Again we turn to our paper security blanket.

That data resides in a computer implies added expense, artificial formalization, and insecurity that cannot be ignored. We will see later that this insecurity is well based, and we will discuss methods of protecting the data (e.g., from erasure).

LIMITATIONS OF THE INPUT PROCESS

Information retrieval is only one area in which our use of computers is constrained by the current state of the art. The very process of inputting data has limitations.

We might understand this more by asking a pointed question: why don't all computer scientists automate their literature files? An automated literature index could provide quick access to abstracts for writing papers. Why do they use cards (if anything) and a recipe box for a literature index? There are a number of reasons:

1. It is often expensive to interact with computers because a terminal usually costs at least a few hundred dollars.
2. Portable terminals are usually more expensive and not very light.
3. Portable terminals require access to a telephone wherever they are used.
4. Almost all terminals are based on typing input.
5. Getting data into a computer system is a lot of work and takes a lot of time both to input and index properly.

6. Ultimately, the effort of organizing and preparing the material would probably not be perceived as worthwhile.

Because insiders do not automate their literature files, it is not too surprising that physicians interested in indexing literature often give up, if they start at all. The solution, of course, is to have someone else input the literature data and index it—that is what modern on-line literature databases (e.g., Medline, Dialog, and Source) are all about. The hard work is done by someone else. All the physician needs to do is to make intelligent requests.

Another aspect should be considered. To the health care provider, as to other human beings, reality is a continuum. To input reality into a computer requires that we classify, categorize, and quantify it (break it into a finite number of categories) before it can be processed in any way. Computers cannot cope with human reality. Instead, categories must be imposed on the information.

There are two ways of getting information into computer-processible form. One way is to input everything as it is into the computer, and then to write programs that carry out the quantification process. This approach has worked only in very limited areas—such as in processing pathology reports—because it is extremely difficult to write a program to dissect the structure and meaning of medical reports.

The more common approach is to quantify data before putting it into a computer. The full text may also be typed in and then the quantified data is used as index data to retrieve relevant reports. This process of encoding data into categories based on explicit criteria has been called taxonorics. Taxonorics represents an attempt to define a precise way of stuffing continuous reality into computer-compatible pigeonholes, while distorting reality as little as possible (Figure 9-1).

Collecting, categorizing, and inputting information usually forces placing a coding clerk between the information source (the health care provider or patient) and the computer. This often leads to delays and to transcription errors. Frequently special forms are provided for gathering data. Even when properly designed, these forms themselves can be a source of errors. Obviously, errors can occur even if the individual at the source personally categorizes the information, because different people may have different interpretations of supposedly standard terms. When the data is finally ready to be entered into a computer system, errors may occur during the input device's reading of computer-compatible media (such as OMR or OCR forms), and in further typing steps if they are needed. Many errors can occur in a data collection and input process (Figure 9-2). The propensity for errors has resulted in extensive research on their prevention, detection, and correction. A solution to some of these problems is to use a modern data-entry software package. The health care provider or patient is presented with a form on the terminal screen. The program asks precise questions and reminds the person about how to categorize the data to be input. The program checks everything input to make sure the responses are reasonable. In some systems even the consistency of a given item with others is checked. It will, however, still require time

FIGURE 9-1
Reality versus computer representation.

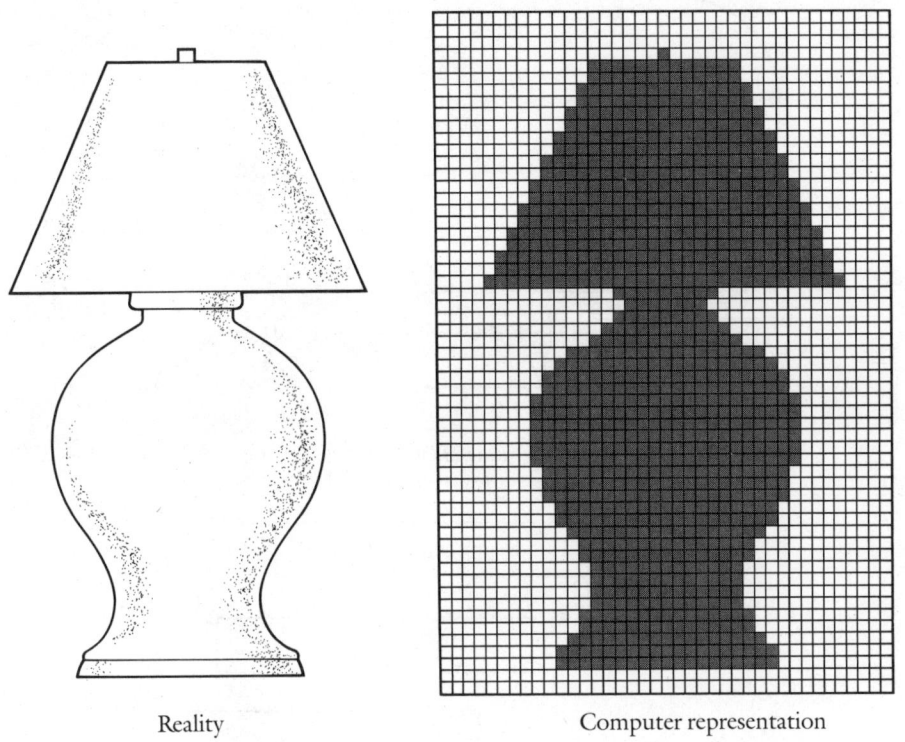

Reality   Computer representation

for the health care provider to accept the computer as the primary record-keeping device.

A practical example of the limitations imposed by the computer's need to deal with quantified data (both for input devices and for processing) is seen in hospital-discharge summary-abstraction systems such as PAS/QAM in the United States, or the HMRI system in Canada. The information we are attempting to collect includes diagnoses, procedures, and critical events recorded during hospitalization. Medical records staff members provide this information, usually on special forms using numeric codes. Unfortunately they have no stake in our feedback from these systems, so their primary motivation in filling out the forms is to clear the backlog of charts. There is no real control of the completeness or accuracy of the data, although in some places spot-chart reviews are done periodically. Once the encoded data is fed into a computer system, only very limited quality control can be performed, such as detect-

FIGURE 9-2
How data collection becomes garbage collection.

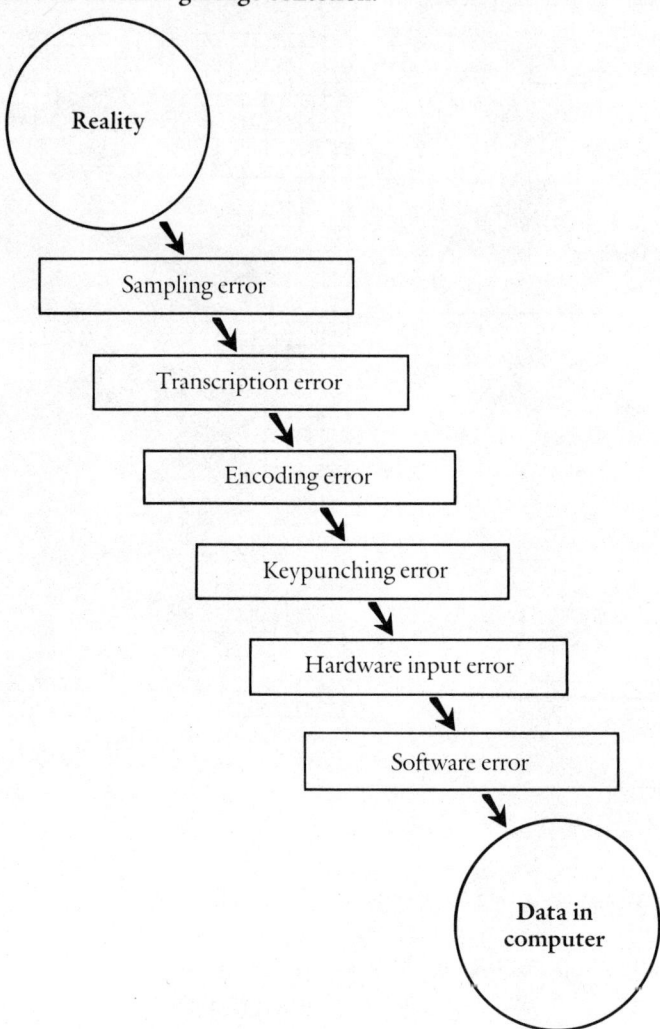

ing blank or mutually exclusive codes (e.g., pregnancy and male). The process is usually completed long after a patient has been discharged from the hospital. Feedback (output) from these systems to the institutions generating the data may run even months late. It is understandable why information generated by such systems is sometimes inaccurate or incomplete. That these systems work as well as they do is probably the result more of devoted people than of technology. Incorrect or absent codes that make it past quality control checks are a kind of noise added to the original reality. Reconstructing reality from this data gives a picture of unknown validity.

If abstracting the medical record is so problematic, anyone would worry about putting the major part, or all, of the medical record, into a computer system in a form suitable for processing. The effort to do so is often perceived as much too great for the improvement effected by automation. Even today, with inexpensive terminals more widely available, there would remain the inconvenience of using a finite set of available devices that would (according to a variant of Murphy's law) always be located somewhere other than where they were needed.

Clearly, there is no point in putting data into a computer unless it is to be used to generate useful output. The cost of input virtually demands that computer-based records become a vital and active part of patient care. This high cost should deter us from simply computerizing a medical record that has become a pro forma repository of medical observations or a medicolegal documentation system. If we cannot use the computer-based data to its fullest, then it is using us, and we would probably be financially better off with a filing cabinet and a few clerks.

HOW OUTPUT LIMITS US

We have considered the input process as a limiting feature in computer applications, but input is only half of the two-way channel between the user and the computer. In what ways do hardware and software inhibit the full realization of the potential of computer systems in the output process?

We have already alluded to one way in which output technology constrains us. It is not always available when and where we want it. Terminals are often inaccessible, or at least not easily available to the health care staff person who is constantly on the move. Even when terminals are available, standing in line to use them is unacceptable; yet the more terminals, the greater the cost.

Furthermore, the format of computer output often leaves a great deal to be desired. It can be cramped, styleless, voluminous, and inscrutable. It may be difficult to see abnormal values because most printers print only in one color and because it is often difficult to underline or otherwise highlight important items.

Another problem is determined by the limitations of the programs we know how to write. Our systems lack the ability to select only data of interest or significance for output. We are only beginning to discover ways to turn computer systems into information integrators.

Even if these obstacles are overcome, we may not get the output we want—only the output someone else wanted us to have. This is because it is still rare to have report-writer programs available to us that are easy to use and with which we can tell the computer exactly what we want. Generally we get generic reports meant to meet a large class of users' needs.

Budget, expediency, or ignorance of available alternatives may also create constraints, especially regarding the availability of graphic output. Long waits for slowly typed output, or the hard-to-read, poorly aligned, capitals-only character set of some line printers, undermine user acceptance of any system. Providing columns of numbers instead of graphics fails to use the computer's ability to manipulate and represent information in a more digestible and condensed form. The superiority of graphs over numerals has long been appreciated in health care, hence the popularity of the temperature, pulse, respiration (TPR) chart. A review of present hospital systems leaves one with the conviction that developers were unaware of present-day graphics technology.

A further problem associated with computer output is that people accept it on blind faith. They will not believe newspapers, they doubt what is said on TV, but they trust computers for some unknown reason. They assume that something produced by a computer must be correct. From what we have already seen it is clear that people generate and enter data, and write programs to process that data. People make mistakes. Computer programs can be based on human misconceptions, or programs can be affected by human problems in mapping our conceptions into the simple steps of which computers are capable. People who are uncritical of computer output are guilty of the ultimate buck-passing. It is our responsibility to question computer output, because the computer is not programmed to question itself. Errors often may live forever undetected. Where a human may at least harbor a spark of doubt about human output, a computer will never question its own errors.

SOFTWARE AND ITS LIMITS

The greatest of all problems mentioned above is one not determined by input and output devices, but our inability to write programs that distill the essence out of large amounts of data. To take a case in point, if we walk into the Coronary Care Unit (CCU) and ask, "How is Mrs. Jones doing?" the staff person may reply, "Fine." This person may have formulated a clinical judgment based on masses of data, but with all irrelevant particulars excluded. Mrs. Jones is likely far from "fine" or she would not be in the CCU, but in context that reply might be logical and meaningful. Computers cannot in general make such qualitative evaluations because they seldom contain models for disease processes. A person seeking information from most CCU computer systems could get lots of data but no succinct response. On the other hand, the reassuring impression we received about Mrs. Jones may not have been based on all available data, and in this respect decisions based on the output of a computer system that collected exhaustive data might be more sound. A great deal of research in the area of artificial intelligence is now trying to address this problem.

The inability of computers to comprehend relationships among multiple pieces of data is evident in monitoring systems in which alarms are often based on single parameters deviating from a specified range. Alarms go off constantly instead of only at those points where there is truly a clinical crisis. Unless a program has been developed that meaningfully integrates multiple parameters and makes a judgment, an alarm is really nothing more than a befuddled request by the equipment for a human to evaluate the situation. Too many false alarms will ultimately lead to ignoring or disabling the alarm system. A survey carried out a few years ago found that most alarm systems (e.g., on cardiac monitors) were disabled. A failure to recognize a deteriorating trend among several parameters, any one of which may still be within the arbitrary normal range, is even more sinister because staff personnel can be lulled into a false sense of security.

Another analogy is to consider our sense of vision. Seeing involves two levels of acuity. Centrally we see sharply and in high detail. Peripheral vision has lower resolution. We can concentrate on an object, yet be aware of its context. This ability to keep detail and context together is still a matter for research as far as computers are concerned.

COMMUNICATIONS: DESIGN VERSUS REALITY

It is sometimes said that the future of computer technology lies in great networks of interconnected computers that can intercommunicate and share data in a distributed database or data bank. On a smaller scale, networks of computers encompassing several hospitals or physicians' offices could be useful for a variety of services and medical research endeavors.

However, the ease with which we can communicate with remote computers and they with each other cannot be taken for granted. In the simplest case—connecting a remote, portable terminal to a central computer—even using an ordinary acoustic coupler is not perfectly convenient. A telephone is required, and noise on the line can and does sometimes interfere with data transmission. The data-transmission speed achievable with these devices also leaves something to be desired. This speed cannot be much improved unless one is willing to sacrifice portability or to install a high-speed (and more expensive) modem.

Because they are standardized communications schemes, networks have limitations associated with them. Special hardware is usually required, and hardware cost, speed restrictions, and rigid communications protocols restrict their universal use. We must choose hardware and software very carefully to be compatible.

THE HUMAN FACTOR

Just as hardware and software technologies limit health care–computer systems, so also the people who develop and use these systems have limitations. The importance of the human factor is reflected in the failure of many health care–computing projects.

Most of us are optimists by nature. We believe that diligent effort must ultimately be rewarded by progress. Health care providers are among the most optimistic of people. With death and sickness all about us, we persevere, trying to help our patients.

Therefore, people in health care tend to look with hope to any new tool that promises to help them in patient care. Those who sell computers have been quick to exploit this optimism, sometimes encouraging health care providers to believe that proven and reliable computer products exist for many problematic areas in health care. In reality, some good products do exist, but there are many false fronts, lemons, and unsupported systems.

The failure of people to appreciate the limitations of technological advances has been demonstrated repeatedly. For example, we are presently living with the sober reality of atomic energy. Remember the days when we were told there would be enough nuclear fuel to serve the world's energy needs cheaply, safely, and forever? Those were optimistic times. Few envisioned that nuclear power plants might contaminate our environment. Nor did many consider the problems of nuclear proliferation.

In the days just after World War II, popular science magazines assured us that by 1980 we would all be flying our own airplanes to work. Our communities, they prophesied, would consist of long rows of houses with roads at the front door and airstrips at the back door.

Analogously, health care providers who imagine that computer systems will soon solve all their problems are usually victims of false optimism. Not separating what is essential from what would be desirable, and what is practical from what would bankrupt our institution, has undermined many health care–computing projects.

We must all be aware that computers are merely machines that require explicit and correct programs to function. We draw from this knowledge the obvious conclusion that unless we thoroughly understand a process, nobody can program a computer to imitate that process. Health care is not nearly the hard or purely scientific discipline that computer professionals might wish it to be or need it to be to pin down a program. As health care providers, in many cases we do not yet know how to express what we are doing in a logical sequence—because we truly do not know how we work. From a medical history and a physical examination we draw on a variable store of information, past experience, educated guesses, and intuition to reach a preliminary differential diagnosis. We order laboratory tests, formulate a working diagnosis, and initiate treatment. We recognize that often others will use different treatments for the same disease. No health care provider could begin to state in detail how a "universal" health care provider assesses patient data and prescribes treatment, except in very limited areas. No computer programmer can write a program that does this either. The limits of our understanding of the processes at work in diagnosing, investigating, and treating patients circumscribe the way in which we can use computers to support that care.

ON CREATIVITY

Just as an overactive imagination can be the user's biggest limitation, so an underactive imagination can cause systems developers to impose their limits on the potential of existing technology for the health care field.

The biggest problem in this respect is caused by the uncreative developer who is content to computerize an existing process. Sometimes, considerable modification of a process is needed to tune it properly before automation should even be contemplated. Even more significantly, if computers are to be used to advance health care, we ought to give some priority to employing them to do things we are presently not able to do without their help.

A truly creative person with an adequate background in both computer science and health care, and with the ability to see things that never were but might be achieved in health care computing, is still a rare find. A computer programmer can write a program, but it takes a person who knows what the real problems are to figure out which program to write. The limited availability of high-level, innovative personnel imposes yet another restriction on our use of computers in health care.

A SERIES OF HURDLES

Although it may at first appear necessary and possible to automate a given health care application, the cost of technology may be the first barrier to actual implementation. If this is not the case, then implementation may trip over any of several more hurdles. We must include here the constraints caused by the rather simple ways in which computers can process information. We find it extremely difficult to program them to do some of the things that people find easy: using associative reasoning, retrieving relevant past experience, distilling intelligence from masses of data, and guessing intelligently at solutions to complex problems. Part of the reason for this is that the programming tools available to us are still fairly difficult to use and are restricted in scope. A more fundamental limitation, however, is that we do not understand what is involved in many of our activities well enough to write programs to imitate them.

If we accept this reality we must finally cope with the limitations of current input-output and storage technology. Sometimes our attempts to realize a useful system may be blocked by the devices that must be used. Until we have inexpensive input devices that can accept scribbled notes and listen to speech, we will have difficulties in getting much of day-to-day reality into a system. Until we have reasonably inexpensive output devices that can produce highlighted, graphic, and even verbal, output we will be constrained in using them.

Computer memory with the versatility and associative power of human memory is not available in any form. Devices and software that permit computers to be interconnected in networks are still expensive and restricted in capability.

All of these factors place limits on using computers in health care. Each day, however, the picture changes: better and more affordable devices are constantly being introduced (voice output devices are an excellent example); better and more user-oriented software is becoming available; more effective and easier to use database systems are coming into their own. We all should become aware of the current practical limits of technology, structure our needs within these limitations, and anticipate a brighter future that will relax the limits on what we can do.

CHAPTER 10

WHAT ARE THE ISSUES?

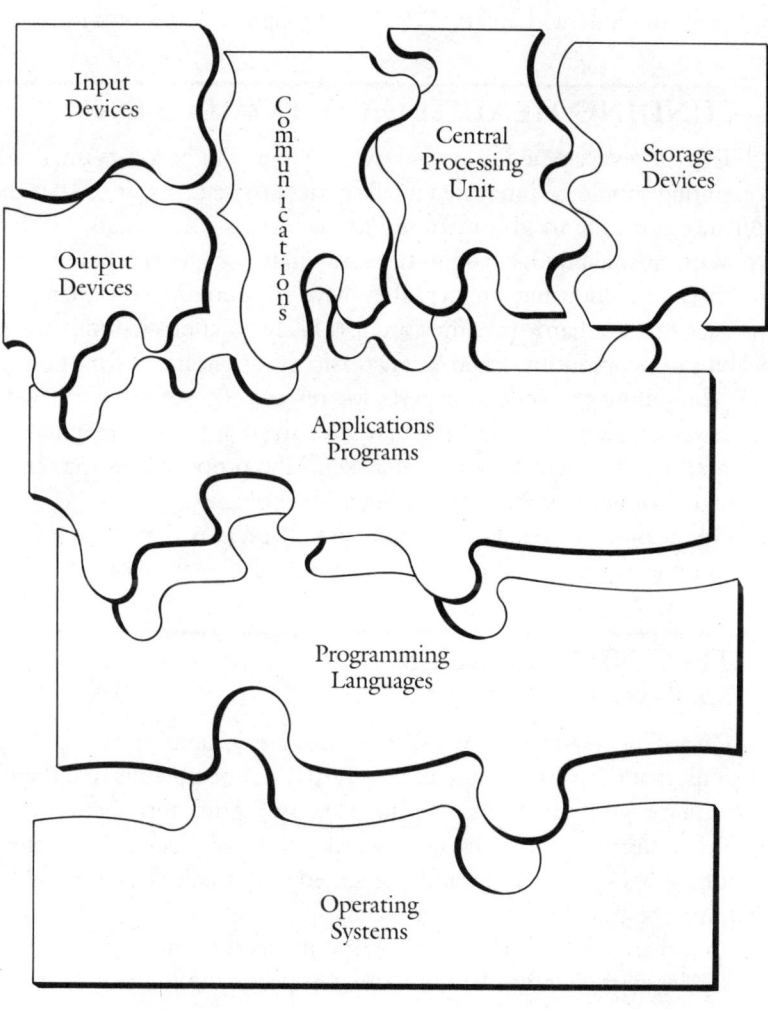

The call of automation sounds sweet to the ears of the health care community and of hospital administrators who have acquired a taste for expensive technology. It is now taken for granted that clinical judgment alone will be insufficient to establish a diagnosis or to determine the appropriate treatment for most patients. Given a marketplace such as this, it is not surprising that vendors will try to woo health care workers with sweet refrains about automation.

Healthy skepticism does not imply a negative attitude. It does imply, however, a serious effort to evaluate the claims of those with computers to sell.

Fortunately, many distinct issues in health care computing can be addressed separately and can serve as foci of an evaluation. Each of these issues will be considered in depth in subsequent chapters. For now, though, we will provide a brief overview.

FUNDING HEALTH CARE COMPUTING

There is a very practical reason why anyone who becomes involved in health care computing should be interested in all of these issues: sooner or later they will have to convince someone to give them money to support their plans.

Many hospital budget committees and granting agencies have been stung by failed health care–computing projects they have supported. Now that they have learned their lessons the hard way, they are less likely to approve funds for poorly justified health care–computing schemes. Increasingly, applications for grant funds for health care computing are sent to experts for review. These reviewers will be totally unimpressed by grand claims. What they want to see is that the researcher has considered the practical, problematic issues at stake in the proposed project, and has developed strategies for anticipating and coping with problems.

One reason for reading the following chapters is that these issues must be dealt with in one's next funding application for a health care–computing project.

TECHNICAL ISSUES
SOFTWARE ENGINEERING

One of the most vexing issues in health care computing is perhaps one of the least obvious, that of software engineering. It may not be obvious that there are many ways of writing a program and that some ways are significantly better than others.

Programs that are written in a "quick and dirty" fashion, that are written in low-level languages, or that are undocumented may totally frustrate other programmers who may be called on to change them.

And change is often required—not only because the first shot at a program often misses the mark, but also because errors in programming may become apparent only after weeks, months, or occasionally years of routinely using a program. It is probably a safe statement that no computer program of any complexity works perfectly. It is usually not possible to *prove* the correctness of programs. The best that can be done is to test them thoroughly, and there are formal techniques for doing this. However, many programs are pushed into active service without adequate testing. Latent bugs may lie hidden only to emerge much later, causing the program to fail.

Users of computer systems do not need to become experts in software engineering, but they should be aware of its importance to appreciate the necessity of acquiring competent help before buying or writing programs. Programs must be selected or written at least as carefully as hardware is chosen or developed, and they should be examined not simply on the basis of what they do but on how they do it. Chapter 12 introduces the basics about the how.

Human Engineering

The commitment to automation often implies substantially restructuring an organization. Many businesspeople work with computers at arm's length, through an intermediary. In the health care field, however, physicians, nurses, and other health care personnel work directly with the computer in a hands-on situation. They are therefore intimately interested in how easy the machine is to use. Complex, obscure, or unnecessarily difficult-to-use computer systems can be a genuine hardship to a user. Human engineering, the art of making systems easier to use, is therefore essential in developing any health care–computing scheme.

In any working environment, health care included, those who have wished to introduce new procedures, new forms, or new data-collection methods have always been aware that they are, in essence, disrupting the way in which their colleagues conduct their business. Computers have the potential of causing a greater disruption of current practice. They may also make future change quantitatively and qualitatively more difficult.

Human engineering and the impact of computers on the human clinical environment will be examined in Chapter 13.

Privacy and Security

Much has been written about the privacy and security of computer records, probably because it is easy to say something—although seldom something significant. We all recognize that personal data must be protected from unauthorized, prying eyes. However, having paid lip service to this issue, we face a much more difficult task when we try to *do* something about it. Many health care–computer installations are lacking in even elementary physical security precautions against vandalism and fire. It appears that our concern does not lead to a willingness to spend money to correct a deficiency.

The advent of automation has brought with it several new and substantial privacy and security problems. The relative ease with which computer-stored information can be organized and retrieved makes it much less difficult to find things that were once scattered around in many paper medical records. Without actually stealing anything tangible, an unauthorized party can sometimes invade a computer system over the telephone and make an illegal copy of the desired data. The ability to transmit data between systems poses an even bigger problem. It is now possible to collate data from two or more separate databases to piece together information that would not be available from any one separate data source. Finally, the extreme miniaturization of computer-stored records makes the physical theft of computer-based information potentially much more damaging than the theft of paper charts in the past. Someone who steals one magnetic tape might get the equivalent of several truckloads of paper charts.

Despite the enhanced threat to privacy and security that health care automation may pose, this issue predated automation. Privacy and security of data have always been important in health care. The computer, then, focuses our attention on some old problems and increases the urgency of solving them. We can no longer be comfortable with sweeping this issue under the rug. We will address this issue in Chapter 14.

Economics

Because money for health care is becoming less freely available, we are being faced with the necessity of considering the cost justification of innovations. Everybody knows that computers are expensive. However, we need to examine in detail how much money we can afford to spend on computers and how much money they might save us. Expressions such as cost-effectiveness are used despite the problem of agreeing on precise definitions of clinical effectiveness unless something as dramatic as mortality statistics is involved.

Cost justification analysis should be part of the planning process of any health care worker who is contemplating using a computer system. We will provide an introduction to this important area in Chapter 15.

Functional Specifications and Contracts

Functional specifications and contracts are both economic and legal issues. Too many computers are purchased or leased for health care purposes in the complete absence of written agreements of any kind. Very few health care–computing systems are acquired on the basis of an enforceable contract guaranteeing their performance relative to some specification. In many cases, hidden costs and extras will add considerably to an original quotation. In the worst cases, hardware and software simply fail to perform as promised or as the user expected. The difference in the understanding of what a system is supposed to do as viewed by the user and by the supplier can be enormous in the absence of written functional specifications to which both have agreed and in the absence of the contract that formalizes the agreement.

Such an important issue cannot be ignored by health care professionals who work within constrained budgets that cannot cover the cost of spectacular failure. We detail the considerations in a functional specification in Chapter 16.

MANAGEMENT ISSUES
Managing Systems Development

Successful applications do not just happen: they are made. In the case of in-house systems development or implementation, effective management of the process is an essential ingredient for success, timeliness, and affordability. Even when outside systems developers aid in a health care–computing project, the responsible manager is well advised to have some idea of the nature of the development process. There is a great deal more involved in project management than hiring a programmer and getting on with it. These topics will be considered in Chapter 17.

Organizing For Automation

Chapter 18 addresses how institutions might organize for health care–computing projects. The radically different requirements of hospital business computing for administrative purposes, and health care research computing in support of individual research projects, make separation of responsibilities essential to successful computer implementation. The overlapping concerns of the health care community and hospital administration in the area of computer services to patients make an effective and understood structure mandatory for institutional cooperation.

The means by which the end-users of health care–computing facilities can promote and defend their own interests are also given consideration in this chapter.

EDUCATIONAL ISSUES
Training Health Care–Computing Specialists

A well-trained and experienced individual is necessary to take effective responsibility for a health care–computing project. The sort of person required has the ability to bridge the gap between computer science and health care. Many health care–computing projects have failed because their proponents were unable to find anyone to bridge this gap adequately.

The health care community has acknowledged the role of data processing in its affairs, and therefore there is a growing demand for health care–computing specialists. A few institutions of higher learning are beginning to respond to this perceived need, and in Chapter 19 we will look carefully at the ways in which this educational need might be met.

Conspicuous Computing and Consumer Education

Not only health care–computing specialists but also those of us who are the consumers of health care computing need to be educated. It is no accident that we often feel differently about computer technology than we do about any other kind of technology that is used in health care. What is it about computers that makes them different?

To some extent, computers have been *oversold* as a general solution to all problems. There are many health care workers who believe it is easy to program a computer to do almost anything they can imagine. Much of the blame for this unreasonable level of expectation must fall on the computer industry itself. The advertisements for health care–computer systems for every area from radiology departments to the physician's office are long on promises, but short on performance specifics.

The disorder is what we call conspicuous computing—using computerization as a means of making ourselves look sophisticated or progressive. The techniques of consumer motivation (creating needs that were not previously felt) have been just as effective in selling health care–computing products as they have been in selling automobiles. We will examine this phenomenon in some detail in Chapter 20.

THE FUTURE OF HEALTH CARE COMPUTING

Each of the issues that must be examined in an evaluation of the impact of computers on the health care environment has a prehistory extending well back into the precomputer era. If we remember this fact, we will know that the computer is only another tool for doing many of the things that we have been doing for years without computer assistance. Indeed, a noted computer scientist and philosopher, Joseph Weizenbaum, has pointed out that computers are *conservative* influences as often as they are harbingers of change. Could it be, for instance, that in health care, computers have come along just in time to save our hopelessly large and inefficient medical record departments, when in fact the whole system should be rethought and redone?

On the other hand, there is a good probability that computers will continue to provide an ever-increasing variety of valuable services to health care—services that could not be rendered in any other way. It seems likely, for example, that advances in health care–related artificial intelligence techniques may soon be with us, in the form of computer-assisted diagnosis and treatment planning. In the more distant future, it may be possible that the Bionic Man and the Bionic Woman of science fiction may approach reality.

In the final chapter, therefore, we indulge in some crystal-ball gazing in an effort to see where all of this intense effort in health care computing will take us within our lifetimes.

WHO CARES?

Why are these issues important to you? It is very tempting to pass off discussion of these problems as mere philosophy in a rush to get moving with some real system. Such an attitude, although understandable, is dangerous. Many a *real* health care–computing system has ended in a *real* fiasco. Everyone who works in health care computing is aware of at least as many failures as successes. Naturally, the successes find their way into print. The health care worker who is contemplating the first brush with automation may thereby receive misleading impressions about the ease with which computer systems can be developed and employed.

It is not so easy. Computer programs are still difficult to write, and many projects can be brought to completion only by skilled professionals. Technical know-how alone is not enough to ensure success. Knowledge of the issues involved in health care computing is essential to achieving worthwhile results.

If computers could write their own programs, then software engineering would not be an issue. If all health care workers found computer systems easy to use and helpful to their normal way of doing business, then human engineering would be unimportant. If we could trust everyone to respect the privacy of sensitive, personal, health care data and if computers were invulnerable to fire and other natural catastrophes, then perhaps there would be no security issue. If computers were really inexpensive, then the study of economic issues would be superfluous. If no one had ever bought the wrong computer through simple ignorance, then functional specifications and contracts would be a waste of time. If computers could set their own priorities, fund themselves, and keep all of their users happy without human intervention, then management issues would not exist. If the workforce were full of health care–computing specialists and if advertising were not so effective, then the education of health care–computing specialists and of consumers would not trouble us.

Those who dismiss the issues involved in health care computing as mere philosophy do so at their own risk.

CHAPTER 11
A STORY OF FAILURE

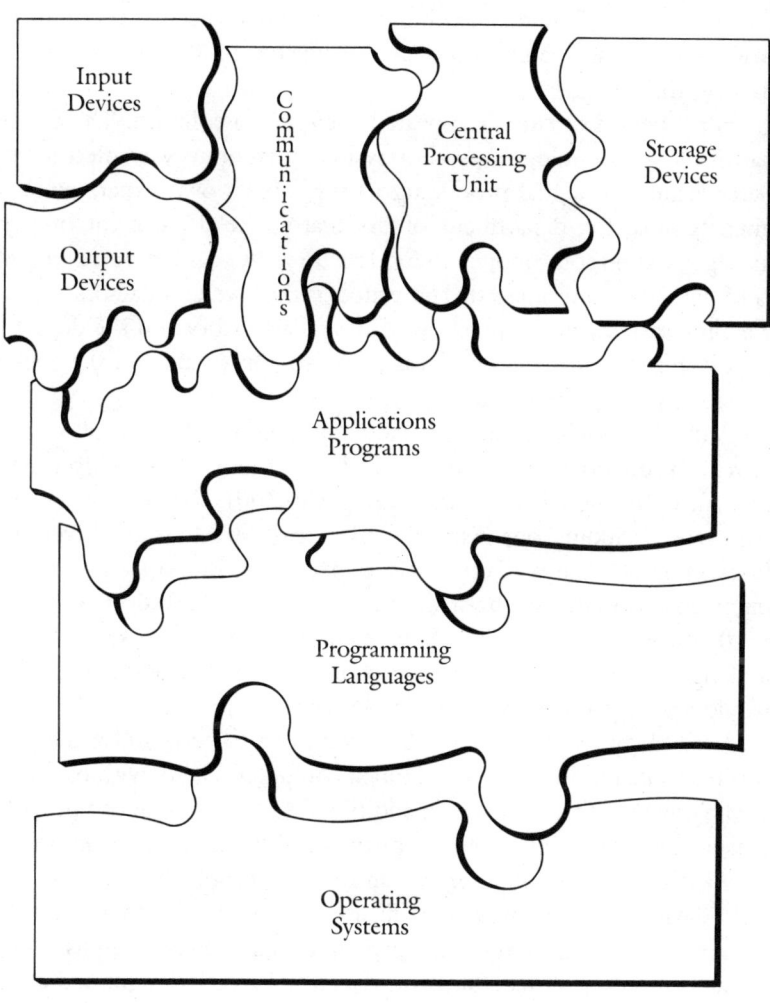

CHAPTER 11

About 10 years ago a project was begun in a big city hospital to create a psychiatric patient information system. The long-term objective was to do treatment evaluation on psychiatric inpatients and outpatients. It was recognized that this was an ambitious project. The initial focus was to be on the support of psychiatric process monitoring of the inpatient population.

It took a full year to develop a formal proposal for funding from external grant agencies. It was then found that the department of psychiatry could not get sufficient funds to establish the system from these sources. Research funding agencies called the project a service. The hospital budget committee called it research. Falling between two categories and failing to secure a sufficient funding commitment are the tragic flaws in this story.

For a period of time it appeared there was a solution. The closely affiliated department of psychology's psychophysiology laboratory wanted to establish a computer facility for signal processing to support its own experimental treatment program. Unlike the department of psychiatry, the department of psychophysiology managed to find some money to fund its computer system. It was therefore decided to pool the computing interests (unrelated as they were: a database system and a signal handling system) of the psychophysiology laboratory and the department of psychiatry. The psychiatric database was going to get its start on the back of the psychophysiology computing system.

Although psychophysiology had enough money for a small real-time computing system to support its experiments (a PDP-11/40 with a 2.5 Mb cartridge disk drive, and analog-to-digital hardware costing $40,000), the cost of the database systems hardware (including one disk drive of at least 50 Mb, tape drives, and communications equipment) and of the software needed to support a psychiatric database was unfortunately in the neighborhood of $100,000 to $150,000. Still at least $60,000 to $110,000 shy of the amount of money needed for a database system, psychiatry went looking for other users who might contribute to developing a computer system that would serve information storage and retrieval functions.

Cardiology was also looking for a computer to perform ECG analysis. Cardiology was persuaded to invest in a combined computer facility with psychophysiology, and cardiology therefore donated an additional $50,000 to the computer facility, some of which was used to buy a second cartridge disk, adding only another 2.5 Mb.

At this point, a computer system that had originally been conceived as a psychiatric database facility was now firmly dedicated to two real-time signal analysis applications—psychophysiology experiments and ECG analysis. The entire purpose of the computing system, and consequently its very design, had drastically changed from the original proposal for the psychiatric information system to a signal processing facility. Ninety thousand dollars had already been spent in total, but it had been spent on a real-time computing system. Thus the psychiatry department was still about $60,000 to $100,000 short of what it needed. Vital hardware and software components for the database system were still lacking. This would have been an excellent point for the psychiatric database proponents to throw in the towel, but they did not.

There was still neither enough mass storage nor the right software to support the psychiatric database management system, so the facility started looking for more money. It was not difficult to find more users, but it was difficult to find *paying* users. An additional $17,000 was obtained from a research grant (this money was absorbed in simply making the system able to handle multiple users simultaneously); $15,000 was contributed by the psychology department (which wanted to use the computer for scoring and interpreting psychological tests); and $10,000 was added to the pot (mostly for another 2.5 Mb disk) by an outside agency that wanted to use the computer system to store data on psychiatric outpatients (at last there was a file storage and retrieval application, even though the amount of data was small enough for a 2.5 Mb disk).

At this point, $126,000 had been spent on computer hardware and software. But a lot of money was still needed to turn the computing system into a full-scale database facility!

At least $30,000 was needed for a reasonable-capacity disk drive of 50 Mb or more, and two of them would have been better. Further price tags included at least $10,000 more for a tape drive and another $10,000 for appropriate database management software. But there never was any money to buy these things. Thus, on top of the $126,000 already paid out, $50,000 to $80,000 was *still* needed. Remember, a basic database system would have cost only $100,000 to $150,000 in the first place.

During this time a substantial amount of money had to be sought constantly to pay for hardware maintenance. This was running about $12,000 per year and it absorbed any available funds that might have been able to contribute to obtaining capital equipment and software.

At least it was easy to fund the programming staff; their salaries were available, unlike funds for capital equipment. The programmers could do something about the lack of software, so they created some file management software and other programs, some of which were already commercially available, but for which funds did not exist. They were reinventing the wheel because the computer facility could not afford to buy existing commercial software. To add to their woes the programmers were faced with a complete revision of the computer's operating system and of the programming language by the company that had originally supplied it. The revised operating system and FORTRAN compiler were very different from the originals, and they had drastic effects on existing applications software, most of which had to be rewritten.

To make matters worse, the facility had no money for ordinary operating costs. In desperation, the facility turned to the hospital administration, which agreed to pay for one half of an annual hardware maintenance contract *if employee health records were kept on the "psychiatry" computer*.

And so it went. Among other interests, surgery wanted to keep some surgical records on the system in exchange for a small amount of funding, but this offer was turned down. However, the pulmonary function laboratory was brought in, and their test-reporting system was implemented quite successfully.

But the system, conceived of drastically conflicting interests, failed to serve most of its users well. As a psychiatric database facility it had never yet existed, because there never had been enough funding to get that going. To be sure, $126,000 had been found, but most of it had been found for other computing purposes. The computing facility lacked enough continuing financial backing to meet even ordinary maintenance costs.

There are enough problems here that the facility would probably have collapsed under its own weight, given time. This, however, was a time of financial constraint and this injured project was fair game for the administration. It cut the salaries of the computing staff, and ultimately took over 100% control of the computer system because it felt it could make use of the facility for administrative data processing services.

The administration finally was caught in the same web, and they began to realize that signal processing and accounts receivable have a "few" differences. Ultimately the computer was disposed of, but not until more money had been invested.

There, in a simplified form, is the sad tale of one unsuccessful health care–computing installation. It generated a few papers and even a few partially satisfied customers. But it was still a failure.

What can be learned from this disaster, 4 years in the making?

The most obvious lesson is that no matter how hard one ignores the economic issues, they catch up with one anyway. Because of hopeless financial constraints, this project was doomed.

Although this project was strapped by lack of funding, it was not a cheap failure. In addition to the $126,000 spent on hardware and software, $200,000 was spent on salaries over a 4-year period, $52,000 on hardware and software maintenance, and $20,000 on paper forms and other expendables. In round figures, this disaster cost about $400,000, and that was not nearly enough to guarantee an effective return on the large investment.

Put simply, there is sometimes not enough money to support the intentions of those who want to start and carry on a health care–computing project. They are therefore compelled to seek the support of outside interests to generate a "critical mass" to afford hardware, software, and support personnel. But the wider a computer installation casts its nets to serve more and more users with unrelated interests, the more inexorably hardware, software, and human capacity fall behind increasing demands. The more one tries to do, the bigger the system required to do it, and the more it costs merely to keep existing users happy. Also, 50% to 80% of the programmer's time will be spent maintaining the past (i.e., doing software maintenance). When it is impossible to afford a small system to do one job, it will almost surely be impossible to afford a more expensive system to do several jobs!

Using a retrospectoscope, we see that not only economic issues but also management issues were ignored in this facility. The original purpose was to establish a psychiatric database system. There should have been a firm stand on this specification. As soon as psychophysiology came along with its own funding, psychophysiology should have been encouraged to establish its own specification and to seek to develop its own separate resources—not as a means of supporting the database project, but as a legitimate end in itself. Unfortunately, it was probably psychology that suffered the most in this failure. From the database point of view, this experience simply proved the truism that one cannot get more than one is willing to pay for. The moment one starts compromising one's computing goals the outcome of the battle is already in question. To attempt to establish a database management system with no money is ludicrous.

Several more positive lessons were learned. It was found that a pulmonary function report generator can be developed cheaply. It was learned that a minicomputer has an incredible capacity, and that even a diversity of mismatched applications such as the ones outlined here could not saturate it. Another way of looking at this would be to say that the facility made the same mistakes with $100,000 worth of hardware that some people have made with $1,000,000 systems. Today it is possible to make the same mistakes for only $10,000 with microcomputer systems. But they still were mistakes and it is still a failure.

Some interesting points about software engineering and about the people who write programs were also learned the hard way. One cannot mix database and real-time environments because most programmers are not good at both kinds of applications. Furthermore, software packages developed by other users and provided "as is" are best avoided. One particular communications software package was purchased from another university; it was undocumented and unsupported. Three months of programming effort were wasted in attempting to make it work. Eventually, the equivalent commercial communications package was bought from an established company, and it worked the first day.

This project demonstrated painfully the problems of managing personnel adequately. Too often one forgets that programmers are people with feelings. Writing a computer program is a creative act. If one requires a programmer to spend many months in developing a functioning program and then pulls out of a project and never implements that program, the person who created it is going to be offended. For such a reason, one of the programmers in this project resigned even before funding for his position was cut off, vowing never to work in the health care environment again.

In summary, then, this story of failure demonstrates how disregarding the important issues in health care computing can prevent the success of a project.

CHAPTER 12
SOFTWARE ENGINEERING

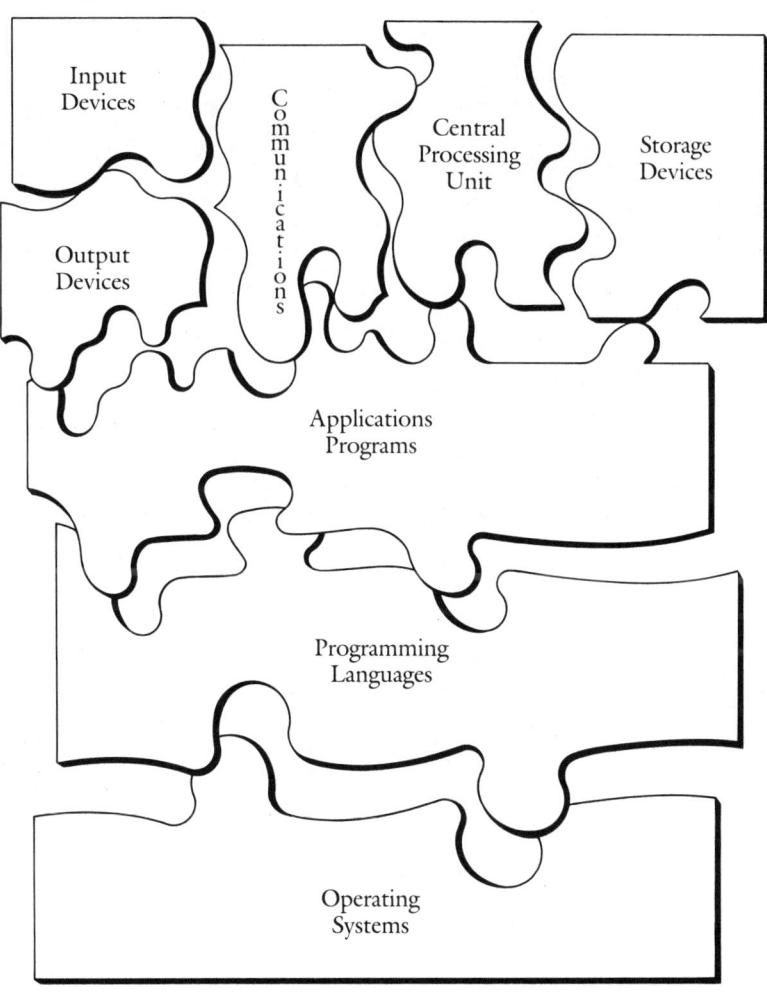

CHAPTER 12

One of the most critical issues that affects the users of computer systems is one that users are least likely to understand—software engineering. Software engineering refers to using formal methods for designing, writing, and testing computer programs (software). Users of a health care–computing system might wonder why such techniques should concern them. In an atmosphere in which users think of computers as "black boxes" that automatically accept input and correctly produce the required output, concern over software engineering might appear to be superfluous. Such an attitude, however, is dangerous and unrealistic, because the issue of software engineering has an overwhelming impact on the schedule, budget, and even the success and long-term survivability of a health care–computing endeavor.

A computer program that is flung together with a primary regard to expediency, with little concern for sound design, bears a relationship to proper software that is roughly analogous to the relationship between chicken coops and houses. Both chicken coops and houses fall under the generic term "buildings," but the latter can be a home fit for a king, whereas the former may barely keep the rain off the chickens! "Chicken house programming," like "chicken house carpentry," results in a low-quality product.

Unfortunately for many naive users, the weaknesses of inferior programming may not be immediately recognizable to the untrained eye, and the results of sloppy work may not manifest themselves until long after the unskilled programmer has departed. The principle of *caveat emptor* applies here, and buyers are advised to inform themselves of the features that distinguish programming expertise from slipshod approaches.

WHY ENGINEER SOFTWARE?

The bottom line of software development is economics. As we stressed earlier, software development is the most expensive component of a computer system, often exceeding hardware costs by a factor of two or more.

Software development is expensive because it takes so long to produce finished programs that work according to specifications. There are four interlocked phases in creating useful software: design, coding, testing, and maintenance. These four phases, and estimates of the amount of time commonly devoted to each, are outlined in an excellent article by Zelkowitz.*

In the design phase, someone must identify the problem that needs to be solved by automation and then develop an appropriate programming strategy for solving that problem. Zelkowitz estimates that in larger applications, this phase may account for about 11% of the entire software development effort.

The second phase of the process, coding, is the activity people commonly think of as programming. It is the actual writing of statements in a programming language.

---

*Zelkowitz, M.V.: Perspectives on software engineering, ACM Computing Surveys **10**:197, 1978.

But to view coding as the main effort of programming is quite misleading, because this activity may account for as little as 7% of the total software development effort in a large application.

Once code has been written, testing it may account for another 15% of the time spent in creating software.

According to Zelkowitz, 67% of the time and money expended on creating a large software system is accounted for by the fourth and final phase of the process: software maintenance. Unhappily, it is impossible to detect all or even most errors in a program that appears to be functioning properly. Many errors will become apparent only after a program has been in use for weeks, months, or occasionally even years. As each of these errors is discovered, it must be corrected, thus program modifications become necessary. Additionally, user requirements in a given application change constantly, and users' changing needs will necessitate periodic software modifications.

Not only is software development expensive, but also, unfortunately, there is no assurance of its ultimate success. The large investment, both of time and of money, in hardware acquisition and software development does not pay off in terms of useful results until software is designed, written, tested, debugged, and found to be working correctly. If for any reason the programming process halts short of the delivery of the intended software product, the entire investment is a loss. When problems are encountered in software development, deadlines are missed, budgets are exceeded, priorities change, and the result may be a large commitment for very little practical return. In such circumstances, it has been common to see good money thrown after bad to salvage something worthwhile out of a programming fiasco.

Anything that could reduce the risk in software development and that could help to assure the favorable outcome of the process would be desirable. However, the inherent limitations of the programming process severely restrict the potential for instituting any such procedures.

An interesting constant in software development has been discovered. When all four phases of the development process are considered, it would appear that a programmer working alone produces, on the average, fewer than 20 lines of tested, working program per day. This low figure reflects the enormous proportion of the programmer's time that must be spent in design and testing. Because many programs routinely run into hundreds (or even a couple of thousand) of lines of code, the total output of user-ready software that one programmer can produce in 1 year is not large.

Often in a health care environment, time is an important consideration in software development. Once a need has been perceived, a medical research goal, a patient-care priority, or an administrative plan may demand rapid implementation. For instance, a 2-year development period could render needs obsolete before they had been met. The necessity to conduct several projects simultaneously, or a very large project within a reasonable amount of time, will demand the addition of extra programming staff members in a health care–computing laboratory.

Unfortunately, when two or more programmers work on the same project, the time-saving realized is not directly proportional to the number of programmers. In fact, adding more programmers to a team also introduces more problems of communication among the programmers as they attempt to coordinate their efforts, and this necessary communication occupies an increasingly large segment of each programmer's time. Zelkowitz estimates that if one programmer is capable of writing a 5000-line program in 1 year, five programmers working as a team could produce only 20,000 lines of code per year—not 25,000 lines, as one might have expected. The bigger the team, the less efficient it is. This is a limitation of larger programming projects.

Because a programmer's productivity in lines of code is about the same no matter what programming language is used, it makes sense to employ high-level programming languages with powerful statements rather than low-level assembler-type languages.

However, no matter what language is used, the cost per statement is very high. It makes sense to do everything possible to obtain the highest quality software in return for this big investment. In an effort to minimize errors, maximize program efficiency, and reduce testing and software maintenance time to a minimum, the discipline of software engineering has developed. This discipline is predicated on the observation that a formally designed piece of software is more likely to approach perfection more quickly than an equivalent program that has been thrown together by old-fashioned ad hoc methods.

To most health care workers, even the elementary concepts of computers and computer programming may be mysterious. To such readers we recommend gaining a firm understanding of general, introductory computing concepts. Once the basics have been grasped, the computer-system user is in a position to look more closely at the four phases of software development, to which we now turn.

THE DESIGN PHASE

Details of the various techniques that have been developed for software design are beyond the scope of this book. Here we will enumerate a few of the more common methods only briefly. Interested readers can find greater depth in the sources listed in Appendix III. They should realize, of course, that entire university courses are devoted to this subject.

One of the better-known techniques is variously called top-down development, or simply structured programming. Basically, this technique is a method of structuring and analyzing a problem in a progressively refined manner, from the highest or most abstract level down to the lowest or most detailed level, progressively adding more and more detail to the subsystems, the structures, or the modules that have been identified in preceding steps. In other words, design progresses from a global overview of the problem, down to the precise programming tactics that must be used to cope with each small step of the solution. Programs are made as modular as possible.

Algorithms that are used frequently are placed in subroutines that can be invoked as many times as necessary by the main program. Another distinguishing feature of structured programming is that the logic flow within every module is kept as simple as possible. Statements are executed in sequence from the top, or beginning, of the program to the bottom, or end. Whenever the logic flow must go backward (i.e., back in the direction of the beginning of the module), it is permitted to do so only through a carefully designed looping syntax, the use of which minimizes the chance of logic errors. The logic flow in a carefully structured program resembles a river that flows from top to bottom, invoking subroutines and clearly discernible loops along the way.

Another fairly popular design technique is hierarchical input, process, and output (**HIPO**). HIPO is largely a documentation technique that emphasizes the clear, logical structuring of the processes in a program. According to a HIPO technique, a program should be represented somewhat like an organizational chart with a hierarchy of logical subsegments. In turn, each of these segments can be expanded to demonstrate the input it receives, the process it carries out, and the output it produces. The overall logic of a program thus becomes evident at a glance, and on the detailed level, the precise operation of each logical module of the program can be examined easily.

Meta stepwise refinement is a design method by which programs are broken into progressively smaller and smaller sections, subsections, and sub-subsections until the level of individual statements in a programming language is reached.

In addition to these design techniques, the development process itself can be organized to facilitate efficient programming that is as free from error as possible. In the chief programmer team concept, the programmers assigned to a task are organized as one chief, one backup chief, a programming secretary (whose job it is to perform all the necessary paperwork and documentation to ensure there are no misunderstandings between team members working on different parts of the project), and a number of programmers, each of whom will be assigned to do specific tasks.

Another interesting approach to the programming process makes use of the structured walk-through. A programmer who designs a module of a program must justify the work in a conference to a devil's advocate, whose job it is to find errors in that program. When such meetings take place on a regular, frequent basis throughout the development cycle, logical errors may be discovered early.

Another successful technique that has been used in some places is maintaining a systems development library of routines that have already been tested and proven correct. Thus, programmers working on new projects can string together these already tested routines and can thereby avoid duplicating a lot of development effort.

Documentation

Inherent in the design of any software system should be writing all the documentation required to make software a usable product, as opposed to a mysterious "black box." The three levels of documentation are user documentation, program documentation, and systems documentation.

User documentation permits the end-users of a piece of software to employ it for the purpose for which it was intended, without reference to any other information. The users should be provided with a "cookbook" instruction manual or equivalent material presented on the CRT screen that illustrates how they are to provide input to the program and what kind of output they will receive from it. A few sample interactions between user and program will probably be included.

Program documentation, by contrast, provides all the details that permit a computer programmer other than the original developer to understand and, if necessary, to modify a program. The purpose of each program will be described. The acceptable range and types of input will be identified, and the kinds of output that can be expected will also be specified, with examples. Each logical segment, or module, of the program will be identified. For each segment, the necessary input will be documented. The logic, defined algorithms, and calculations used in each segment will be specified and referenced. The output produced by each logical module will also be stated. Finally, a complete listing of the source program will be given, so that any programmer who reads this document will be able to correct or modify the program in the future.

Systems documentation is the final level of documentation that permits a systems analyst or a programmer–analyst to see where each program fits into the overall software environment of the computer system being used. Few programs stand alone, especially in database applications or in systems in which many commonly used routines are invoked by numerous programs that are otherwise unrelated.

This documentation should be created throughout the entire software development process. No software development effort is complete until this essential work has been done.

THE CODING PHASE

As we have seen, coding a program should be a relatively straightforward job, provided that an adequate design has been carried out. This part is the work that programmers love to do and that naive employers usually expect to see them doing. However, it should be remembered that to competent programmers who are familiar with the language they are using, this is the easiest and least time-consuming phase of software development.

THE TESTING PHASE: EXTERMINATING BUGS

Those who have had much experience with software have usually learned the hard way that they should never trust a program that appears to be working properly. They know that a "debugged" progam that has been "thoroughly" tested is simply in a quiescent phase of its existence.

Bugs in programming are side effects of the software development process. Some bugs are obvious. Mistakes in the syntax of programming statements (e.g., using a command improperly) will often prevent a program from operating at all, and such errors must be corrected before any output can be produced. But the most pernicious kind of bug arises from logical errors in the program itself. Although every individual line of code may be syntactically correct, the effect of the programming may be erroneous (i.e., it may not produce the kinds of calculations, data manipulations, or output that are required).

There can be several sources of such errors. If systems analysts do not understand the nature of the problem they are attempting to solve, they will not be able to design an appropriate program. However, even if they do understand the problem, they may still make errors, and the design may not solve the problem at hand. On the next step down the hierarchy, programmers may misconstrue the systems analyst's intentions. When this is the case, the programmer may create a "perfect" program—but one that misses the point entirely. On the other hand, a programmer may understand what is required but may have problems in translating specifications into the appropriate coding, and thus may inadvertently write a program other than the one intended.

Some logical bugs produced by each of these problems or a combination of them announce their presence to all by producing garbled output. Other bugs are more subtle in their effect, but are still detectable by wary users. For instance, a progamming error that produces an incorrect result in a statistical test may yield numerical values that are plausible but are actually erroneous. We are aware of a "home brew" statistics package that had been used by physicians for over a year before anyone noticed an error. Who knows how many papers with false statistical "conclusions" have been published, thanks to such programs? Reviewers rarely run checks, and they rarely have the raw data even if they wish to check it.

When a statistical software package has been widely used on a particular machine for a long period of time, most bugs will eventually be detected and corrected; users will thus have reasonable confidence in the package. But even so, users remain responsible for checking the accuracy of results.

Although subtle programming errors are frustrating enough, they are unfortunately not the most obscure. The most occult bugs in a progam may lie dormant in parts of the code that have never even been tested. This is because most of the time it is impossible to give all conceivable sets of input to a computer program. The potential variation in input may be infinite. At most, those testing a program with simple data usually have to settle for input at the extremes of the expected range of values, plus a few samples from within that range. Sometimes programmers will include special routines in their programs that will identify and reject input that falls outside of a specified range of acceptable values. Sometimes they will even make sure that these routines function properly by throwing a few erroneous input sets at the program. But not always. After months and months of crror-free execution, a program may be thrown into disastrous turmoil by a data-entry clerk who makes an incorrect key stroke (e.g., putting a negative sign in front of a number where none was expected). Many other input errors can fool a program that works perfectly if it is given correct input.

In very general terms, we can identify four levels of program testing. The first and easiest is to submit a few sample sets of typical data to a program, and to verify the correctness of the results produced. At a second and slightly more rigorous level, programs can be tested with a broad set of sample input that varies at regular intervals throughout the range of possible correct input.

Neither one of these levels of testing does anything to determine what happens when a progam encounters improper input. What happens, for example, if a clerk makes a typing error and gives the computer alphabetic characters when it wants numbers? Programmers should always anticipate such problems—but sometimes they do not. When they do anticipate such problems, developers may include error-detection routines in their programs. Unfortunately, it is common for software developers to feel they have discharged their duty by including these routines in their work, and they are not always moved to test them.

The third level of software testing, therefore, throws a complete spectrum of input at the computer, including input that is out of range, or even of the wrong data type. The resulting output is scrutinized to determine whether the computer detected these mistakes. For example, a statistical program that assumes zeroes for missing data would yield patently incorrect results. When data is missing, the program must detect the fact and report it to the user.

It is seldom possible to proceed beyond this kind of program verification. The ultimate and fourth level of program testing consists of producing mathematical proofs for the logic of a program. Proof for even the simplest of routines may run into many pages of complex mathematics; embarrassingly, some simple programs that have been "proven" correct by such a method have subsequently been shown to be in error. Rigorous proof for a typical large program is probably impossible at present.

SOFTWARE MAINTENANCE

Most "completed" software, then, harbors errors. In programs of any complexity it may be impossible to eliminate all bugs. An operating system, for example, will always contain several serious errors when it is first released. The most rigorous testing by the company that supplies the software will have failed to reveal these hidden problems. Only as users subject the operating system to an enormous variety of uses will some of the bugs emerge. Efforts to correct bugs in systems programming may introduce new bugs of their own. Patches to fix the problem in an operating system may themselves have to be patched in the future. For this reason, software maintenance is a never-ending process that requires continuing monetary commitment.

Frederick P. Brooks, Jr., in his highly readable *The Mythical Man-Month: Essays on Software Engineering* (Addison-Wesley, 1975), explains software maintenance thus:

A program doesn't stop changing when it is delivered for customer use. The changes after delivery are called program maintenance, but the process is fundamentally different from hardware maintenance. . . . Program maintenance involves no cleaning, lubrication or repair of deterioration. It consists chiefly of changes that repair design defects.

In this sense, the term "maintenance" is a misleading euphemism. Nothing is being "maintained." The term simply denotes the eventual detection and correction of errors that should not have occurred in the first place.

Software maintenance is an expensive process that Brooks estimates to be typically 40% or more of the cost of developing a program. As we saw, Zelkowitz thinks this figure may be closer to 70%. Interestingly, the cost is influenced by the number of users; more users find more errors!

Therefore, it is wishful thinking for the user of a health care–computing system to avoid a software maintenance contract, in spite of its high cost. The user can pay the developer now or pay even more later.

So significant are the demands of software maintenance that Brooks has seriously suggested that the first version of any large software system should be thrown away, and that the whole thing should be rewritten a second time to correct all of the design mistakes that were incorporated in the first working version. Another excellent book on software maintenance is *Principles of Software Maintenance,* by James Martin (Prentice-Hall, Inc., 1983).

PROJECT MANAGEMENT

Throughout the development process, the importance of overall project management cannot be overemphasized. The necessity of close project management has been repeatedly demonstrated by software development projects that have severely overrun their schedules under the benign neglect of a management that does not know what is going on. Frequent checkpoints and demonstrable benchmarks of progress in the development of a software system are the only reliable ways of determining how close to schedule a given project may be. Function is the only reliable measurement of success. The number of lines of "completed" code that have been written means nothing. Confident assertions that a program is 90% complete often have really meant that 90% of the effort (e.g., testing, debugging, and software maintenance) remains to be done.

THE BOTTOM LINE

The current limitations of software engineering usually come as a shock to computer-naive users who might expect any product that they buy—including a computer system—to function properly. Our inability to prove the validity of most software comes as no surprise to programmers, but it naturally leaves users with a sense of profound insecurity.

The modern programming techniques that have been developed in an effort to cope with this problem are limited and only partially successful. Furthermore, the techniques of software engineering are rather recent developments. Although these techniques are now taught in many undergraduate computer science curricula at the university level, the majority of the programmers now in the labor force have had little (if any) formal exposure to them. To make matters worse, these modern programming methods are initially time-consuming and confining in comparison to ad lib, unstructured programming. In the small software development group, these techniques are often ignored in the interest of expediency, as overworked programmers try to turn out as many functional programs as possible in a short time. This situation often arises in a health care–computing laboratory. When rushed, however, programmers tend to design their programs while they write them; in other words, without any advanced planning.

These observations have important implications for computing in the health care environment.

In the health care field it is exceptional to see the kind of design or coding of applications software that would meet any criteria of good software engineering or that could pass any standard testing process. Commercial developers of health care–computer systems are seldom asked by their clients to prove that their software products have been intelligently designed, documented, or, for that matter, tested. This problem is serious enough that the FDA in the United States is looking toward regulating health care–computing software. Developers have their corporate reputations to protect and they may have large, highly trained, and highly paid staff personnel at their disposal. Yet they may not be wise enough to take these matters into account.

On the other hand, it is assumed that in-house developers will naturally do their very best on behalf of their health care employers. Unfortunately, "best" is frequently interpreted—both by developers and by their health care employers—in terms of the speed of generating untested, unstructured, undocumented programs. Many in-house health care–computing departments are so small and so underfunded that they cannot afford a proper program development team. Consequently, the disciplined, professional approach to programming to which the team approach commends itself is the exception and not the rule in health care–computing laboratories. Traditional (i.e., sloppy) programming and all its pitfalls are typical of what one finds in applications software in a health care environment.

The inherent unreliability of almost all software, both at the systems level and at the applications level, means that health care workers have a responsibility to mistrust computer output, especially in a new system. To assume that programmers understand how to evaluate output concerning what may be to them an arcane health care subject is dangerous (e.g., a computer-generated pulmonary function report may seem acceptable to a programmer, but only a health care specialist can reasonably be expected to evaluate the output for clinical correctness). Until a program has proved its reliability in many uses, the outputs of which have been verified, high suspicion of that program's output is mandatory. Even after extensive testing, a kernel of suspicion should remain.

Although the realities of software engineering have important implications for health care workers who hire others to develop software for them, these realities also have an important message for computer hobbyists. When the home computer revolution occurred, it was common for computer-naive health care providers to assume that with a little training they could program their own computers. Anything may be possible, but the complexity of good computer programming for anything except trivial tasks obviously excludes it from the realm of hobbies. The average health care provider has neither the time nor the training to be able to program useful health care applications. Developing a few "adding machine" routines for accounts receivable on an office microcomputer may be within the capability of health care providers who are interested in dabbling with computers. If they make mistakes, they hurt no one but themselves. (On the other hand, it is highly doubtful that any junior programmer could write the software for a coronary care monitoring system.)

That is not to say, however, that users have no part in the software engineering process. On the contrary, in small development operations a health care worker who knows something about computer programming, if only as a hobby, can at least help improve the quality of the programmer's work by playing the devil's advocate. Sitting down with the programmer and performing a structured walk-through of the program may help the programmer to see logical problems before they become buried in a "completed" program.

In the planning stage, even computer-naive health care providers have a vital part to play in explaining to software developers precisely what they require.

The physician, hospital administrator, or other health care worker who becomes deeply involved in health care computing will need to keep up with current developments in the software engineering field. Fortunately, there are several avenues of continuing education that are open to such individuals.

In the forseeable future, new, very high-level languages may put applications development in the hands of the users. These systems do not require the intricate programming of today's systems.

Finally, a variety of university courses and short commercial courses on software engineering intended for the business community are becoming available.

This continuing effort at self-education will obviously not transform a health care professional into a computer scientist. However, educated users are more likely to get what they want than naive clients with more money than technical knowledge. Customers who appreciate the general principles of sound software engineering are the most likely to obtain substantial results in return for their substantial investments.

CHAPTER 13
HUMAN ENGINEERING

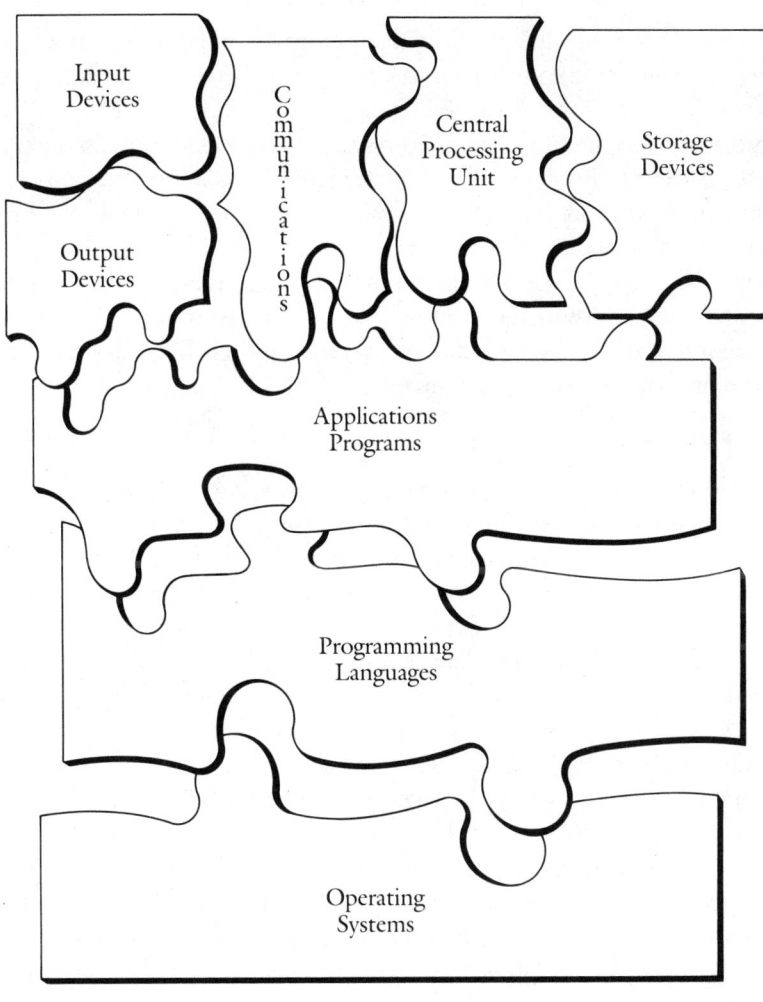

CHAPTER 13

Human beings and present **digital computers** are basically incompatible. There are vast differences in the ways in which people deal with information and the methods by which computers can input it, manipulate it, and output it. In the practice of health care computing, these differences will have an important impact on the ease and success with which any given application can be realized.

Earlier we discussed the limitations of current hardware and software technology. To avoid excessive repetition, these points will be summarized quite briefly here. The discussion will concentrate on ways to make the best of existing limitations.

HUMANIZING TECHNOLOGY

Human output differs substantially from computer input, and vice versa. A frustrating communications barrier therefore exists between user and machine. Computers have only a limited capability to be adapted toward a humanlike approach to information input and output. To make matters even more discouraging, in general, with current technology, the more humanlike the input and output, the greater its cost. In most applications there comes a point beyond which one cannot justify the added expense incurred by further adapting the computer to the user's way of doing business. Even in those rare cases in which money is no object, absolute technological limitations are eventually reached. No amount of money can yet buy a computer system that will listen to ordinary, everyday speech and will then formulate its own programs on the basis of information it learns in a conversation.

HUMAN ENGINEERING

Fortunately, with a little thought and planning it is possible for a systems developer to make the best of the current technological constraints of computer systems. The systems developer can design a system so that the average user finds it fairly easy to use, in spite of the inherent awkwardness of the technology. This sort of design is called human engineering. Systems that are well engineered are now often called user friendly. Be careful of that claim, however; it seems that all systems today are claimed to be user friendly—we have never seen a system advertised as user unfriendly!

Human engineering (also called ergonomics) is the rather fuzzy area that deals with designing mechanized devices for efficient use by human beings. As such, it is really an expression of the systems developer's consideration for the end-users of the system. This consideration is expressed particularly in software, which the developers will prepare remembering that for many of the people who will ultimately use their programs, this may be their first experience with that type of program, or any program. Human engineering strives to calm the user's anxiety and to dispel confusion. Software writers who strive to human engineer their products use programs almost as an extension of their own personalities to guide the user step by step through the execution of what may be to the user a confusing and complex process.

The personality of the programmer is quite evident in the character of a program.

The instructions and clarifications output by a program should ideally reflect a polite and helpful attitude. Unfortunately, it is not uncommon for users to be confronted with computer instructions that are cryptic, ambiguous, unnecessarily computer-esque, or even downright condescending.

The objective of human engineering is that we get systems so easy to use that we can find no reason not to use them—they are simply more efficient and workable than manual methods.

Most users care nothing for the technicalities of computer science. They care only about the quality of the service that the computer system provides for them, and this is a reasonable expectation. They have spent their money for a working product.

The demands of human engineering are evident in the interface between the computer and its end-users (in the input and output processes), and in special user requirements such as the security of data and systems reliability. Each of these areas will now be examined more fully.

THE INPUT PROCESS

Inputting data is often a tedious, error-prone, and time-consuming aspect of a user's interaction with a computer system. Human engineering of the person–computer input interface requires considering both hardware and software features of the system.

Before going any deeper, we should recognize that a well-lighted but nonglare environment with a comfortable chair and desk is part of a well-engineered data-entry setup. These things reduce fatigue and actually increase productivity.

There already exists in the marketplace a wide variety of input devices. With this equipment, end-users can deal with a computer system in a hands-on mode. The convenience of use and the suitability to the user's purposes will largely determine the acceptability of a computer system in the user's eyes. Input devices should therefore be chosen with regard to their functional features. They should not simply be selected by default because one is familiar with them.

The most familiar sort of input device is some variation on an ordinary typewriter keyboard. For certain kinds of data entry such as the input of text, a typewriterlike keyboard is the only acceptable choice. It will therefore be necessary in most computing environments that data-entry personnel will have to know how to type.

In some health care–computing situations, however, the demand that people using input devices have typing skills may severely limit the usability of a system by physicians, nurses, and other clinical or laboratory personnel who do not have clerical training. In an effort to reduce problems of this sort, special keyboard arrangements for nontypists have been developed. It is now possible to buy a keyboard on which all of the letters are arranged in alphabetical order. There also exist available keypads in which each key produces a function rather than a single letter.

In many circumstances, there are better input devices than keyboards. One example is the popular "mouse," which allows a user to move a cursor around the screen instead of typing. Many of these are not expensive, and they should be used whenever they are required. Why ask nontypists to answer multiple-choice questions from a typewriterlike keyboard when they could more easily point with a light pen or even with their fingers at selections on the screen of a VDT? Such input devices are inexpensive and readily available. Devices are now commercially available that allow the user to speak 100 or more letters, words, or phrases and the device will recognize these and cause the computer to carry out the requested function. This can make it easy to use onscreen menus.

When numerical data must be entered as input, several input devices can reduce the drudgery. A variety of OMR and OCR devices can be used to input numbers and responses to multiple-choice questions on a medium that is directly readable by the computer. This technique permits those who have no typing skills to record data on computer-processable media, thereby eliminating a time-consuming and error-susceptible transcription step by a data-entry clerk.

When inputting data from graphs or other continuous curves, it is not necessary to make frequent measurements along the curve to determine discrete X and Y coordinates and to then type these numbers into a computer. Instead, a cursor connected directly to the computer can be traced over the length of the curve. Coordinates are determined by the computer and data is collected automatically, thus saving a great deal of time and effort. Alternatively, the signal can be digitized either directly or from a tape recording using an analog-to-digital converter (e.g., to input values from intracardiac pressure recordings).

When human engineering plays an appropriate role in the development of the computer system, the developer will be aware of the spectrum of devices available on the market and will select those devices that will serve the needs and skills of the end-users of the system.

Analogously, programming techniques that direct the input process should also reflect the needs and sophistication of systems users. In an input procedure, much potential confusion can be prevented if a computer is programmed to request individual data items interactively. It can specify in plain language the data it is expecting and indicate the criteria to be used in giving a response (such as what the term "mild" means). This technique is called prompting.

Human engineering also means that the systems developer respects the varying levels of familiarity and expertise among different possible users of the system. Although prompting may be an essential aid to one user, it may be a repetitious, boring, and unacceptably time-consuming irritation to a more sophisticated user who has been using a program for some time and who knows what input the computer wants. Sometimes the user should have the option of selecting or suppressing prompting instructions. HELP features are extremely important. It should be possible for a user to type "HELP" or "H" or "?" at any time and get an explanation of what is required at that point.

Another aspect of programming flexibility should also be considered; sometimes a computer program that guides the user through a rigid step-by-step sequence of operations may impose unreasonable constraints on the user. When the computer demands that a user provide a series of answers to questions during an input sequence, it frequently is programmed to expect perfect responses to questions. In this situation, the user is given no opportunity to go back and revise portions of the input if they have been entered incorrectly. The user who has made a mistake may therefore be forced to delete the entire record that has just been entered and to enter it again, this time perfectly. Thus the first effort has been wasted and must be duplicated—perhaps because of one small mistake. Input programs should also check for obvious mistakes such as values out of range, letters entered where numbers are expected, and items too long or too short in terms of the numbers of characters. Thoughtful consideration of the human-engineering issue involved would motivate a programmer to design software that did not require perfection of the people using a program.

When printed forms are used for data collection, these forms should be designed so that data can be recorded on them easily. They should also be organized in such a way that the data-entry personnel who read this information and enter it into a computer system can do so conveniently and without missing anything. The data should be recorded in the same order that the computer requires it.

On a more complex level, it is also advisable that the developer require the computer to perform tedious or error-prone tasks whenever possible, to unburden data-entry personnel. Sometimes it is necessary to encode information before the computer can classify or process it. When these codes are numerous or not readily apparent (as when an arbitrary numeric coding scheme is used), people tend to have a great deal of difficulty. They become frustrated and they make mistakes, because a simple slip of the finger on the input keyboard can misencode something. It is far better if the computer itself performs any encoding, if possible, or shows the user the textual version of any numeric code in time for the user to notice a mistake. The objective is to allow people to input data in a humanly understandable way or at least (by using mnemonics) in a way that will make errors detectable.

THE OUTPUT PROCESS

Computer output should also reflect a consideration for the people who will have to read it. Again, human engineering both of hardware and of software is important.

The physical output medium used is one obvious consideration. There is no reason to produce hard copy unless a permanent record is required. Making printed output (as contrasted to video screen output) is generally slower, is definitely noisier, and requires a continuing expense for paper. Economics is not the only factor at stake. When confidential information is recorded on paper, that paper has to be guarded or disposed of carefully, whereas images that have faded from a videoscreen tell no tales. Today it is possible to provide well-formatted, color, and even graphic data on CRT screens.

Other features of output are equally important. Speed and quietness are considerations of human engineering that must be treated separately in any application. Nor should it be assumed that the printed word is always the best choice. Pictorial representations are often preferable to lists of numbers. In nuclear medicine, for example, multicolor images on videoscreens are used to demonstrate strikingly the differential uptake of various radioactive materials in organs of the body. For soft-copy (CRT display) output, the required technology is readily available and presently in use. Today hard-copy graphics output is more expensive but does exist, even though there are limitations. Still the best practical hard-copy output for these images is a color photographic technique.

The quality of print (i.e., solid-looking type versus dot matrix) is also a human engineering consideration. For instance, when computer-produced documents are being used principally for internal archival purposes, the relatively low quality of dot-matrix print might be acceptable. On the other hand, when computer-generated documents are to be sent to patients or to health care providers in other centers, one would probably wish to use letter-quality print. The developer should consider this point. The old-fashioned and barely legible upper-case-only typeface produced by many line printers is becoming obsolete with more modern printing developments. Serious consideration to more legible alternatives should be given as a routine aspect of human engineering the output of any computer system. Letter-quality printers are now even available relatively inexpensively for personal computers.

Not only hardware but also software should be designed in such a way that output is legible, that important or abnormal values are in some way highlighted, and that the overall result is pleasing. A few systems still in existence will print the number "3" as "003." The information content of a one-digit integer is obscured by meaningless leading zeroes and a useless decimal point. The usual reasons for such output are lazy programming, or software that is simply old and primitive compared to what is available today. If a developer presents shoddy output to a user, the user should send the developer back to the drawing board with instructions to come up with output that respects the needs of humans—not with artificial output that reflects computer constraints.

Human-engineered output (or the lack of it) is also manifested in the manner in which programs handle errors during execution. Many operating systems provide error-indication facilities for both users and programmers. Whenever the computer desires to report an error condition, the user should get a detailed explanation of what has happened and what is required of the user. This kind of human engineering makes a great deal more sense than computer systems that report only a cryptic error code and then expect the user to go away to look up its hidden meaning in a reference manual.

PRIVACY AND SECURITY

The security of sensitive data entrusted to a computer system is an important aspect of the human engineering of computer systems. The systems developer has a responsibility to recognize the potential harm that may come to patients if some of the data collected on the system should be accessed by unauthorized persons or should be irretrievably destroyed. This issue is dealt with more fully in the following chapter.

RELIABILITY

Another important goal of human engineering is to design systems with a minimum potential for frustrating their users. Bizarre or awkward input procedures and poorly designed output can be quite frustrating. Nevertheless, users will forgive a system that is reliable. Systems reliability is taken for granted. Users rightly insist that if they must make the effort to adapt themselves to a computer system, the system must be available when they need it. No other feature of human engineering elicits so little praise or so much condemnation as the reliability of computer systems.

Unreliable computer systems can waste a great deal of users' time. Consider the case of an interactive time-sharing system that "crashes," destroying several hours' work for each of a dozen or more users. If such failures occur even infrequently, users may get frustrated and give up. The system that has been thoughtfully designed will provide fail-soft routines that salvage users' work and save it at the time of systems failure, so that when the system is repaired the users can be brought back **on-line** with little or no loss of their data.

The more an organization comes to rely on automation, the less it can afford computer down-time. It is costly to leave clerical personnel sitting idle because of a computer failure. While a computer is out of service, large backlogs of work may accumulate—so large that extra help at overtime rates may be needed to catch up. There is also cumulative frustration and damage to the user's confidence in the system.

In health care environments, the results of systems failure could be much more serious than financial loss. Monitoring systems connected to critically ill patients must never be out of operation. Computer-driven laboratory reporting systems are relied on for timely, vital data; these systems dare not fail for more than a few minutes at most. Short of total hardware redundancy, there is no way to guarantee that a system will have zero down-time. In critical applications such as monitoring systems, this expensive reality may have to be faced and financed. In applications such as laboratory reporting, a well-rehearsed manual backup procedure may suffice to tide one over a system failure. The necessity of maintaining adequate backup methods in critical applications is a consideration of human engineering that unfortunately receives less attention than it deserves. Some commercial laboratory reporting systems are marketed without regard to backup of any kind. Their unexpected failures have on occasion thrown a hospital's entire laboratory service into complete disarray.

Computer systems are only machines, and therefore they will fail sooner or later. The developer who does not think of the consequences of failure in systems designed for use in health care fails to serve all of the user's requirements.

COMPUTERIZING PEOPLE

Although it is critical to design computer systems with a consideration for people's requirements, it is equally important to make the best use of the human resources in an organization—not primarily to serve the computer system, but to permit people to interact with the computer as comfortably as possible.

Computers are often a disruptive influence in the health care environment. Those who will use them firsthand will be forced to modify how they used to do their daily work manually. Such disruption will necessitate a period of user training, during which productivity will be low and levels of frustration high. The systems developer should prepare for this situation.

First, wherever possible, the developer will bring the most "programmable" staff members into the closest interaction with the computer. In the health care environment, it will be easier to schedule clerks' time for user training than it will be to schedule physicians' time.

But the developer should strive to soften or even to negate user resentment by demonstrating that the computer returns a benefit to all users that is greater than the sacrifice they must make to use it. A secretary will probably learn to appreciate a system that helps produce the repetitious numerical data of a report in one half of the time it previously took to type the data on an ordinary typewriter. Note that even a large benefit to a third party is unlikely to win the devotion of the individual who is roused from a comfortable routine to learn new, automated techniques. Each individual user must be convinced that the computer system helps him or her personally. "Payback" is the catchword here. If the user perceives payback, the system's probability of success is improved.

BEASTS OF BURDEN

In human interactions, the sort of person who possibly irritates us the most is the petty functionary who is unfriendly, and who is officiously insistent on scrutinizing every detail at the expense of getting the job done.

In many ways, computer systems are patterned after this kind of exasperating individual. Many machines are programmed to be impersonal and unfriendly. They dogmatically enforce whatever foolish procedures they have been programmed to support. They are incapable of differentiating important information from a mass of trivial data unless programmed to do so.

Worst of all, computers have become a sort of "intellectual beast of burden" that some human masters falsely assume can relieve them of their responsibility to think. Periodically, there are celebrated cases in which checks for huge sums of money are erroneously paid out. Similarly, we know of a poor fellow who received several nasty notices and finally a letter from a collection agency because he would not pay a bill of

$0.00. (When ultimately he was threatened with legal action, he solved the problem by mailing in a check for $0.00!)

If computers are intellectual beasts of burden, they deserve the same respect as camels, which—as the joke has it—are horses designed by a committee. These beasts are clumsy, ill-tempered, and difficult to work with. However, when handled skillfully, they will perform essential services efficiently.

For the foreseeable future, it will continue to be necessary for humans to get around the built-in limitations of hardware and software technology as best they can. The time may come when health care workers will be able to use a computer simply by discussing a problem with it. However, until science fiction becomes reality, they will have to adapt their normal way of doing business to the limitations of computers. Human users will continue to be forced to express themselves in ways that computers can understand. Similarly, for a long time humans will have to tolerate the sorts of output that computers are capable of providing.

Regardless of their limitations, users of computer systems can demand that their systems will be intelligently human engineered to the furthest practical extent that technology and budget allow. Before accepting any health care–computing system, users must defend their own interests by asking several critical questions: Am I getting something I can use without having to learn a whole new set of skills? Is this computer system really a human-engineered product that I, as a health care professional, can use easily? Is it the product that I truly need? How good a product is it?

Much can be learned about the role of human engineering technically complex consumer products by considering automobiles. Although a car is complicated and has thousands of parts, its user interface (i.e., the way in which a driver interacts with it) is simple enough that almost any adult can operate it properly. There are many kinds of motor vehicles, but driving one is similar to driving any other, whether one gets behind the wheel of a taxi, a compact, or a limousine. Over the years, there have been many technical improvements in car design. Engines have become more powerful; the center of gravity has become lower; tires have grown wider; structural safety features have improved. However, although drivers have benefited from all of these improvements, they have been insulated from any disruption of customary driving skills and habits. The environment of the driver's seat has remained relatively unchanged. When one compares cars to many other kinds of machines and considers the very low level of preventive maintenance that most cars receive, one concludes that cars are astonishingly reliable. When anything does go wrong with them, parts and servicing are readily available.

In short, the automobile is a human-engineered consumer product that, although complex, is easily operated by its end-user, the driver. In the same way, health care–computing systems ought to be human engineered so that they too are usable products, and readily understood and operated by health care professionals. Computer scientists may design and implement a system, but their presence should be no more

FIGURE 13-1
Human engineering. The computer system has to fit the environment.

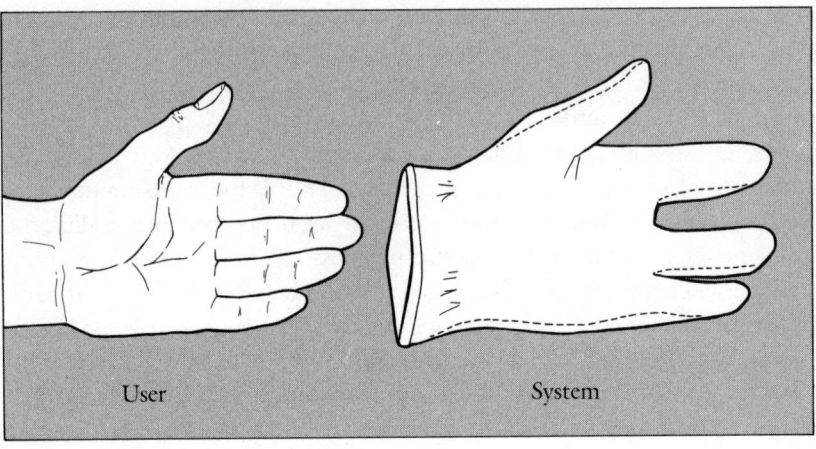

obvious to the end-user of a health care–computing system than the input of an automotive design engineer should be to the average driver.

In general, health care–computing systems have a long way to go before they can be favorably compared to such products as automobiles. The current limitations of hardware and software technology impose real constraints on the extent to which human engineering of computer systems is even possible. When a particular health care–computing application is undertaken, a compromise is always struck between technological feasibility and the ideal system that the user would like to have if money and present-day scientific achievements were unlimited (Figure 13-1). Throughout the life of a health care–computer application, this compromise may have to be periodically renegotiated as budgetary constraints, user needs, or technological advancements throw new factors into the equation.

Human engineering, as it applies to health care computing, is the human science by which the best possible compromise is struck. Human engineering of health care–computing systems is a goal to which every developer should aspire. It is certainly an issue that all health care professionals should consider when they decide to become computer users.

CHAPTER 14
PRIVACY AND SECURITY

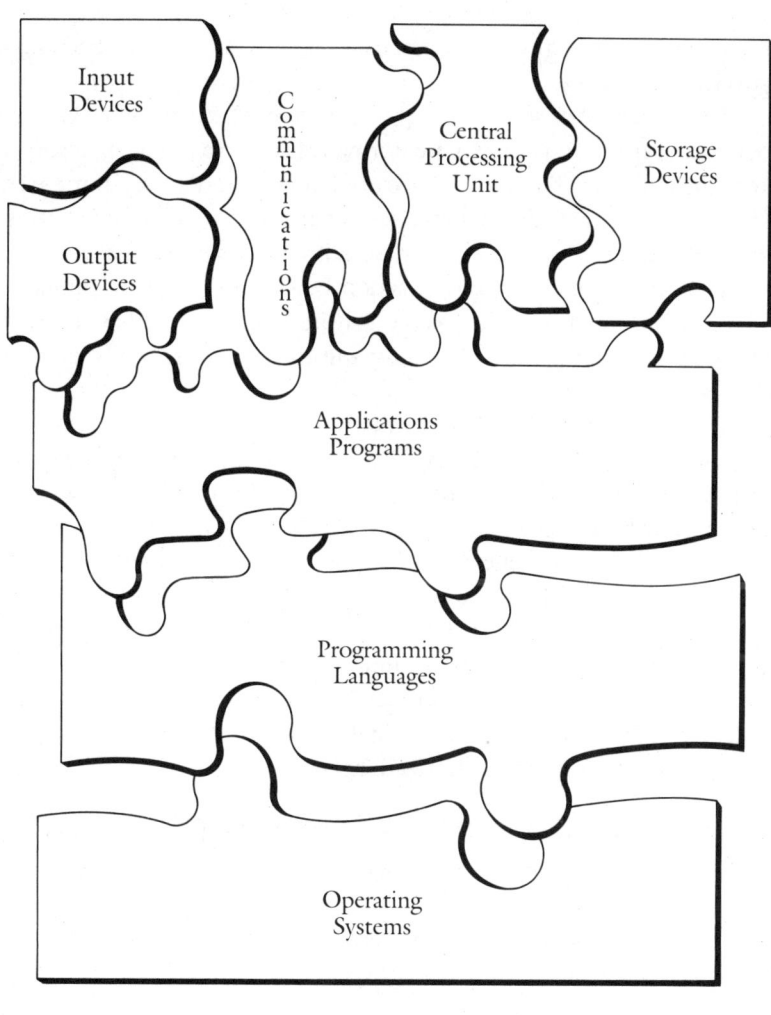

CHAPTER 14

PRIVACY

The privacy of personal data is a problem for society to resolve. It concerns the kinds of information about individuals allowed for entry and storage in records systems of all kinds. As the IBM series *Data Security and Data Processing* (1974) notes, privacy is concerned with (1) how and what information will be collected, (2) how and by whom it will be used, and (3) how it can be reviewed, modified, and corrected.

A hermit may be able to lead a completely private existence. If a person never comes into contact with government or society, it may never be necessary to divulge anything about that person to anyone. However, as soon as some nosy do-gooder comes along offering welfare assistance, the hermit will then become known to some government agency.

To interact with society, we pay a price in terms of privacy. If we install a telephone, our name and number are normally listed in a public directory unless we pay to keep them private. There is a choice on that matter, but only at some cost to ourselves. If we take a job, we will be forced to pay income tax. The data relating to our income must be divulged to the appropriate authority; here we have no choice. Similarly, when we buy property, the transaction becomes a matter of public record.

Some information is inviolably private (e.g., no one has the right to know our religious affiliation). However, most information—especially that relating to health care—is rarely so private.

Data about the health of individuals is in some cases very sensitive. Therefore, the existence of any kind of record concerning individual health poses a risk to those individuals—the risk that this confidential information will fall into unauthorized hands. At the same time, medical records are essential to the process of modern health care. Indeed, they are beneficial to the individual. Some personal health care data must be collected by health insurance agencies to protect themselves from financial disaster in the case of illness, and from a health care point of view, medical records can be potentially lifesaving in some circumstances.

Thus there is a built-in conflict between the right of patients to privacy and the need (or even the governmental demand) for them to divulge some of this information to certain authorized agencies for their own protection and benefit.

The conflicts between the rights of individuals and the requirements of society's institutions are difficult to resolve. But they are not subject to arbitrary resolution by data processing experts. Although such experts do have a definite role in informing the public about their perception of the problem, privacy issues must be faced and solved by society itself, expressing its collective will through government and law. Privacy is a vital issue in modern society, not a mere data processing problem.

SECURITY

On the other hand, the security of data is neither a social nor a legal issue. Rather, it is a problem with which organizations must cope—a procedural matter that involves the responsibility of organizations to protect the information they are authorized to collect from unauthorized or accidental modification, destruction, and disclosure. Privacy may be society's problem, but security is one's own problem.

The security of personal data has always been a problem for health care. The duty of physicians to keep secret the things they learn about patients is embodied in the ancient Oath of Hippocrates. Centuries ago, court physicians kept few, if any, medical records on their influential patients, in case the records should fall into the wrong hands. Even into the early twentieth century little emphasis was placed on medical records. This is reflected in the sparse and clinically inadequate chart-keeping at that time, both in private practices and even in the largest North American hospitals.

Times have changed. Today, medical records of various kinds are an indispensable part of the whole health care system. Indeed, it is considered to be malpractice for a physician to keep inadequate clinical records.

The security of these records is often poor. There are many hospitals in which anyone wearing a white lab coat can walk into the medical records department, demand any patient's chart, and get it. This situation, oddly enough, is especially true in teaching hospitals where the constant turnover of postgraduate students makes their personal recognition by medical records staff members improbable.

In the private physician's office, the situation is not much better. How many offices are safe from deliberate breaking and entering, and the theft of medical records? Often, the filing cabinets in which records are kept are not even locked at night.

SECURITY OF COMPUTER-BASED HEALTH CARE DATA

When a computer system is used to store health care information, the security problem becomes even more significant. A computer-based databank can store a huge amount of sensitive information in a physically small and rapidly accessible space, thereby increasing the potential damage that could be caused by accidental or deliberate destruction or disclosure to unauthorized parties. Computer software tools actually facilitate the ease with which people can browse through data and link together various pieces of independent medical databases, thereby gleaning information that was never intended to be inferred from separate, unlinked data items.

Medical records are used for patient care, health insurance, costly and time-consuming research, and essential medicolegal documentation. Thus, the continuing existence and physical integrity of medical records is necessary to many aspects of the health care system.

The entire problem of security is getting more complicated by the day as health care institutions increasingly perceive computers as an economical means of storing and manipulating health-related data (in much the same way that big business now uses computers for its data). We may expect increasing problems unless adequate measures are taken to ensure the security of health care data that is kept on computers.

What can be done to guard against security problems?

THREATS

First, we must recognize the potential threats to the security of computer-based data so we can protect ourselves against them. In *Data Security and Data Processing*, the following are the threats that IBM distinguishes:

1. Errors and omissions. Human fallibility has not greatly improved since Alexander Pope said that "to err is human." The most frequent cause of data disasters is human blundering (e.g., the programmer who accidentally erases a whole data file, or the data-entry clerk who puts the wrong identification on a record so it can never be retrieved again). Similarly, there may be an unintentional failure to perform a human role (e.g., someone may fail to record a necessary piece of data or may record erroneous data in a health-related database).
2. Dishonesty. Some sinister human actions involve purposeful, criminal intervention by unauthorized individuals in computer-based records systems. Much publicity has surrounded celebrated computer frauds in the business community, in which huge sums of money have sometimes been embezzled. In health care, computer fraud might also take place, especially where health insurance information is concerned, or when someone does fraudulent research. However, the more probable criminal threat to the security of computer-based medical records concerns the unlawful disclosure of confidential health care data to unauthorized third parties. Health care–computer installations must protect themselves against such third parties, because of insurance company representatives who would like to get their hands on their customers' health care data.
3. Vandalism. In Ontario, Canada, a minor scandal erupted in 1978 when a newspaper broke a story that programmers in the provincial Ministry of Health were amusing themselves by collating lists of persons who had been treated for venereal disease. The story was later shown to be largely, if not completely, a fabrication. The point is that it was possible, and proper preventive mechanisms were only put in place after the event. Potentially more destructive is the disgruntled employee who seeks vengeance on the boss by deliberately trying to destroy irreplaceable data. This possibility is not simply theoretical. It has sometimes happened in industry, with devastating consequences. Also, a re-

mote, but real, possibility is the random vandalism of computer installations and their data by outside persons, even by terrorists.
4. Natural disasters. A number of natural disasters could destroy computers and their health care data, with potential interruption of patient care, research protocols, or hospital business functions. Fire in or near the computer room or the data library is always a tremendous danger. Fire can originate in the storage area where paper supplies are kept. Electrical fires caused by malfunctioning components in computer hardware can also occur. The presence of smoke can damage both computer hardware and the magnetic storage media on which data is stored. Even people smoking can pose a serious threat to the integrity of magnetically stored data—not only because smoking is a fire hazard, but also because particulate smoke material gets into hardware and storage media, and can interfere with the correct reading and writing of data. Water damage caused by firefighting efforts, leaking roofs, and faulty plumbing can also destroy computer hardware and stored data.

The Magnitude of the Threats

Unlike conventional paper records, the records stored on a computer system are miniaturized and centralized in one place. One disk pack may contain the equivalent of a couple of rooms full of ordinary paper medical records. Although obviously beneficial from an operational point of view, this extreme condensation of health care–related data poses potentially very serious security problems.

The blundering programmer who accidentally types the wrong command on a terminal can destroy an entire data file with a single flick of the finger—a feat obviously impossible in conventional records systems. The crook who steals a magnetic tape containing health care data may get the equivalent of a dump truck full of ordinary charts. Fire, smoke, or water damage, even if confined to a small area, can wipe out a computer system and all of the data it contains.

The ability of computer systems to be programmed for easy retrieval and correlation of huge amounts of data is among the principal motivations for using them. With appropriate programming, we can discern relationships among data that were not previously apparent because of the prohibitive amount of work required to correlate and cross-index old-fashioned paper charts. Paradoxically, this very strength of computer systems is also one of their largest security liabilities. The elegant software tools designed to assist legitimate users in retrieving data and in appreciating the relationships among data can greatly facilitate the ease with which unauthorized persons can make illegal use of that data. Communications links designed to permit the rapid, authorized transfer of information between different systems can serve as a huge breach in the security of any computer facility. Unauthorized users who can circumvent a system's built-in security measures can rummage through data deliberately kept separate and can look for interesting interrelationships. They can make copies of the data they want without having to steal anything physical. More frighteningly, they can perpetrate these crimes over long distances, using nothing more complex than telephone lines—possibly to interconnect two systems to extract "interesting" data relationships!

Health care records contain some particularly sensitive data about individuals. Should such data fall into unauthorized hands, it can be put to uses that have nothing to do with health care and may be damaging to individual patients. In Canada there are documented instances of the questionable use of provincial health insurance records by the federal police. Thus it has appeared that government itself may pose one of the security threats to health care–related data.

Protective Measures

Considering the spectrum of security threats to health care–computing systems and the data they contain, what protective measures should be instituted to prevent the disasters we have discussed? Industry has responded to security needs in business data processing with a variety of countermeasures designed to prevent or limit the extent of security breaches of data processing systems.

Backup. A variety of backup procedures should be instituted against the realistic possibility that data may be inadvertently or deliberately destroyed, damaged, or modified because of any of the human or natural causes just outlined.

Duplicate copies of all important data must be kept. It usually is sufficient to perform such a system backup at the end of every working day, so that in the event of disaster one day's work, at most, will be lost. Sometimes data is duplicated immediately on a second disk drive so a "hot" backup is always available. A data processing installation can even improve on this by keeping a computer-maintained transaction log that records every interaction between users and the system. Using yesterday's backup file and today's transaction log, one can totally restore a destroyed database right up to the point when the destruction occurred.

Obviously, it is useless to store backup files (tapes or disks) in or even near the computer room. Although this procedure might save one from the consequences of a programmer's mistake, it cannot help one if a disaster destroys the backup files along with the computer system. Backup materials should be housed in another building, preferably in a fireproof vault.

If a computer system is essential to the normal operation of some aspect of health care service (e.g., a laboratory reporting system), there must be adequate backup for the entire system in the event that the computer is destroyed or (more probably) put out of service by a minor electrical fire or malfunction. In many cases, the cheapest adequate solution is to have a predefined manual backup procedure to which one can resort if necessary. In other cases it may be mandatory to arrange for the processing of one's data on someone else's computer system in the event of disaster. This kind of arrangement should be negotiated before a disaster strikes. Special data processing facilities are being established in highly secure buildings to face the need for backup machines after a disaster.

Even relatively minor problems can terminate data processing operations, and adequate backup procedures should take these possibilities into account. A fire confined to a storage area can still destroy all program documentation or the supply of a particular preprinted form, such as checks or medical records forms. There must be an emergency copy of all documentation and a supply of such forms in a secure location, or one should have a good working relationship with a printer who is responsive to a customer's needs in an emergency.

Physical security. The time has gone when computer installations could be displayed as showpieces behind glass. The computer room should be physically secure against intrusion at all times. In practical terms this means a lock on the door, no display window in the computer room, a security patrol, and strict limitation of access to the computer facility to authorized staff members.

In large, expensive, and critical industrial data processing centers, physical security measures are elaborate and may include passcard entry to the computer room, a combination lock on the door of the computer center, or keys. Often terminals are located remotely from the main computer, and not even programmers are allowed into the computer room—only the operators are permitted there. All repair personnel are accompanied.

In most health care–computing situations the installation will be much more modest. Therefore, more simple security measures will have to suffice.

Fire protection. A sprinkler system is worse than useless (water can damage a computer). Fire-extinguishing gas, nontoxic to humans, is a standard fire-protection measure in computer rooms. Any water system should not go directly to the sprinkler heads, but rather be controlled by a valve outside of the computer room.

Fire prevention is equally important. Computer rooms should be kept clean, and mounds of scrap paper must not be allowed to accumulate. Books, manuals, and paper supplies should be stored elsewhere, because a fire may start either among such supplies or be fueled by them. Considering the destruction that smoke can cause, it would be desirable to keep all paper supplies far away from the computer room instead of next door. Perhaps the fire inspector for the institution can help one institute a good program of fire prevention. Smoking must be prohibited in the computer room and in data libraries housing magnetic media. Naturally, all the electrical safety rules must be respected in an effort to prevent electrical fires caused by overloaded power lines and other causes. The assistance of a qualified electrician will be required for every system, except for a microcomputer, which uses standard wall current.

Computer defenses. Computer systems can be programmed to defend themselves against security breaches.

First, software can be designed to identify would-be users signing on to the system. Usually an account number is used for this purpose. Such items as passcards or keys on the terminals have also been used, thus combining some aspects of physical and systems security.

Second, the system might try to verify that users are who they claim to be. Verification can sometimes be accomplished through the use of passwords, known only to the authorized user. To make sure that a password remains secret, the user can change it at will. This good idea is often thwarted by lazy users. The most common passwords used on any system are probably the user's first name, the user's last name backwards, or a variation on this. Because most criminal security breaches are caused by inside workers, this lazy practice is a serious security problem. In more elaborate installations, handprint or voiceprint identifying machines are used to verify the identity of computer-system users. In general, these facilities are beyond the means or the needs of the average health care–computer installation. When terminals can access the computer by telephone via a modem, a good procedure is to have the computer require the user to hang up after sign-on and then to have the computer call the number back. This permits access to a single phone for a given password.

Third, once a verified user has been signed on to a system, the system can restrict the user's activities to those functions the user has been duly authorized to perform. A database management system lends itself to this kind of approach. It can be programmed by the database administrator to permit specific users to have access only to those data items they require for their work and not to the rest of the database. The database administrator can further specify whether a given user is permitted to change certain data items, add new data items, or merely view them without modifying them. With more sophisticated systems, the administrator can further state at what hours given individuals are allowed to use the system. Such measures, in addition to the physical security measures just outlined, may effectively prohibit unauthorized access to the database by inside workers after business hours.

Fourth, the computer system can be programmed to keep a detailed record of all transactions between users and the system that notes the identity of the user, the time, and the terminal used for every action, as well as the operation performed and the data transacted. This detailed record is in the transaction log to which we previously referred. It serves not only as a means of backup in the event of systems failure, but also as a security check for the system. If a user should be informed that his or her account was last opened at a time when the user was not using the system, then the security breach can be immediately reported to the appropriate authority, and the user can change the password, preventing further incursions.

Fifth, very sensitive data can be ecrypted (scrambled), both for transmission over data communications lines (to prevent wiretappers from understanding it), and for recording on magnetic storage media (so that thieves could not understand it even if they stole it or copied it). The National Bureau of Standards (NBS) has developed an encryption algorithm, which it recommends for use in sensitive data processing facilities. This algorithm depends on a random numerical key that results in millions of possible encryption mechanisms, thus making manual deciphering impossible. However, it has been pointed out by some critics that a very large computer system could be used to crack the NBS encryption procedure by simply trying one key after another until sensible output was produced.

Procedures. In addition to all of the previously mentioned measures, a health care–computing installation can institute operational procedures to limit security risks. There should be a ritual at the end of every day in which a designated person responsible for backup must produce backup files and must take them away to another location for safekeeping. Someone must be delegated responsibility for keeping scrap paper out of the computer room. This person must throw away or destroy unclaimed printed output after a well-known and publicized interval of time. Otherwise, unclaimed output will clutter the computer area and pose a fire hazard.

To reduce the possibility of criminal intervention in a sensitive health care database (such as one concerning health insurance information or data on potentially compromising personal details), division of responsibility among programmers may help to ensure that no single individual acting alone could seriously compromise the database. If no single person knows everything about how a system works, it is unlikely that anyone will be able to interfere significantly with its security programming without the collusion of at least one other inside worker. This has been appreciated in industrial data processing for a long time. Even in a minicomputer-based database management system, one person should be made the database administrator, with the clear understanding that no one else will be allowed to alter the security parameters for the various data items.

Finally, it may be helpful to establish a policy regarding after-hours work in sensitive health care–data processing facilities. If it is understood that nobody is permitted to use the system at night, then this policy can be stated to security personnel. In some installations, of course, this policy may be impractical.

Conceptual security. We recommend the creation of a new term, "conceptual security." This type of security involves *not* keeping certain kinds of databases when the benefits to the patient or to society do not truly balance the risk of the violation of privacy. It is simply too easy and inexpensive today to buy a computer system, set up a data collection process, and capture and store virtually any kind of data. Unless there is net value (e.g., as determined by a human experimentation committee), we advise against permitting establishment of such databases.

THINKING THE UNTHINKABLE

Many computer facilities that house health care data are small, and the smaller the operation, the more likely are its proprietors to assume that a serious breach of security could not occur in their facility.

This is wishful thinking. Even though a computer system is too small or too unimportant to attract sophisticated criminals, serious breaches of security can still occur through simple carelessness. A VDT thoughtlessly located in plain view of unauthorized personnel or the general public can display confidential health care information for all to read. Hard-copy output discarded into wastebaskets can be retrieved and read by anyone, including custodial staff. Because it may be nearly impossible to prevent this kind of accidental disclosure, many health care–computing facilities use codes such as numbers or alphanumeric constructions rather than actual names to identify patients. By such a strategy, at least casual observers would not know whose information they were reading. All of these codes, however, are easily cracked by anyone who has an interest in so doing.

Even more insidious are situations in which health care workers themselves, even with the best intentions, inadvertently breach the trust of patients. A physician in an institution may wish to contact a colleague's patients to solicit their participation in a research protocol. Locating appropriate potential research cases through a centralized computer facility may be a trivial problem. However, you may appreciate the negative feelings of a patient who is suddenly contacted by a physician with whom the patient has never had previous contact. What right had that physician to know anything about this patient? What right had the patient's own physician to divulge confidential information to another physician not involved in the patient's health care?

The ethical way to proceed in such cases would be for the patient's own physician to contact the patient and ask permission to give the patient's name to the would-be researcher. Only if that permission were forthcoming (preferably in writing) should the researcher feel free to contact that patient personally.

Regarding research protocols, several additional points should be kept in mind. A guiding principle should be that only as much data as is needed for research will be collected. Information greed not only wastes computer resources by needlessly filling up secondary storage media, but also is an unnecessary invasion of the patient's privacy. If possible, data collected for research purposes ought to relate to some benefit that accrues to the patient. Many patients who present themselves for treatment in teaching centers are under the mistaken impression that they are required to give certain personal information to receive service. This is a kind of implicit blackmail, and the ethical institution should make it clear to patients the division between data required for their treatment and data required for purely academic purposes.

To arbitrate and regulate such matters, it would be desirable if all health care databases could be registered and reviewed by some organization of peers. Rules and guidelines for using health care data stored on computers ought to be formulated. Who has control over the data? Under what circumstances, if any, may this data be divulged to parties not directly concerned with treating patients? Who gets access to computer-based health care data? Where does data dissemination stop? With physicians? With paramedics? With research assistants? With computer people? With secretaries? With epidemiologists? With government? Does any moral consideration prevent some people who are legitimately involved in some aspects of patient care from accessing computer-based health care data?

None of these questions is easy to answer. They are privacy issues, and unlike the problems of systems security, they are not the exclusive domain of the health care–computing specialist.

Elementary physican security precautions are effective and often inexpensive. A lock on the door and at least a CO_2 fire extinguisher in the computer room are two good investments. Bigger installations that can afford them should consider more expensive gas fire-extinguishing systems to protect their investments.

Simple security procedures should be implemented. Backup of important data should be conducted daily, and backup files should be stored securely, away from the computer room.

The greatest possible use should be made of the computer's built-in software-security mechanisms, whatever they are. At the very least, each user should have a secret password that is changed frequently at random intervals.

Regarding the uses to which data may be put, any information that is traceable to individual persons (whether for health care service or for medical research purposes) should be totally inaccessible to agencies or persons not specifically involved with the care of those patients or with the research protocols for which the data was collected and to which those patients have previously agreed. Exceptions should be made only with the explicit, informed, written consent of the patients involved.

When data is to be aggregated for statistical purposes, all personal information identifying patients should be purged from the data before it is handed over to outsiders. It is unacceptable to rely on promises extracted from outsiders that they will not use or publish personal information. The originators of health care data are responsible for it, both legally and morally. Security is their responsibility, and that means keeping the personal health care data entrusted to them strictly to themselves.

It is obviously easier to make suggestions than to implement workable solutions. The idea of proposing rigid standards that will be universally acceptable to all computer-based health care databases in all kinds and sizes of installations is ludicrous on technical grounds alone. Computers are not "universal" machines. They are devices tailored to specific purposes for specific institutions by specific people. Certainly, the precise methods of data security employed must differ from place to place according to individual circumstances while still remaining ethical. There is no physical way to make a minicomputer system as secure as a big computer system costing millions of dollars. However, despite the difficulties, security standards must be formulated and enforced in every health care–computing facility. Perhaps the most important positive intervention of all is raising everyone's awareness of security problems and creating an attitude to make security everyone's problem and responsibility.

Those who use computers in the health care environment dare not assume that serious and even potentially destructive breaks in security and the consequent violation of the privacy of patients cannot happen in their installations. Such problems have already happened repeatedly in business, and they will increasingly happen in health care unless measures are taken at a practical, local level to ensure the security of data entrusted to the growing number of computers used in and around health care.

CHAPTER 15
ECONOMICS OF HEALTH CARE COMPUTING

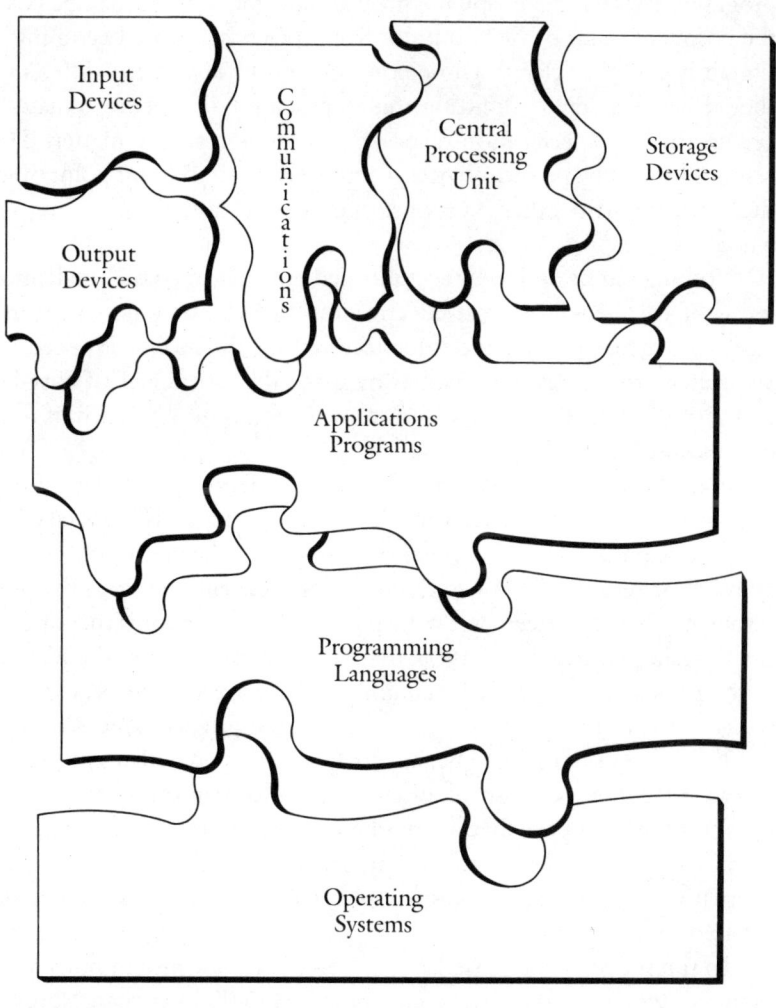

CHAPTER 15

Because economics is a highly technical discipline, a comprehensive survey of it is beyond the scope of this book. Fortunately, most health care–computing projects would benefit even from a simple economic analysis. Such an analysis is possible and we will begin by defining some useful terms.

Cost justification is the process by which one elucidates the two sides of the economic equation; on one side is the cost of doing something, and on the other side is the result that is achieved for the investment. A cost justification is something that can be applied to a process, a person, or a piece of equipment. It can be constructed from a variety of different points of view. A computer program to improve health care diagnoses may simply be a cost add-on from the hospital's point of view, but it may also be highly cost justified from the point of view of society. Conversely, a computer program to identify patients for consideration for early discharge to a home care program may save the hospital a great deal of money and may be cost justified from the hospital's point of view, but not from society's. Before beginning a cost justification, it is crucial to clarify whose point of view or how many different points of view should be considered. Omitting this step is a pitfall that traps many naive analysts. Frequently, the specification of point of view is a simple matter. The organization responsible for the project obviously represents an important point of view. However, there may be many others: a sponsoring organization, the employees, or society as a whole.

Nothing can be said to be cost justified unless it surpasses predefined thresholds in terms of cost-benefit or cost-effectiveness analysis, or unless in some other way it passes a test that permits the value received for the money invested to be evaluated. We will approach cost justification by using the techniques of **cost-benefit analysis** and cost-effectiveness analysis, and we will attempt to give each of these terms a precise and useful meaning.

In the term "cost-benefit analysis," "cost" refers to the dollar value of all resources used by the project. Related to health care computing, it is the total expense associated with the acquisition of a computer system or with the use of computer resources, plus all other project-related noncomputer costs. "Benefit" refers to the dollar value of all resources created or freed up by the project. In this case, it is the total economic result that is realized through the use of that same computer system or resource. Benefit has nothing whatever to do with clinical effectiveness or the benefit to patients or to society. It is merely the economic results of the project expressed in dollars.

The concepts of cost and benefit are best explained with a simple example based on 1 year. Suppose it presently requires six clerks to perform some job without any computer support. Suppose they are working at maximum capacity in a situation in which it will soon be necessary to hire additional help. A computer system is considered as an alternative to hiring three more people. The costs of the computer system are summarized in Table 1.

To run the computer-based system for 1 year, one programmer and two clerks are required, for a personnel cost component of $55,000 per year. Note that many other

TABLE 1
Cost and benefit of a theoretical computer system, based on 1 year

Present manual system	
6 clerks @ $15,000 each	= $ 90,000
Proposed computer system	
Cost	
Hardware and software	= $ 40,000
Staff programmer @ $25,000 + 2 clerks @ $15,000 each	= $ 55,000
	$ 95,000 = C
Benefit	
Immediate benefit	
Reduction of 4 clerks @ $15,000 each	= $ 60,000
Billing for accounts receivable, previously written off	= $ 5,000
Future benefit	
Computer eliminates need to hire 3 more clerks @ $15,000 each	= $ 45,000
	$110,000 = B

Benefit/cost = B/C
 = $110,000/$95,000
 = 1.16

Net benefit = B − C
 = $110,000 − $95,000
 = $15,000

potential costs have been assumed to be nil for the sake of simplicity. In addition to reducing the number of clerks required, the computer system enables the two remaining clerks to perform $1\frac{1}{2}$ times as much work as six clerks could do manually.

The financial benefit of the computer system is also shown in Table 1. In this simplified example, there is a reduction of four persons in the clerical staff for an annual salary savings of $60,000. In addition, we must consider that without the computer system three more clerks would have to be hired to cope with the workload that the computer system can now handle. The salary savings of three fulltime clerk equivalents ($45,000) per year is added to the total benefit of the computer system. In this particular example, we will further suppose that introducing a computer system makes it possible to bill for $5000 per year of additional accounts receivable that were previously written off as too costly to collect with the old manual system. The total benefit is $110,000 per year.

Cost-benefit can be expressed either as a benefit/cost ratio or as a net benefit figure. Let

    B = The present value of all current and future benefits accruing from the project.

    C = The present value of all current and future costs of the system.

Thus, the benefit/cost ratio is simply B/C and the net figure is B − C. If the benefit/cost ratio is greater than 1, or equivalently, if the net benefit is greater than 0, the project, person, or technology being evaluated is cost-beneficial. If the ratio is 1, or equivalently, if the net benefit is 0, one is financially neither better nor worse off after introducing the new system. If the ratio is less than 1 (net benefit negative), the system is a financial loser.

Referring again to Table 1, we can compute the benefit/cost ratio of our example system. According to the above formula, it is $110,000/$95,000 = 1.16. The net benefit of the computer system is $110,000 − $95,000 = $15,000.

Several potentially tricky points should be explained. First, if the organization responsible for the project is a private profit-making organization, all costs and benefits should be calculated on an after tax basis. Further details regarding such a case can be found in any good accounting text.

Second, present value is required in the calculations to account for the fact that a dollar of cost (or benefit) now is more valuable than a dollar of cost (or benefit) that will occur at some point in the future. The formula for present value calculations is:

$$P = \frac{F}{(1 + r)^n}$$

where P = the present value, F = the future value, n = the number of years in the future at which the value F will occur, and r = the annual discount rate.

Third, one must define the period of time for which one will evaluate the project, but frequently it is simpler (and equally valid) to use 1 year of the project as the time unit for analysis.

Finally, it should be stressed that the mere observation that something new will break even financially is not sufficient evidence to declare that it is cost justified. There is no point in making the change to something new if its only justification is that it pays for itself. The benefit/cost ratio should in most cases be greater than 1, thus indicating significant actual financial savings through using the new procedure (Figure 15-1).

COST-EFFECTIVENESS

As with cost-benefit, "cost" here refers to the total financial commitment required to establish a new process. The cost is expressed in dollars. "Effectiveness," on the other hand, refers to the salutary health care or societal effects of the new process. A cost-benefit analysis is expressed in quantifiable terms; cost-effectiveness is usually qualitative, subjective, or subject to disagreement. Effectiveness is often difficult to measure at all, and therefore it is inherently prone to a wide margin of error. Effectiveness can be measured (or, more frequently, estimated) by using a variety of parameters, very few of which have scientific validity. In rare cases in which one can demonstrate a cause-and-effect relationship between a process and mortality, one has

FIGURE 15-1
The benefit/cost ratio.

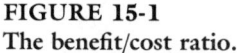

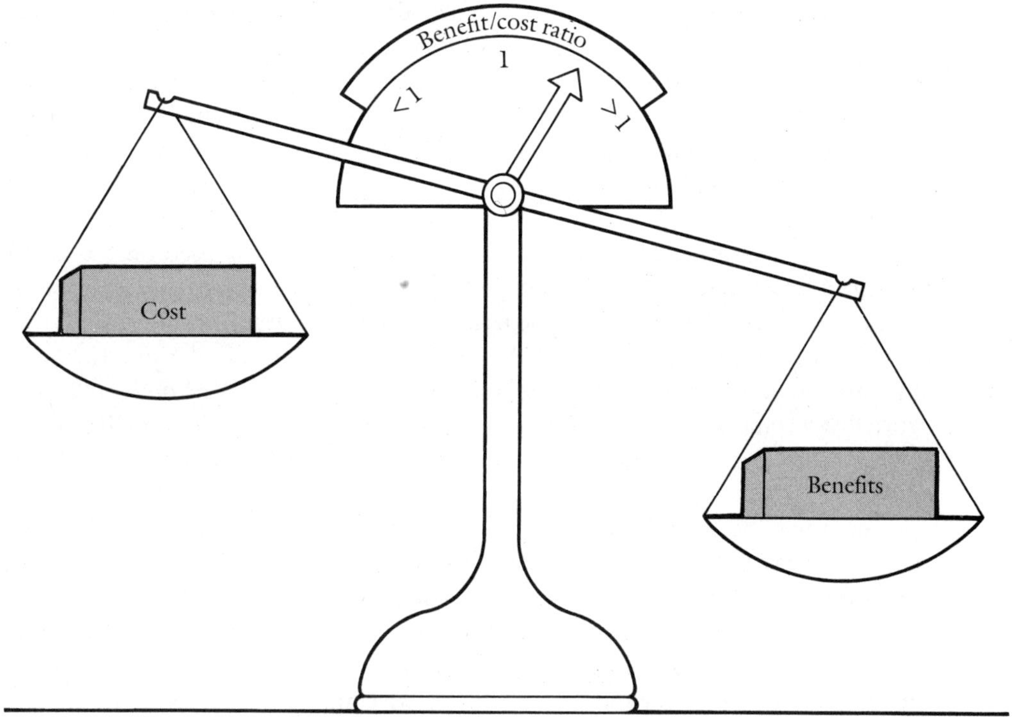

a watertight cost-effectiveness calculation. It could legitimately be stated that lives are saved at a cost of so many dollars per life. When a hard endpoint such as mortality is not available, we must use softer endpoints such as morbidity. When it can be proved that a certain new process reduces a hospital stay or pain or that it increases the quality of life in some measurable way, this too may be a measure of clinical effectiveness. Of course, length of stay in a hospital is a notoriously unreliable measurement of actual morbidity.

Unfortunately, most claims of clinical effectiveness are not even as objective as a measurement of a hospital stay. Most of the time, morbidity is evaluated in intuitive terms. It represents little more than a subjective evaluation of the severity of a disease, sometimes made by the patients themselves, but more often stated by their optimistic health care providers.

The inability to measure morbidity in reproducible ways makes the formulation of an effectiveness/cost ratio for situations with a soft endpoint a treacherous problem. Even when effectiveness can be measured in terms of some parameter, it is usually difficult to prove a connection between the new process and the improved effectiveness claimed for it. Even when cause, effect, and accurate measurement can all be demonstrated (e.g., in a randomized clinical trial), it still remains a problem to decide how much a day of feeling better or another day of a life is worth. When are we morally justified in deciding that it is too expensive to save someone? This is as much a problem for philosophers, theologians, sociologists, and ordinary citizens as it is a question for health care–computing specialists. A cost-effectiveness argument can raise as many moral and economic problems as it solves, especially when the cost is great and the effectiveness (in purely numerical terms) is relatively small. There are no easy answers.

For these reasons, a cost-effectiveness argument is generally used only as an adjunct to a good cost-benefit argument when one attempts to cost justify a health care–computing system. It should be noted that if a cost-benefit argument is strong enough, a computer system can easily be justified on purely financial grounds without any consideration of cost-effectiveness. On the other hand, it may be quite difficult to prove that a computer system will have such an impact on the quality or effectiveness of health care that the consideration of financial benefit will be no object in its evaluation.

One way of accomplishing a cost-effectiveness analysis is to ignore the proof of cause and effect and to use the current outcomes in a process such as the "gold standard." If it can be shown that introducing a computer reduces costs and the effectiveness (e.g., patient status after treatment) remains the same, then the process can be considered cost-effective. This is a risky move, however, without a long-term study. Other work has been done that defines the effectiveness of a test result as being positive if the result is available in time for its potential use in making a decision, and negative (e.g., the money to do the test is wasted) if it is late. If a computerized process, even a costly one, makes the results of some essential urgent test available in time, then it is worth it. Even if a manual process would have cost less, the result would be too late to be of clinical value and the money would have been wasted.

Cost, benefit, and effectiveness are normally expressed in the context of some unit of time. One speaks of the cost of a computer system as being written-off over a period of time in terms of so many dollars per year. Similarly, one speaks of a benefit of some number of dollars per year. A benefit/cost ratio is meaningful only when the time periods for benefit and cost are similar. Likewise, effectiveness/cost ratios can be assessed only when the timeframe for both the numerator and denominator is the same.

COSTS: THINK OF EVERYTHING

It is easy enough to construct a misleading cost-justification argument; all one needs to do is to overlook some of the costs. In practice, such an omission occurs more frequently than one might hope, not so much from malevolent intentions as

TABLE 2
Costs and savings of computer systems

COSTS	
Hardware	Supplies
Software	Environmental costs
Hardware maintenance	Miscellaneous
Software maintenance	Inflation
Staff	

SAVINGS	
Decreasing staff	Collecting more money
Increasing staff efficiency	Decreasing use of more expensive methods
Reducing staff turnover	Discounts for hospitals and educational institutions
Saving supplies	

from simple ignorance of all the costs of a process involving a computer. It is not unusual for the computer-naive to get in over their heads financially when they invoke this expensive technology.

Such problems can be avoided when one knows what the costs will be from the very beginning of a data processing project. Then one can plan an appropriate budget. Table 2 lists the various kinds of expenses that can be associated with a health care–computing system. There are many such expenses. Let us look at these costs, one by one.

Hardware

Some of the costs of a computer system are obvious. Hardware is usually the first cost that comes to mind in pricing a health care–computing system. When equipment is rented or leased, the user agrees to a certain monthly payment, and the computation of the annual cost is simply the monthly figure multiplied by 12. Leasing is always more expensive than outright purchase. The lessee, who does not have enough capital to buy the equipment, effectively borrows the money from the lessor and pays the lessor a profit. Even on a 5½-year lease at the low rate of 2.25% of the list price of the capital equipment per month, the costs are 48% more than the original purchase price of the equipment. An alternative to leasing is to borrow the money from a bank and pay commercial interest rates. Which way to go is an accounting decision.

Computing the annual cost of hardware purchased outright is slightly more tricky than computing the annual cost of rented or leased machines. The capital outlay must be amortized over a given number of years. The interest this money could have earned if it had been invested is added to the annual cost of the hardware to demonstrate how much the purchased hardware costs rather than merely how much one paid for it initially. It should be noted that the annual interest is determined on the depreciated value of a piece of equipment. An accountant's advice is required in specific cases.

When amortizing a purchase price, one can accidentally calculate unrealistically low annual costs if one inadvertently assumes that a computer system will last forever, or if one falsely believes that a user can recoup a large portion of the purchase price of hardware by selling it as a used product. Usually, the life expectancy of computer hardware is about 5 years and rarely more than 7 years (and even less when using microcomputers; consider 3 to 5 years for these). After that, equipment becomes old, out of date, and often unreliable. Maintenance will become prohibitively expensive, because (with the exception of certain popular makes) spare parts will become difficult to find and will be exceedingly costly, even if they are available. For these reasons, a 7-year-old used small computer system is worth almost nothing in resale value. A standard amortization period is 5 years.

Because equipment wears out, one has to budget for the eventual acquisition of new equipment to replace it. A certain percentage of the total capital cost of the equipment should be put aside every year to finance the acquisition of new hardware. This is not an additional item of cost, but it is an important budgeting reminder.

Simple rental of computer systems is rare for anything except for the most expensive systems (e.g., hospital information systems) or for very inexpensive microcomputer systems (e.g., those marketed for use in physicians' offices). The user agrees to rent the computer for a fixed number of months or years, during which time its owner will maintain it. At the end of that time, the computer system will be worn out or no longer useful, and will revert to its owner. Rental payments are sometimes referred to as "silly money" by people in the data processing industry, because rental is usually far more expensive than any other means of acquiring the services of a computer system. The user simply pays out money continuously, never acquiring any equity in the system.

In a lease, however, the user generally is paying something toward eventual ownership of the system. When the lease expires, the user may have the option of either purchasing the equipment outright for a variable sum or extending the lease for a fraction of the original monthly charge. When a computer system has been leased for 5 years, it may have several more years of fairly trouble-free service left in it. Such an approach is therefore attractive under some circumstances.

When one can afford to buy computer equipment outright, the choice between purchase and leasing may be difficult to make. The advice of an accountant is required in considering these two options.

Hardware may be the most obvious cost in a computer system. However, it should be noted that over the lifetime of most projects, hardware accounts for less than one quarter of the total cost.

SOFTWARE

Software falls into two broad categories: systems software (the set of programs required to make machine resources available to the user) and applications software (programs written for particular users). Systems software is sometimes included in the purchase or lease price of hardware (bundled), but usually it is priced separately (unbundled).

When systems software must be acquired separately from hardware, it too may be purchased outright with an initial lump sum payment, or it may also be leased (monthly license payments). The annual cost of such software would be its purchase price amortized over a projected number of years with interest added. Sometimes the purchase price of such systems software is prohibitive to smaller organizations. (Some database management systems for use on big computers cost over $100,000.) In these cases, users may have to lease software, with arrangements analogous to hardware leasing agreements.

Hardware Maintenance

With rented systems, the supplier usually takes responsibility for hardware maintenance. However, in purchased or leased systems, it is the purchaser or the lessee who must arrange and pay for hardware maintenance. There are three ways of handling the maintenance problem: on a contract, on a per-call basis, or with one's own in-house maintenance staff personnel.

The first and most worry-free way is to acquire a maintenance contract from the supplier. Most leases require that one obtain such a contract. For an annual payment, usually between 8% and 10% of the initial hardware purchase list price, the supplier or a representative agrees to keep the hardware functioning properly, all labor and parts included. Usually it is possible to get the supplier to agree to maintain its system for several years, say 5. However, at the expiration of a maintenance contract the whole situation becomes negotiable. If a particular machine has been a money-loser for its supplier, or if a machine is old and hard to maintain, the supplier may then refuse to renew a maintenance agreement when it expires. It is important to check on the company's previous behavior in this regard before committing oneself.

The second way of arranging hardware maintenance is the way most of us maintain most things in our homes: on a per-call basis. In this case there is no maintenance contract. Whenever the computer breaks down, the owner simply calls the supplier, who then charges for labor and travel by the hour (usually with a minimum charge) and for any replacement parts required. When a machine is reliable, this procedure can be the cheapest option. It is, however, rather like gambling. As machines age, they often become very expensive to maintain on a per-call basis. An advantage of a maintenance contract is that most companies give first priority for servicing to installations with such contracts, whereas per-call servicing is relegated to second priority.

The third way of performing hardware maintenance is for the owner to take the do-it-yourself approach. With large and expensive computer systems that are prone to break down frequently because of their complexity, it may be economically sound to hire fulltime preventive maintenance staff personnel and to keep frequently used spare parts on site. Most health care–computer installations are much too small to merit this kind of treatment, but large ones can use this approach profitably.

The precise terms of maintenance agreements vary substantially from supplier to supplier. Parameters such as hours of service, guaranteed response time to calls for service, guaranteed up-time, mean time between failures on the system or on its major components, mean time to repair, and availability and location of spare parts should all be considered before signing a maintenance agreement.

Software Maintenance

The necessity of software maintenance was previously discussed. Updates, correction of errors, and revisions of systems software (e.g., operating systems or programming languages) are not normally supplied gratis except when systems software maintenance is explicitly included in a software leasing agreement (and that may or may not be part of a hardware leasing agreement).

Software maintenance for applications programs is a separate consideration altogether. When a developer creates a health care–computing system and fulfills the terms of the user's functional specification, the resultant system should do what the user specified. In fact, the realities of human nature and communication dictate that what the user wants is only approximately expressed by the functional specification. The user may have failed to tell the developer something important; the developer may have misunderstood the user; or the user may have changed the original plans over time and may have thought of new things for the system to do, not realizing the programming implications of these "little" changes. Because of these possibilities, it is desirable to arrange for applications program maintenance ahead of time. The user may set up a software maintenance agreement with (this does not cover the cost of altering or improving software according to user wishes, only repairing bugs and making improvements of general value to all customers) the original developer or may retain responsibility for software maintenance if access to an in-house programming team is available. The latter approach may not be possible if the original developer retains the copyright to the software. Users who would like to take charge of program maintenance must clarify this point before buying or leasing software.

The annual cost of a systems software maintenance contract in the minicomputer marketplace generally runs to about 10% to 15% of the original purchase price of the software. For applications programs, the cost of software maintenance (additions and improvements) can, over the life of a project, easily amount to four times the cost of software development, much of it absorbed in the salary costs of an in-house programming group. It is thus an enormous expense if the software is developed and maintained at one's own site, and if one has no way of charging others to recover costs.

It is easy to ignore, or bury, the cost of software maintenance. In practice, many health care–computing installations seem to forget to budget for this item. Recognizing the problem and facing the cost are parts of an economic analysis.

Staff

In an in-house data processing situation, salary-related costs can be the single biggest item in the annual budget. Those who doubt the veracity of this claim are invited to peruse the job opportunities section of any newspaper. Data processing is voracious in its appetite for people, and these people command salaries that indicate the demand exceeds the supply. Those who like statistics can read the frequent data processing salary reviews in *Datamation* magazine.

A full in-house data processing team will consist of the manager, analysts, programmers, machine operators, data-entry personnel, and sometimes even hardware technicians. Even an application that does not require in-house programming staff members will still have salary costs that relate to data entry and systems operation. The cost of clerical help for data entry is frequently omitted from the total costs of a small computing application! It is common to read claims that a computer system has reduced departmental staff member requirements, but these claims may conveniently ignore that other staff members had to be added to run the computer system or that new duties fell on staff members previously unaffected, such as physicians or nurses. Such self-congratulatory reports either are dishonest or reflect self-deception. If it takes a programmer, an operator, and a data-entry clerk on half-time to replace two secretaries, where are the savings? It is possible to realize savings, perhaps by reducing staff members, increasing staff members' productivity, changing staff members' roles, or reducing management requirements. It is important to document the real personnel costs and savings when one creates a budget.

Supplies

The input, output, and storage media used by a computer system are expensive supplies, and often they are significant items in the data processing budget. Ordinary input media such as punched cards are not particularly expensive individually, but they do tend to be used in great quantity. On the other hand, specialized input media such as custom-designed, preprinted OMR forms can cost 10¢ to 25¢ each or more. Similarly, output media such as perforated fanfold paper for a line printer are moderately expensive. The cost of such media increases substantially when one requires custom-designed printed documents such as paychecks or specially printed health care reporting forms. Multiple copies are very expensive compared to single-part documents. Each type of printing device requires its own kind of ribbon, which must be replaced regularly to produce legible output. Some of these ribbons are no more expensive than a typewriter ribbon, but the big, special ribbons for some impact line printers are considerably more costly.

Magnetic storage media are another class of supplies that can be very expensive. When one acquires a disk drive, one disk pack is usually included with it. However, it is usually necessary to have at least one extra disk pack for backup purposes, and often an installation will need several interchangeable disk packs for several different applications. At a minimum, a disk pack will cost $500 to $1000; sophisticated disk packs that contain read heads (data modules) can cost up to $2500. Floppy disks cost $5 to $10. Magnetic tapes, used for backup purposes or for archival storage of large amounts of data, cost about $10 to $15 each. A large number of tapes are required by many installations of even moderate size.

The employees of a health care–computing establishment will use a variety of common office supplies—everything from scratch pads to paper clips—and these items must also be included in the budget.

Environmental Costs

Another hidden cost of computer systems that usually goes unstated, if not forgotten, relates to the physical environment in which the computer system must be housed. Most microcomputer systems take up the space of a desktop and the cost of this is usually ignored. But floor space is never free of charge to any organization unless there is no other good use of that space. If a computer room in a hospital could have been rented to a couple of physicians for their offices or used for that much-needed expansion and streamlining of the emergency department, then the floor space is costing the hospital money. Two methods of calculating the cost of floor space are available. One is to determine the actual cost from the accounting records. The figure must take into account the depreciation cost of the building plus interest (calculated on a square-footage basis so it can be applied to the space in question) and charges for such things as heat, light, building maintenance, and housekeeping. The other method is to determine the fair-market rental value for equivalent space in the same neighborhood. Frequently, this second method is by far the easiest.

A number of modifications to the computer room beyond those that would be needed for other uses are often necessary, and their costs must be included. Special air conditioning is needed for everything except microcomputers. Special electrical work is often necessary, sometimes for peculiar voltages and usually for high amperage. Even for microcomputers it is usually necessary to have an isolation transformer or a surge protector. A good grounding system is a necessity. Electrical conduits or raised floors under which electrical cables can run are also frequent modifications that must be made for a computer room. Fire alarms, gas fire-extinguishing systems, locks, and other kinds of physical security systems are expensive but necessary.

Finally, the potentially numerous communications links between a central computer and peripheral terminals will have to be installed and paid for. If telephone lines are used for communication, one will be charged for the installation and the monthly use of the phone.

Miscellaneous

Lawyer's fees, printing costs for documentation, shipping bills, insurance, and many other operating expenses should come out of a miscellaneous account.

One additional factor that plagues any budget should not be forgotten: inflation. The budget that one plans today is based on this year's dollar value. By the time one obtains the money budgeted for and has spent it, one may be surprised to discover that the purchasing power of one's dollar has fallen considerably. Although this is a serious menace to good budgeting, it is less of a problem to cost justification because costs and savings tend to inflate together.

SAVINGS

Although optimism can lead one to ignore important costs inherent in a computing system, pessimism can also cause one to neglect ways in which significant monetary savings can be achieved. The spectrum of potential savings that can be realized in a health care–computing situation are considered here.

REDUCING PERSONNEL COSTS

Often cited as the source of savings in a computer system, staff reduction is a goal that is not always reached. The problem of claiming a clerical staff reduction while ignoring a data processing staff increase has already been noted.

Most of the search for benefits should rest on productivity enhancement. But personnel savings can sometimes be accomplished by the outright elimination of jobs. The wisdom or morality of replacing people with machines will perhaps never be determined to anyone's satisfaction, but we can sometimes use computers in this way. An inherent problem with using computers to replace people is that all labor slack may be removed from the overall process. When there are no computers, existing staff can usually get by if one person is ill or on vacation. However, when a computer has reduced staffing requirements to the bare minimum, unexpected personnel shortages may have to be covered by paying people to work overtime (provided they are willing to do so), or by hiring temporary personnel. The latter procedure can be difficult because of the need for special training in using the system.

The effect of computer systems in most health care–computing applications is so local that on the average it is difficult to prove any net saving in staff. Indeed, it is generally observed that additional people must be hired to run the computer. At the same time, existing staff members are still occupied doing the same old jobs, even though the computer may enable them to do more of the same sort of thing. The reason for this situation is that most health care–computing schemes are designed to be innovative rather than merely to automate existing processes. As such, they are add-ons to the services rendered by the institution, and therefore are new items in the institutional budget. This situation is merely a reflection of the way we choose to employ computers in health care; it does not imply that computers are useless or unreasonably expensive; often they are the cheapest possible means of implementing a novel idea.

Increasing Productivity

A computer system that is able to increase the productivity or efficiency of existing staff may permit an increasing volume of work to be accomplished without hiring more people. This potential benefit does not have an immediate effect; it is a future salary savings that is realized only after a period of time. As such, it is one of the greatest potential cost-saving features of any computing system. Note, however, that to compare future cost savings with present costs, the future cost savings must be converted to their equivalent present value by using the formula presented earlier.

Reducing Staff Turnover

Educating a new clerical person to work in the health care environment is expensive. For the first few weeks or months in a moderately specialized job, a new person will have low productivity. When a critical and somewhat complex office procedure (such as issuing reports) depends on one person, the entire health care operation can be thrown into confusion when that person quits. Therefore, anything that reduces the turnover of staff saves money, because it will reduce the necessity for employing temporary personnel or for hiring existing personnel to work overtime.

When computer systems can relieve clerical personnel of boring, tedious tasks and can free them for decision-making roles more suited to their human abilities, the systems will also increase the employees' inclination to stay in their jobs. For example, a secretary who has to type the same kind of invoice 20 or 30 times a day is likely to be frustrated. However, if a computer (even a word-processing terminal) does all the repetitious work and the secretary has to provide only a few details for each invoice, the secretary can then get the job done more quickly, more accurately, and with less frustration.

Saving Supplies

Although computer storage media, printed forms, and other expendables must be included in the cost of a computer system, these costs may be partially offset by savings in the file folders, filing cabinets, and paper used in the manual system the computer is replacing. There may be significant savings to be realized regarding larger projects in printed forms. The computer can reduce the need for expensive forms and the staff members required to handle them. Certain kinds of output devices are also able to decrease the cost of physiological recording media such as ECG paper.

Collecting More Money

It costs money to create an invoice. Someone must think of the item to be invoiced and issue the appropriate instructions. Secretaries have to type up the invoice, enter it onto the books, and mail the invoice to the client or company that has incurred the debt. Someone will have to address the envelope, put the invoice in the envelope, meter and mail the letter—or maybe deliver it if its circulation is internal. There must be some means of checking whether or not the debtor has paid the invoice, and there must be a mechanism for "reminding" delinquent accounts when payment is overdue.

In health care, a physician or an institution has a legitimate right to expect remuneration for services rendered. However, some of the minor services performed for patients are worth so little money individually that it would be prohibitively costly to issue invoices to patients for them. Sometimes people even forget to bill their services.

Many companies market microcomputer systems for the physician's office, and larger companies have systems for hospital accounting that handle all aspects of accounts receivable. Now it is profitable to bill $1 or $2 and to collect on delinquent accounts. In an environment in which physicians and hospitals are paid by patients or their insurance companies on a fee-for-service basis, computer systems will demonstrate the ability to save money in the overall operation of the business and to improve the collection of accounts.

Decreasing Reliance on More Expensive Methods

If computer-assisted diagnosis and patient management facilities are perfected, it might be possible for a physician to diagnose and to treat patients on the basis of fewer tests than are generally used at present. The ideal computer support would permit a physician to use only those tests that have the greatest potential for yielding an important result.

The potential also exists for appropriate computer systems to save money by eliminating a reliance on marginally useful tests and procedures and to extract the maximum from tests done to reduce requesting unnecessary tests.

Discounts and Tax Savings

Educational institutions and some health care facilities (though normally not private physicians' offices) are eligible for a variety of discounts of the commercial costs of computer systems. It is a common practice for computer hardware manufacturers to grant discounts of from 10% to 20% to educational institutions that buy their products. A medical school might benefit from this savings. In Canada, educational institutions and hospitals are normally exempt from federal sales taxes and duties on computer hardware. One should not neglect to consider these possible savings if one is in a position to qualify for them.

ADDING IT UP

In the United States an organization that purchases computer equipment will receive a 10% tax deduction in the first year, called an investment tax credit. This is a financial benefit. Optimism colors even conservative estimates of savings. The further one must reach into the future to find potential savings the less likely one is to realize that savings. Any claims of yet-to-be-realized cost reductions in a proposed computing system should be regarded with suspicion. It is easier to talk about saving money than it is to put it into the bank.

However, pessimism may make us blind to the importance of significant changes that may be required in an old process to fully benefit from savings that could be realized through a total commitment to automation. One may be naturally reluctant to relinquish all features of an old manual process to a computer system because the change seems to be very big and difficult. Such an attitude can rob an organization of potential monetary savings.

Unsubstantiated claims for cost-benefit and cost-effectiveness justification are quite prevalent in noncommercial data processing circles. Regarding cost-effectiveness, finding examples of computer systems' increasing any measurable parameter of the quality of health care is almost impossible. The utmost skepticism is indicated in evaluating such claims.

At this point in the evolution of health care computing, the most convincing argument for cost justification remains a provable benefit/cost ratio that is substantially greater than 1. When economic benefits only equal costs, there may be little justification for the inconvenience of changing one's way of doing business unless a demonstrable and affordable improvement in effectiveness will also be experienced. When the monetary benefit of a computer system cannot be projected to meet its own cost, cost justification rests on an estimate of enhanced effectiveness relative to the unrecovered costs. Not only is the proof of enhanced clinical effectiveness through automation exceptional, but also the assessment of how much money any given amount of effectiveness is worth remains a matter of public policy or personal judgment.

When a very large and expensive health care–computing project is contemplated (e.g., in multiinstitutional, regional, or even statewide applications), a pilot project on a smaller scale is usually undertaken to assess the workability, costs, savings, and clinical value of the scheme. On the basis of such a model system, health care workers and the people who control the purse strings can decide whether it is appropriate to proceed with full-scale implementation. In such potentially expensive projects, the advice of professional economists would be very useful, both for designing certain aspects of the pilot project and for analyzing its results.

The economics of computing are as much a part of the health care computing scene as any of the other technical issues we have discussed. Accurate forecasting of total cost and appreciation of the many ways in which computing systems can save money for their users will help health care workers to plan for the systems they will use, and will go a long way toward guaranteeing the long-term survivability and success of their projects.

CHAPTER 16
FUNCTIONAL SPECIFICATIONS AND CONTRACTS

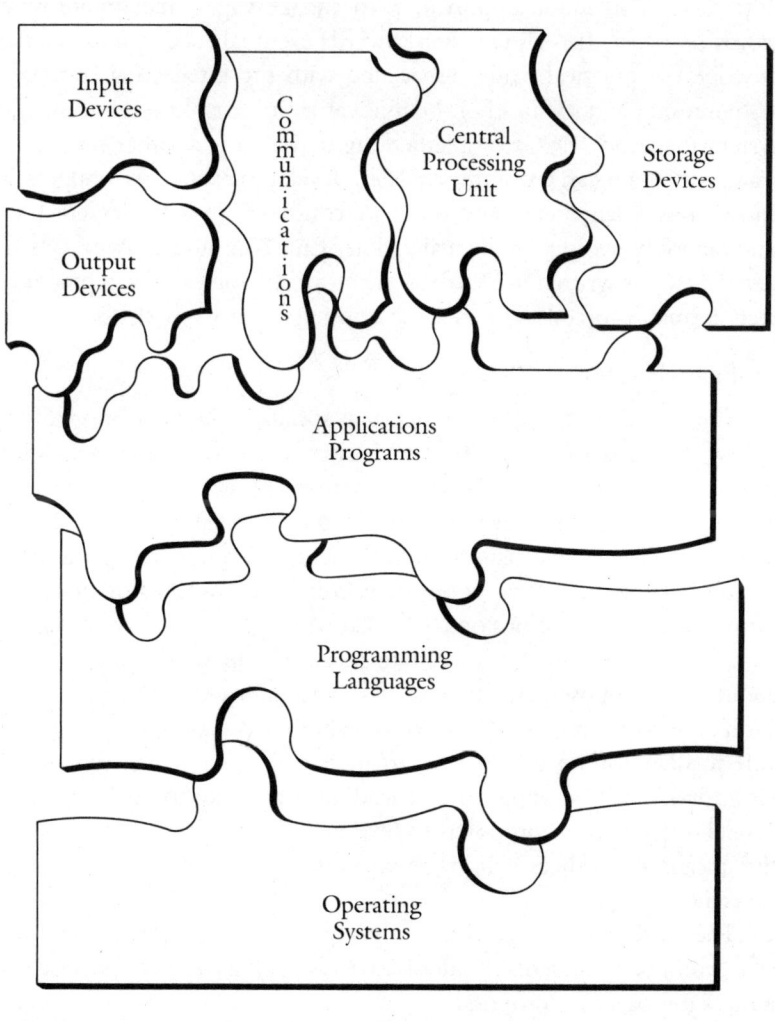

CHAPTER 16

A functional specification is a formal description of the way in which a completed computer system is expected to perform from the point of view of its users. This chapter will discuss in detail what this specification should contain, including the functions that a computer system is to perform, the kinds of input it must accept, the sorts of output required, and other special requirements placed on the selected system.

WHY A FUNCTIONAL SPECIFICATION?
REALITY VERSUS DREAMS

The first purpose of the functional specification is to organize and spell out the requirements of the people who think they need a computer. Writing a functional specification gives the person or organization contemplating the acquisition of a computer system an initial opportunity to change vague and grandiose dreams to real words on paper. It is a giant step towards eventual success if one makes the effort to describe the practical reality associated with the intellectual concept of the perfect system residing in the head of the innovator. It is easy enough to imagine a computer system that reads ECGs; implementing a system is another matter. Selecting hardware, performing an economic analysis, developing software, budgets, and timetables, and writing maintenance and purchase contracts are inconvenient but real problems that cannot be avoided in the realization of any computer system. When the functional specification is written, it is a focal point for the logical development of ideas in concrete terms. It forces us to consider contingencies we wish we could overlook.

PEER REVIEW

The second purpose of a functional specification is to be an instrument of peer review. It forms a part of a proposal when a would-be user is seeking approval and funding for a possible health care–computing project. (The outline of the contents of a complete proposal is detailed in Chapter 21.) The written specification can be studied and challenged. Unscrupulous users who want a computer for status, for fun, or for some scheme they know their colleagues would not sanction should avoid putting their specifications on paper. Conversely, ethical proponents of a health care–computing project will not hesitate to answer in writing the numerous questions about their proposed systems that less scrupulous people might find embarrassing. Would-be computer users who know what they want and why they want it will be able to demonstrate competence to their colleagues in the functional specification. Good work will be apparent; misleading activities should be exposed. One of the results is that what is proposed to be done is communicated to other potential users; this means that others will know what is going on and can contribute toward the objective.

Therefore, those reviewing budget proposals and grant applications for health care–computing systems should always insist on a detailed functional specification as an integral part of a proposal.

GUIDANCE TO DEVELOPERS

The third reason for writing a functional specification is that it is essential when one proceeds to request quotations for hardware and software from systems developers or suppliers.

People sometimes hear that computers are extremely versatile, and they therefore assume that these machines can do almost anything. But this very versatility is a problem, and it makes the functional specification a necessity in realizing any computer system, health care or otherwise.

So many different kinds of computer hardware and such a diversity of systems software and applications packages are commercially available that it is not easy to select the optimum system. Some hardware and some software may be nearly interchangeable, but this is the exception and not the rule. The functional specification forces the user or the user's agent to determine what is needed. It is always a good idea to go shopping with a shopping list.

When several competing commercial computer systems (turnkey systems) purport to serve the same kind of application (e.g., radiology-reporting systems, coronary care unit–monitoring systems, and computer systems for the physician's office), a potential user will have to make a choice. To make a rational choice, one must know exactly what is needed before one can compare these needs to the features, strengths, and weaknesses of the existing range of products.

When no commercial system is available to serve an application, development of a new system may be undertaken. In most cases, the user will not be competent to present the developer with a list of specific hardware and software needs. Determining the appropriate items is the developer's job. However, with an approved functional specification in hand, those who require a computer system can approach a company or a systems developer with some intelligence. They will be able to tell the developer what they want their computer system to do (Figure 16-1). It is neither fair nor reasonable to present a developer with a vague request to be transported into the modern age through the magic of computerization. Many computer companies love such ignorant users; they can sell them almost anything. However, the ethical health care–computer systems developer will be unwilling to do anything until the customers know why they want their new system and express these reasons in a written functional specification.

Selecting companies to approach for quotations is not a random process. By the time one has completed the whole proposal for a computer system (of which the functional specification is only one part), one should have a good idea of which companies are in the running.

In presenting the functional specification to a systems developer as part of a request for a proposal, a quotation, or a tender, remember that someone is being asked to do a lot of work. It will require a big effort on the vendor's part to read the document, understand it, and assess the company's ability to fill the needs. If money is available and is earmarked to be spent on a computer system, then the request deserves

176 *Concepts and issues in health care computing*

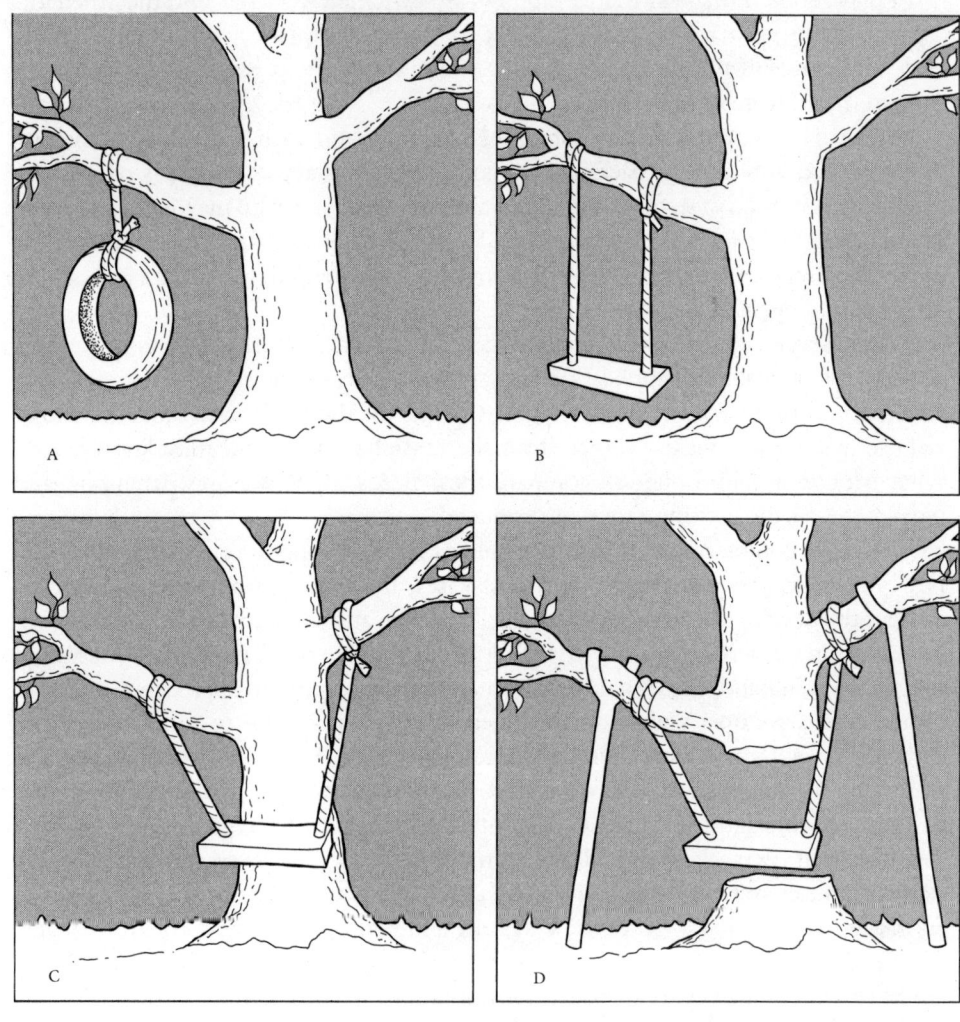

FIGURE 16-1
Why a functional specification? A, What the user really needed. B, What the user *said* was needed. C, What the developer *thought* the user said. D, What the user finally *got* when the misunderstanding was cleared up.

a considered response. On the other hand, many health care institutions and departments have acquired bad reputations in data processing circles for requesting proposals for grand computing schemes that always seem to fall through at the last moment. Not only is it deceptive and inconsiderate to put one or more developers to work assessing a proposal if there is no intent to follow through with a purchase from one of them, but it is also self-defeating. Once a department or institution has acquired a reputation among computer vendors for "crying wolf," it will have to overcome a formidable psychological barrier before any of its future requests will be taken seriously.

CONTRACTS

When an outside systems developer is to be hired to furnish a health care–computing system, the fourth reason for formulating a functional specification is a legal one. Through a process of negotiation with the developer, the user's original "ideal" functional specification will be modified to conform with the very best deal available. Then it can be incorporated into a contract between the user and the systems developer. The obligations of each party and the costs that have been mutually agreed on are specified in this document and signed as a binding agreement. This contract helps users to be sure they get what they pay for. Anybody can buy a collection of components. The onus should be on the vendor to make the hardware and software do what they are supposed to do. The functional specification serves as the standard against which the developed system can be compared. The precise legal requirements of a formal contract will vary. Legal counsel is always required.

A contract in itself can guarantee very little. If it becomes necessary to resort to the letter of a contract to enforce a system developer's duties to a client, it is already too late. Progress can be made only in the spirit of mutual cooperation and understanding. But the ability to write a contract at all indicates that both parties understand each other and agree to the same ground rules.

When an in-house systems development group is charged with creating a health care–computing system, it may be wise to formulate what amounts to a pseudo-contract with them, to direct and enforce their agreed-on performance.

THE FORMAT

The format of a functional specification can vary a great deal, but it should incorporate several key sections if it is to serve its four purposes. The format suggested here is couched in general terms so it can be used as a suitable model in a request for proposals or quotations, or in a final contract. (Of course, details of equipment, software, and terms of acquisition would have been negotiated and specified before they could be used in a contract.)

THE INTRODUCTION

The introduction will state in a nutshell what one wants a computer system to do. One writes about what one knows: the environment, needs, problems at present, and what one wants to achieve. This section will express the problem domain from the user's viewpoint (e.g., one should say at the start whether one is talking about a system for physiological measurement, a system for an admitting database, or whatever). This brief introduction will start the reader thinking along appropriate lines to piece together the details of subsequent sections into the desired overall picture. The writer should present an abstract or summary of the rest of the document in this introduction or in a separate section.

The External Specification

The external specification describes the obvious external features of the required system, without stipulating how the functions are to be performed.

In viewing the computer system as a magical "black box," how does the user want it to perform? First, specify the application(s) it is to serve. Second, describe the data to be input and the results to be output for each application. This description will include a generic description of the types of data involved, an estimate of the amounts of input and output to be processed per unit of time (along with any peak periods), and some physical description of the input and output. Will people be available to type the data in directly, or will forms first be used to capture the data? What level of user is involved? For instance, it should be clear to someone reading this section whether one can accept a slow and noisy impact printer for the printed output, or whether one will require a silent, high-speed electrostatic device.

The functional specification is a document for the future, as well as for the present. Difficult though it may be to anticipate future computing needs in any environment, it must be done here. It cannot be assumed that any given computer system is capable of any arbitrary modification, expansion, or, for that matter, contraction. Some kinds of health care–computing systems (especially those that are essentially computer-containing instruments, such as CT scanners) are almost impossible to change.

If one anticipates that in the future one or one's developer will foresee the need for additional internal memory, more secondary storage, more on-line terminals, or more powerful software, one must let the developer know these plans at this stage, because he or she has no way of anticipating them. In the interest of providing the least expensive system that meets the immediate functional specification, the developer's inclination will be to cut all frills in the proposed system and possibly to exclude the ability for future expansion or changes. The option of growing with the system may cost money for expansion potential in the short term, but to sacrifice this option could cost a good deal more money at some time in the future when upgrading to an entirely different or larger system may be mandatory.

Try to give the developer a feel for the general range of capabilities that will be expected from this system. State both the minimum acceptable level of performance and the maximum performance that could possibly be required, such as:

> This system will support no fewer than four and not more than eight interactive terminals simultaneously. It will not need to communicate with any other processors. The storage of 100,000 patient records is required and should be expandable to not more than 200,000. The length of each record. . . .

This kind of information should tell a knowledgeable developer not only what is needed now and what could be needed in the future, but it should also tell what is not expected from the system.

The following material may not usually be necessary except for producing a complete request for proposals (RFP) based on the functional specification.

SOFTWARE TOOLS

The types of systems software one may insist on being present (e.g., to ease future development) should be specified in the software tools section. The generic type of operating system (real-time or time-sharing) should be specified, if one knows what is needed. If not, sufficient detail on how one will use the system should be present so the developer can offer an appropriate suggestion. The types of programming languages one wishes to use (e.g., FORTRAN or BASIC) must also be stated here; one should at least specify whether one wants high-level languages or assembler-like languages. Specialized software utilities such as database management systems, query languages, and report generators should also be described in this section. One should not forget to consider the software security features one expects.

In other words, this part of the functional specification describes in general terms the software utilities one requires the developer to include and use in the final product.

HARDWARE

At this point, a user probably will not know precisely the makes and models of hardware that will ultimately be chosen for the system. A detailed hardware picture is not essential, and too much detail may overly constrain potential suppliers. However, some users may have a good idea about the general characteristics of the hardware that will be required. The more that is known, the more that can be specified. To give really detailed specifications, users will generally need technical help.

The approximate type of computer—whether it is to be dedicated to a single user, shared, devoted to real-time acquisition of biological signals, or used by many users for database activities—should be known at this point. The approximate size of its internal memory may also be discernible and therefore specified. On the basis of the external specification, it should be possible to project the type (e.g., disk or tape) and capacity (in bytes) of secondary storage. The number and characteristics of terminals, other input devices (e.g., card readers or optical mark document readers) and output devices of all kinds can also be stipulated. Performance characteristics can sometimes be specified in terms of ranges of values (e.g., one may specify a line printer, the speed of which falls between 60 and 120 lines per minute). This approach leaves some leeway for manufacturers to present their wares as possible alternatives. If one specifies nonnegotiable characteristics for hardware, one should be sure that such hardware really exists in the marketplace and that it is within one's price range; otherwise, one may bias the application towards a high cost, or specify needs beyond anybody's means to satisfy them.

APPLICATIONS SOFTWARE

It is usually possible to describe in general terms the special applications software one will need. One may want to state that the software must be written in a high-level language and that a structured technique of programming should be used. One may go so far as to describe the appearance of questions and answers on a CRT screen, and one may devise a mockup of some printed output on a typewriter. In so doing one is specifying precisely what one wants programs to do. One should describe the kinds of reports one must generate, the processing one needs done, the files one must keep, and the methods one requires for entering data, correcting data, and unloading old data from the system.

There remains a final point about the software provided with a system. Who owns the copyright? If the systems developer owns it, will that developer's company permit the user to modify the software if the need arises later, or will the company insist on making such changes itself? The cost of such changes must be considered in a final contract.

One should state the requirements for a software maintenance contract and the support one will need.

DOCUMENTATION

Documentation standards are critical if the system is to be modified in the future. One expresses here the kinds of literature one will need. The user will undoubtedly ask for a users' manual that will explain to computer-naive users how to use the system. However, the user should also request the detailed systems documentation that future programmers can use to change and debug the system (if the vendor will permit that). Systems manuals for the operating system, programming languages, and other software utilities should be requested in this section. In addition, it would be a good idea to ask for detailed systems-level documentation about the applications program(s).

THE SCHEDULE

The schedule commitment the user hopes to contract with the developer must be finite; otherwise development or installation might trickle on forever. It must also be formulated with a realistic knowledge of the practical limits of program development (if any) and systems delivery. It does no good to demand the impossible, although there is considerable merit in demanding what experience has proved reasonable.

The projected dates for placing an order and for installing the computer system on the premises must be stated. When software development is to continue in-house, a detailed schedule for various milestones in software development will have to be worked out. When dealing with an outside developer, the user must at least specify the date for the beginning of testing, the period for parallel operation with the old manual system (if any), and the projected date for total switchover to the automated system.

It would be wise to include in the schedule a period of user acceptance testing and a final date for accepting or rejecting the system, along with a specified acceptance test procedure (ATP).

If a company wants one's business badly enough, many points about the schedule will be negotiable. One might negotiate for them to earn a bonus by completing a system early. Conversely, one may be able to stipulate a financial, maintenance, or equipment penalty they will pay as compensation if they fail to meet a deadline at any stage. In these kinds of arrangements it is very important to define landmarks clearly, unambiguously, and irrefutably.

GENERAL TERMS OF ACQUISITION

The functional specification will eventually form a part of a contractual agreement with some systems developer or company. When one first presents the functional specification to various companies for quotations, one will use this document to elicit from them their interest in the contract and their willingness to meet its terms.

Therefore, one should suggest the general kind of arrangement into which one is willing to enter. If one intends to purchase the system outright, one should say so. If, however, one wants to lease or to rent it, one should state that and further specify the length of the lease or rental period one wants.

This is also the place to spell out how maintenance of the system will be conducted. Normally, the user will want to stipulate a hardware maintenance contract and a software maintenance contract. It would be greatly to one's advantage if one could find suppliers who would undertake responsibility for all aspects of the maintenance of the system, regardless of the origins of the many parts of which the system may be composed. One should state here that this is the kind of arrangement one is looking for.

Numerous details about hardware and software maintenance contracts must eventually be negotiated. How long will a contract last? What response time to service requests will be the maximum acceptable? Will the final contract stipulate that spare parts be kept on the user's site? At the company's site? Or not at all?

• • •

Developing a functional specification is a time-consuming project requiring considerable expertise in health care computing. If a health care establishment does not have access to such expertise, it will need to acquire it from a paid consultant. Trying to proceed cheaply now, without benefit of a knowledgeable expert, will usually result in wasting money later.

However, those who will ultimately use a health care–computing system should be wary of seeking help from those who have a particular product to sell. Products should be selected to suit the true functional specification. On the other hand, a functional specification that is deliberately fashioned to match a certain company's available product line is not worthy of the name. It is best to rely on independent consultants or on one's own staff.

The functional specification has important implications for the future of the health care workers and health care institutions that may ultimately acquire a computer system. Therefore it is a high-level management document. It reflects the opinion of those in authority and carries their sanction. All of the participants in the creation of a functional specification are identified in this document so there can be no doubt about the authority it carries. Because the written functional specification is the principal means by which developers of health care–computer systems tailor their computer solutions to the user's problem, the ability to formulate this document intelligently does not merely separate the professionals from the amateurs; it frequently determines whether a health care–computing system is an appropriate tool or a useless add-on that creates more problems than it solves.

We have now examined how to undertake the essential prerequisite to systems development—writing a formal functional specification. When this has been done, a health care–computing project is ready to move from the planning phase into the actual process of systems development. Whether one entrusts systems development to an outside agency or to in-house health care–computing experts, the rigorous demands of the development process necessitate adequate management if the end result of the process is to be successful. We now turn our attention to these management issues.

CHAPTER 17

MANAGING HEALTH CARE–COMPUTING PROJECTS

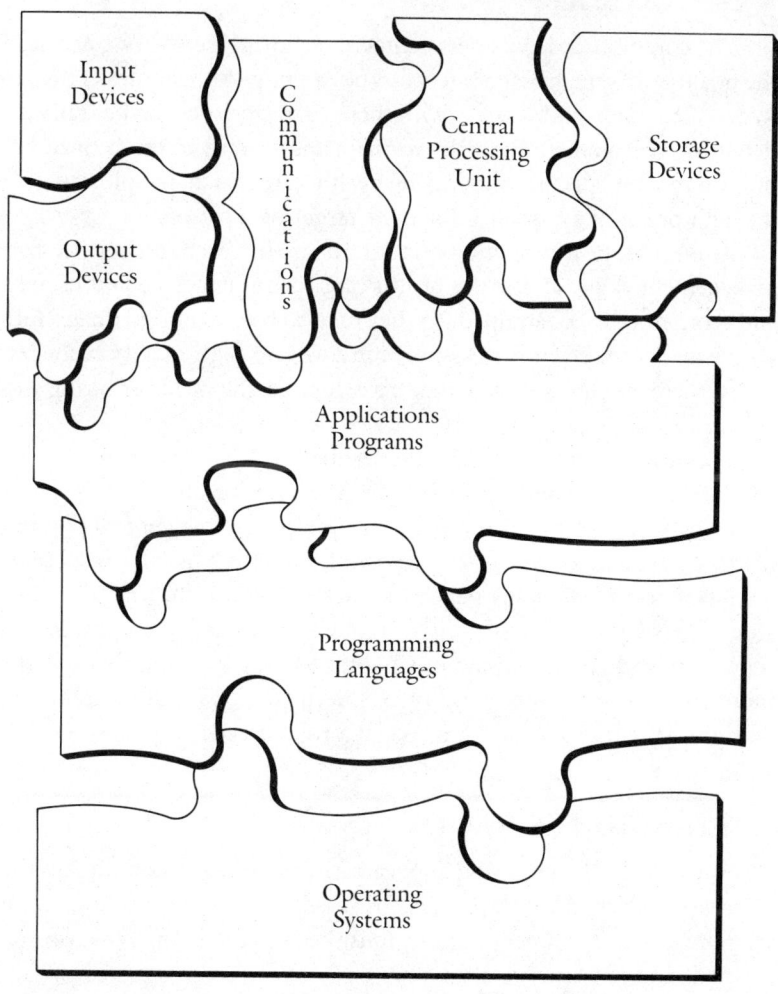

CHAPTER 17

Successful computer applications do not just happen. The successful use of computers in solving health care problems depends ultimately on good management, which might be defined as the coordination of various human and technical elements towards a specific end. Perhaps more than anything else, good management of the systems development process will reflect an understanding of the many issues involved in this line of work. Common sense will take the manager who knows what to expect a long way.

In this chapter we will be reflecting mainly on larger projects. Even if a small project is undertaken on a personal computer, it would be wise to follow at least the basic concepts of this material.

ATTRIBUTES OF THE HEALTH CARE–COMPUTING MANAGER

The commonsense business acumen, technical know-how, and leadership that are the qualities of any manager are to some extent personality traits that are not common to everyone. Men and women with these characteristics can be trained in the skills and details of management, both by formal education in business or health care administration and by specific training in health care. Such people can then be groomed through practical experience for their target occupation.

At present, however, the typical graduate in computer science has no training in management skills, and many health care–computer installations are relatively small and economically constrained, so they tend to hire recent graduates rather than people with experience. Even if the opprtunity to hire high-quality management personnel exists, there is often a basic failure to recognize the need for hiring them. This failure can lead to disaster.

The best way of altering this predestination for failure is to prevent it by taking on a person who is properly trained in managing computer systems development. If this recommended pathway is not possible, however, some general pointers about project management may be of use to a person thrust into a health care–computing management position without any particular background for the job. This approach might be seen as crisis intervention. It is certainly no alternative to prevention (i.e., hiring a trained individual, as we saw in Chapter 8), but it should be of some help. We will therefore look at the successive phases in the life of a health care–computing project, with special emphasis on the manager's role in each of them.

FEASIBILITY STUDY

A health care–computing application falls or flies depending on the care and completeness with which it is planned. A feasibility study should be the first step in this planning process. Three questions must be answered: (1) What do we need? (2) Will it work? and (3) Can we afford it?

These questions are obvious and brutal. The first important step in answering them is to define what needs to be done: there has to be a problem and automation must be potentially capable of solving it. Alternative solutions not requiring automation should be considered very seriously at this stage, because computers often (though not always) call for the greatest initial capital outlay of any method. Big financial risks are taken early in the process of automation; there is no satisfactory means of "testing the water" before getting seriously involved. If computers appear to be a necessary part of the solution, a good study will consider using existing computer systems such as university computer centers, service bureaus, or already installed in-house systems that might be shared through some arrangement with their present owners.

A person managing the feasibility study has the responsibility of considering each alternative and of explaining the implications of each in writing. If all of the alternatives are proved to be impossible or uneconomical, then obtaining a new in-house computer is an option that can be seriously considered.

It must also be determined if the project is feasible. Are there any commercially available systems to choose from? Has anyone else done this before? If the answers are "no," a wise person will look hard at the project and wonder if it is not just too early to move ahead—at least in that direction.

As we have implied, economic considerations play a paramount role in a feasibility study. Precise cost estimates are naturally impossible until detailed specifications have been written and quotations have been obtained from suppliers. Nevertheless, a ballpark estimate will at least determine whether a project can potentially be paid for, either by obtaining funds from internal sources or by persuading an outside agency to foot the bill. Every researcher who depends on grants knows a certain level of support exists beyond which a project is unlikely to be funded by any given agency. The general estimate of costs should include everything—hardware, software, the maintenance of both, supplies, personnel, and other miscellaneous expenses (see Chapter 15). Enough leeway should be left for inflation and the unwarranted optimism that pervades most budgets. Any other approach is self-destructive. Many health care–computing applications that might have worked have failed because of inadequate financing.

THE PROPOSAL

A feasibility study can have one of three outcomes: (1) the decision to scrap or shelve a project, (2) a recommendation to tackle the same problem in some other noncomputing way, or (3) a decision to proceed to a formal proposal for computer support, suitable for peer review and with a clear plan for funding. The contents of a proposal are described in Chapter 21.

During the peer review process, the manager's responsibility is to provide requested information, to answer questions, and to play the role of an advocate for the proposal. Often the primary responsibility for proving the value of the proposed work will fall to some other health care worker (e.g., a clinical department chief who is seeking budget approval for a computer system). The health care–computing manager's role is to assist clients in any way possible. The manager who anticipates objections will be in a good position to answer them. A good way to prepare for public advocacy is to be a devil's advocate in private.

Once a proposal has been approved in principle and adequate funding has been obtained, the health care–computing manager is then in a position to approach actual implementation. Using the part of the proposal called the functional specification, which we mentioned before, the manager can now take one of several approaches. The manager may work with outside developers in a systems house, may buy a package if a suitable one exists, or may elect to use or to establish an in-house health care–computing group to begin the implementation.

THE DEVELOPMENT/ACQUISITION PERIOD

Whatever implementation method is used, the manager will play several different roles simultaneously throughout the development process. What are these different roles?

THE OVERSEER

Until development or acquisition is complete, the manager must ensure that things are done and done on time. The manager's responsibility is to make certain that the development schedule is honored and that identifiable landmarks of progress are achieved on time. In an in-house data processing group, the manager will thereby help to contain costs within the budget. Even in a one-person software development "group," if it takes 6 months to complete a project that was scheduled for only 3 months, the labor cost will be double the estimate. The importance of realistic scheduling and sticking to this schedule cannot be overemphasized. As the adage goes, a project gets to be a year late a day at a time!

When an outside developer has been contracted to create a health care–computing system, the pressure to meet a deadline is still required. The best way to guarantee that development does not drag on longer than anticipated is to specify formally delivery dates for documentation, hardware, and systems testing in a contract, with appropriate penalty clauses for late delivery. Even little slip-ups should not be placidly tolerated by the customer.

THE INTERPRETER

Throughout the development/acquisition, the data processing manager will play an important role in facilitating the communication between systems developers and those who will ultimately use their systems. This role applies whether development is done locally or through an outside systems house.

On the one hand, the manager has an important responsibility to defend the interest of users. The manager will be their watchdog, ensuring that developers do not misunderstand the specifications and that they do not try to change the specifications unilaterally. In this capacity, the data processing manager exercises control over the developer to make sure the developer meets contractual obligations. Such considerations apply even if the developer is an in-house programming team. Economics demands that such a group meet the schedule just as an outside developer would.

On the other hand, the data processing manager will also exercise expectation control over the users. Once a computer-naive user perceives a "dream system" becoming a reality, there seems to be a natural tendency for the user's imagination to run wild. The user may begin to attribute the yet-to-be-delivered system with all kinds of magical properties not suggested in the functional specification. If this kind of wishful thinking is allowed to continue unopposed, the user inevitably will be disappointed when the real system (that does no more than meet the functional specification) is delivered. Users have a reputation for forgetting what was in the specification. The data processing manager must always remind users that they are responsible if the systems developer fails to read their minds. Just like developers, users are bound to the contractual process, and they cannot modify the specification unless they are willing to pay both in dollars and in postponed delivery time.

THE QUALITY CONTROL OFFICER

The manager of an in-house systems development team is personally responsible for ensuring that all of the issues raised in this book are adequately covered. An intimate understanding of software engineering, human engineering, administrative issues, economic analysis, management, and organization is essential for the person in this position, because the project will survive or die depending on how well the manager understands these problems.

The health care–computing director dealing with an outside agency employed to create a health care–computing application will have to look over the shoulders of these developers to ensure they are living up to stated standards of product development.

TURNKEY SYSTEMS

Sometimes the development process can be considerably shortened when one or more prefabricated computer products (or turnkey systems) exist in the marketplace. When the purchase of a turnkey system from a developer is contemplated, the project manager has the responsibility for becoming familiar with each of the competing offers of various companies and for comparing the abilities of each with the client's requirements. It may be necessary at times to leave deliberately a certain amount of slack in specifications to allow for the situation when a preexisting computer product that may be quite satisfactory for its stated purpose may nevertheless not be precisely the system one is looking for. The more exactly a system must be tailored to stated specifications, the more it will cost and the longer it will take to be developed. Consequently, custom-tailored systems cost more than turnkey systems.

On the other hand, it is not very probable that every health care–computing requirement is at present met by an existing commercial computer product. Exceptions to this observation may be computer-containing instruments such as CT scanners, in which the computer is dedicated to performing a fixed role that does not change from user to user. However, for most kinds of health care–computing applications, the individual requirements of different users will vary enough so that at least some modification or configuration (alteration supported in the software itself) of a turnkey system will be required before it will work to any one user's complete satisfaction. Modifying an existing product is often faster and cheaper than designing a new computer system "from the ground up," but it is still a minidevelopment process, subject to all of the requirements of larger systems development efforts.

THE MOST IMPORTANT JOB

Project management is of paramount importance in realizing any successful health care–computing application. It may be fair to say that professional management of systems development is the feature most responsible for separating amateur dabbling from significant health care–computing work that achieves useful results.

One person must be clearly in charge of developing each health care–computing application. Committees of users have their functions, which are to arrive at a consensus and, with the assistance of the data processing manager, to discern needs, to investigate possible solutions, and to review the state of the budget. Intelligent decisions in data processing are not made by committees, however. Those users who do not know what they are doing in the computer marketplace are easy prey for hungry vendors who may not truly understand the requirements of health care computing. The health care–computing manager is the one person who speaks the language of both the users and the systems developers. Such a person is the one health care–computing users must rely on in most cases for getting their requirements satisfactorily met within a reasonable time frame and within a budget they can afford.

One who is in this position in one's own personal projects should not ignore these points either. Low-cost computing has as one effect given more people the opportunity to fail at a lower cost!

The need for competent management is not restricted to the systems development process. Someone will have to assume continuing responsibility for the day-to-day operation of every health care–computing facility, and someone will have to be in charge of the never-ending process of software maintenance and of responding to changing computing needs in the health care environment. Nor is management an issue confined to individual applications or installations. Within institutions such as hospitals many computing projects at many different phases may be carried out for radically different purposes in different departments. The division of management responsibility for health care–related computing on a divisional, departmental, or institutional basis can be problematic, but it must be faced. The next chapter, therefore, looks at these issues.

CHAPTER 18
ORGANIZING FOR AUTOMATION

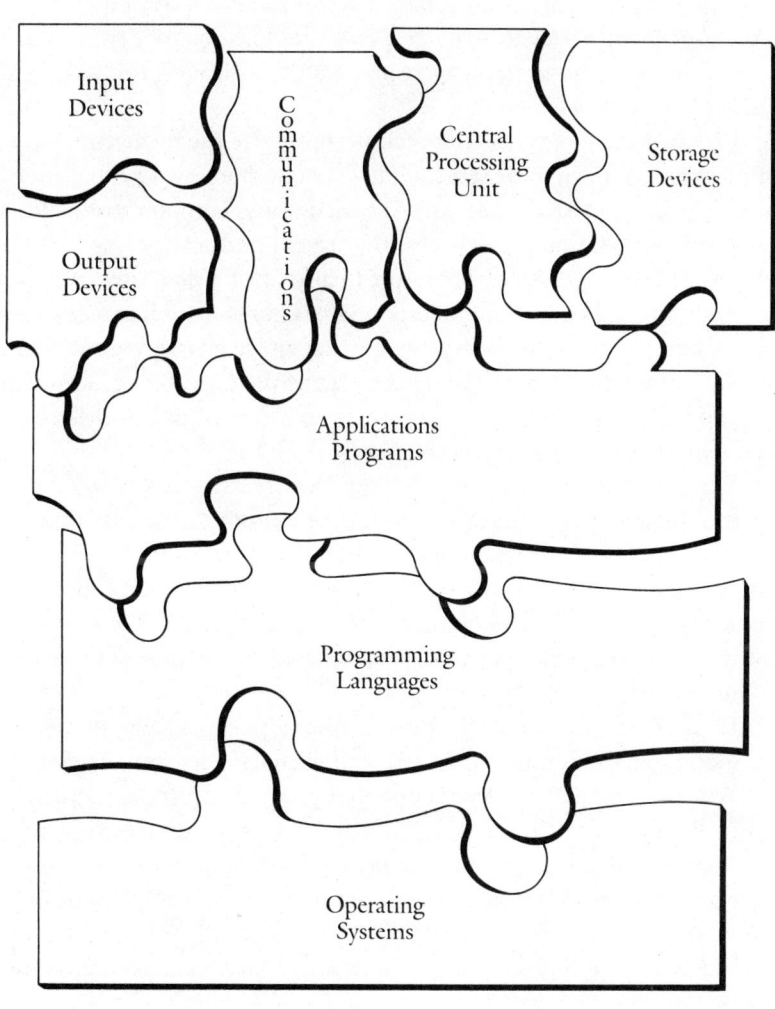

CHAPTER 18

Acquiring data processing technology implies a substantial commitment on the part of the user. The degree to which users are willing to reorganize their approach (obviously in sensible ways) to doing business (health care or other) will largely determine the success of their computing ventures. In the health care environment there is an understandable hesitation associated with making a wholehearted commitment if it implies that the health care milieu itself may be affected by the change.

What are some of the major factors we must consider?

First, acquiring computer hardware is a big decision because it involves a large financial outlay. Once hardware is obtained, the user is locked into it. Even with a lease, one cannot simply unilaterally divest oneself of a computer, and one can usually resell purchased hardware only at a loss. The original decision to acquire hardware must therefore be one the user is prepared to live with for at least several years to justify the investment.

Even when a computer user seeks to minimize the financial commitment by renting a system or paying for services on a system shared with other users, the monetary outlay is far from trivial. As any knowledgeable computer user knows, any shared system also has unique drawbacks: the overall performance, as far as any one user is concerned, can be significantly lower than that of a dedicated system.

Another hardware-related reason that accounts for reluctance in committing oneself to automation is the realistic worry that an already expensive "starter" system will grow and thereby become even more expensive. The predilection of computer hardware for seemingly spontaneous generation is one of its less desirable characteristics. The wise user fears this phenomenon.

The informed user may become even more hesitant to embark on automation after realizing that software development can be a more expensive proposition than hardware acquisition. Even when one can buy a complete software package that approximates one's needs, there will be costs associated with modification and maintenance. Sometimes software development will be undertaken. Only with great care can software development costs be kept under control, because they tend to build up little by little.

Even when software development proceeds successfully, programming triumphs are soon taken for granted, and users start clamoring for more sophisticated software.

When software development does not proceed according to plan, a greater danger exists. Because of the investment already made in hardware acquisition and software development, there is a natural tendency for desperate users to throw good money after bad in an effort to force systems development to completion. When projects bog down and fall behind schedule, more programming staff personnel may be hired. Instead of having a positive effect, this action may only further complicate the programming effort and put a project even further behind schedule than it would have been without additional help, as we saw in Chapter 12.

The ultimate fear concerning a commitment to computer systems is that the first system one acquires may not be the proper system to do the intended job. The financial loss in such cases can be devastating.

Obviously, timid dabbling in automation is no answer, for that will certainly fail to produce anything of value. Knowing this, one must be fully aware of the level of commitment and must organize the environment in which the computer will be used to maximize the chances of success. Organizing for automation should be an important prerequisite to installing a computer system in any health care environment, but usually this is perceived only in retrospect after a policy of ad hoc management has failed to achieve the desired results.

We can, however, learn from the mistakes of our predecessors.

THE IMPACT OF COMPUTER SYSTEMS

Metaphorically speaking, a computer can have the same effect on an unprepared environment as does spicy food on an unaccustomed stomach: the results can be catastrophic!

To start, the computer will often force the user to redefine ways of doing business. The procedures necessary for collecting data and entering it into the computer system will usually represent a significant departure from procedures used before automation. When an automated process is introduced for which there was no manual predecessor, health care personnel may find themselves required to fill out data collection forms or to use terminals at virtually every step of their activities. Under these circumstances, it is natural for personnel to become irritated at having to collect data for someone else's purposes and to focus that irritation on the computer as the source of the added burden. A computer-based data management system may demand certain kinds of data from health care providers before it will issue reports they require for hospital records. This kind of procedure is often mandatory if complete, reliable data is to be collected. Still, it is a type of blackmail, and health care providers may resent it.

The impact of automation is not limited to its effect on end-users. Staffing requirements in an organization (in the hospital as a whole, in a service area, or in a department) will be altered, sometimes drastically. New job roles such as analyst, programmer, and operator may be defined. Data processing people may become part of the health care environment for the purpose of program development, and someone may be required to oversee and operate a computer system once it is working. Secretaries may find themselves redefined as data-entry personnel when a computer system takes over some of their clerical duties.

The economic impact of a computer system is usually sizeable. Even if hardware is relatively cheap, software development costs are generally high, and they have nowhere to go but up. A lot of money will be tied up in a computer system—money that is not going to be available for other purposes.

Thus computers have an enormous potential to disrupt any environment in which they are employed.

Not only does the computer determine in many cases how business will be conducted, but it also may establish a precedent that succeeding generations of users will be forced to follow. A functioning computer system that has finally been perfected at great expense and with great effort is not lightly modified or discarded. Thus, whenever a computer is used for some ongoing purpose, the danger exists that it will actually limit innovation and change. Ideas that do not conform to any automated approach may be discarded and their merit may be ignored. Technology begets technology. Each step along the road to automation makes it increasingly difficult for an organization to return to the methods used before computers. Once the automation revolution has overthrown the old order of manual methods, it will be difficult to overthrow the powerful new dynasty that has been established.

EVOLUTION VERSUS REVOLUTION

The cataclysmic approach to change may be effective in eliminating something that does not work, but it does nothing to recover the time, effort, and money that may be wasted if the change fails to produce the desired effects. A more rational approach to a change as major as introducing automation is to proceed in an orderly, stepwise, conscious, and prepared fashion that lends itself to adjustments in direction as they become necessary.

Because the way an institution functions is affected by data processing activities, businesses are now beginning to include data processing personnel in the upper management team. The vice president of data processing is a newcomer to managerial

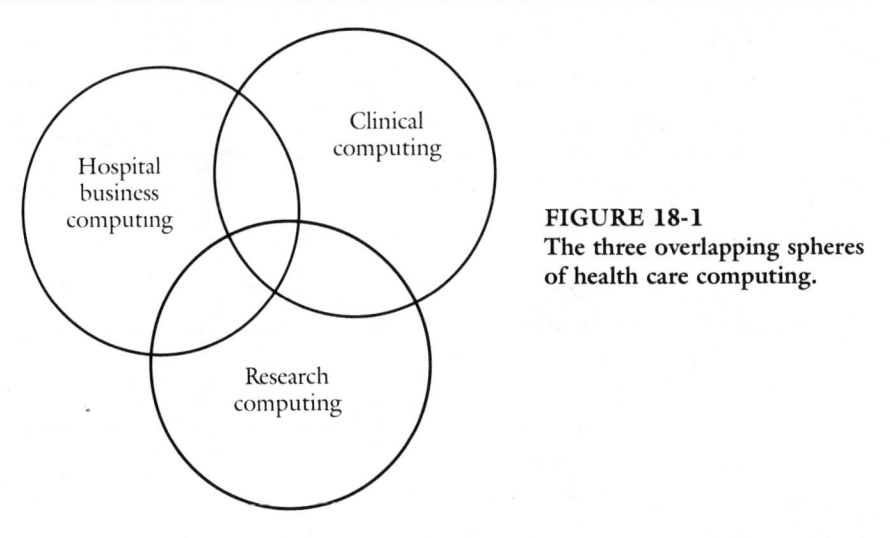

FIGURE 18-1
The three overlapping spheres of health care computing.

ranks, whose arrival signifies that businesses are beginning to appreciate the overwhelming importance of data processing in their everyday activities.

Within health care institutions, the data processing picture is usually not as clearcut as it is in businesses. Three separate kinds of activities involving computers may exist in a hospital: ordinary business computing, computer service relating to patient care, and computing for medical research. Despite areas of overlap, the three spheres of health care computing are mostly independent (Figure 18-1). Organizing the management of data processing in the health care environment is therefore somewhat more complex than in most industries, where there is only one data processing department. It would be helpful, therefore, to look more closely at the organization of data processing activities within a health care environment.

POLITICS OF COMPUTING

Because so many aspects of an organization's activities are dependent on data processing, it follows that those who control data processing are in a position of considerable power within that organization. That such power can be used in both productive and counterproductive ways makes possible a convincing case for both those who favor a centralized approach to health care computing and those who favor a decentralized approach.

In support of the establishment of a computer center in health care institutions where computers are used, one can cite several theoretical advantages. Such an approach makes it theoretically easier to coordinate the computing needs of the whole organization. Central control over health care automation facilitates the peer review of proposed projects. Such projects can be assessed by disinterested individuals for feasibility, necessity, and affordability. On this basis, institution-wide computing priorities may be established. In general, a central computer facility can possess bigger, more expensive, and more powerful hardware and software than could each of several smaller installations (this is often referred to as the economy of scale). The maturation of microcomputer systems is slowly making this argument obsolete, but there is still a long time to go before it no longer applies generally. Furthermore, a central facility will be more likely to attract highly competent people to the data processing effort than any one small application could either attract or afford.

When smaller applications can reasonably share the same equipment and personnel, it makes sense for them to join forces to produce a whole that would be greater than the sum of its separate parts. Centralization of the computing effort also creates an environment that facilitates continuous performance monitoring of various projects. It can be determined by a central authority when development should be terminated because of a final success or failure. In this way an institution can avoid squandering money on projects that have no reasonable hope of future success. Applications can be reevaluated periodically, and their priorities in an institution's overall health care–computing scheme may be changed as various landmarks of progress or unexpected problems arise.

Up to this point, the case for a health care–computing center sounds irresistible. However, this approach is not without serious drawbacks. A single computer center in any institution can become the focus of a power struggle among individuals or departments with totally unrelated or even conflicting interests. A person with limited technical know-how but big ambitions can easily hire the technical expertise necessary to run a computer center. Thus, controlling computers can provide a fairly easy pathway to a powerful management position. The computer center will determine what projects can and cannot be done in an institution. The manager who is not equally responsible to all interests will be at liberty to assign a high priority to pet projects and to give lower priority to rival projects. It is easy enough simply to tell an unwanted user that a project is not feasible. Naive users will not know when they are being bamboozled.

The diverse nature of health care–computing projects alone makes the approach of the single computer center unreasonable for most health care environments. Administration, health care services, and medical research are spheres of interest that must each be adequately separated and expertly staffed if health care–computing efforts are not to become bogged down in managerial conflicts and overlapping responsibilities.

Administrative Computing Versus Patient-Care and Medical Research Computing

First, there must be a clear division between patient-care computing and the ordinary kinds of business data processing activities found in most big businesses, including hospitals. Obviously, nonadministrative medical staff members should not have power over administrative computing functions relating to the everyday business of the hospital. Payroll, accounts receivable and payable, and housekeeping schedules lie squarely in the realm of hospital administration and must not be subject to outside interference.

Similarly, physicians or basic scientists who obtain their research funding from outside agencies must have the academic freedom to determine the nature of their own research and the methods they employ. Their research should be subject only to the normal processes of peer review and not to be the interference of the hospital administration.

However, the distinction between medical science and hospital administration becomes somewhat more blurred in health care–computing activities that are conducted for purposes of patient care. An uneasy relationship has always existed between medical interest in up-to-date technology and the administrative realities of controlling the hospital budget. Health care automation is making available certain kinds of patient care not previously available, and it threatens to upset the balance. A CT body scanner may improve the quality of health care, but it is tremendously expensive to obtain and operate. In such areas, administration and even government must have input in managing a health care–computing function.

PATIENT-CARE COMPUTING VERSUS MEDICAL RESEARCH COMPUTING

It is equally important to distinguish and separate the commitments to health care service and medical research. These areas are both important, and therefore clear priorities need to be established separately for each and they must be prevented from interfering with each other. Funding, responsibilities, and accountability will be different for each area.

In many ways, these two areas are in conflict with each other. Research projects have a natural tendency to expand in scope and in number. Unless limitations are placed on the research load, burgeoning research applications may slowly squeeze out ordinary service functions in a shared computer facility. Budgeting for both functions together is a real problem. Furthermore, a project that begins with a research grant sometimes goes on to become a patient-care application after the expiration of that grant, and may then need to be supported by service funding from the institution itself. An automated procedure that is initially the object of experiment may be proved valuable or essential and brought into routine service. At this point, the hospital administration becomes interested, further complicating the issue.

On the other hand, those who wish to acquire a computer system to serve specific service goals should realize that growth and improvement in health care delivery and administration occur through research. Without medical research, the theory of the four humours would still represent the ultimate understanding in human physiology! In health care computing, progress is not going to be realized by merely implementing commercially available systems.

A reasonable balance between service and research is the foundation on which computing can best serve the health care community. It is incumbent on those who administer health care–computing systems to ensure peaceful coexistence and helpful cooperation between these two fields of health care–computing interest and yet ensure their autonomy.

AVOIDING CONFLICTS

In the spirit of preventive health care, the best way to deal with the headaches that can be caused by overlapping management is to organize for automation in such a way that management conflicts are avoided in the first place.

MANAGEMENT'S ROLE

A practical solution is to recognize the fundamental differences between the requirements of research computing versus those of health care service and administrative computing, and to separate the management of each so they do not step on each other's toes (Figure 18-2).

FIGURE 18-2
The very different goals of hospital business computing and patient care computing can lead to rivalry if management responsibilities are not clearly divided.

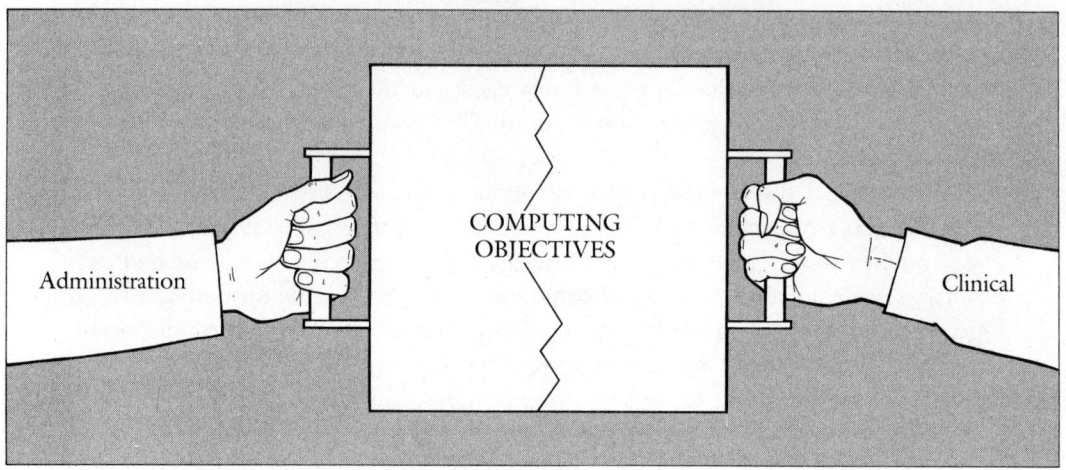

With business and patient-care computing, the overriding necessity is for stability, reliability, security, and fiscal responsibility within the institution. The evolution of data processing here is slow and deliberate, because mistakes are extremely costly and could have potentially disastrous consequences for the institution. Computer applications for these functions in a hospital will develop as the result of numerous conferences, deliberations, and meetings. When so much is at stake, domination by computer enthusiasts cannot be allowed. Full institutional backing is required before any change can be made.

However, in medical research computing exactly the opposite requirements exist. Much of clinical research depends on insights and inspirations of single individuals or small groups of colleagues. The funding process normally grants money to individual researchers for the specific purposes of achieving their own particular aims. Computing requirements for medical research projects are in a constant state of upheaval and modification. Those who wait for stabilization or a consensus will wait forever, miss their opportunities, and achieve nothing. The success of any given medical research project is never guaranteed at the outset, nor can it be essential to the life of an institution. Many medical research ventures have served a useful purpose by identifying a blind alley so that others will not have to repeat the same mistakes. Therefore, computing requirements in medical research should be geared to the small, incisive, leading edge of investigation, not to the safe, predictable requirements so necessary for the stability of hospital business and patient care.

Recognizing the vast differences between business and patient-care computing and the innovative requirements of medical research computing, management should be separated into a department of administrative data processing (responsible for business and patient-care computing) for the large, central data processing functions of running the hospital, and a separate administration for research computing. In turn there should be a specially trained manager within administrative computing responsible for the fiscal system. Administrative and research computing will have no areas of mutual responsibility except in those cases in which they agree their jurisdictions clearly overlap. An excellent arbitrator of questions of responsibility in given applications is the person in charge of funding. Research funds support research computing. The hospital budget supports hospital service computing.

On the management level, the department in charge of hospital service computing is the same as the data processing department in any other kind of business. Its head may be a vice president within the hospital administration, although in most institutions this person carries the title of director.

On the other hand, the person who heads research computing will have functions unique to the health care–computing environment. A director of research computing will exert a leadership function among researchers and health care innovators within an institution, will motivate users to the advantages of automation when there is reason to believe such advantages exist, will coordinate the development of shared resources, and will move projects from the planning stages to completion. A director of research computing will be a source of expertise, a person who possesses knowledge of the details that must be attended to in implementing health care–computer research support applications, and will keep them running smoothly. This individual will assess the feasibility of user requests, establish reasonable schedules, and be concerned with the financial realities of running computer services. Because of a unique expertise, the director may often be called on to assist health care personnel in preparing their grant applications for research projects that will require expenditures for data processing.

One of the best ways in which the health care–computing expert can assist researchers is by helping them to make the most of their rather limited financial resources. Computers are expensive, and usually any one researcher cannot obtain enough money for adequate hardware acquisition and software development; hence the motivation for shared computer facilities and development. When possible, the person in charge of the facility should control reinvention and thus enable the researcher with a new project to make use of hardware and software that is already developed or possibly underused. Equipment, development effort, and cost can thereby be contained at the relatively low level with which most research projects can cope. When new kinds of hardware must be acquired or new software developed, the director of research computing will be able to set realistic budgetary goals and to direct these new developments so they will benefit future users, as well as current ones. This kind of cooperation under one unified management is essential if many little research projects requiring health care–computing services are to succeed at all.

In short, this is also a management position of high responsibility. It should never be viewed as a consultative role. Unless one person is in charge of this area, it will be directionless, and no user will be served particularly well. The director must be independent, having no special obligations to any one user or group of users, because he or she is responsible for all clinical-computing endeavors within the division, department, or institution.

There are, of course, constraints on the power of this position. The director of research computing's role should be to help the various unrelated health care users in getting their diverse jobs done. Clearly, funding for medical research is granted on the merits of individual studies. The director has no control over setting the budget for various projects and should have no power to usurp funds that were allocated for some other purpose. The director of research computing may be responsible for several physical installations, ranging from simple personal computing systems to large time-sharing systems. Although encouraging users with similar interests to band together in shared facilities when it is in their best interest to do so, the director of research computing must recognize that the primary responsibility will be to individual users or to voluntary association of users.

The director's responsibility for budgeting is to try to arrive at realistic estimates of cost, and to assist in efforts to persuade those who control the purse strings that these costs are necessary.

THE COMPUTER ADVISORY COMMITTEE

Whether or not a research-computing project succeeds or fails is strictly a matter between the researcher and the funding agency. However, when applications are designed for rendering some service to patients, there is an overlap of interest between researchers and the hospital administration. This overlap is best dealt with through a body that might be called the computer advisory committee, made up of representatives from health care computing and administration. Examples of applications subject to both health care and administrative management include admitting/discharge/transfer systems, patient registration schemes, radiology reporting systems, and laboratory reporting systems. The committee should involve the physicians, nurses, and health care–computing experts who are responsible for the selection, development, implementation, and daily operation of computer services for patient care, and the hospital administrators who are responsible for efficiently running the service departments and who will have to find the means of paying for developing the systems.

When a health care–computing project combines both research and service goals, the computer advisory committee should review the project to clarify the implied partnership of the hospital with the research funding agency. The project should be considered service-related to the extent that the hospital is required to finance it. The research-related aspects of the project should be clearly delineated, and it should be made clear that the institution will assume no financial liability for them. The service-related aspects should be considered in the same light as any of the other service applications we have just considered.

THE USER'S ROLE

If the computer advisory committee is somewhat like the "board of directors" in relation to patient-care and administrative computing that directly concerns the institution, the users' committee might be analogous to the "stockholders." Users have an important role to play as a pressure group that lobbies to make sure its own legitimate interests are met.

In hospital business computing, input from the comptroller, accountants, and administrative and junior management personnel will be important in identifying areas in which automation ought to be considered. Often, financial reasons are the primary motivation for undertaking a data processing application in business. However, some nonmanagement personnel, such as clerical staff personnel, should not be forgotten, because they will have to use a computer system with their own hands. Their perception of existing problems in the current method of performing any administrative function and their desire for improvement are very important.

In computing applications concerned entirely with medical research, a somewhat different situation exists. Here the individual is the motivating influence. The computing goals of medical research often require less of a cooperative effort than do business and patient-care data processing. After all, the individual researcher obtains funding for individual projects. If a project has been reviewed and approved through the proper channels of peer review, the researcher should be able to request and to obtain those computer services for which money has been approved. Therefore, the role of the director of research computing is to assist the researcher in achieving project goals—not to direct the research or to hinder it in any way.

The voluntarily cooperating association of research users who agree to pool their resources must also have a means of expressing collective priorities and desires. They do this through a research user's committee, which should meet regularly.

REALITIES IN HEALTH CARE COMPUTING

Today computing in the health care environment is moving rapidly towards decentralization. The needs of medical research computing are so radically different from ordinary business and patient-care data processing functions seen in the administrative sphere that these two kinds of computing cannot be combined. Their managerial philosophies, objectives, and fundamental hardware and software requirements are often mutually incompatible.

Within the business and patient-care computing sphere it is also true that physical installations are going to proliferate. Increasingly, computer-based health care instruments are appearing on the market that are totally self-contained. When development of a totally new system is undertaken, it is inappropriate to attempt to combine some kinds of disparate applications such as signal processing and database management. Different kinds of systems are required to support these completely unrelated areas; programmers with different sets of skills are required for each (see Chapter 1).

At the same time, the average medical research application has such a small budget that the separate acquisition of facilities is impossible in many circumstances. The economic necessity of pooling resources and avoiding duplication whenever possible makes it incumbent on users with compatible requirements to band together in users' groups.

When computing is to be invoked as a means of delivering health care to patients, some method of effective management must be worked out so that all of the parties with a legitimate interest in the project can be represented.

Establishing effective management is the key to success. A successful implementation does not occur haphazardly, but is carefully planned to deal with budgets, schedules, varying levels of user enthusiasm, and ever-changing requirements to its completion.

Organizing for automation is just as important as finding the right hardware and obtaining the proper software. Only when this responsibility is unambiguously assigned and only when managerial authority is clearly delegated can one hope to avoid wasting energy in internal political squabbles.

In this section we have seen that good management is as much a part of health care computing as computer hardware or software. It seems unfortunate, therefore, that many of the people who must take on roles of managerial authority in health care computing have not had any specific training to prepare them for their jobs. Recent innovations at some universities would appear to support the belief that health care computing is a distinct profession with discernible demands and challenges, for which an appropriate academic curriculum should and can be devised.

Therefore, in the following chapter we will look more closely at the kind of training that could best prepare someone for a career as a health care–computing specialist.

CHAPTER 19
TRAINING HEALTH CARE–COMPUTING SPECIALISTS

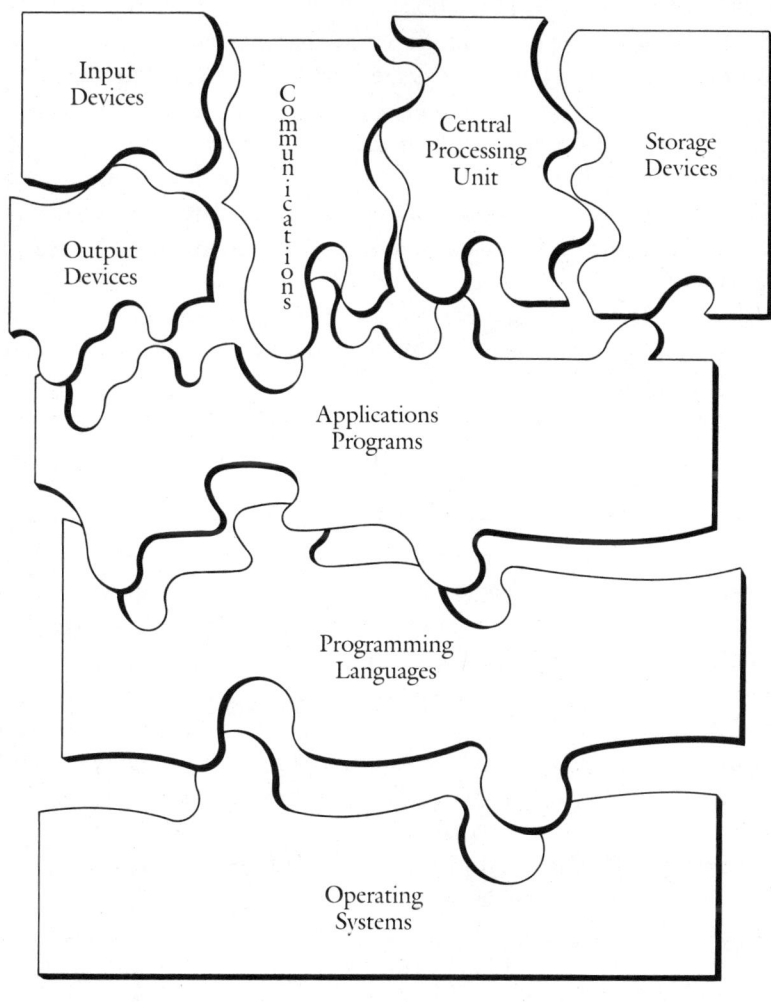

CHAPTER 19

It may sound redundant to say that the expertise of a graduate in computer science is in computer science, but the point is worth emphasizing. Business has long appreciated that a computer science graduate seldom knows enough about the business environment to be useful without additional business-oriented academic and on-the-job training. This is because substantial differences exist between what is taught in a computer science department and what business data processing requires. For example, although COBOL is eschewed as a rather dull and cumbersome programming language in the academic environment, it still remains the principal programming language in the business community.

However, it is not only the computing details that separate academic computer science and the computer science of the business world. Businesses are especially interested in accounting, which is reflected in their data processing needs. Accountancy is not normally studied by computer scientists. Indeed, the entire framework of modern business, from its organizational methods to its basis in economics and the profit motive, has very little in common with the academic scene. Even the management and economics of computing projects are only rarely covered in an undergraduate computer science program. Computer science academicians are not likely to teach their students about the kinds of information that will be required to develop a management information system or, for that matter, about how to apply such a system effectively—even if they do teach them about information systems!

Business, then, needs data processing services that are directed to its particular needs. As such, a commercial enterprise would prefer to hire a person holding a bachelor's degree in computer science and a degree in business administration in preference to a Ph.D. in academic computer science. Innovation in computer science is usually not what interests business.

The academic community has responded to the needs of business by instituting in some business schools a strong computer science curriculum specifically directed to business applications.

Compared to business, the health care system is slow in adopting computer technology and the successful use of computers in health care is still not perceived as being dependent on people who are knowledgeable in both computer science and health care. The health care environment presents computer professionals with unique problems that their training usually does not anticipate. Previous experience with the business community will not greatly help these professionals either. Hospitals are like businesses in the sense that they are big institutions composed of many different departments. But they are unlike businesses in many important respects.

For one thing, the degree of autonomy exercised by each department within a hospital is generally greater than one might expect to find in a business enterprise of a similar size. Whereas in businesses the profit motive is the overriding consideration that all departments must respect, in hospitals (especially in a country with government-run health care) there may be no such motivation. Just like a corporation, different hospital departments frequently come into direct conflict with each other as they compete for the same dwindling supply of dollars. However, their conflicts will often be resolved on other than a profit-related basis. The high degree of departmental independence is not confined to interdepartmental rivalry. It is fair to say that there is not even a true employer-employee relationship between most health care institutions and the health care providers who work in them. Frequently the health care provider in a hospital works under a complex financial agreement in which fee-for-service plays a part. Each health care provider is therefore his or her own boss to some extent—an observation underlined by the difficulty that our health care institutions have in merely enforcing the completeness of their medical records! Establishing any kind of cooperative health care–computing venture in such an environment challenges diplomatic and administrative skills.

On the assumption that it is possible to get agreement in principle for a health care–computing venture, financing it is uniquely frustrating in the health care environment. A business need only satisfy itself that a piece of equipment or a procedure will save money or increase revenues to justify its use. In health care, however, only some hospitals share such a motivation. In Canada, for instance, the government-run form of health care places hospitals under tight financial constraints. This often precludes expending large amounts of money now to save more later. Even increased efficiency in dealing with a particular kind of health care problem can be interpreted negatively, because this simply means that more such cases would be treated, with increased overall costs to the government!

Even when money can be found for health care computing, the computer professional's frustrations are far from over. The very structure of health care decision making is inscrutable. The computer scientist called on to implement useful computer-based systems in support of health care objectives may be required to do research to discover an approach on which to base the programming. If health care providers have not been able to elucidate a general approach for evaluating and treating broad classes of patients, the computer scientist will obviously have trouble in doing so. At the very least, the computer scientist soon discovers that many problems are not computer-related, but that they involve the clarification, explication, and formalization of health care processes themselves.

SKILLS OF THE HEALTH CARE–COMPUTING SPECIALIST

To meet the unique challenges of applying data processing techniques to the health care environment, a person will require a combination of computer science training and some background in health care. Such an individual will also need an understanding of areas that fall somewhere between the two disciplines but that are generally not dealt with in either one of them, such as managerial skills.

COMPUTER SCIENCE BACKGROUND

The health care–computing specialist will have a sound background in computer science. This person must have theoretical and practical knowledge of hardware and software, a good grasp of operating systems and compilers, and an understanding of database management systems (an area central in health care applications). Excellent knowledge of computer graphics and at least one course in artificial intelligence are also important. At the applications programming level, the health care–computing specialist should have experience with a variety of programming languages and techniques, and at least one course in software engineering. This person's knowledge would not be complete without some training in the economics of computing; a course or experience in managing software development would also be beneficial. In short, this person is expected to be a better-than-average computer scientist, not merely a programmer. The salary will reflect this fact.

HEALTH CARE BACKGROUND

Those who will direct the development or the application of computers in health care must have some knowledge of the specific problem areas in which their computer system will be used. A basic understanding of hospital administration is essential in developing an admission/discharge/transfer system. Those who work on automated radiology reporting systems have to know about the problems radiologists encounter and that automation might reasonably be expected to solve. The same analogy holds for every other applications area in health care. Most of the time health care providers will be quite unable to think about problems specific to their specialties in an organized, analytical way, nor will they be able to state these problems clearly enough to permit automation to proceed rationally. The responsibility of the health care–computing expert is to uncover and clarify these problems and to evaluate the potential role of computers in solving them. To do this, the computer scientist must be thoroughly integrated into the health care environment and must be completely at home with health care personnel. When health care providers use the jargon of their respective specialties, the health care–computing specialists must know what they are talking about.

There are a number of ways in which a non–health care professional can obtain some familiarity with the health care environment. Perhaps one of the best ways is for such a person to undertake an apprenticeship under someone who is already expert in a particular health care–computing area, and who has already become very familiar with the particular health care problems under consideration. One way of accomplishing this is to do a thesis project under the supervision of such a person. An additional useful approach to the health care education of a computer scientist would be reading appropriate books about clinical decision making, physiology, and other health care topics. Those who need more in-depth knowledge in a particular area might be able to arrange to study or audit specific basic science courses in a health care institute (e.g., a school of medicine or school of nursing). Those working in teaching hospitals will have access to a wealth of rounds and formal lectures in specific subject areas (e.g., cardiology), some of which may be very useful.

Non–health care professionals should not underestimate their own abilities to master selected areas of basic science that pertain to specific special-interest areas in health care computing. The undergraduate physiology programs can be useful to anyone who has ever taken a university biology course.

In addition to an overview of the health care environment, at the departmental or specialist level, health care–computing people must acquire some understanding of the economics of health care systems. A global view of the health care system will assist the computing expert when called on for an opinion regarding the difficulty, expense, and priority of various possible health care–computing applications.

SPECIAL TRAINING

Some of the background of the ideal health care–computing specialist cannot be obtained from a university computer science course, health care training, or immersion in a health care milieu.

Generally speaking, managerial skills make or break a computing venture. In business, data processing managers are trained on the job as they rise through the hierarchy. In health care, however, installations are small, and computer-knowledgeable personnel are correspondingly few. Salaries are generally not competitive with business, so the turnover of computing personnel in health care institutions tends to be high. It is therefore difficult for health care either to attract high-level data processing managers as replacements or to retain the services of those who have received on-the-job training. This situation is unfortunate because the degree to which a health care–computing project meets its goal on time and within budgetary constraints is determined to a huge extent by management skills.

Most computer science curricula teach virtually nothing about the basics of acquiring computer equipment and services in the real world. However, a data processing manager obviously has to know about selecting systems in the marketplace. He or she must be familiar with existing products and their comparative strengths, weaknesses, and prices. Similarly, an appreciation of the reputations, past records, and relative competence of companies providing hardware and software services should be an integral part of a data processing manager's knowledge base.

A grasp of the economic issues of data processing in the real world includes familiarity with contracts, leases, rental agreements, and software and hardware maintenance agreements. The manager will need to be familiar with all the arcane terminology of these contracts, so common to business.

The health care data processing manager needs to cultivate associations with the sales representatives of various companies. Most of these are honest, decent people, whose principal objective is to serve their customers with the most appropriate products their respective companies have to offer. However, some people are inherently more knowledgeable, or more hard working, or simply easier to get along with than others. A good working relationship with the local sales representatives can be a decided asset to any data processing manager.

The same is true about in-house relationships. It would be helpful to have a course that exposes the problems of interpersonal relations and teaches effective strategies to avoid and solve problems.

An additional and vital aspect of the training of a health care–computing specialist should be reviewing previous health care–computing applications and analyzing why they have either succeeded or failed. Some good general lessons can be learned from such a critical evaluation, and such an education may save a future health care–computing practitioner from wasting time on an insoluble problem or from trying to invent what could be bought over the counter. Often a course or two providing an introduction to health care computing is available at larger universities, and even more in-depth courses (e.g., on the application of database systems to health care) are sometimes available. Taking such courses periodically as refreshers is a good idea to become familiar with what is going on in the world of health care computing. Such courses are also run by associations, management consulting firms, and computer vendors.

Once equipment has been obtained and software has been acquired or developed, the health care–computing specialist must then manage a data processing application. Setting a budget (and sticking to it), establishing a schedule (and meeting it), guiding implementation, and supervising staff are not easy tasks. They require technical know-how, vigilance, meticulous organization, and even diplomatic finesse.

Good public relations between computer personnel and the health care community can be realized only by genuine understanding and goodwill on the part of both computer science personnel and health care personnel. The health care–computing specialist is a person who would exemplify this cooperative spirit, because he or she will be the most visible proponent of computer services in a health care environment.

UNIVERSITIES MEET THE CHALLENGE

Institutions of higher learning are becoming aware of the unique skills required by the health care–computing expert. An increasing number of them are responding to this need by establishing courses or even whole curricula specifically directed towards educating people to fill this role. In general, two approaches have been taken: degree programs in health care information science, and supplementary education in health care computing for graduates of other programs.

DEGREE PROGRAMS

Some universities (e.g., Stanford University) have chosen to establish separate institutes granting degrees in health care information science or health care information processing. These academic institutes are often hybrid organizations combining a variety of personnel from other academic areas, such as computer science, health care, biomedical engineering, biostatistics, and industrial engineering. The precise composition of such interdisciplinary institutes varies from place to place. The purpose of such institutes is, in general, twofold. First, students in the institute receive specific training in health care information processing. Often only graduate students are accepted. Admission requirements may include degrees in either computer science or in health care. Second, the institute is a liaison between the health care community and computer scientists. Ideally, it would be a resource for advice.

The following are those universities offering such an approach to health care information processing that replied to our inquiries by January, 1982:

Universities with degree programs in health care information science
Duke University
Georgia Institute of Technology
Hunter College (New York)
Stanford University
University of California–San Francisco
University of Victoria (Victoria, B.C., Canada)

SUPPLEMENTARY COURSES

A second kind of response by the academic world to the challenges of health care computing is supplementing existing curricula in computer science with additional courses provided by other departments to qualify a computer science graduate as a specialist in health care computing. This approach seems less redundant than establishing a separate institute of health care information science with a wide variety of courses that partially overlap those already being offered by the computer science department. Health care–computing experts ought to have the benefit of the best possible training in computer science, and it must be conceded that the most qualified teachers of computer science are to be found in that department. Introductory courses in health care–computing are necessary, but not sufficient, to train a health care–computing expert. In-depth knowledge of computer science is mandatory.

The supplementary courses should concentrate on the knowledge that will transform a computer scientist into a health care–computing expert. Biomedical engineering, health care, industrial engineering, business administration, and computer science itself are departments that could individually or collectively offer some of these courses.

There are universities in North America that offer supplementary courses in one or more departments. Examples of such courses are the economics of health care computing, health care decision making, database systems in health care, health care image processing, organization and management in health care systems, product evaluation and selection, and many specialist-oriented courses (e.g., computers in cardiology, radiology, laboratories, or administration).

Regardless of which approach a university may take to training health care–computing experts, an essential part of this training should take place in the health care environment. The "ivory tower" is not the place to learn about the practical needs and frustrations of computing in health care. Students must get out into the health care community to conduct their term projects, systems analysis assignments, and theses on a practical level. Encouraging such participation will be to the advantage of the health care personnel with whom such projects will be carried out.

CONTINUING EDUCATION: KEEPING UP

A sound academic background is a firm foundation on which to build a career in health care computing. To maintain knowledgeability in the field, a health care–computing expert will need to keep abreast of ongoing developments.

SPECIALIST JOURNALS

A number of scholarly journals are devoted entirely to health care computing. These journals offer editorials, review articles, and individual project reports. Addresses for the journals listed here are provided in Appendix II.

Journals devoted to health care computing

Australasian Physical and Engineering Sciences in Medicine
Automedica
CES Computer Enhanced Spectroscopy
Computer Medicine
Computer Programs in Biomedicine
Computerized Radiology
Computers in Biology and Medicine
Computers and Biomedical Research
Computers in Healthcare
Computers and Medicine
Computers in Psychiatry/Psychology
Cyberdent
Engineering in Medicine and Biology
Healthcare Computing and Communications
International Journal of Bio-Medical Computing
Journal of Clinical Computing
Journal of Educational Computer Research
Journal of Medical Systems
M.D. Computing
Medical Computer Journal
Medicine and Computer
Methods of Information in Medicine
Micro MD Journal
Physicians and Computers
Sigbio Newsletter
Software in Healthcare

BOOKS

The books written on health care computing are increasing in number every year. An up-to-date list of these books appears in Appendix II.

MEDICAL/NURSING/ALLIED HEALTH JOURNALS

Other publications in the health care literature (not specifically devoted to health care data processing) occasionally offer review articles or articles concerning specific applications in health care computing. A MEDLINE search of the *Cumulated Index Medicus* shows that in 1 year, approximately 3,000 articles concerned with some aspect of computers or automation appeared in the health care literature alone.

OTHER TECHNICAL JOURNALS

Non-health care technical literature, such as the publications of the Association for Computing Machinery (ACM) or the Institute of Electrical and Electronics Engineers (IEEE), occasionally publish interesting review papers about some aspect of computers in health care. These publications are also very useful for maintaining up-to-date knowledge about computer science in general.

Trade journals in data processing frequently provide excellent review articles about computing machinery and software practices, written by acknowledged experts in their fields. *Datamation, Computer Decisions, Infosystems,* and *Mini-Micro Systems* are some of these journals.

SYMPOSIA AND CONFERENCES

Several important health care–computing meetings take place regularly, and the proceedings of these conferences are required reading for anyone who wishes to know about the state of the art. The Medinfo International Conference occurs every 3 years. Annual conferences include the Symposium on Computer Applications in Medical Care (SCAMC), which covers a wide range of health care–computing interests, the Canadian Organization for the Advancement of Computers in Health (COACH), and Computers in Cardiology. A partial list of other symposia and conferences follows.

Symposia and conferences
Artificial Intelligence in Medicine
Computers in Ophthalmology
Health Care Management and Informatics
International Congress of the European Federation for Medical Informatics
  (EFMI-IMIA)
Medcomp (International Conference on Computing in Medicine)
Medical Informatics in Ambulatory Care (International Conference on Medical
  Informatics)
Society for Computer Medicine
World Association for Medical Informatics

Health care conferences are increasingly providing a platform for scientists who are using computers in an innovative way to advance health care knowledge. Some of them have also sponsored tutorial sessions about using computers in relevant specialty areas. The annual meetings of the American Heart Association, the Radiologic Society of North America, the Society for Critical Care Medicine, and the Canadian and American Hospital Associations have provided tutorials in computing. Similarly, other health care specialties have their own annual meetings, the proceedings of which may from time to time contain some important papers on using automated techniques.

Most of this reading material is available in computer science or health care libraries. Almost all of it is available by private subscription. However, some excellent trade journals, such as *Datamation,* are circulated without charge to qualified applicants.

HUMAN INTERACTION

Reading alone is not likely to provide the intellectual stimulus to keep up with health care computing. It is just as important to remain involved in a project or with an institution where things are going on. By continuing interaction with others, one acquires new ideas, new viewpoints, and new techniques.

Attendance at one or two conferences per year is an excellent and enjoyable way to meet other people in the field and to learn from them.

In addition, membership in societies and special interest groups is strongly recommended. Organizations such as the ACM and the IEEE have special interest groups with their own newsletters, meetings, and workshops.

GETTING STARTED

Students increasingly have the opportunity to obtain specialized training in health care computing. However, such opportunities did not exist even a few years ago, and they are still available only at a small number of universities. Therefore, many of the people who are now working as health care–computing specialists or who will be thrust into such roles in the near future will have to possess the initiative to obtain basic or continuing training for themselves.

The health care providers, computer scientists, or hospital adminstrators who are becoming involved in health care computing are probably best advised to start gradually, appreciating that they will have to spend some time and money on self-education.

It would perhaps be wise to establish a liaison with a local university's computer science department. One should arrange to meet one or two of the professors and discuss the plan one has in mind in a brainstorming session. It may be that the project that one proposes is exciting enough to be the basis for a project for one or more computer science graduates or undergraduates. (Professors are always looking for practical projects for their students; the students, in turn, are gratified when their work is useful to somebody besides themselves.)

Would-be health care–computing experts can improve their knowledge about computer science by reading journals, proceedings of symposia, books, and specialized publications. Even those health care providers or hospital administrators who may have studied some computer science as undergraduates may be shocked at the progress that has taken place within the past decade, if they have not kept up with modern developments.

It would be worthwhile for health care professionals interested in health care computing to attend specialty conferences in their own field at which tutorial sessions on data processing are offered.

At a deeper level of commitment, a physician, hospital administrator, laboratory technologist, medical records librarian, head nurse, or other health care worker with an interest in some aspect of health care computing could audit courses on the subject at a nearby university. Finally, those who wish to gain a working knowledge of health care data processing may be able to arrange a sabbatical with some specialist in the field. Six months or a year will not transform a health care professional with inadequate computer science training into a health care–computing consultant, but it will at least enable such an individual to approach specific health care–computing applications with some confidence and basic knowledge of the many factors involved in their success.

Finally, everything we have said about continuing education for health care–computing specialists also applies to those who must teach themselves something about this discipline.

THE HEALTH CARE–COMPUTING SPECIALIST

Increasingly, we may see physicians, degree nurses, and hospital administrators taking postgraduate university work in health care information science, as they recognize the commitment necessary to obtain a useful background in this subject. At the very least they should learn enough to become adequate and secure users of key products.

However, the average health care worker has such limited experience in computer science that he or she may not be able to overcome the deficiency. Our hope here is that newer tools (such as very high-level languages) will deliver more power directly to the user. If this can be done and the user can directly program an application, then the day-to-day dependence on experts and the long waits for products will be reduced.

Although few health care workers will ever become health care–computing specialists, all will benefit from increased knowledge. Appreciation of the issues involved in health care computing, an understanding of the problems facing health care–

computing specialists, and knowledge of the ways in which they should deal with these problems will greatly enhance users' chances of obtaining the computer services they really require.

Therefore, in the preceding chapters we have looked at the technical issues facing health care–computing projects. In this chapter, we have considered the kind of background and training that a health care–computing specialist ought to have—as much for the enlightenment of the health care workers who rely on their services as for the education of those who wish to become expert in this field.

However, one further aspect of user training should be considered—how to recognize, face, and conquer "the big sell." The user's education as a consumer of health care–computing goods and services cannot be neglected. We now turn our attention to this subject.

CHAPTER 20
CONSPICUOUS COMPUTING

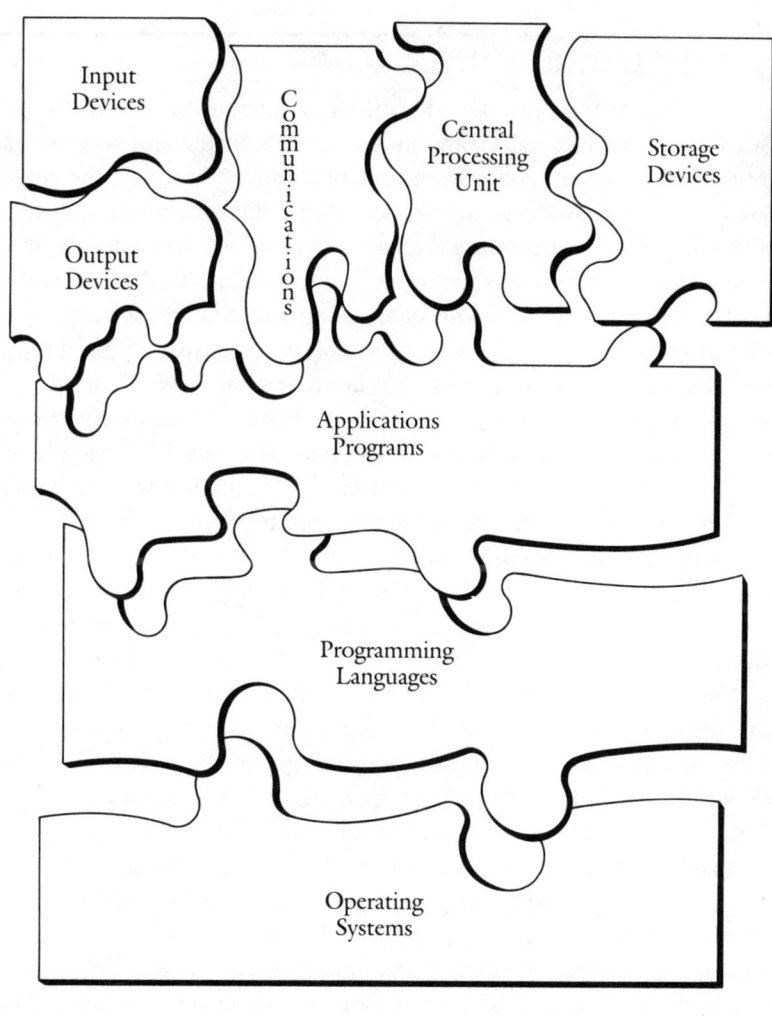

CHAPTER 20

Most of us are aware that computers have made possible many remarkable things. This is not to say that all of these things are necessarily good. Those of us who have ever tried to explain to a bank that it has made a mistake know differently. Nevertheless, computers are generally acknowledged to be a tangible manifestation of the progress and the ingenuity of humankind.

Computers are making substantial contributions to health care, and their technical applications are abundantly published. But the sociology of computing in the health care environment is seldom considered. We believe that, quite apart from any scientific or economic consideration, fantasy and self-aggrandizement are factors responsible for some uses of computers in health care.

CONSUMER EDUCATION

In recent years, consumer education has done much to draw the buyer's attention away from promotional claims in the auto industry and toward practical considerations such as fuel economy and safety features. Similarly, the consumer of health care–computing products and services should become aware of pitfalls for potential buyers in today's marketplace. Let us therefore look more closely at some of these.

Our society believes in science as a source of knowledge and truth. Apart from a few heretics who are suspicious of anything scientific, most people—especially those who think of themselves as scientists—believe that just about everything associated with science represents progress and improvement. The offspring of science is technology, which we can loosely define as the implementation of the lessons of science. The technological imperative—the compulsion to do things simply because they can be done—appears to be a side effect of our fascination with technology.

The computer is the apex of technological development. It is complicated, fast, powerful, and mysterious. It is even difficult to conceptualize, because it performs some functions that used to be considered uniquely human (such as reasoning), yet it is a machine, a tool. A mystique therefore surrounds the computer and everything it touches.

One who is not driven by the technological imperative will be enticed by many to join the computer revolution. It is important to say here that we are not criticizing those who discern needs and use technology fruitfully. It is the irrational users we would like to examine. To motivate potential customers industries use sales gimmicks that we disdain, but to which we are all susceptible. Glossy four-color brochures fill the mailbox of the most casual inquirer. Salespersons come to one's door at the drop of a business reply card. Computers are styled to turn one's head and to get one's attention. Colors are picked with care. Computer chassis are larger than necessary because big is impressive. The true economy and real necessity of a computer system seldom figure in the sell. There is a subtle emphasis on what the computer can do for the product. People who once sold us big fancy cars convinced us that by buying them we could show the world how successful we were. Now, responding to consumer pressure, they have cleverly learned to sell us half the car (for the same money) so we can project self-images of common sense, thrift, and conservation-mindedness.

So with computers. Those of us who are susceptible to consumer pressure at home are also susceptible to the same pressure in our health care facilities. Clever advertising is being used to create needs that health care personnel have not previously felt, and at times the pitch is to the ego—not to real needs. This creation of needs leads to conspicuous computing! For those dazzled by technology the computer turns plain arithmetic into higher mathematics. It transforms a common laboratory into a hotbed of innovation, dignifies ordinary record keeping with the mantle of database management, changes dabbling into a research project and elevates one above one's colleagues. The very presence of such expensive equipment in a department is evidence of being at the leading edge of the discipline.

Those who oversell the computer solution foster the belief that computerization heralds a new era—a quantum leap for the organization or the department.

Too often it is a leap into space. Without knowing precisely why they want a computer, prospects become customers. Under these conditions, acquiring a computer is often an act of faith. A small computer can cost as much as a car, and most minicomputer systems are sometimes more expensive than a house. However, there are no Ralph Naders, no Better Computing Bureaus, and often not even a lawyer hired to uphold one's end of a deal in a contract—if there is a contract. *Caveat emptor* never applied more strongly. The same consumers who would demand guarantees for the functioning of a $50 toaster are remarkably trusting when spending the institution's or the granting agency's money on a health care–computing system!

Computer advertising promises products that work. It assures the consumer that a particular system will solve specific problems. The careful buyer can get such a product (e.g., in an instrument such as a CT scanner in which the built-in computer functions as part of a larger machine; the built-in computer's purpose is well defined, and its functional performance is understood and guaranteed).

The same can also be true of a turnkey computer system that is supposed to work as soon as it is plugged in and turned on (e.g., radiology reporting systems, monitoring systems, admitting/discharge/transfer systems, and cath lab data acquisition systems). The computer system is intended to *be* the instrument—not just to be a controller *in* the instrument, as in the CT scanner.

But a computer system is truly an instrument only to the extent that it is a useful product. The dangers are twofold. First, the general product, designed as a solution to everyone's problem, may not fit one's specific needs, and getting the company that supplies it to do the modifications may be difficult. Second, some systems are put together in a way analogous to assembling the parts of a kit: computer from here, software from there. To continue the automobile analogy, this approach is like buying a crate full of parts to convert a Volkswagen into a dune buggy. The advertising shows a picture of the finished product, but if one assembles the vehicle and it does not run, it is one's own responsibility.

If one purchases the wrong kind of computer instrument, or if one inadvertently assembles a computer monster, then one has only two options. One can either get rid of the computer or one can change the entire department to fit the system such as it is. The latter approach at least spreads the suffering around. There are many places one can visit to see how this is done, but clearly it is not the solution.

At a stratum of complexity above turnkey systems are computer systems that do not even pretend to be finished products. Let us call them general purpose systems. Some hospital information systems require an incredible amount of work to make them do what the specific institution needs. To use the automobile analogy again, what one acquires is the whole assembly line. One will need analysts, programmers, and data clerks to design, tool-up for, assemble, and test whatever the final product may be. Here one must be extremely careful and get professional help.

The ultimate danger is not just failure; the financial losses can be very high.

Disaster will most likely occur if one proceeds solely on the sales pitches of vendors. So, one should actively prepare oneself against being motivated by the glossy brochures and the grand promises. One should not swoon at the thought that computerization will change one into The Bionic Health Care Worker.

Educated consumers of computing products and service for the health care market will know *what* they want and *what* they are getting into. Their knowledge and critical thinking can save them from being gullible marks for sharp salespersons and can help them to get the kinds of systems they really need.

In the long run, knowledgeable consumers will be a boon not only to themselves and to the agencies that ultimately bear the cost of health care computing, but also to the health care data processing industry. No businessperson wants to fight with dissatisfied clients—it is simply bad business. From all points of view, then, the best customer is an educated consumer!

CHAPTER 21

FUNDING HEALTH CARE COMPUTING

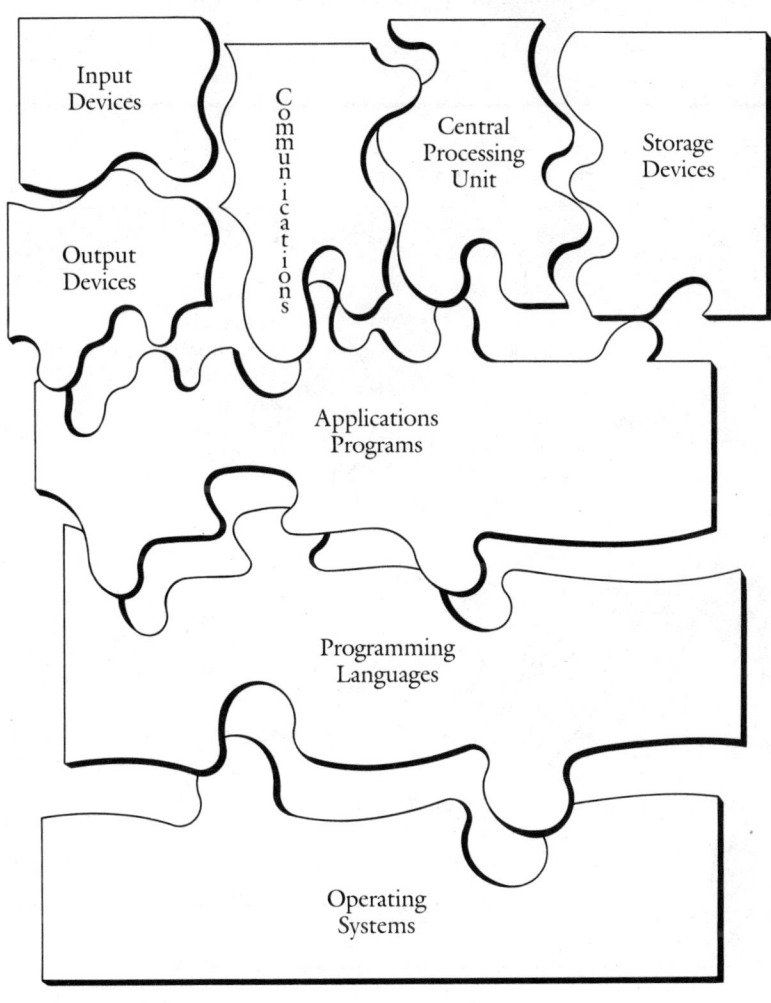

CHAPTER 21

APPLYING FOR MONEY

Medical research projects and pilot projects testing innovative methods of health care delivery cost money. When computers play a part in such projects, they are often a significant cost component. Health care workers who want to undertake expensive work of this sort can obtain funding from a variety of external funding sources (e.g., National Institutes of Health [NIH], National Library of Medicine [NLM], or the Medical Research Council—Canada [MRC]). One who needs only minimum computer services may be able to foot the bill personally for something such as an office computer. Somewhere in-between is the usual process of including and defending a budget item for a computer-based system in a hospital budget request. Usually, it will be necessary to find a separate source of money.

Whether approaching their own departments or an agency for money, health care

FIGURE 21-1
The two sides of the funding problem.

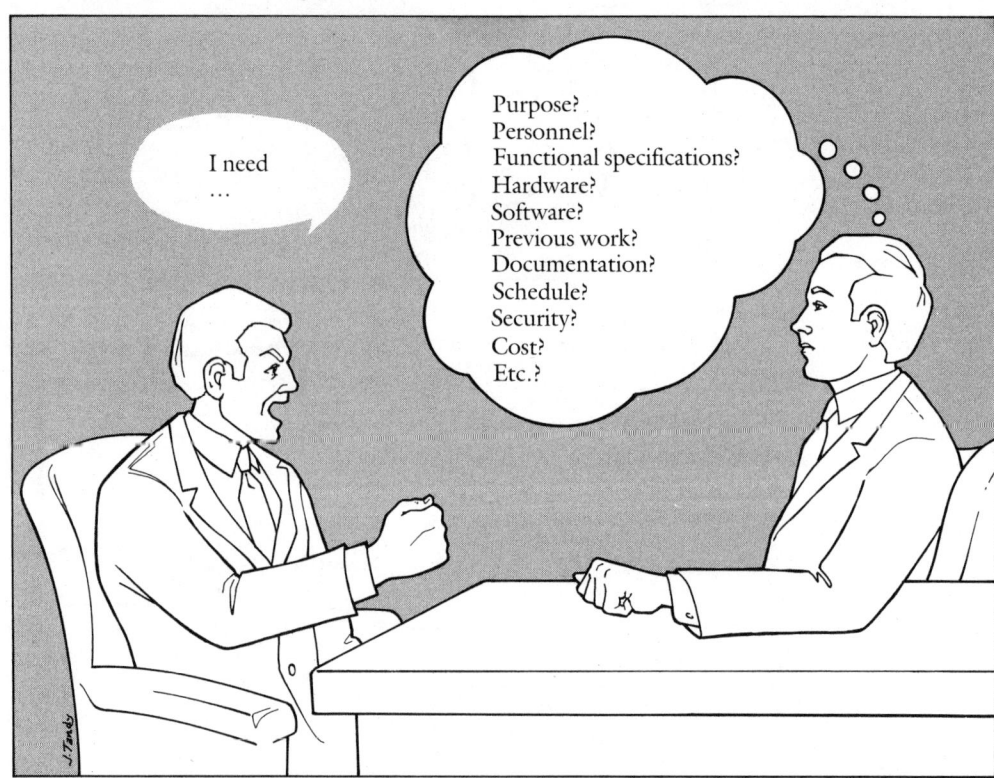

workers will have to convince peers that the proposal is sound (Figure 21-1). A written document is normally the vehicle in which an applicant delivers arguments to those who will decide the fundability of the project. A proposal for a computer system to be used in a health care environment can be constructed so that it anticipates and answers convincingly most of the pointed questions a referee might have. The model proposal will demonstrate that the applicant has considered every one of the critical issues in health care computing and is not just overly optimistic. It will further illustrate that the advocate of the proposal has realistically addressed potential problems and therefore has a good chance of surmounting them.

A PLAN FOR A FORMAL PROPOSAL

A general plan for a formal proposal for a health care–computing system is presented in the following list:

Summary
Introduction to the problem
Functional specification (précis)
Previous work
Critical analysis and comparison
Selection or plan
Economic analysis
Schedule
Operational detail
Appraisal of system
Appendices
    Relevant publications
    Existing systems to choose from
    Functional specification (details)

A document similar to such a plan would be quite suitable for applications for funding from most agencies. Naturally, the precise form will have to be modified somewhat in accordance with the requirements of the various agencies approached, but we can examine generally most of the parts such a document should contain.

SUMMARY

The summary part of the document might be considered an abstract. In technical proposals, this section is often called the "Executive Summary." It is usually not more than five pages long and is devoid of technical jargon. The salient facts of the proposed project should be stated in such a way that those unfamiliar with health care computing can understand the essence of what is being proposed and what its total cost is.

It sometimes happens that a referee is so busy that there will only be time to read this summary. Therefore, this section must be concise, clear, and informative. It may be the most important section of the entire proposal.

Introduction to the Problem

In the introduction to the problem, the problem for which automation is proposed as a solution should be stated and then detailed. The problem area is dissected into component parts and considered judgments made about what parts of the problem will be easy or difficult to solve.

This section would be a good place to demonstrate that one has considered alternative solutions to that problem that do not call for a computer. The reasons why each alternative will not work should be stated. If one cannot state such reasons, one should not be talking about an expensive computer system.

For research projects, experimental methods and justification for the anticipated outcome are fundamental components of any application for funding. It is the responsibility of the applicant to provide this information in the context of the field of research.

When a computer system is proposed as a tool for carrying out a scientific research project, the use of this (probably expensive) instrument will have to be justified. If a small fee for performing a few statistical calculations on a computer system is proposed, there should be no problem. However, at the other extreme, when the computer system itself is the subject of the research (e.g., when an automated decision-making system is proposed as part of a novel method of health care delivery) adequate information must be included in the proposal to demonstrate to reviewers that the approach is sensible and potentially successful.

Functional Specification

Functional specifications have already been explained extensively in Chapter 16. At some point in the formal proposal, one should state the kind of automated solution required to deal adequately with the problem(s) outlined in the previous section. If one has decided to concentrate only on some big, fairly straightforward problem areas and deliberately to avoid small but knotty problems, the functional specification should reflect this choice. This section states what one wants the proposed system to do when it is installed and working.

The functional specification is a comprehensive statement reflecting a broad understanding of many of the issues we have discussed. In addition to the ultimate expected performance of the computer system, other related issues, such as security, must be addressed. It is quite possible to relegate the details of the functional specification to an appendix to make the overall document more readable.

If the proposal is approved, then this functional specification serves as a guideline for suppliers when one requests quotations from them. Finally, it will be incorporated with modifications into a contract.

Previous Work

The previous work section demonstrates that the person making the proposal has done the necessary homework and is intent on avoiding reinvention in cases in which development is proposed. First, there should be a review of the literature about previous similar work, if any. One should include a list of key references. If there are few or even no such references, one should document this and state how this conclusion was reached. If there are one or two particularly relevant review articles, it is often wise to include reprints of them as appendices to this document. This section might not be included or would be quite abridged in an intrainstitutional proposal.

If there are acknowledged experts in the field under consideration or people who have successfully completed somewhat similar work, their names, addresses, and telephone numbers should be included if possible. This attention to detail will make the referees' work easier.

There may be computer products available commercially to perform the kind of work one is contemplating. If one were proposing the acquisition of an automated extensive care unit monitoring system, one should indicate in the proposal the commercial systems available for the purpose and give an evaluation of each one of them. It will suffice to identify the commercial products in this section and to list the companies that supply them, together with the names, addresses, and telephone numbers of local representatives of those companies. The salient features and quoted prices for all of the commercial systems mentioned in this section should be included as another appendix to the entire document. It would not be reasonable to include in the body of the document a detailed analysis of many possible systems, only one (if any) of which will ultimately be proposed.

CRITICAL ANALYSIS AND COMPARISON

In the critical analysis and comparison section, one should compare the functional specifications to the work that has previously been done at other centers or to the presently available commercial products (turnkey systems).

The purpose of this section is to whittle down the field to a list that includes only those products or previous projects that are capable of meeting the functional specifications one has stipulated. If there is no existing work that would suit one's purposes, one should state this here and indicate that one intends to develop a new system or to tailor one (or have it tailored) to meet specific needs.

SELECTION OR PLAN

If one can use a commercially available computer system or a system from some other center, one should specify one's choice in the selection or plan section.

It may be necessary to modify an existing product so that it matches the functional specification. If one takes this approach, one should assess the feasibility and cost of such changes.

On the other hand, one may get to this stage and find out that for the sake of simplicity or for economic reasons, one should modify the functional specifications to match one of the available products! If this is one's honest conclusion, it may be better to go back, rethink the needs, and change the original functional specifications (or at least the phasing or priorities for meeting needs) accordingly.

If there is no existing system capable of meeting the functional specifications, then one puts in a plan for developing a unique system. One should state whether one will be establishing an in-house data processing team or will hire outside developers, and give an accurate impression of the size of the proposed operation and the general length of time one expects development to take (note section on operational detail).

Economic Analysis

At this point in the proposal, one should enumerate the current and projected costs of implementing the automated solution one selected in the previous section. The meaning of cost-benefit justification should be formally defined in the document for the sake of readers who are not familiar with this term, and one should then provide an analysis in detail. Similarly, one should probably define cost-effectiveness before attempting to make some kind of analysis. Remember that very few people have ever demonstrated a computer system to be clinically effective by any quantitative criterion. Referees are not likely to be impressed by claims of improved quality of health care in the absence of compelling arguments or evidence to this effect.

Schedule

One should state the schedule for the development, testing, and implementation of the proposed system. In the schedule, one indicates how the performance of the development team will be monitored. What milestones are to be used? What is the schedule for achieving these milestones? The schedule for testing and debugging the system, for installing it on the premises, and for running it in parallel with manual procedures, together with the date on which one plans to commit oneself exclusively to automated methods, should be listed.

Operational Detail

The operational detail section of the proposal should discuss how the computer system will be managed on a day-to-day basis, once it is operational. The overall process in which the computer may be only one cog should be outlined, and the computer's role in this process should be detailed. How will the computer impact on the people using it and on the way they do business?

Equally important is a consideration of how quality control of the automated system would be ensured. It is relatively easy to define a data collection system in support of clinical trials. It is difficult, on the other hand, to guarantee that data essential to the success of the research will be collected and input into the computer system correctly.

Appraisal of System

How will one know whether the computer system has achieved the goals one set for it? What is the acceptance test procedure (ATP) that must run correctly before the system can be accepted from a developer? One should include the details of these tests. How will failure be recognized if it occurs, and what will one do to cut losses if necessary? It has often happened that a computer system directed to a specific purpose has seemed like a good idea in the proposal, but has been unworkable in the implementation. Given such experience, it only makes sense for the applicant to leave open reasonable escape routes. There is nothing shameful about an honest experiment that ends in honest failure. Indeed, this kind of experience may be a valuable lesson to future workers in the area.

APPENDICES

The four appendices already mentioned (relevant survey articles, analysis of available systems from which to choose, the details of the functional specifications, and the details of the ATP) will be included at the end of the application for funding. In addition, any other relevant appendices that do not logically belong in the body of the text can be included here.

Generally speaking, one should keep the body of any document as thin and to-the-point as possible. Referees do not have much time to wade through a large stack of paper. They want to get at the facts of the proposal and be secure that further details and documentary evidence are available in appendices if required.

• • •

It is desirable to structure an application for funding in the previously outlined way for two reasons. First, a well-planned and persuasively stated proposal is much more likely to evoke a favorable response than a vague request will. Enlightened self-interest should be motivation enough for the would-be user of health care–computing systems to accept this somewhat compulsive format.

But the second reason for making an organized, thoughtful proposal goes far beyond personal interest. Society can no longer sanction the expenditure of large sums of money on questionable medical research or flashy health care gadgetry. The perception that computers are supposed to be modern and progressive does not qualify them for use in the health care environment. They are costly and difficult to employ intelligently, and when misused, they can have a deleterious influence on health care. Those who would embark on a course that involves automation, therefore, have a responsibility to consider all of the issues implicit in a move towards health care computing, and a proposal such as the one outlined here helps the person originating a computer project to remember all of the issues.

The effort required to produce such a document is considerable, but it is worthwhile. Those who make the effort and who know enough about health care computing to perform the task adequately may be satisfied that they are proceeding in an informed, reasonable, and ethical manner. Their goals, their reasons for using computers, their logic in making their selection, and the financial implications of their proposals will all be laid out plainly, so their peers can also make a reasonable, informed decision.

It is impossible to know with certainty where automation will lead the healing arts. The benefits health care may reap from computers may be limited only by our imagination. But the potential dangers—financial and ethical—are sufficiently plain that everyone who works in this expanding field has a personal obligation to keep both eyes open. Everyone who proposes, designs, or introduces computer systems in the health care environment must understand the issues underlying health care automation.

Through our continuing efforts to cope with all of the implications of the grand new technology at our disposal we can determine whether computers will be abused as agents of dehumanization, or whether computers will be incorporated as our faithful servants.

CHAPTER 22
THE FUTURE OF HEALTH CARE COMPUTING

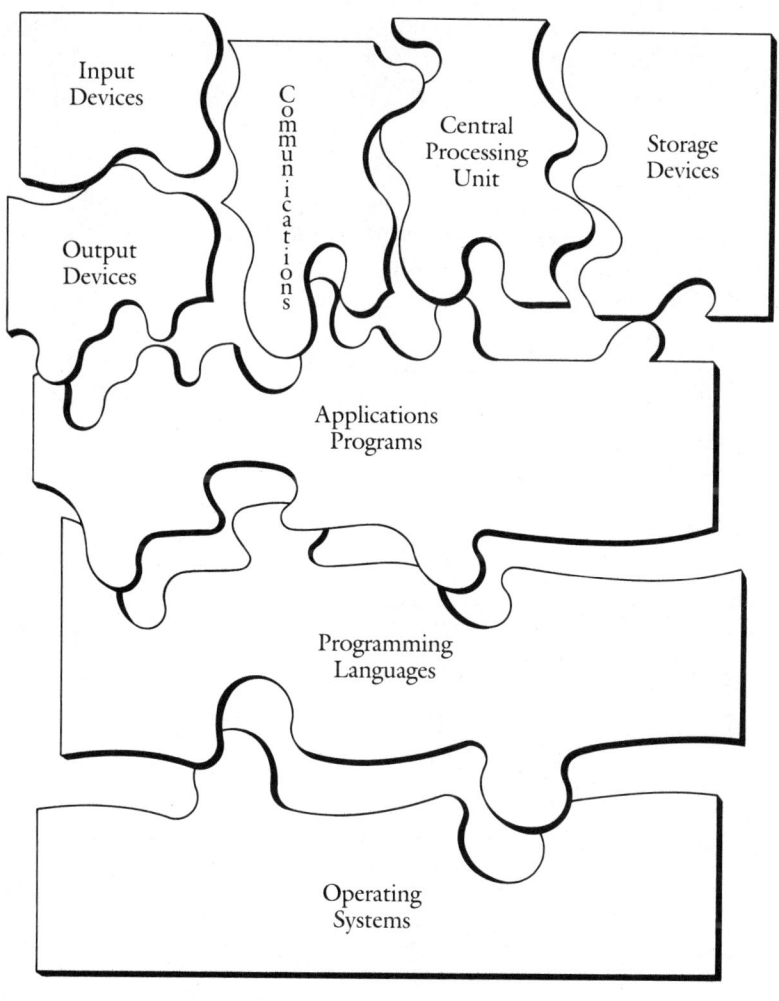

CHAPTER 22

Many predictions about the future of technology have been inaccurate in the expected length of time it would take for events to occur. Greater inaccuracies come, however, not from what we know, but from what we do not know. We cannot usually foresee real revolution.

Regarding computers, this has certainly been true.

Twenty years ago, ambitious engineering students and faculty members sometimes built their own computers at great expense and with hundreds of hours of effort. The home-brew computers these pioneers developed were just novelties. They could not be programmed easily and once programmed they often could not save the program for later retrieval on a mass storage device. The output of these machines was usually very restricted. These interesting projects in electrical engineering were done to try new ideas and to gain experience—not usually to support an application as mundane as business or health care.

However, today the situation has changed beyond the wildest dreams of even the visionaries of the last decade. For less than $20, one can purchase a basic calculator that performs arithmetical, trigonometric, some algebraic, and even statistical functions. For less than $200, one can purchase a programmable calculator similar in physical size but with the ability to store many hundreds of programming steps. Firmware read-only memory modules, providing preprogrammed packages for applications such as statistics or accounting, can be purchased separately and are plugged into the calculator as required.

Today we are able to obtain complete microprocessor-based systems (with disks, tape, and terminals) that are far more powerful than the computers of yesteryear, but whose price is less than a single terminal was just a few years ago.

Twenty years ago, these commonplace realities would have seemed like fantasies. Because the modern computer reality has so richly outdone the most optimistic predictions of its advocates, it would not be unreasonable for us to imagine that the future impact of computers on health care may be bound only by our imagination and not by technical limitations.

WHY USE A COMPUTER SYSTEM IN HEALTH CARE?

How computers serve health care will always depend on our insight into their relevance and on how we choose to use them. We can now already distinguish several important roles for computers.

PERSONNEL AUGMENTATION

Computer systems can be used to augment human resources wherever there exists a tested, working, and proven manual process where it is necessary to expand capacity, increase speed, or eliminate redundancy. A computer properly integrated into such a situation can enhance the productivity of existing personnel so they can handle an increased workload more easily or an existing workload more quickly or less expensively. Computer systems used in such situations should be less expensive than hiring additional people to cope with the increased workload at the same level of quality, and they should not decrease the overall effectiveness or usefulness of the procedure. Preferably, the computer should enhance the environment, not dehumanize it.

To illustrate how computers can enhance the roles of humans within an organization, let us consider how a fully automated cardiac pacemaker registration system could operate in a typical hospital.

With high labor costs it was expensive to maintain active, long-term followup on every patient who had ever received a cardiac pacemaker in our hypothetical hospital. Analysis of pacemaker failure in cohorts of patients with similar types of pacemakers was out of the question. Consequently, the standard procedure for replacing a pacemaker was either to wait until it started to malfunction and the patient got into trouble, or to replace an implant long before it was expected to wear out. Either way the situation was undesirable. After computerization, however, all recipients of a cardiac pacemaker have been registered on a computer-based system for several years. Patients who have pacemakers can telephone at regular intervals, and by placing simple-to-use electrodes under their arms, they can transmit a rhythm strip to the computer over the telephone. The computer notes if there is any impending malfunction in the pacemaker and issues warning letters to the patient and the health care provider, as required. It has thus been possible to prolong the useful life of a pacemaker implant, thereby saving money, inconvenience, and surgical morbidity for the patients. Moreover, when it is discovered that a particular kind of pacemaker is failing prematurely, it is a simple matter to locate and recall all patients with similar equipment for prophylactic replacement. This feat would have been impossible without some kind of up-to-date registry. Thus, computers can be used in a pacemaker clinic to enhance the clinical effectiveness of the existing clinic staff personnel. They can now anticipate and prevent emergencies, rather than merely respond to them. Patient care has been improved.

A completely automated system such as the one described here could be implemented by simply combining features of partially automated pacemaker followup systems already in existence throughout the world.

Management Augmentation

When an existing process is soundly conceived, useful, and efficient, but very tedious or complex, maintaining and managing that process may be difficult. The amount of paperwork involved in documenting and ensuring that all of the steps in a complicated procedure are carried out may be burdensome. In such cases, computers can serve a policing or disciplinarian role, because these machines are capable of attention to even the most tedious details of a management process. Moreover, the system can measure parameters of performance and provide information to management, so that various aspects of a complex process can be quality-controlled or modified as required for increased efficiency.

As an extension of management augmentation, a computer can be used to implement a very complicated process that because of its intricate and consequently expensive management requirements could not be implemented in any other way. In such cases the computer is used as the framework on which a new process is built.

One good example in health care research is using a computer to manage clinical trials. Accurate and complete patient identification and documentation, as well as continuous monitoring of the data collection process itself (protocol management), can reduce the cost of carrying out trials with a significant decrease in the effort necessary for quality control. Systems now exist in experimental form that can do this.

Brain Augmentation

An ideal use of computers is to augment people's ability to handle information and to make decisions. Computers can perform feats of calculation, information storage and retrieval, and data manipulation that would be impossible to accomplish manually.

An extension of this capability is using computers to simulate processes to refine our understanding of a phenomenon. Physiological and biochemical models are two examples relevant to health care. Similarly, a computer can be used to model a complex procedure, so that we may study inherent time delays, costs, and bottlenecks.

In the near future, we might expect significant advances in computer-aided diagnosis and decision making. These are essentially modeling problems, and as we gain more insight into the ways in which health care providers approach clinical management, it will become increasingly more possible to assist them in this process by using computer-based models.

WHEN A COMPUTER SYSTEM IS INAPPROPRIATE IN HEALTH CARE

We have examined general roles for computers in health care both now and in the future. However, computers are sometimes proposed or used for irrational reasons. One would hope that in the future we would be able to avoid what we might call the antiroles of computers in medicine.

Robot Health Care Providers

We believe that computers should not be used as a means of directly diagnosing or recommending treatment to human patients without the supervision of human health care providers—even when this is already possible. Computers must be used to assist but never to replace the health care provider. Many of the decisions a health care provider must make have as much (or more) to do with assessing the emotional status of the patient, intuition, and perceiving the patient's willingness to endure treatment, as they do with purely technical matters. The warmth, concern, perception, sensitivity, and compassion that are integral to the healing arts can never be replaced by technology, and those who attempt to do so are ignorant of the capabilities of computers and of the complexity of human processes. Another factor to be considered is the raw reliability of computer hardware and software in such systems. Is current technology really up to direct patient interaction without overview? We think not for several years.

SELF-AGGRANDIZEMENT

Because computers are expensive, and because their implementation has a drastic impact on all users, these machines are potentially disruptive tools, subject to abuses of local political power. Disaster is the result when the hospital administration, one health care department, a clique, or an individual has a stranglehold on data processing within an institution through the control of a centralized computer facility or its development staff. Those who crave technology as a means of demonstrating scientific leadership or of otherwise impressing their colleagues can waste a great deal of other people's time, effort, and money, once they perceive the computer to be the most prestigious vehicle for an ego trip. As automation makes ever greater inroads into the health care scene, all concerned parties must beware of people who want computers for various kinds of self-aggrandizement.

SUPPORTING OBSOLETE METHODS

A common abuse of computers is to use them to prolong outmoded management practices. State-operated health insurance plans are one example. Some existing centralized systems are too large to serve adequately the people who depend on them. In one Canadian province, for instance, it is estimated there are more employees working for the provincial health insurance plan than there are physicians in the whole province. The system is inefficient and technically obsolete. Without computer support it would probably have been changed.

If there were no computers, such unmanageable centralized schemes would be replaced by a network of much smaller local offices that would be able to process their business in a more timely and efficient manner, probably with less danger of making mistakes and with more potential for correcting errors.

Although health care is no longer the growth industry it once was, it will continue to grow in the future. We should beware lest computers be used to prop up obsolete procedures in health care administration when decentralization or innovation is really indicated.

ROBBING PEOPLE OF WORK

There is a risk, not only in health care but also in all types of business, that in the future computers will take over more and more of the interesting and challenging aspects of work, causing people to lose their skills, leaving them with only boring, "watching the gauges" functions. We would hope that in the future, health care will avoid using computers merely to replace human beings unless significant savings or measurable improvements in health care delivery can be effected by so doing. In other words, automation should proceed because of necessity.

ENSHRINING THE THEORETICAL

Whenever a computer system is used in the health care environment in the future, let us hope it is used in accordance with proven, well-thought-out principles.

Because computers require quantifying and simplifying reality into discrete parameters that can be measured, stored, retrieved, and processed, there will always be a danger they will be used to oversimplify reality, especially when the original conception of reality is faulty. Computers do just what we tell them—the ultimate embodiment of the "we only followed orders" personality. All of the thinking must be done by people before they bring a computer into the picture. Until we have systems that can "learn" we must follow this advice.

A PROMISING FUTURE

If computers were to be applied in health care to exploit their positive aspects, and if health care could avoid their potentially bad features, then the future of health care computing might be rosy indeed. Let us try to imagine where computers in health care are going.

HARDWARE ADVANCES

First of all, computers are going out of sight—and ultimately, out of mind. The trend in computer hardware is toward miniaturization. This trend will probably continue. Currently, computers and their peripheral devices are becoming portable and affordable, but there is still a ways to go until they are truly convenient and easy to use. To succeed as commonplace, everyday instruments, they will have to become even less obtrusive, more portable, more powerful (of the class currently called work stations), and easier for the average person to use (e.g., using a mouse or touch screen input, and voice and/or graphic output).

Computer systems in health care will become more justifiable on purely economic grounds because they will become cheaper, and therefore they will become more common in everyday health care. Microprocessor technology has already drastically influenced the design and the cost of computer hardware, but this effect is just a start.

The coming years should see the widespread use of computer-controlled devices that can be implanted in the human body. As the machinery of computers becomes smaller and smaller, computers will be able to become parts in more elaborate instruments such as "intelligent" pacemakers, artificial limbs, and perhaps, someday, even a long-term artificial heart. (One already exists that holds patient data, as well as a summary of the last 48 hours of antiarrhythmic pacing!) It is not at all difficult to imagine that the miniaturization of computer hardware and the development of new power sources and transducers will soon make The Bionic Man a matter of commonplace experience, not of science fiction.

One can imagine that a means will be found to interface computers with the human nervous system. Such an advance would make possible the creation of artificial eyes, ears, and voice generation. Some research examples of each of these already exist.

Intelligent, implantable devices that are capable of measuring such variables as heart rate, rhythm, and blood pressure and blood chemistry could automatically infuse antiarrhythmic drugs to control arrhythmias.

Implantable devices containing a computer could also be used beneficially in high-risk patients. An implantable device might be designed for patients with a history of severe heart disease. When the computer detected a dangerous arrhythmia, it could automatically dial an ambulance to take the patient to a hospital. This kind of device is realizable today. The communications technology and the computer itself already exist. Here the big limit is in understanding arrhythmias. When they have been understood, the development of appropriate control software will be possible. This area will be the subject of intensive research in the near future.

Advances in digital communications and storage devices will also have a profound influence on the use of computers in health care. The ideal of a "cradle-to-grave" medical record is now possible. Given the mobility of our population and the relative expense and awkwardness of communications facilities we still are a ways from a practical system. However, as it becomes cheaper and easier to transmit volumes of data over distances, the distributed database of medical records will become a reality. We also expect imminently the use of new optical or laser disk technology to store radiographs and other images, making them easily retrievable.

Another approach to the lifelong personal medical record may be a record that patients carry with them wherever they go. It is not difficult to conceptualize a tiny storage device that could be implanted in a patient's body (subject, of course, to the patient's approval!). At a hospital there would be a device for reading this history and for updating it as required. This has been done on a minor scale in pacemakers already.

SOFTWARE ADVANCES

Software development will begin to keep up with advancing hardware technology. We are actually able to look forward to computer systems that can respond to "natural language" in the form of typed input or even in the form of speech. Commercially available terminals already exist that can recognize 100 different words spoken to them. Eventually computers may be able to interpret drawings and pictures as easily as we can. The overall trend in the future should be towards computer systems that ordinary people can use and program effectively with little prior training. Although they will be far more common, computers will become infinitely less conspicuous.

In graphics, computers as parts of computed tomography instruments have already been used to show health care providers what their own eyes cannot see. We have graphic computer output in three or more dimensions (e.g., one of these additional dimensions may be time). Computer-generated movies, though already impressive, are still in their infancy, and much more elaborate 3D (holographic) output is ultimately in the offing.

When hardware and software advance sufficiently, people will be able to interact with the computer more directly. Already patients can have their blood pressure checked by a machine in many shopping centers. Would it be unreasonable to predict that at some future date a patient may be able to undergo an automated routine checkup? The patient could converse with a computer that would ask relevant questions and listen to the spoken answers. Then the machine would make some biological measurements, using a few attached devices such as those to measure blood pressure, heart rate, and ECG. These sorts of machines would be used principally for routine physical examinations. If anything significant were found, the patient would be instructed to see a human health care provider. It has already been conceded that an annual routine physical examination for every citizen would be economically impossible. Computers might help make it possible, given the (admittedly questionable) assumption that a good reason exists for conducting such screening examinations of symptomless people.

In the near future, we would expect to see tremendous advances in the development of health care knowledge-based systems, including the delivery of practical useful products. We are already learning effective ways to represent our understanding of pathological processes and treatment strategies. By using sophisticated artificial intelligence systems, we will be able to test, check, and verify hypotheses with an ease not previously imagined. At the very least we can expect such programs as these to be scrutinizing the diagnoses we make, the treatments we recommend, and the efficiency of the overall patient management process.

ADVANCES IN OUR ATTITUDES

As the field of health care learns to rely on the methods of systems analysis to employ computers effectively where they are most needed, it may learn to use these and other analytical tools to study more objectively the things that are done in health care. Dogmas will be evaluated and empirical procedures will be increasingly questioned. The tendency of the health care establishment to adopt potentially hazardous investigations and treatments that have not passed objective tests of efficacy or cost justification may slowly come to an end as computers make large and complex evaluations of treatments and investigative procedures easier to carry out. Large cooperative studies have always been difficult to manage; automation is already simplifying such studies and may thereby encourage them.

The computer has arrived at a time when health care providers are becoming aware that clinical research is a professional activity in its own right. Computers may be one of the most powerful tools for future clinical researchers. Automation may thereby greatly reduce the reliance of medical science on the inconclusive case studies whose results are due to data dredging. Computers may assist in bringing in a new era in which demonstrable conclusions replace results that are merely sampling effects.

Automation may also help the field of health care to make a good adjustment to the problems induced by extreme specialization. The average patient is bewildered by the increasing compartmentalization of health care into specialties, subspecialties, and sub-subspecialties.

In fact, the general practitioner is often confused. Any specialist is well aware of the numerous inappropriate referrals he or she receives. Any social worker is aware of the many patients whose welfare seems to be overlooked, because each of several agencies assumes that somebody else is responsible for the client. Interns and residents know that the more specialists involved in a case, the more likely something will go wrong. Automated systems may someday help general practitioners and their patients to navigate through the increasingly complex maze of specialists, hospitals, and social services, making sure that the vital central factor—the patient—is not forgotten in the shuffle, that adequate records are kept, and that the quality of the overall process is maintained.

A POSITIVE INFLUENCE

Assuming that proper respect is paid to the practical issues in health care computing, there is reason to presume that automation will play a substantial and beneficial role in the future of health care. If we use these machines to do the things we cannot do manually, to help us do what we do not have time or staff to do presently, and to encourage us to look at health care from a more scientific viewpoint, then we will be using computers appropriately, and we can expect the maximum benefit from them.

How we choose to use automation will determine its ultimate impact on the future of health care, for it seems probable that computer technology, like all the rest of technology, will advance faster than we know how to use it in the service of humankind.

GLOSSARY

Access To retrieve information from some **storage device** such as **internal memory,** disk, or tape. The access time is the time it takes to locate data, retrieve it, and place it in a **register** where it can be operated on. The access time for data in internal memory is usually 1 μsec (microsecond) or less, whereas for a disk it is typically greater than 10 to 15 millisec. See also **Random access memory.**

Acoustic coupler A device for changing a sequential train of pulses, corresponding to a **binary** number, into sounds of a given frequency, which are piped into the mouthpiece of a standard telephone receiver. The reverse process is achieved by changing the received sounds back into a train of pulses.

Address The numerical designation given to a memory **location.**

Algorithm Sequences of logical steps that carry out specific **tasks,** operations, and transformations of data. An exact description of the solution to a problem.

Alphanumeric The set of all alphabetic and numeric characters.

Analog computers Computers that perform operations on continuous signals. Their output is in the form of continuous signals, such as voltage fluctuations or waveforms.

Analog-to-digital converter An **input device** for changing continuous physical (analog) signals into digital form (i.e., discrete numbers). A digital-to-analog converter does the opposite and has application in electronic and electromechanical **output devices.**

Applications package A self-contained collection of **programs** designed to serve some specific set of requirements (an application). A good commercial example would be the SPSS statistics package that is sold as a unit.

Applications program A **program,** written by users or supplied by a company, that serves a particular need or set of needs. Examples of an applications program would be a program to generate a specific report or a program to perform a particular set of calculations. Most of the time, a high-level **programming language** is used.

Arithmetic unit That part of the **central processing unit** that carries out arithmetic operations such as add or subtract, increment or decrement.

Assembler A **programming language** that allows the use of mnemonic codes for machine instructions and symbols for variables, which are then processed and turned into **machine language.**

Asynchronous In asynchronous transmission, data is sent one **character** at a time, and the time of arrival of characters at the receiver is arbitrary (see Figure 3-2).

Backup The process of creating a computer-compatible duplicate of information stored on a **computer system.** Also the procedure for redundantly recording information. Backup hardware usually refers to a duplicate or equivalent of any **peripheral device** or of the computer itself. Backup procedure usually refers to a procedure, ordinarily paper-based, for manually recording and managing information during a systems failure.

Words in the explanations that are themselves defined in this glossary are printed in **boldface.** For other, more complete sources of definitions of data processing terms, see *International Microcomputer Dictionary* (SYBEX, 1981).

Bar code One of a variety of schemes for representing numeric or **alphanumeric** (letters and number digits) sequences, typically as black stripes of varied width and spacing. One variation of these appears on many consumer packages.

Batch operating system For an adequately detailed explanation of this topic, see Chapter 6.

Binary Refers to numbers of base 2. Such numbers can be composed of only the digits 0 and 1: numbers are thus strings of 0s and 1s, in which each digit position towards the left represents an increasing power of 2. The number "101" (101_2) is read from right to left as $(1 \times 2) + (1 \times 2) = (1 + 4) = 5$. Computers use binary numbers because such numbers are easy to represent as on and off states in simple circuits and because they are easy to process, since rules for logical and arithmetical operations in base 2 can be implemented in simple circuits.

Bit Constructed from the words **BI**nary digi**T**, bit refers to a single digit of a **binary** number (e.g., the binary number 101 is composed of three bits). The bit is the smallest unit of information in the computer. It can represent the response to a yes/no question or any two-state information. It represents a switch in an on or off state, or, on storage medium, a magnetized or nonmagnetized state.

Bug An unintentional error in a **program**. See also **debugging**.

Bundled Refers to the fact that the cost of the **software** is included in the overall price of a **computer system**. This often means that the software cannot be obtained separately (cf. **unbundled**).

Byte The number of **bits** required to encode one **character** of information in any given **computer system**. In most **minicomputers**, two bytes of eight bits each form one **word**.

Cathode ray tube (CRT) An electronic tube (e.g., the familiar television picture tube), in which an electron beam is deflected in patterns and hits a phosphor, which makes its output visible to a human. Sometimes called a visual display unit (VDU) or a video display terminal (VDT).

Central processing unit (CPU) The part or parts of computer **hardware** that carry out data manipulation (**processing** or moving data) and control the sequence of operations performed by the computer. One important part of the CPU is the **arithmetic unit,** which performs arithmetic. Another part is the **control unit** that supervises the sequencing of operations. The **internal memory** contains the **instructions (programs)** that determine what is to be done and in what sequence.

Channel A pathway for data into or out of a **computer system**. Usually it is made up of multiple parallel wires, each of which transfers one **bit** of a **byte** or **word** simultaneously.

Character Any letter, digit, or punctuation mark. Characters are usually represented by a **binary** code composed of eight or nine **bits**. Such a code, and any piece of information eight or nine bits in length, is usually referred to as a **byte.**

Coding The process of representing information in some other form. To encode data involves changing it from one form such as decimal to another form such as **binary**. To decode data means to change it back from encoded to original form. When referring to a **program,** coding refers to the action of writing the programs in a given programming language.

Compiler A **program** that translates a human-readable **source code** into a more machine like **object code.** The object code may be an intermediate code to be further translated into **machine language,** or it may actually be machine language.

Computer Usually refers to an entire **computer system** (the **processor** plus all **peripheral devices**). Actually it should refer only to the **central processing unit,** although it may also include the **internal memory.**

Computer-aided instruction (CAI) Using a **computer system** in education. In health care training, computers have been used to provide multiple-choice quizzes or even to simulate patients or physiological systems.

Computer output microfilm (COM)   A device for producing photographic film output directly from a computer. Such devices are very high speed, often using an electron beam on a **cathode ray tube** to produce light patterns that can be recorded on film.

Computer system   Always refers to the entire **hardware** package and would most properly also include all **software.** The emphasis is on a working whole.

Control unit   That part of the **central processing unit** that directs the sequence of operations, such as which **instruction** is to be **executed** next.

Cylinder   On a **disk** pack, a cylinder is a stack of **tracks,** all of which are equidistant from the central axle. In a disk pack, the nth cylinder consists of the nth track on each surface of every platter. Because the **read/write** heads of a disk pack are ganged, it increases efficiency to store related data on cylinders so that all data can be read without having to reposition the heads.

Data access arrangement (DAA)   A mechanism sometimes required by the telephone company that goes between a device and the telephone line on which the device will transmit or receive. Its claimed purpose is to prevent electrical damage to the telephone system.

Data definition language (DDL)   A special group of commands used in **database** management systems that allows the definition of the structure and contents of the database.

Data-entry clerk   A staff person whose role is to transcribe or to input directly into a **computer** via some **input device.**

Data management language (DML)   A group of commands that give a **programmer** a standard method of storing and retrieving data when using a **database** system.

Data processing consultant   An expert in using computers in specific applications environments (e.g., a business data processing consultant or a health care data processing consultant).

Database   An organization of information into files for central access, modification, and retrieval.

Dataset   See **modem.**

Debugging   The process of discovering and correcting errors in **programs.**

Digital computer   A device that performs calculations and manipulates data composed of discrete elements such as numbers. Most modern digital computers work in the **binary** number system.

Disk   A type of storage using oxide-coated circular platters. Data is stored on the platter along **tracks** as magnetized regions. Information is recorded or retrieved by inserting the disk into a disk **drive,** which contains a read/write head that moves over the spinning disk in line with a track.

Diskette   Sometimes called **floppy disks** or flexible disks. A diskette is an oxide-coated, flexible-plastic magnetic recording **medium. Access** time is slow, often exceeding 100 μsec, and capacity is small, usually less than 1 megabyte. However, diskettes are relatively inexpensive.

Distributed processing   Using a mix of local and remote computer power, available for solving a user's problem.

Documentation   User documentation: an instruction manual or its equivalent that provides users with sufficient information to use a system. Systems documentation: a description of **hardware** and **software,** contained in a variety of manuals. **Program** documentation: a concise, complete expose of what a program does and how it does it, on both an overall basis and on a detailed basis. Documentation is most important when someone other than the original **programmer** must correct or extend a program.

Dot matrix A method of producing **characters** for viewing by either brightening or darkening an appropriate combination of dots in a two-dimensional array. Most dot matrix representations are 5 horizontal points × 7 vertical points, or 7 horizontal points × 9 vertical points.

Down, down-time Period of time during which a **computer system** is not functioning. Scheduled down-time is the time during which the system is not available, not because it has failed but because it is performing functions such as **backup,** or because preventive **hardware** maintenance is being done. Unscheduled down-time is an unexpected systems failure.

Drive A mechanical mechanism on which a magnetic secondary-storage **medium** is mounted to make its data accessible to the **computer** (e.g., **disk** drive or tape drive). A drive contains all electrical and mechanical components necessary to **read** or **write** data on its medium, but it often excludes its controller, which controls the flow of data between the computer and the drive.

Dumb terminal A **terminal** that does not possess any intrinsic data processing capability and that acts as a pure **input** or **output device.**

Execute To perform the operation indicated by an **instruction.** If the instruction is "add," to execute "add" is to carry out the addition. To execute a **program,** a **computer** does what is specified by the instructions that make up the program.

Fail-soft Describes a mechanism that permits a **computer system** to continue in operation, although at a reduced capacity or with reduced **resources,** after a failure of part of the system.

Firmware instructions, routines, and **programs** Today these are typically implemented in **read only memory (ROM)** and are available for **execution** but not for alteration.

Floppy disk See **diskette.**

Flow charting A graphic representation (by using blocks and arrows) of the logical sequence of the **execution** of a **program.**

Full duplex The ability of a communications linkage to send and to receive simultaneously on the same line.

Gigabyte (Gb) One billion **bytes;** 1000 **Mb.**

Half duplex A communications linkage that can send and receive, but not simultaneously. Sometimes the term "simplex" is used for a linkage that can only send or receive.

Hard copy Any human-readable output from a **computer** that is produced on paper or other permanent **media.**

Hard disk A disk that is rigid (made of metal or fiberglass) as opposed to being flexible—as is the case with a **floppy disk.**

Hardware The physical devices included in a **computer system.**

Hard-wired Physically (and usually permanently) connected to a **computer,** usually by an electronic conductor. Hard-wired **programs:** on old computers, programs actualized in the form of interconnections of wires on **patchboards.** A method still used on **analog computers** to process continuous signals instead of digital (numerical) information.

Input device A machine capable of accepting data and making it available for **processing** in a form acceptable to a **computer.**

Instruction One of the fundamental operations that can be performed by a computer (e.g., "add").

Intelligent terminal A **computer peripheral device** that, in addition to providing input and output facilities, also allows some **processing** and often storage of data. Intelligent terminals can sometimes operate in a stand-alone mode (not connected to any other computer) for the purpose of data collection. When a data collection session is complete, the **terminal**

can then be connected to the main computer and the data can be transferred from the intelligent terminal to the main computer.

Internal memory The storage facilities in a **computer system** where **programs** and data are placed immediately before **execution.** It is usually the highest-speed memory on a computer system, although sometimes small higher-speed cache memories are made part of the internal memory.

Interpreter A **program** that translates the statements written in some **programming language** and executes them one statement or one group of statements at a time. No **object code** is produced. An example is the BASIC interpreter used on many **microcomputers.**

Interpreting Using a special version of a **keypunch** machine to print in human-readable form across the top of **punched cards** the information that is represented by their punched holes.

Joystick A device for inputting **X-Y** coordinates by movements of a lever to drive the motions of a cursor on a graphic screen—up, down, left, and right.

Kbyte (Kb) One "thousand" **bytes.** See **Kilo (K).**

Keypunch A keyboard device for producing cards with punched holes.

Kilo (K) For our purposes, 1000. In "computerese," usually means 1024 (2^{10}—the closest number to the decimal number 1000 in the **binary** system).

Light pen A small penlike **input device** used to point out choices or to draw lines on a **cathode ray tube.** Electronics associated with the light pen enable the **computer** to determine the position on the screen at which it is being pointed.

Line printer A high-speed impact **hard-copy output device.** Line printers usually use a rapidly rotating chain containing several copies of their **character** set. Multiple hammers, one in each print position, strike the chain at the time when desired characters are in position. Thus, when the chain is appropriately aligned, multiple characters of any given line are printed simultaneously. This printing process is much faster than hard copy **terminals** that print only one character at a time.

Location The place in or on a **storage device** where a single piece of data or a single **instruction** is stored.

Machine language The **instructions** of a **computer system.** These are usually **binary** numbers and are idiosyncratic to any given type of computer.

Macro The name given to a **routine** written in **assembler** and used as a unit by the assembly-language **programmer,** who usually uses symbols to invoke the routine.

Magnetic-ink computer-readable (MICR) A special **character** font printed with magnetic ink. This is the well-known character set often used by artists to depict **computer** printing. It was first used for **processing** checks in banks. Such characters are still frequently seen on checks, although more human-readable **optical character recognition** fonts have replaced MICR characters in most other applications.

Magnetic memory Any memory device using magnetic fields as a means for storing data.

Magnetic strip card A small card resembling a credit card to which a strip of magnetizable material is affixed. Data can be **read** from or written onto this magnetic strip. An example of a common application for these cards is in the entrances to the subway system in Washington, D.C. In health care, these cards are useful for containing identification or clinical information on ambulatory patients.

Management consultant A person involved in advising administrators, especially regarding organizational matters. Consultants are becoming increasingly involved in data processing and its impact on the organizations that use it.

Mass storage device A **secondary memory device** holding large amounts of data.

Maxicomputer Those computers most commonly found in large computer centers, typically with prices in the million-dollar range (e.g., IBM's model 3033 or 3038).

Mean time between failures (MTBE) The average length of time that will elapse between successive failures of any device.

Mean time to repair (MTTR) The average amount of time it takes to restore a failed device to functioning status.

Medium Any carrier on which data may be recorded (e.g., paper, disks, magnetic tape, paper tape, or **punched cards**). Plural: media.

Megabyte (Mb or Mbyte) One million **bytes**; 1000 **Kb**.

Memory size The total amount of memory of a given type (such as **internal memory**) in a **computer system**.

Microcomputer Usually refers to a complete **computer system** built around a **microprocessor CPU**.

Microprocessor Usually refers to a **central processing unit (CPU)** formed on a single integrated circuit chip, though sometimes a few chips are used. Early microprocessors had 8-**bit words,** though some now have 16-bit words, making them virtually miniprocessors-on-a-chip.

Midicomputer Colloquial term sometimes used to describe computers in the fuzzy zone between large **minicomputers** and small **maxicomputers** (e.g., Digital Equipment's PDP 11/70 and DEC system 20, Hewlett-Packard's HP3000, or Interdata 7/32).

Minicomputer An imprecise term usually referring to computers of moderate price (less than $500,000; e.g., Digital Equipment's PDP 11/34, Data General's Nova 3, or Hewlett-Packard's 21MX). Most have 16-**bit words.** It is increasingly difficult to make a meaningful distinction between the upper limit of minicomputers and the lower limit of **maxicomputers,** or between the lower limit of minicomputers and the upper limit of **microcomputers.**

Modem A device for changing serial **binary** numbers into a signal that can be transmitted over standard telephone lines, or the reverse. Derived from words **MO**dulate/**DEM**odulate. Synonym: **dataset.**

Mouse An input device for interacting with a computer. The mouse can be moved over a surface (such as a desk top) and it will provide coordinate data to the computer that can be used to move a cursor on the screen.

Multiplexer A device for mixing data coming from or going to low-speed devices and sending it along one high-speed line, or the reverse (e.g., a linkage between two cities handles 240 **characters**/second, and **terminals** are capable of printing 30 characters/second; therefore communications from eight such terminals can be mixed—usually by interdigitation in time, i.e., time-division multiplexing—by a multiplexer and sent along the one 240-character/second line; a demultiplexer is used to obtain the eight original independent character references). Also refers to the device on a **computer system** into which terminals plug and that passes the data from many terminals onto the computer's input and output channel.

Multistream batch operating system For an adequately detailed explanation, refer to Chapter 6.

Network An intercommunicating group of **computer systems** or **terminals**.

Node One of the **computers** or **terminals** in a **network**.

Object code See **object program**.

Object program (object code) The code resulting from the compilation process (see **compiler**).

Off-line Not directly **computer**-accessible. In the case of a **drive,** not attached to the computer. In the case of **media,** not mounted on a drive.

On-line Opposite of **off-line.** An on-line application is one in which the user is directly dealing with a **computer.** Contrasted usually with **batch processing,** in which data is collected now and processed later.

Operating system (OS) The main systems **programs** that provide methods of accessing systems **resources** and that schedule **access** to those resources. The operating system often provides other services, such as specific programs called "utilities" for **backup** or accounting security. Synonyms: supervisor, executive, or monitor.

Operator A person who performs functions needed during normal systems use, such as feeding in cards, changing tapes or disks, initiating special **programs,** or handling paper for the printing facilities.

Optical character recognition (OCR) An OCR reader is a device for scanning and recognizing printed **characters** and transforming these into **computer**-readable form.

Optical mark recognition (OMR) An OMR reader senses the position of pencil marks on a card or a form, thereby providing a means of inputting multiple-choice data into a **computer.**

Optimizing compiler A **compiler** that attempts to correct inefficiencies in the logic of **programs** to improve **execution** times and **internal memory** requirements.

Output device A machine for transforming data coming from the **computer** into a form readable by people or readable by other machines. In the latter sense, a storage **medium** like tape could be considered to be an output medium under some circumstances.

Paper tape A continuous thin paper **medium,** usually about 1 inch wide, on which data is recorded as round punched holes. Once created, the paper tape cannot be altered. In most applications, this medium for storing data has become obsolete.

Parallel interface A method of transmitting data a whole **word** or **byte** at a time from device to device, where a separate line is assigned to each **bit** being transferred to achieve a high rate of data transfer.

Patchboard An electrical panel that allowed wires to be plugged in to interconnect circuits in historical computers that used such a method of **programming.**

Peripheral device Any **hardware** device other than the **central processing unit** (e.g., **input, output,** or **storage device**).

Phoneme A quantum of sound with a given frequency and timing, characteristics that, when concatenated with other such quanta of different characteristics, can be used to generate a reasonable facsimile of human speech.

Plotter A device for producing graphic **hard copy** in which lines, curves, and **characters** are produced by moving a pen according to coordinates supplied by a **computer.** It can work in a pen up mode for moving without drawing and in a pen down mode for drawing dots or continuous lines.

Polling The process whereby a **computer** indicates to a **terminal** that it can transmit its data to the computer.

Printer-plotter Typically, an electrostatic **output device** (working in a way similar to a Xerox copier) that is capable of producing both **characters** (for text) and graphic output. These devices are also available for producing characters only or for graphic output only.

Processing Manipulating data; performing **(executing)** computations.

Processor See **central processing unit.**

Program A list of instructions written in some **programming language** that controls what a computer will do (e.g., a series of arithmetic commands—such as A + B − C—tells the computer which calculations to perform on a specific set of variables).

Programmer The person who creates logical and error-free lists of **instructions** in a **programming language** for solving a problem. Some programmers are also responsible for defining the **program** itself. See **programmer/analyst.**

Programmer/analyst A person who performs the combined functions of a **programmer** and a **systems analyst.**

Programming language (language) A set of **instructions** (or symbols) and syntactic rules for using and combining them, for writing **programs.** There is a continuous evolution of high-level programming languages towards the point where the instruction **(words)** and the syntax (grammar) are as close to natural language as possible.

Project manager A person who takes responsibility for enforcing the goals of a project (e.g., a project manager ensures that appropriate work is performed by **programmers,** that schedules are met, that appropriate communication occurs between developers and users, and that a project stays within its budget).

PROM Programmable **read-only memory (ROM).** A ROM that is alterable by the user.

Pseudorandom-access memory Memory in which it is possible to skip over most, but not all, **locations** to **access** any one desired location (e.g., **disks** are said to be pseudorandom-access devices because one can skip rapidly to the desired **track;** it is then necessary to wait until data on that track moves sequentially into place for reading).

Punched card Commonly referred to as the "IBM" card. Patterns of rectangular holes, aligned in columns, can print up to 80 **characters** of information on a single card. Once created, a punched card cannot be modified, unless more information is added in previously unused columns. Punched cards are rapidly becoming obsolete.

Query language A set of commands employed by a user to extract from a **database** data that meets specified criteria.

Random access memory (RAM) A kind of **internal memory** whose **locations** can be accessed and the contents retrieved with the same access time for all locations. Usually refers to electronic (as opposed to magnetic) internal memory.

Read To retrieve data or an **instruction** from some storage **location** or **medium.**

Read only memory (ROM) Memory from which it is possible to **read** data but whose data cannot be changed.

Register A temporary electronic storage **location** in which **instructions** or data are placed while being subject to some arithmetical or other operation. Usually a register has the same **bit** length as a standard **computer word.**

Remote job entry (RJE) A process for permitting batch input of **programs** or data to a **computer system** in situations in which the user is distant from the computer. Data or programs to be transmitted are assembled into messages following one or another industry-standard format and are transmitted according to a standard protocol. Usually methods are employed for detecting errors and initiating retransmission when errors are detected. Ordinarily, at least a small **processor** and local **storage devices** (**internal memory** or small **secondary memory devices**) are employed to use optimally the long-distance communications link. Data is transmitted at speeds exceeding 2400 BPS via **modems.**

Resources Any **hardware** or **software** capabilities offered by a **computer system** (e.g., file management problems, the **central processing unit,** and the **line printer** are all resources). The major concerns with resources are that they be available and that they be used as completely as possible so one can get the maximum amount of work out of them.

Routine A self-contained collection of **program** statements that perform some very specific subsection of an overall program. The same routine may be invoked numerous times within the same program. Thus it is useful to separate routines from the main body of a program, so that routines can be invoked many times without the necessity of repeating their statements many times.

Secondary memory device Those devices (excluding **internal memory**) that are used for storing **progams** and data. One can usually **write** data onto these devices and **read** from them, although some secondary memory devices are read-only.

Semiconductor memory Electronic memory whose individual memory cells (each storing a **binary bit**) are made up of transistor-like devices.

Sense light A light whose on-off status is controlled by a **program.** There are also sense switches, switches whose on-off status can be **read** by a program.

Sequential access memory Memory devices such as tape on which, to **read** or **write** data at a specific **location,** all data intervening between that location and the current position must be read or passed over. Thus the more data to be passed over, the longer it takes to get to the data of interest.

Serial interface An **input** or **output device** for a **computer system** that effects data transmission or reception. For output it transforms **parallel** data into a sequential train of pulses. For input it transforms data from a sequential train of pulses into parallel **binary words.**

Smart terminal See **intelligent terminal.**

Software The **programs** that cause the **computer** to perform specific functions.

Software engineering A relatively new field that addresses the efficient development of reliable and error-free **software.**

Software maintenance The ongoing process of detecting and removing errors from existing **programs.** Commercially, this usually refers to the process of the manufacturer's supplying and installing new versions or corrections to old versions of **software** products such as **operating systems, progamming languages,** and **applications packages.**

Software package Usually refers to an **applications package,** but could refer to all of the **software** in a **computer system.**

Software transportability The ability to take a **program** written and working on one **computer** and run it without modification on a different computer.

Source code The **program** in its original **programming language,** before it is translated into **machine language.**

Storage device See **secondary memory device.**

Stored program The concept in which **instructions** are kept in **internal memory** for **execution** in the same form that data is kept. A **program** can be designed to alter itself as required when stored in this way.

Structured programming An attempt to achieve better organization of **programs** and better program **documentation** to make programs more understandable, more error-free, and more efficient. This also involves the stepwise refinement of the problem itself, until a stage is reached where there is a simple correspondence between the logic of the program solution and the **instructions** or **routines** available in some **programming language.**

Supercomputer Usually refers to the most powerful computers. Such computers are normally capable of **executing** many millions of **instructions** per second and often have specialized **hardware** for calculating, **processing** arrays of numbers, handling large volumes of input and output, and speeding up processing. They are extremely expensive and are used only for the most complex computations. One example of a supercomputer is the CRAY 1.

Synchronous Synchronous transmission occurs according to a fixed time standard. In the case of synchronous communications, each **bit** transmitted as part of a message is expected at the receiving end within a fixed, limited time interval. A continuous string of **characters** is sent, with no blanks except between messages (see Figure 3-3).

Systems analyst (analyst) In general, a person responsible for the first attempts at stepwise refinement of a problem. A systems analyst defines a problem in data processing terms and may indicate to **programmers** the directions for specific data processing solutions.

Systems house A company that develops **hardware** and/or **software** systems to user requirements.

Task Any procedure or set of procedures that must be performed by a **computer** (e.g., executing a user's **program,** in which case the program is the task, or executing some portion of a program).

Teletype An old-fashioned **input** and **output device,** used for creating **hard copy** output at low speed.

Terabyte (Tb) A trillion **bytes;** 1000 Gb.

Terminal Any device for providing input and/or output to and/or from a **computer.**

Testing The process of subjecting a **program** to the conditions under which it must normally function to see that it works correctly.

Time-sharing operating system The section entitled "Time-Driven Operating Systems" in Chapter 6 explains this term in sufficient depth.

Touch screen A device (also called a touch sensitive display: TSD) that can sense the position of a finger pointed at a given region of a CRT screen. Sometimes touching the screen is required, but some systems will sense without actual contact a finger brought in proximity to the screen.

Track A term that applies to magnetic storage **media**—**disk** or tape. Refers to the area that can be magnetized by a magnetic recording head. On a tape **drive** there are normally seven or nine heads that record seven or nine linear tracks on the tape. This is the same idea as the multitrack cassettes for music. On a spinning disk, a single track is a circle. There are several hundred concentric circular tracks on a disk; the one on the outer rim is the longest track, whereas the one closest to the spindle is the shortest. However, all can contain the same number of pieces of data.

Trackball Similar to a **joystick,** but uses a ball moved by the palm of the hand of a human operator instead of a lever held by the fingers.

Transaction logging The process of redundantly recording everything that users input into a **computer.** Used in conjunction with a **backup** copy of systems data for restoring data stored on the **computer system** to its original condition in cases in which the **database** is inadvertently destroyed.

Turnaround time Can be measured in many ways, but nominally is the elapsed time from the submission of a job to a **computer system** until all output has been produced.

Turnkey system A **computer system** marketed as a complete product, meeting the specified needs of a given spectrum of users.

Unbundled Refers to the fact that the cost of the **software** is not included with the cost of the **hardware** in the overall price of a **computer system** (cf. **bundled).**

Up, up-time The period of time during which the **computer** is functioning normally.

Wand An **input device** used to read optical **bar code** labels by sensing the optical pattern of the light and dark areas.

Word The number of **bits processed** as a single unit in an arithmetical operation.

Word processing The computer-assisted production of text or documents.

Write To record data on a memory device.

X-Y digitizer An **input device** that allows the motion of a pen or cursor to be transduced and fed to the **computer** as a series of X-Y coordinates.

APPENDIX I

PEOPLE ACTIVE IN HEALTH CARE COMPUTING

Abdella, Thomas N.
Dept. of OB/GYN
University of Tennessee College of Medicine
800 Madison Avenue
Memphis, TN 38163

Acord, B.A.
Dept. of Clinical Engineering and Academic Computer Services
GWU Medical Center
Washington, D.C. 20037

Alderman, E.
Stanford University School of Medicine
Division of Cardiology
Stanford, CA 94305

Alexander, Mary Jane
Research/Evaluation Methodology Unit
Rockland Research Institute
Orangeburg, NY 10962

Anderson, Garland D.
Dept. of OB/GYN
University of Tennessee College of Medicine
800 Madison Avenue
Memphis, TN 38163

Ash, Stephen R.
Arnett Clinic
2600 Greenbush
Lafayette, IN 47904

Ashton, John M.
Professional Systems Corporation
3858 Carson Street, Suite 220
Torrance, CA 90503

Ayers, W.R.
Georgetown University Medical Center
Washington, D.C. 20057

Ball, Marion J.
Dept. of Computer Systems and Management Group
Temple University Health Sciences Center
Philadelphia, PA 19140

Balsam, Jeff
Professional Systems Corporation
3858 Carson Street, Suite 220
Torrance, CA 90503

Banks, Gordon
University of Pittsburgh
1360 Scaife Hall
Pittsburgh, PA 15261

Barnett, G. Octo
Laboratory of Computer Science
Massachusetts General Hospital
Boston, MA 02114

In developing a list such as this one, inevitably key persons will be omitted. This list was developed from several international meetings' lists of authors and from a survey of approximately 100 key persons in the field. It covers only the United States and Canada.

Barrett, Suzanne M.
Laboratory of Computer Science
Massachusetts General Hospital
Boston, MA 02114

Beardsley, Robert S.
University of Maryland School of Pharmacy
Baltimore, MD 21201

Bellman, R.
University of Southern California School of Engineering
Dept. of Electrical Engineering
University Park
Los Angeles, CA 90007

Bise, Bernard
Dartmouth Medical School
Dept. of Community and Family Medicine
Hanover, NH

Blum, Bruce I.
The Johns Hopkins University
Baltimore, MD 21205

Blum, Robert L.
Stanford University, Dept. of Computer Science
Margaret Jacks Hall
Stanford, CA 94305

Bourque, Michel
Computer and Biostatistics Center
Clinical Research Institute of Montreal
110 Pine Avenue, West
Montreal, Quebec, Canada H2W 1R7

Boyer, J.
Dept. of Radiology
University of Pittsburgh
RC 406 Scaife Hall
Pittsburgh, PA 15261

Brannigan, Vincent M.
Dept. of Textiles and Consumer Economics
University of Maryland
College Park, MD 20742

Brierly, C.F.
c/o *Computers and Medicine*
American Medical Association
535 North Dearborn Street
Chicago, IL 60610

Bron, K.M.
Dept. of Radiology
University of Pittsburgh
RC 406 Scaife Hall
Pittsburgh, PA 15261

Brown, Bob
Medical Association of Georgia
938 Peachtree Street
Atlanta, GA 30309

Caceres, C.A.
Clinical Systems Associates, Inc.
1759 Q Street
Washington, D.C. 20009

Caldwell, Robert M.
The University of Texas
Health Science Center at Dallas
Dallas, TX 75235

Califf, Robert M.
Dept. of Medicine
P.O. Box 3531
Duke University Medical Center
Durham, NC 27710

Campbell, B.C.
Rush–Presbyterian–St. Luke's Medical Center
1753 West Congress Parkway
Chicago, IL 60612

Cardus, D.
Dept. of Physiology
Baylor College of Medicine
1333 Moursund Avenue
Houston, TX 77025

Carlsen, Ruth H.
The Clinic Center
U.S. Dept. of Health and Human Services
Bethesda, MD 20205

Casiraghi, E.
c/o *Journal of Clinical Computing*
166 Morris Avenue
Buffalo, NY 14212

Castleman, P.
Bolt Beranek and Newman, Inc.
50 Mouton Street
Cambridge, MA 02138

Chadwick, M.
University of California
San Francisco, CA 94143

Chi, E.C.
New York University
New York, NY 10003

Chung-Bin, A.
Therapeutic Radiology
Rush–Presbyterian–St. Luke's Medical Center
1753 West Congress Parkway
Chicago, IL 60612

Clark, Kathy H.
University of Minnesota Medical School
Minneapolis, MN 55455

Clayton, P.D.
Dept. of Medical Biophysics and Computing
University of Utah
325 Eighth Avenue
Salt Lake City, UT 84143

Collen, M.F.
Kaiser-Permanente Medical Group
3700 Broadway
Oakland, CA 94611

Conklin, George S.
Rockland Research Institute
Orangeburg, NY 10962

Conley, Bernard E.
National Center for Health Services Research
Hyattsville, MD 20782

Conneally, P.M.
Dept. of Medical Genetics
Indiana University School of Medicine
Indianapolis, IN 46223

Connelly, Donald P.
Dept. of Laboratory Medicine and Pathology
University of Minnesota Health Sciences Center
Minneapolis, MN 55455

Cornfield, J.
Dept. of Biostatistics
George Washington University
Washington, D.C. 20052

Counte, M.A.
Rush–Presbyterian–St. Luke's Medical Center
1753 West Congress Parkway
Chicago, IL 60612

Covvey, H. Dominic
Clinicom International, Inc.
208-93 Lombard Avenue E.
Winnipeg, Manitoba, Canada R3B 3B1

Cox, J.R., Jr.
Dept. of Computer Science
Box 1045
Washington University
Saint Louis, MO 63130

Cradduck, Trevor
Dept. of Nuclear Medicine
Victoria Hospital
391 South Street
London, Ontario, Canada N6A 4G5

Craig, Thomas J.
Rockland Research Institute
Orangeburg, NY 10962

Craven, Nancy H.
Clinicom International, Inc.
208-93 Lombard Avenue E.
Winnipeg, Manitoba, Canada R3B 3B1

Crowe, S.
U.S. Dept. of Health and Human Services
National Institutes of Health
Bethesda, MD 20205

Cunningham, J.R.
Princess Margaret Hospital
500 Sherbourne Street
Toronto 5, Ontario, Canada

Dayhoff, M.O.
National Biomedical Research Foundation
Georgetown University
Washington, D.C. 20057

Dayhoff, Ruth E.
Dept. of Physiology and Biophysics
Georgetown University Medical Center
Washington, D.C. 20007

Demuth, N.K.
20281 Ramona Lane
Huntington Beach, CA 92646

Dennison, Darwin
School of Health Related Professions
State University of New York at Buffalo
New York, NY 14214

Distefano, J.J.
Engineering and Medicine
4731 Boelter Hall
UCLA
Los Angeles, CA 90024

Dixon, W.J.
Health Science Computing Facility
UCLA School of Medicine
Los Angeles, CA 90024

Dlugacz, Yosef D.
Rockland Research Institute
Orangeburg, NY 10962

Drazen, Erica
Arthur D. Little, Inc.
Acorn Park
Cambridge, MA 02140

Edelstein, Sylvia Z.
National Institutes of Health
7550 Wisconsin Avenue
Bethesda, MD 20205

Edmunds, Linda
University Hospital
Health Sciences Center
State University of New York at Stony Brook
Stony Brook, NY

Eisenberg, M.F.
School of Engineering and Applied Science
George Washington University
Washington, D.C. 20052

Elashoff, R.M.
UCLA Cancer Center
924 Westwood Boulevard
Suite 515
Los Angeles, CA 90024

Ellis, Lynda B.
University of Minnesota Medical School
Minneapolis, MN 55455

Farmer, James J.
Medical College of Ohio
Dept. of Pathology
C.S. 10008
Toledo, OH 43699

Feigenbaum, E.
Dept. of Computer Science
Stanford University
Palo Alto, CA 92605

Fenna, Don
University of Alberta Hospital
112 Street and 83 Avenue
Edmonton, Alberta, Canada T6G 2G3

Fiddleman, Richard H.
The MITRE Corporation
1820 Dolley Madison Boulevard
McLean, VA 22102

Fischer, Pamela J.
School of Hygiene and Public Health
Johns Hopkins University
Baltimore, MD 21205

Fischer, Susan
Rockland Research Institute
Orangeburg, NY 10962

Fishman, Irene G.
National Institutes of Health
7550 Wisconsin Avenue
Bethesda, MD 20205

Franklin, Kenneth
Uniformed Services University of the Health Sciences
4301 Jones Bridge Road
Bethesda, MD 20814

Gabrieli, Elmer R.
Medical Data Center
1630 Statler Bldg.
Buffalo, NY 14202

Gafke, G.P.
Applied Physics Laboratory
Johns Hopkins University
Baltimore, MD 21205

Gall, J.E.
Management Engineering
El Camino Hospital
2500 Grant Road
Mountain View, CA 94042

Gardner, R.
Latter-Day Saints Hospital
Salt Lake City, UT 84103

Garfinkel, D.
Moore School of Electrical Engineering
University of Pennsylvania
Philadelphia, PA 19174

Gatewood, Lael C.
University of Minnesota
Minneapolis, MN 55455

Geotowski, C.R.
TELEMED Corporation
2345 Pembroke Avenue
Hoffman Estates, IL 60172

Gersting, J.M.
Indiana University–Purdue University at Indianapolis
P.O. Box 647
Indianapolis, IN 46223

Glaser, E.M.
University of Maryland School of Medicine
Baltimore, MD 21201

Glazener, Tull
Regenstrief Institute
Indianapolis, IN

Glicksman, A.S.
Dept. of Radiation Oncology
Rhode Island Hospital
593 Eddy Street
Providence, RI 02902

Glueck, B.
c/o *Journal of Clinical Computing*
166 Morris Avenue
Buffalo, NY 14212

Goldstein, Larry
Harvard School of Public Health
677 Huntington Avenue
Boston, MA 02215

Golin, M.
c/o *Computers and Medicine*
American Medical Association
535 North Dearborn Street
Chicago, IL 60610

Greenes, Robert
Dept. of Radiology
Peter Brent Brigham Hospital
Boston, MA 02115

Grobe, Susan J.
University of Texas at Austin
School of Nursing
Austin, TX

Gross, Cynthia R.
National Institutes of Health
7550 Wisconsin Avenue
Bethesda, MD 20205

Guerrieri, J.A.
8522 N. Obeto Avenue
Chicago, IL 60648

Haas, Jeff
Regenstrief Institute
Indianapolis, IN

Hammon, G.L.
University of Texas System
P.O. Box 7759
Austin, TX 78712

Hammond, W.E.
Box 2914
Duke University Medical Center
Durham, NC 27710

Harbort, Bob
Emory University Hospital
Atlanta, GA 30322

Hardin, Richard C.
Massachusetts Health Data Consortium, Inc.
400-1 Totem Pond Road
Waltham, MA 02154

Harris, D.K.
c/o *Computers and Medicine*
American Medical Association
535 North Dearborn Street
Chicago, IL 60610

Hart, Richard J.
Medical Information Management, Inc.
6436 West Langley Lane
McLean, VA 22101

Harvey, A.C.
Winnipeg Clinic
425 St. Mary Avenue
Winnipeg, Manitoba, Canada R3C 0N2

Hattwick, Michael A.
Medical Information Management, Inc.
6436 West Langley Lane
McLean, VA 22101

Hearon, J.Z.
Mathematical Research Branch
National Institute of Arthritis, Metabolism and Digestive Diseases
Bethesda, MD 20014

Heinmets, F.
Dept. of Physiology
University of Massachusetts Medical School
Worcester, MA 01601

Henley, R.R.
Office of Medical Information Systems
University of California, San Francisco
San Francisco, CA 94122

Herron, J.M.
Dept. of Radiology
University of Pittsburgh
RC 406 Scaife Hall
Pittsburgh, PA 15261

Hierholzer, Walter J.
University of Iowa Hospitals and Clinics
Iowa City, IA 52242

Hill, Claire
Information Strategies, Inc.
1088 Orange Avenue
West Haven, CT 06516

Hodder, Richard
Uniformed Services University of the Health Sciences
4301 Jones Bridge Road
Bethesda, MD 20814

Hodge, M.
21238 Sarahills Drive
Saratoga, CA 95070

Holden, A.D.C.
Dept. of Electrical Engineering
University of Washington
Seattle, WA 98105

Horacek, Milan
Dalhousie University
Halifax, Nova Scotia, Canada

Huang, H.K.
Dept. of Radiological Sciences
University of California
Los Angeles, CA 90024

Hudson, Donna L.
School of Medicine
University of California, San Francisco
Fresno, CA 93703

Imirie, J.F., Jr.
Foster McGraw Hospital
Loyola University of Chicago
2160 S. 1st Avenue
Maywood, IL 60153

Jacobs, S.E.
223 Burchell Avenue
Highwood, IL 60040

Jacquez, J.A.
Dept. of Physiology
University of Michigan
Ann Arbor, MI 48104

Jeffreys, Brian
The Mt Sinai Medical Center
Cleveland, OH 44106

Jelliffe, R.
Dept. of Clinical Pharmacology
University of Southern California
Los Angeles, CA 90007

Jelovsek, Frederick R.
Dept. of Obstetrics and Gynecology
Duke University Medical Center
P.O. Box 3974
Durham, NC 27710

Johnson-Hurzeler, Rosemary
The Connecticut Hospice
61 Burban Drive
Branford, CT 06405

Johnston, M.
Discourse, Inc.
511 11th Avenue, S.
Minneapolis, MN 55415

Kahn, S.A.
Applied Physics Laboratory
Johns Hopkins University
Baltimore, MD 21205

Kay, Donald R.
University of Missouri
Columbia, MO 65211

Kennedy, W.H.
Dept. of Radiology
University of Pittsburgh
RC 406 Scaife Hall
Pittsburgh, PA 15261

Kerlin, Barbara D.
The MITRE Corporation
1820 Dolley Madison Boulevard
McLean, VA 22102

King, A.
12 Jackson Street
Denver, CO 80206

Kingsland, Lawrence C. III
Information Science Group
University of Missouri
Columbia, MO 65211

Knight, J.
c/o *Journal of Clinical Computing*
166 Morris Avenue
Buffalo, NY 14212

Kunitz, Selma C.
National Institutes of Health
7550 Wisconsin Avenue
Bethesda, MD 20205

Kuzmak, Peter M.
The Johns Hopkins Hospital
Baltimore, MD 21205

Landahl, H.D.
Dept. of Biochemistry and Biophysics
University of California, San Francisco
San Francisco, CA 94102

Laska, E.
Rockland State Hospital (MSIS)
Orangeburg, NY 10962

LeBlanc, Robert
Hopital du Sacre-Coeur
5400 Ouest, Boulevard Gouin
Montreal, Quebec, Canada H4J 1C5

Ledley, R.S.
National Biomedical Research Foundation
Georgetown University Medical Center
3900 Reservoir Road N.W.
Washington, D.C. 20007

Lehr, James L.
Dept. of Radiology
University of Chicago
950 E. 59th Street
Chicago, IL 60637

Lemmon, Larry
Regenstrief Institute
Indianapolis, IN

Levy, A.M.
University of Illinois School of Medicine
School of Basic Medical Sciences at Urbana-Champaign
Medical Science Bldg.
Urbana, IL 61801

Lindberg, Donald A.
University of Missouri
Columbia, MO 65211

Lloyd, Stephen C.
University of South Carolina School of Medicine
Columbia, SC

Losos, Frank J.
Dept. of Pathology
Montefiore Hospital
3459 Fifth Avenue
Pittsburgh, PA 15213

Lubs, H.A.
Medical Center
University of Colorado
Denver, CO 80202

Ludwig, Dana
University of California, San Francisco
San Francisco, CA 94143

Lyman, M.
Dept. of Pediatrics
New York University Medical Center
New York, NY

MacDonald, R.C.
Regenstrief Institute
Indianapolis, IN 46202

Mantel, J.
Radiation Physics
Sinai Hospital of Detroit
6767 W. Outer Drive
Detroit, MI 48235

McAlister, Neil H.
Family Practice Unit
Toronto Western Hospital
Toronto, Ontario, Canada M6J 1T9

McColligan, Elizabeth E.
Dept. of Biomedical Engineering
The Johns Hopkins University
Baltimore, MD 21205

McDonnell, G.
Massachusetts General Hospital
Dept. of Medicine, Harvard Medical School
Boston, MA 02114

McHugh, M.
School of Nursing
The University of Michigan
Ann Arbor, MI

McLatchey, John
Massachusetts General Hospital
Boston, MA 02114

Mertz, S.L.
Arnett Clinic
2600 Greenbush
Lafayette, IN 47904

Miller, Perry L.
Dept. of Anesthesiology, Yale University
School of Medicine
New Haven, CT 06510

Miller, R.A.
University of Pittsburgh
1360 Scaife Hall
Pittsburgh, PA 15261

Mitchell, F.
Kaiser-Permanente Hospital
1910 W. Sunset Boulevard
Los Angeles, CA 90026

Mohler, W.
National Institutes of Health
DCRT
Bethesda, MD 20205

Moore, R.
Box 701 Mayo Memorial Bldg.
University of Minnesota
Minneapolis, MN 55455

Morgan, M.M.
Massachusetts General Hospital
Dept. of Medicine, Harvard Medical School
Boston, MA 02114

Morowitz, H.J.
Dept. of Molecular Biophysics and Biochemistry
Yale University
New Haven, CT 06520

Muses, C.A.
International Research Center
844 San Ysidro Lane
Santa Barbara, CA 93103

Myers, J.D.
University of Pittsburgh
1360 Scaife Hall
Pittsburgh, PA 15261

Mylopoulos, John
University of Toronto
Toronto, Ontario, Canada

Nelson, Eugene C.
Dartmouth Medical School
Dept. of Community and Family Medicine
Hanover, NH

Newton, C.
Dept. of Biomathematics
UCLA School of Medicine
924 Westwood Boulevard
Los Angeles, CA 90024

O'Neill, Michael J.
The Johns Hopkins University
Dept. of Mathematical Sciences
Baltimore, MD 21205

Orthner, Helmuth F.
Office of Academic Computer Services
Dept. of Clinical Engineering
George Washington University Medical Center
Washington, D.C. 20037

Ostrow, Harold
National Institutes of Health
Bethesda, MD 20205

Ostrowski, Maureen
California Primary Physicians
929 South Georgia Street
Los Angeles, CA 90015

Palumbo, Francis B.
University of Maryland School of Pharmacy
636 W. Lombard Street
Baltimore, MD 21201

Patrick, E.A.
Jewish Hospital
Cincinnati, OH 45229

Pauker, S.
Tufts New England Medical Center
171 Harrison Avenue
Boston, MA 02111

Pearson, R.E.
c/o *Journal of Clinical Computing*
166 Morris Avenue
Buffalo, NY 14212

Perreault, Robert
Physichiatric Research Center
Hopital du Sacre-Coeur
Pavillon Albert-Prevost
6555 Ouest, Boulevard Gouin
Montreal, Quebec, Canada H2V 4B3

Perry, H.
Srere Radiation Therapy Center
Sinai Hospital of Detroit
6767 West Outer Drive
Detroit, MI 48235

Peterson, L.H.
Bockus Research Institute
19th and Lombard Streets
Philadelphia, PA 19146

Piggins, Judith
Massachusetts General Hospital
Dept. of Medicine, Harvard Medical School
Boston, MA 02114

Pipberger, H.V.
VA Research Center for Cardiovascular Data Processing
Veterans Administration Hospital
50 Irving Street NW
Washington, D.C. 20422

Polli, G.J.
c/o *Computers and Medicine*
American Medical Association
535 North Dearborn Street
Chicago, IL 60610

Pople, H.E.
University of Pittsburgh
1360 Scaife Hall
Pittsburgh, PA 15261

Potvin, John
Faculty of Medicine
University of Toronto, Room 2306
Medical Sciences Bldg.
Toronto, Ontario, Canada M5S 1A8

Pratt, A.W.
Division of Computer Research and Technology
National Institutes of Health
Bethesda, MD 20205

Priest, Stephen L.
Brockton Hospital
Brockton, MA 02402

Protti, D.J.
Health Information Science Dept.
University of Victoria
Box 1700
Victoria, B.C., Canada V8W 2Y3

Pryor, Allan
Dept. of Biophysics and Bioengineering
Latter-Day Saints Hospital
325 Eighth Avenue
Salt Lake City, UT 84103

Pryor, David B.
Dept. of Medicine
P.O. Box 3531
Duke University Medical Center
Durham, NC 27710

Rautaharju, Pentii
Dept. of Preventive Medicine
Dalhousie University
Halifax, Nova Scotia, Canada

Ray, R.D.
University of Illinois College of Medicine
The Abraham Lincoln School of Medicine
Dept. of Orthopaedic Surgery
840 South Wood Street
Chicago, IL 60612

Reich, Steven D.
University of Massachusetts Medical Center
Worcester, MA 01605

Reuben, R.
Tufts New England Medical Center
171 Harrison Avenue
Boston, MA 02111

Richardson, Mary Ann
Rockland Research Institute
Orangeburg, NY 10962

Riordan, Daniel
Uniformed Services University of the Health Sciences
4301 Jones Bridge Road
Bethesda, MD 20814

Robbins, G.
Cardiovascular Information Research Laboratory
3300 N.W. 56
Oklahoma City, OK 73122

Roberge, Fernand
Institut de Genie Biomedical
Universite de Montreal
Hopital du Sacre-Coeur
5400 Ouest, Boulevard Gouin
Montreal, Quebec, Canada H4J 1C5

Romano, Carol Ann
Dept. of Nursing, Clinical Center
National Institutes of Health
Bethesda, MD 20205

Rome, H.P.
Section of Psychiatry
Mayo Clinic
Rochester, MN 55901

Rosasti, Robert A.
Dept. of Community and Family Medicine
P.O. Box 3531
Duke University Medical Center
Durham, NC 27710

Rothmeier, J.
Medical Center
Dept. of Biomedical Computing
The Commonwealth of Massachusetts
University of Massachusetts
55 Lake Avenue North
Worcester, MA 01605

Rotolo, L.S.
National Biomedical Research Foundation
Georgetown University
Washington, D.C. 20057

Ruchkin, D.S.
Dept. of Physiology
University of Maryland School of Medicine
Baltimore, MD 21201

Ruddle, F.H.
Dept. of Biology
Yale University
New Haven, CT 06520

Rutman, E.L.
Mayo Clinic
Rochester, MN 55901

Saba, Virginia
Division of Nursing, BHPr, HRA, PHS
Hyattsville, MD

Salloway, J.C.
Rush–Presbyterian–St. Luke's Medical Center
1753 West Congress Parkway
Chicago, IL 60612

Sandberg, A.
Medical Methods Research
Kaiser-Permanente Medical Group
3700 Broadway
Oakland, CA 94611

Sashin, D.
Dept. of Radiology
University of Pittsburgh
RC 406 Scaife Hall
Pittsburgh, PA 15261

Schlager, David D.
Family and Community Health Associates
810 Bonneview Road
York, PA 17402

Schmitt, Otto H.
Veterans Administration Medical Center
54th Street and 48th Avenue, South
Minneapolis, MN 55417

Schultz, Samuel
Center for Nursing Research
The University of Michigan
Ann Arbor, MI 48109

Schwartz, Marc D.
Carvi Interactive Video Systems
New Haven, CT 06511

Schwartz, W.
Tufts New England Medical Center
171 Harrison Avenue
Boston, MA 02111

Schwirian, Patricia M.
The Ohio State University
Columbus, OH 43214

Shakun, Ernest N.
R.S. McLaughlin Examination & Research Centre
University of Alberta
Edmonton, Alberta, Canada T6G 1K8

Shannon, R.H.
Radiology Association of Spokane
Diagnostic and Therapeutic Radiology
N. 5901 Linwood
Spokane, WA 99207

Shapiro, Alan R.
Medical University of South Carolina
Charleston, SC 29425

Sharp, Gordon C.
University of Missouri
Columbia, MO 65211

Sherman, H.
Peter Bent Brigham Hospital
721 Huntington Avenue
Boston, MA 02115

Shires, David
Dalhousie University
Halifax, Nova Scotia, Canada

Shortliffe, T.
Stanford University School of Medicine
Palo Alto, CA 92605

Shusman, D.
Massachusetts General Hospital
Dept. of Medicine, Harvard Medical School
Boston, MA 02114

Siegel, Carole
Rockland Research Institute
Orangeburg, NY 10962

Sievert, Chester E.
Veterans Administration Medical Center
54th Street and 48th Avenue South
Minneapolis, MN 55417

Silvis, Stephen E.
Veterans Administration Medical Center
54th Street and 48th Avenue South
Minneapolis, MN 55417

Simborg, D.W.
21 Tamal Vista Boulevard, Suite 223
Corte Madera, CA 94925

Simpson, Roy L.
Hospital Corporation of America
One Park Plaza
Nashville, TN 37203

Slack, W.
Beth Israel Hospital
330 Brookline Avenue
Boston, MA 02215

Slasky, B.S.
Dept. of Radiology
University of Pittsburgh
RC 406 Scaife Hall
Pittsburgh, PA 15261

Smith, Jack W., Jr.
Dept. of Pathology
The Ohio State University
333 W. 10th Avenue
Columbus, OH 43210

Smith, Monica
Massachusetts General Hospital
Boston, MA 02114

Smith, R.
Mayo Clinic
Rochester, MN 55901

Speedie, Stuart M.
University of Maryland School of Pharmacy
636 W. Lombard Street
Baltimore, MD 21201

Spencer, W.A.
Texas Institute for Rehabilitation and Research
The Texas Medical Center
1333 Moursund Avenue
Houston, TX 77025

Stacy, R.W.
Dept. of Physiology
Southern Illinois University
Carbondale, IL 62901

Stark, L.
Physiological Optics and Engineering Science
University of California
Berkeley, CA 94720

Starmer, F.
Duke University Medical Center
Durham, NC 27710

Stead, William W.
Box 2914
Duke University Medical Center
Durham, NC 27710

Sterling, T.D.
Computing Science
Simon Fraser University
Computing Science Programs
Burnaby, B.C., Canada V5A 1S6

Sternglass, E.J.
Dept. of Radiology
University of Pittsburgh
RC 406 Scaife Hall
Pittsburgh, PA 15261

Sternick, E.S.
Medical Physics Division
Tufts New England Medical Center
171 Harrison Avenue
Boston, MA 02111

Stewart, R.L.
The Johns Hopkins University
Laurel, MD 20707

Stiennon, O.A.
One South Part Street
Diagnostic Radiology and Computer Medicine
Madison, WI 53715

Stone, Elliot M.
Massachusetts Health Data Consortium, Inc.
400-1 Totem Pond Road
Waltham, MA 02154

Straube, M.J.
Box 2914
Duke University Medical Center
Durham, NC 27710

Streiner, David
Faculty of Medicine
McMaster University
1200 Main Street, W.
Hamilton, Ontario, Canada L8N 3Z5

Strong, Robert M.
Harvard School of Public Health
677 Huntington Avenue
Boston, MA 02215

Studney, Don
Dept. of Medicine
University of British Columbia
Vancouver, B.C., Canada

Sturm, R.
Mayo Clinic
Rochester, MN 55901

Terdiman, J.
Kaiser-Permanente Medical Group
3700 Broadway
Oakland, CA 94611

Thorp, James W.
National Naval Medical Center
Bethesda, MD 20814

Tolchin, Stephen G.
The Johns Hopkins University
Laurel, MD 20707

Truax, Terry
University of Michigan Hospitals
Ann Arbor, MI 48109

Ulrich, D.K.
Purdue University
West Lafayette, IN 47907

Vallbona, C.
Baylor College of Medicine
Texas Medical Center
Houston, TX 77025

Van Brunt, E.E.
Kaiser-Permanente Medical Group
3700 Broadway
Oakland, CA 94611

Vieweg, Bruce W.
Dept. of Psychiatry and Missouri Institute of Psychiatry
University of Missouri–St. Louis, School of Medicine
5400 Arsenal Street
St. Louis, MO 63139

Wallach, Jacques
S.U.N.Y. Downstate Medical Center
Dept. of Pathology
Brooklyn, NY

Walters, Richard F.
Dept. of Community Health
School of Medicine
University of California
Davis, CA 95616

Warner, H.R.
Dept. of Medical Biophysics and Computing
University of Utah
Salt Lake City, UT 84103

Watson, Bruce L.
Boston University Center for Law & Health Sciences
760 Commonwealth Avenue
Boston, MA 02215

Waxman, B.
Division of Health Care Information Systems and Technology
George Washington University Medical Center
Washington, D.C. 20052

Weed, L.L.
PKC Corporation
RR1, Box 630
Cambridge, VT 05444

Weinkam, J.J.
Simon Fraser University
Computing Science Program
Burnaby, B.C., Canada V5A 1S6

Weiss, Sholom M.
Dept. of Computer Science
Rutgers University
New Brunswick, NJ 08903

Whiting-O'Keefe, Q.E.
University of California, San Francisco
San Francisco, CA 94143

Wiederhold, Gio C.
Stanford University Dept. of Computer Science
Margaret Jacks Hall
Stanford, CA 94305

Williams, B.T.
University of Illinois School of Basic Medical Sciences at Urbana-Champaign
1400 W. Park Avenue
Urbana, IL 61801

Williams, Francine
Rush–Presbyterian–St. Luke's Medical Center
1753 West Congress Parkway
Chicago, IL 60612

Wilson, D.H.
Dept. of Medical Informatics
Veterans Administration Hospital
Oklahoma City, OK 73104

Wist, Abund Ottokar
Medical College of Virginia/VCU
Richmond, VA 23298

Wolf, Hermann
Dept. of Physiology and Biophysics
Dalhousie University
Halifax, Nova Scotia, Canada

Wood, E.
Mayo Clinic
Rochester, MN 55901

Woodbury, M.A.
Dept. of Biomathematics
Duke University Medical Center
Durham, NC 27706

Yamamoto, W.S.
George Washington University
Dept. of Clinical Engineering
2300 K. Street N.W.
Washington, D.C. 20037

Yasnoff, W.A.
Rush–Presbyterian–St. Luke's Medical Center
1753 West Congress Parkway
Chicago, IL 60612

Zielstorff, Rita D.
Massachusetts General Hospital
Boston, MA 02114

Zimmerman, J.
Tandem Computer Company
19333 Vallco Parkway
Cupertino, CA 95014

Zimmerman, S.
Dept. of Biomathematics
The University of Texas
M.D. Anderson Hospital and Tumor Institute
Houston, TX 77025

Zuckerman, Alan E.
Dahlgren Memorial Library
Georgetown University Medical Center
Washington, D.C.

APPENDIX II
BOOKS AND JOURNALS IN HEALTH CARE COMPUTING

BOOKS

Title: A Critical Guide to Software for the IBM-PC and PC Compatible: Computers for Professionals in Business, Agriculture, Law and Health
Author: Good, Phillip I.
Publisher and date: Chilton, 11/1983

Title: Visual Display Terminal: Usability Issues and Health Concerns
Author: Bennett, J., and Smith, Michael (editors)
Publisher and date: Prentice-Hall, Inc., 10/1983

Title: Your Health and Your Computer Sub: How Your Computer Can Affect Your Health
Author: Cutting, Robert A.
Publisher and date: Leisure Data, 10/1983

Title: Computer-Assisted Diagnosis and Medical Services: Subject Analysis with Bibliography
Author: Neiderhaus, Lee B.
Publisher and date: ABBE Publishers Association, 12/1983

Title: The Medical Office Computer Handbook
Author: Computer Strategies
Publisher and date: Computer Strategies, 8/1983

Title: Computer-Assisted Instruction and Education: Medical Applications and Subject Analysis with Bibliography
Author: Bartone, Mary R.
Publisher and date: ABBE Publishers Association, 9/1983

Title: Automatic Data Processing, Artificial Intelligence and Computers: Medical Subject Analysis with Bibliography
Author: Bartone, John C. II
Publisher and date: ABBE Publishers Association, 9/1983

Title: Personalized Guide to Computers and Your Dental Practice
Author: Snyder, Thomas L., and Feldmeister, Charles J. (editors)
Publisher and date: The C.V. Mosby Co., 10/1983

Title: Physician's Primer on Computers: Private Practice
Author: Brandejs, Jan F., Pace, Graham, and Weiss, William V.
Publisher and date: Lexington Books, 1979

Title: Library Automation as a Source of Management Information: Proceedings of the Clinic on Library Applications of Data Processing
Author: Lancaster, F.W. (editor)
Publisher and date: University of Illinois Library of Information Science, 8/1983

Title: Using Computers in Clinical Practice: Psychotherapy and Mental Health Applications
Author: Schwartz, Marc D. (editor)
Publisher and date: Hayworth Printers, 12/1983

Title: The Doctor's Computer Handbook
Author: Fell, Peter J., and Skees, William D.
Publisher: Lifetime Learning

Title: Topography of the Brain with Clinical, Angiographic and Radionuclide Correlation
Author: Ramsey, Ruth G.
Publisher and date: W.B. Saunders Co., 1/1977

Title: Ballistocardiography—Research and Computer Diagnosis: Proceedings
Author: Franke, E.K. (editor)
Publisher and date: S. Karger, 2/1973

Title: Physician's Guide to Desktop Computers
Author: Spohr, Mark
Publisher and date: Reston Publishing Co., 7/1982

Title: Locating Ambulance Dispatch Centers in an Urban Region: A Man–Computer Interactive Problem-Solving Approach
Author: Schneider, Jerry B., and Symons, John B., Jr.
Publisher and date: Regional Science Research Institute, 7/1971

Title: Memory Bank for Hemodynamic Monitoring
Author: Ervin, Gary W., and Long, Sylvia
Publisher and date: Nurseco, 11/1983

Title: Computers in Medicine: Current Medical Subject Analysis and Research Directory with Bibliography
Author: Bartone, J.C.
Publisher and date: ABBE Publishers Association, 5/1983

Title: Microcomputers and the Medical Professional
Author: McClung, Christina, Guerrieri, John A., and McClung, Kenneth A.
Publisher and date: John Wiley & Sons, Inc., 11/1983

Title: The History of Database: Computer-Processed and Other Medical Questionnaires
Author: Yarnall, Stephen R., and Wakefield, Jay S.
Publisher and date: Medical Communications, 1975

Title: Health Hazards of CRT's: A Comprehensive Bibliography on a Critical Issue of Workplace Health and Safety
Author: Ryan Research
Publisher and date: Ryan Research, 1983

Title: Current Status of Computers in Medicine: Medical Subject Analysis and Bibliography
Author: Bartone, John C.
Publisher and date: ABBE Publishers Association, 11/1983

Title: Biomedical Computer Programs, P-Series
Author: Dixon, W.J., and Brown, M.B. (editors)
Publisher and date: University of California Press, 5/1983

Title: Calculator Programs for the Health Sciences
Author: Abramson, J.H., and Peritz, E.
Publisher and date: Oxford University Press, 5/1983

Title: The Use of Computers in Perinatal Medicine
Author: Harris, Thomas R.
Publisher and date: Praeger Publishers, Inc., 11/1982

Title: The Impact of Computer Technology on Drug Information: Proceedings of the IFIP–IMIA Working Conference, Uppsala, Sweden, October 26–28, 1981
Author: Manell, P., and Johansson, S.G. (editors)
Publisher and date: Elsevier Science Publishing Co., Inc., 10/1982

Title: Computer Applications in Medical Care
Author: Lindberg, Donald A., Collen, Morris F., and Van Brunt, Edmund E. (editors)
Publisher and date: Masson Publishing Co., 7/1982

Title: A Clinical and Mathematical Introduction to Computer Processing of Scintigraphic Images
Author: Goris, Michael L., and Briandet, Philippe A.
Publisher and date: Raven Press, 1983

Title: Role of Computers in Radiotherapy
Author: IAEA
Publisher and date: Unipub, 1968

Title: Single Photon Emission Computed Tomography and Other Selected Computer Topics
Author: Price, Ronald R., Croft, Barbara Y., and Gilday, David L. (editors)
Publisher and date: Society of Nuclear Medicine, 8/1980

Title: Nuclear Cardiology: Selected Computer Aspects, 1978 Symposium Proceedings
Author: Bacharach, Stephen L., Alpert, Nathaniel M., and Shames, David M. (editors)
Publisher and date: Society of Nuclear Medicine, 1978

Title: How to Select a Computerized Hospital Information System
Author: Ball, Marion J. (editor)
Publisher and date: S. Karger, 1973

Title: Computers for the Physician's Office
Author: Zimmerman, Joan, and Rector, Alan
Publisher and date: Research Studies Press, 6/1978

Title: Computer Graphics in Medical Research and Hospital Administration
Author: Parslow, R.D., and Green, R. Elliot (editors)
Publisher and date: Plenum Publishing Corp., 3/1971

Title: Automation of Clinical Electroencephalography
Author: Kellaway, P., and Petersen, I. (editors)
Publisher and date: Raven Press, 8/1973

Title: CAI Network Evaluation Criteria and Methodology (Seattle, Wash., Nov., 1973)
Author: Medical Communications
Publisher and date: Medical Communications, 1/1976

Title: Computer-Assisted Cardiac Nuclear Medicine
Author: Holman, B. Leonard, and Parker, J. Anthony
Publisher and date: Little, Brown & Co., 1981

Title: Safeguarding Psychiatric Privacy: Computer Systems and Their Uses
Author: Laska, Eugene M., and Bank, Rheta (editors)
Publisher and date: R.E. Krieger Publishing Co., Inc., 1975

Title: Proceedings of the Conference on Information Processing of Medical Records— Lyon, 1970
Author: Anderson, J., and Forsythe, J.M. (editors)
Publisher and date: Elsevier Science Publishing Co., Inc., 1970

Title: Selected Bibliography and Abstracts for Ambulatory Health Care Computer Applications
Publisher and date: Health Administration Press, 6/1/1975

Title: Applying Computers in Social Service and Mental Health Agencies
Author: Slavin, Simon (editor)
Publisher: Hayworth Press

Title: Medical and Health Information Directory
Author: Kruzas, Anthony T. (editor)
Publisher and date: Gale Research Co., 9/1977

Title: Automated Multiphasic Health Testing
Author: Berkley, Carl (editor)
Publisher and date: English Foundation, 8/1971

Title: Computers in the Clinical Laboratory: An Introduction
Author: Toren, E. Clifford, and Eggert, Arthur A. (editors)
Publisher and date: Marcel Dekker, Inc., 5/1978

Title: Computer Techniques in Cardiology
Author: Cady
Publisher and date: Marcel Dekker, Inc., 1/1979

Title: Automated Immunoanalysis
Author: Ritchie, Robert F. (editor)
Publisher and date: Marcel Dekker, Inc., 3/1978

Title: Computer in der Medizin
Author: Chorafas, Dimitris N.
Publisher and date: De Gruyter, 1973

Title: Nursing Research: Design Statistics and Computer Analysis
Author: Waltz, Carolyn, and Bausell, Barker
Publisher and date: F.A. Davis Co., 1/1981

Title: Computer Aids to Clinical Decisions
Author: Williams, Ben T. (editor)
Publisher and date: CRC Press, 12/1981

Title: Computers and the Life Sciences
Author: Sterling, Theodor D., and Pollack, Seymour V.
Publisher and date: Columbia University Press, 1969

Title: Selecting a Computer System for the Clinical Laboratory
Author: Ball, Marion J., and Finley, P.
Publisher and date: Charles C Thomas, Publisher, 10/1971

Title: Computer Application in Mental Health: A Source Book
Author: Crawford, J.L., Vitale, S., and Robinson, J.
Publisher and date: Ballinger Publishing Co., 9/1983

Title: Computers in Laboratory Medicine
Author: Enlander, D. (editor)
Publisher and date: Academic Press, Inc., 1975

Title: Computers in Biomedical Research, Vols. 1-4
Author: Stacy, R.W., and Waxman, B.
Publisher and date: Academic Press, Inc., 1965-1974

Title: Computer-Assisted Medical Decision-Making
Author: Warner, Homer R.
Publisher and date: Academic Press, Inc., 12/1979

Title: Clinical Electrocardiography and Computers: A Symposium
Author: Caceres, C.A. (editor)
Publisher and date: Academic Press, Inc., 1970

Title: Computers in Clinical and Biomedical Engineering
Author: Karanja, Linda (editor)
Publisher and date: Quest Publishers, 5/1983

Title: Systems Analysis and Computer Applications in Health Information Management
Author: Waters, Kathleen, and Murphy, Gretchen
Publisher and date: Aspen Systems, 12/1982

Title: An Introduction to Nursing Research: Research, Measurement, and Computers in Nursing
Author: Sweeney, Mary A., and Olivieri, Peter
Publisher and date: J.B. Lippincott Co., 3/1981

Title: Computerized Transmission of the Heart and Great Vessels: Experimental Evaluation and Clinical Application
Author: Higgins, Charles B., Carlsson, Erik, and Lipton, Martin J. (editors)
Publisher and date: Futura Publishing Co., Inc., 11/1982

Title: Hospital Computer Systems and Procedures, Vol. 2: Medical Systems
Author: Garrett, Raymond
Publisher and date: Van Nostrand Reinhold Co., 11/1976

Title: Computers for Medical Office and Patient Management
Author: Day, Stacey B., and Brandejs, Jan F. (editors)
Publisher and date: Van Nostrand Reinhold Co., 1/1982

Title: Computers, Health Records and Citizen Rights (NBS Monograph 157)
Author: Westin, Alan F.
Publisher and date: National Bureau of Standards, U.S. Government Printing Office, 1976

Title: Analysis Manual for Hospital Information Systems
Author: Doyle, Owen, and Tucker, Stephen L.
Publisher and date: Health Administration Press, 5/1980

Title: Automated Medical Records and the Law
Author: Springer, Eric W. (editor)
Publisher and date: Aspen Systems, 10/6/1971

Title: Microcomputer-Based Aids for the Disabled
Author: Schofield, J.
Publisher and date: Wiley, Heyden & Wiley, 1981

Title: Role of Computers in Medical Practice Management
Author: Ehrlich, Ann
Publisher: Colwell Co.

Title: Computers in Hospital Pharmacy Management: Fundamentals and Applications
Author: Cornell, Joseph A.
Publisher and date: Aspen Systems, 3/1983

Title: Computers in Critical Care and Pulmonary Medicine, Vol. 1
Author: Nair, Sreedhar (editor)
Publisher and date: Plenum Publishing Corp., 7/1980

Title: Computers in Critical Care and Pulmonary Medicine, Vol. 2
Author: Prakash, Omar (editor)
Publisher and date: Plenum Publishing Corp., 2/1982

Title: Computers in Life Science Research
Author: Siler, William, and Lindberg, Donald A. (editors)
Publisher and date: Plenum Publishing Corp., 12/1975

Title: Computer-Assisted Medical Record Systems: An Examination of Case Studies
Author: American Hospital Association Clearinghouse for Hospital Management Engineering
Publisher and date: American Hospital Association Clearinghouse for Hospital Management Engineering, 1982

Title: Computer Applications for Patient Care
Author: Bronzino, Joseph D.
Publisher and date: Addison-Wesley Publishing Co., Inc., 4/1982

Title: Shared Hospital Computer Services Evaluation
Author: Computer Information Services, Chicago Hospital Council
Publisher and date: Healthcare Financial Management Association, 1975

Title: Computer Based Medical Consultations
Author: Shortliffe, Mycin
Publisher and date: Elsevier Science Publishing Co., Inc., 1976

Title: Introduction to Computer Applications in Medicine
Author: Kember, N.F.
Publisher and date: E. Arnold, 1982

Title: Computers in Ultrasonic Diagnostics
Author: Wells, P.N., and Woodcock, J.P.
Publisher and date: John Wiley & Sons, Inc., 9/1980

Title: Functional Mapping of Organ Systems and Other Computer Topics
Author: Esser, Peter O.
Publisher and date: Society of Nuclear Medicine, 9/1981

Title: Trends in Computer-Processed Electrocardiograms: Proceedings of a Working Conference, Amsterdam, 1976
Author: Van Bemmel, J.H., and Willems, J.L. (editors)
Publisher and date: Elsevier Science Publishing Co., Inc., 4/1977

Title: Computers and Brains
Author: Schade, J., and Smith, J. (editors)
Publisher and date: Elsevier Science Publishing Co., Inc., 1971

Title: Introduction to Automated Electrocardiogram Interpretation
Author: Macfarlane, P.W., and Lawrie, D.
Publisher and date: Butterworth Publishers, 1974

Title: Human Congenital Malformations: The Design of a Computer-Aided Study
Author: Gal, E., and Gal, I.
Publisher and date: Butterworth Publishers, 2/1975

Title: Computers in Radiotherapy: Physical Aspects
Author: Wood, R.G.
Publisher and date: Butterworth Publishers, 8/1974

Title: Computers in Radiotherapy: Clinical Aspects
Author: Deeley, T.J.
Publisher and date: Butterworth Publishers, 1972

Title: Computers in Hematology
Author: Cavill, I., and Jacobs, A.
Publisher and date: Butterworth Publishers, 5/1975

Title: Computers in Electromyography
Author: Clifford, J.B., McLeod, H.C., and Nunnally, W.D.
Publisher and date: Butterworth Publishers, 3/1975

Title: Computer Sources: A Practical Guide for Pharmacists
Author: Casler, Robin E. (editor)
Publisher and date: American Pharmaceutical Association, 1982

Title: Hospital Computer Systems Planning: Preparation of Request for Proposal
Author: American Hospital Association
Publisher and date: American Hospital Association, 1980

Title: Biomedical Images and Computers: St. Pierre de Chartreuse, France, 1980, Proceedings
Author: Sklansky, J., and Bisconte, J.C. (editors)
Publisher and date: Springer-Verlag New York, Inc., 12/1982

Title: Digital Image Processing in Medicine: Proceedings
Author: Hoehne, K.H. (editor)
Publisher and date: Springer-Verlag New York, Inc., 2/1982

Title: Memory Bank for Hemodialysis
Author: Cairoli, Oscar, and Voyce, Pamela
Publisher and date: Nurseco, 11/1982

Title: Computer Methods: The Fundamentals of Digital Nuclear Medicine
Author: Lieberman, David E. (editor)
Publisher and date: The C.V. Mosby Co., 12/1977

Title: Computer Projects in Health Care
Author: Giebink, Gerald A., and Hurst, Leonard L.
Publisher and date: Health Administration Press, 10/13/1975

Title: Computerizing a Clinical Laboratory
Author: Aikawa, Jerry K., and Pinfield, Edward R.
Publisher and date: Charles C Thomas, Publisher, 10/1973

Title: Evaluating Automated Hospital Information Systems
Author: Lutheran Hospital Society of Southern California Research and Development Department
Publisher and date: Center Publications, 7/1982

Title: Role of Computers in Medical Practice Management
Author: Erlich, A.
Publisher: Colwell Co.

Title: Computer Applications for Medical Care
Author: Collen, Morris F., Lindberg, Donald A., and Van Brunt, Edmund E. (editors)
Publisher and date: Masson Publishing Co., 7/1982

Title: Managing Computers in Health Care: A Guide for Professionals
Author: Worthley, John A.
Publisher and date: Health Administration Press, 10/1982

Title: The MMPI: Clinical Assessment and Automated Interpretation
Author: Lachar, David
Publisher and date: Western Psychological Services, 5/1974

Title: Hospital Computer Systems and Procedures, Vol. 1: Accounting Systems
Author: Garrett, Raymond
Publisher and date: Van Nostrand Reinhold Co., 5/1976

Title: Clinical Laboratory Computerization
Author: Krieg, Arthur F.
Publisher and date: University Park Press, 1971

Title: Automation and Management in the Clinical Laboratory
Author: Westlake, G. (editor)
Publisher and date: University Park Press, 1975

Title: Computer Applications in Radiation Oncology
Author: Edward, S. (editor)
Publisher and date: University Press of New England, 12/1976

Title: Mathematical Models in the Health Sciences: A Computer-Aided Approach
Author: Ackerman, Eugene, and Gatewood, Lael C.
Publisher and date: University of Minnesota Press, 11/1979

Title: Clinic on Library Applications of Data Processing, Proceedings, 1978: Problems and Failures in Library Automation
Author: Lancaster, F.W. (editor)
Publisher and date: University of Illinois Library of Information Science, 1979

Title: Clinic on Library Applications of Data Processing, Proceedings, 1977: Negotiating for Computer Services
Author: Bivilbiss, J.L. (editor)
Publisher and date: University of Illinois Library of Information Science, 1978

Title: Automation in Analytic Serology
Author: Vargues, R., and Henley, W.
Publisher and date: Thieme-Stratton, 1974

Title: Clinical Chemistry and Automation
Author: Robinson, R., and Wayne, Edward (foreword)
Publisher and date: State Mutual Books, 1971

Title: The Use of Computers in Therapeutic Radiology: International Conference, 1966
Author: British Institute of Radiology
Publisher and date: State Mutual Books, 11/1980

Title: Considerations about the Use of Computers in Radiodiagnostic Departments
Author: DuBoulay, G.H. (editor)
Publisher and date: State Mutual Books, 12/1980

Title: Computers in the Control of Treatment Units: Applications of Modern Technology in Radiotherapy
Author: British Institute of Radiology
Publisher and date: State Mutual Books, 12/1980

Title: Computers in Radiotherapy: Second International Conference, 1968
Author: British Institute of Radiology
Publisher and date: State Mutual Books, 11/1980

Title: Mathematical Modelling and Computers in Endocrinology
Author: McIntosh, J.A., and McIntosh, R.P.
Publisher and date: Springer-Verlag New York, Inc., 4/1980

Title: Mathematical Aspects of Computerized Tomography: Proceedings
Author: Herman, G.T., and Natterer, F. (editors)
Publisher and date: Springer-Verlag New York, Inc., 4/1981

Title: Computers and Mathematical Models in Medicine: Proceedings
Author: Cardus, D., and Vallbona, C. (editors)
Publisher and date: Springer-Verlag New York, Inc., 6/1981

Title: Automation in Hematology: What to Measure and Why
Author: Ross, D.W. (editor)
Publisher and date: Springer-Verlag New York, Inc., 4/1981

Title: The Multi-State Information System: Proceedings of the Fifth Annual National Users Group Conference
Author: Johnsen, Jeffrey (editor)
Publisher and date: Rockland Research, 1981

Title: Handbook of Automated Electronic Clinical Analysis
Author: Thomas, Harry E.
Publisher and date: Reston Publishing Co., 1979

Title: Computers and the General Practitioner
Author: Poyser, J. (editor)
Publisher and date: Pergamon Press, Inc., 11/1981

Title: Computers in Nursing
Author: Zielstorff, Rita
Publisher and date: Aspen Systems, 10/1980

Title: COMAPS: A Computer-Aided Pharmacy System
Author: Robida, Donald G.
Publisher and date: MUMPS, 1976

Title: Computers in Medicine: An Introduction
Author: Enlander, Derek
Publisher and date: The C.V. Mosby Co., 9/1980

Title: An Annotated Bibliography of Biomedical Computer Applications
Author: Automated Education Center
Publisher: Management Information Service

Title: Computer Applications and Techniques in Clinical Medicine
Author: Ludwig, Herbert R.
Publisher and date: John Wiley & Sons, Inc., 1974

Title: Computer Technology in Neuroscience
Author: Brown, Paul B. (editor)
Publisher and date: Halsted Press, 6/1976

Title: Computerized Interpretation of the ECG
Author: Pryor, T. Allan, and Bailey, James J. (editors)
Publisher and date: English Foundation, 1/1980

Title: Computerized Interpretation of the ECG, Part V
Author: Tolan, Gil D., and Pryor, T. Allan (editors)
Publisher and date: English Foundation, 12/1980

Title: Systems Aspects of Health Planning
Author: Thompson, M., and Bailey, N.J. (editors)
Publisher and date: Elsevier Science Publishing Co., Inc., 4/8/1975

Title: Computer Technology in the Health Sciences
Author: Shires, David B.
Publisher and date: Charles C Thomas, Publisher, 6/1974

Title: Computer Diagnosis and Diagnostic Methods
Author: Jacquez, John A.
Publisher and date: Charles C Thomas, Publisher, 12/29/1972

Title: The Computer and Medical Care
Author: Lindberg, Donald A.
Publisher and date: Charles C Thomas, Publisher, 1971

Title: Automated Analysis of Drugs and Other Substances of Pharmaceutical Interest
Author: Hone, R., and Rhodes, C.T. (editors)
Publisher and date: Butterworth Publishers, 1974

Title: Progress in Mental Health Information Systems: Computer Applications
Author: Crawford, Jeffrey L., Morgan, Donald W., and Gianturco, Daniel (editors)
Publisher and date: Ballinger Publishing Co., 3/1974

Title: Computers in Medical Administration
Author: Sondak, Norman, and Kavaler, Florence (editors)
Publisher and date: Artech House, Inc., 2/1981

Title: Computers and Medicine
Author: Schwartz, H., and Sondak, V.
Publisher and date: Artech House, Inc., 8/1979

Title: Computer Assisted Medical Practice: AMA's Role
Author: American Medical Association
Publisher and date: American Medical Association, 1971

Title: Sourcebook on Computers in Pharmacy
Author: American Society of Hospital Pharmacy
Publisher and date: American Society of Hospital Pharmacy, 4/1978

Title: Computers in Psychiatry
Author: American Psychiatric Association
Publisher and date: American Psychiatric Association, 1969

Title: Automation and Data Processing in Psychiatry
Author: American Psychiatric Association
Publisher and date: American Psychiatric Association, 1971

Title: Hospital Management Systems
Author: Brown, M., and Lewis, H.L.
Publisher and date: Aspen Systems, 1976

Title: Medical Information Systems: A New Resource for Hospitals
Author: Hodge, M.H.
Publisher and date: Aspen Systems, 1977

Title: Computing and Operational Research at the London Hospital
Author: Barber, B., and Abbot, W.
Publisher and date: Butterworth Publishers, 1973

Title: A Guide to Medical Computing
Author: Coles, E.C.
Publisher and date: Butterworth Publishers, 1973

Title: Guide to Medical Computing
Author: Hill, D.W.
Publisher and date: Butterworth Publishers, 1973

Title: Advances in Medical Computing
Author: Rose, J., and Mitchell, J.H.
Publisher and date: Churchill Livingstone, 1975

Title: Principles and Practice of Medical Computing
Author: Whitby, L.G.
Publisher and date: Churchill Livingstone, 1971

Title: Medical Data Processing
Author: Anderson, J., Laudet, M., et al.
Publisher and date: Crane, Russak & Co., Inc., 1976, 1977

Title: Topics in Computer Techniques for Electrocardiography, 2nd ed.
Publisher: Cutler-Hammer

Title: Mental Health Information Systems: Design and Implementation
Author: Kupfer, D.J., Levine, M., and Nelson, J.A.
Publisher and date: Marcel Dekker, Inc., 1976

Title: Education in Informatics of Health Personnel
Author: Anderson, J., Gremy, F., and Pages, J.C.
Publisher and date: Elsevier Science Publishing Co., Inc., 1974

Title: Health Informatics
Author: Brandejs, J.F.
Publisher and date: Elsevier Science Publishing Co., Inc., 1976

Title: Decision Making and Medical Care—Can Information Science Help?
Author: Dombal, F., and Gremy, F.
Publisher and date: Elsevier Science Publishing Co., Inc., 1976

Title: Information Systems for Patient Care
Author: VanEgmond, J., DeVries Robbe, P.F., and Levy, A.H.
Publisher and date: Elsevier Science Publishing Co., Inc., 1976

Title: Computer Glossary for Medical and Health Sciences
Author: Sippl, C.J., and Blessum, W.T.
Publisher and date: Funk & Wagnalls, Inc., 1973

Title: Computer Electrocardiography: Present Status and Criteria
Author: Pordy, L.
Publisher and date: Futura Publishing Co., Inc., 1977

Title: Computerization of Clinical Records, Vol. 1
Author: Gabrieli, E.R.
Publisher and date: Grune & Stratton, Inc., 1970

Title: Intensive Care Instrumentation
Author: Hill, D., and Dolan, A.
Publisher and date: Grune & Stratton, Inc., 1976

Title: Computer Projects in Health Care
Author: Giebink, G.A., and Hurst, L.L.
Publisher and date: Health Administration Press, 1975

Title: Computers in Ultrasonic Diagnosis
Author: Hill, D.W.
Publisher: International School Book Service

Title: Computers in Radiology: Proceedings
Author: DeHaene, R., and Wambersie, A.
Publisher and date: S. Karger, 1969

Title: Clinical Applications of Medical Electronics
Author: Portnoy, W.M., Akers, L.A., Rowley, B.A., and Vines, D.L.
Publisher and date: Lexington Books, 1977

Title: Ambulatory Care Systems, Vol. 1: Design of Ambulatory Care Systems for Improved Patient Flow
Author: Rising, E.
Publisher and date: Lexington Books, 1977

Title: An Introduction to Medical Automation, 2nd ed.
Author: Payne, L.C.
Publisher and date: J.B. Lippincott Co., 1975

Title: Records, Computers, and the Rights of Citizens: Report of the Secretary's Advisory Committee on Automated Personal Data Systems
Author: U.S. Department of Health, Education, and Welfare
Publisher and date: The MIT Press, 1973

Title: COSTAR: Computer Stored Ambulatory Record
Author: Barnett, G.O.
Publisher and date: National Technical Information Service, 1975

Title: Evaluation of the Implementation of a Medical Information System in a General Community Hospital
Author: Barrett, J.P., Barnum, R.A., Gordon, B.B., and Pesut, R.N.
Publisher and date: National Technical Information Service, 1975

Title: An Analysis of Automated Ambulatory Medical Record Systems, Vols. 1 and 2
Author: Henley, R., and Wiederhold, G.
Publisher: National Technical Information Service

Title: Health Care Delivery Systems: Role of Computers in the Health Field: Report of the Ontario Council of Health (supplement 9)
Author: Ontario Council of Health
Publisher and date: Ontario Department of Health, 1970

Title: The Role of Computers in the Health Field: Report of the Ontario Council of Health (supplement 9A)
Author: Ontario Council of Health
Publisher and date: Ontario Department of Health, 1971

Title: Computers in the Service of Medicine, Vols. 1 and 2
Author: McLachlan, G., and Shegog, R.A.
Publisher and date: Oxford University Press, 1968

Title: Focus on Medical Computer Development
Author: Ockenden, J.M., and Bodenham, K.E.
Publisher and date: Oxford University Press, 1970

Title: Systems Science in Health Care
Author: Coblentz, A.M., and Walter, J.R.
Publisher: PBI Books

Title: Health and Medical Care Systems: Managing Social Services Systems
Author: Sutherland, J.W.
Publisher: PBI Books

Title: Medical Electronic Equipment, Vol. 2: Monitoring, Recording and Computing Equipment
Author: Dummer, G.W.A., and Robertson, J.M.
Publisher and date: Pergamon Press, Inc., 1970

Title: Biomedical Technology in Hospital Diagnosis
Author: Telder, A., and Neill, D.W.
Publisher and date: Pergamon Press, Inc., 1972

Title: Hospital Computer Systems and Procedures, Vol. 2: Medical Systems
Author: Garrett, R.D.
Publisher and date: Petrocelli/Charter, 1976

Title: Hospitals: A Systems Approach
Author: Garrett, R.D.
Publisher and date: Petrocelli/Charter, 1973

Title: Biomedical Computing
Author: Perkins, W.J.
Publisher and date: Pilman Medical, 1977

Title: Computer Analysis of Neuronal Structures (Computers in Biology and Medicine)
Author: Lindsay, R.
Publisher and date: Plenum Publishing Corp., 1976

Title: Digital Processing of Biomedical Images
Author: Preston, K.
Publisher and date: Plenum Publishing Corp., 1976

Title: Medical Records, Medical Education, and Patient Care
Author: Weed, L.L.
Publisher and date: The Press of Case Western Reserve University, 1971

Title: Computer Processing of Dynamic Images (From an Anger Scintillation Camera)
Author: Larson, K.B., and Cox, J.
Publisher and date: Publishing Sciences Group, Inc., 1974

Title: Computers and the Delivery of Medical Care
Author: Deland, E.C., Frank, W., Stacey, R.W., and Waxman, B.D.
Publisher and date: Rand Corp., 1969

Title: Data Processing in Electroencephalography
Author: Binnie, C.D.
Publisher and date: Research Studies Press, 1977

Title: Mathematical Modelling of Dynamic Biological Systems
Author: Finkelstein, L., and Carson, E.R.
Publisher and date: Research Studies Press, 1977

Title: Computers in Ultrasonic Diagnosis
Author: Woodcock, J.P., and Wells, P.N.T.
Publisher and date: Research Studies Press, 1977

Title: Computerized Axial Tomography
Author: Gambarelli, J., et al.
Publisher and date: Springer-Verlag New York, Inc., 1976

Title: Cranial Computerized Tomography
Author: Lauksch, W., and Kazner, E.
Publisher and date: Springer-Verlag New York, Inc., 1976

Title: Linear Adaptive Decision Functions and their Application to Clinical Decision
Author: Vesely, A., and Vajda, I.
Publisher and date: Springer-Verlag New York, Inc., 1971

Title: Health Research: The Systems Approach
Author: Werley, H.H., et al.
Publisher and date: Springer-Verlag New York, Inc., 1976

Title: Problem Directed and Medical Information Systems
Author: Driggs, M.F. (editor)
Publisher and date: Stratton Intercontinental Medical Book Corp., 1973

Title: Computer Applications in Health Care Delivery
Author: Weller, C. (editor)
Publisher and date: Stratton Intercontinental Medical Book Corp., 1976

Title: Involvement of Computers in Medical Sciences
Author: Shadid, K.M., VanderAa, H.J., and Sicking, L.M.C.J.
Publisher and date: Swets & Zeitlinger, 1969

Title: Medical Data Processing
Author: Laudet, M., and Begon, F.
Publisher and date: Taylor & Francis, 1976

Title: Automation of the Problem Oriented Medical Record
Publisher: U.S. Department of Health, Education, and Welfare

Title: Computer Stored Ambulatory Record (COSTAR)
Publisher: U.S. Department of Health, Education, and Welfare

Title: Evaluation of a Medical Information System in a Community Hospital
Publisher: U.S. Department of Health, Education, and Welfare

Title: Computers, Electrocardiography, and Public Health
Publisher: U.S. Department of Health, Education, and Welfare

Title: Hospitals: A Systems Approach
Author: Garrett, R.D.
Publisher and date: Van Nostrand Reinhold Co., 1973

Title: Computer Techniques in Biomedicine and Medicine
Author: Haga, E.
Publisher and date: Van Nostrand Reinhold Co., 1972

Title: Laboratory On-Line Computing: An Introduction for Engineers and Physicians
Author: Brignell, J., and Rhodes, G.
Publisher and date: John Wiley & Sons, Inc., 1975

Title: Computer Technology in Neuroscience
Author: Brown, P.B.
Publisher and date: John Wiley & Sons, Inc., 1976

Title: Hospital Computer Systems (Biomedical Engineering and Health Systems Series)
Author: Collen, M.F.
Publisher and date: John Wiley & Sons, Inc., 1974

Title: The Minicomputer in the Laboratory: With Examples Using the PDP-11
Author: Cooper, J.W.
Publisher and date: John Wiley & Sons, Inc., 1977

Title: Signal Analysis and Pattern Recognition in Biomedical Engineering
Author: Inbar, G.F.
Publisher and date: John Wiley & Sons, Inc., 1975

Title: The Post-Physician Era (Medicine in the 21st Century)
Author: Maxmen, J.
Publisher and date: John Wiley & Sons, Inc., 1976

Title: Physical Techniques in Medicine
Author: McMullan, J.T.
Publisher and date: John Wiley & Sons, Inc., 1977

Title: Personalized Database Systems (Information Science Series)
Author: Mittman, B., and Borman, L.
Publisher and date: John Wiley & Sons, Inc., 1975

Title: Computers in Neurobiology and Behavior
Author: Soucek, B., and Carlson, A.D.
Publisher and date: John Wiley & Sons, Inc., 1976

Title: Computers in Medicine
Author: Rose, J.
Publisher and date: Year Book Medical Publishers, Inc., 1972

JOURNALS

Australasian Physical & Engineering Sciences in Medicine
Australasian College of Physical Scientists in Medicine
Department of Physical Sciences, Cancer Institute
481 Little Lonsdale Street
Melbourne, Victoria 3000, Australia

Automedica
Gordon and Breach Science Publishers, Ltd.
41-42 William IV Street
London WC2N 4DE, England

CES Computer Enhanced Spectroscopy
Wiley-Heyden Journals
Baffins Lane, Chichester
Sussex PO19 IUD, England

Computer Medicine
Associates, Inc.
Box 455
Mount Arlington, NJ 07856

Computer Medicine
Computer Medicine Society
Box 779
Ealing, London W5, England

Computer Programs in Biomedicine
North Holland Publishing Co.
52 Vanderbilt Avenue
New York, NY 10017

Computerized Radiology
Pergamon Press, Inc.
Journals Division, Maxwell House
Fairview Park
Elmsford, NY 10523

Computers in Biology and Medicine
Pergamon Press, Inc.
Journals Division, Maxwell House
Fairview Park
Elmsford, NY 10523

Computers and Biomedical Research
Academic Press, Inc.
111 Fifth Avenue
New York, NY 10003

Computers in Healthcare
Cardiff Communications, Inc.
6430 S. Yosemite Street
Englewood, CO 80111

Computers and Medicine
Medit Associates Inc.
Box 36
Glencoe, IL 60022

Computers in Nursing
2350 Virginia Avenue
Hagerstown, MD 21740

Computers in Psychiatry/Psychology
Marc D. Schwartz, M.D.
26 Trumbull Street
New Haven, CT

Cyberdent
University of North Carolina at Chapel Hill
School of Dentistry
Chapel Hill, NC 27514

Engineering in Medicine and Biology
Institute of Electrical and Electronic Engineers; Journal of the Engineering in Medicine and Biology Society
345 E. 47th Street
New York, NY 10017

Healthcare Computing and Communications
Health Data Analysis, Inc.
P.O. Box 620370
Littleton, CO 80162

International Journal of Bio-Medical Computing
Elsevier Scientific Publishers, Ireland, Ltd.
Box 85
Limerick, Ireland

Journal of Clinical Computing
Journal of Clinical Computing, Inc.
166 Morris Avenue
Buffalo, NY 14214

Journal of Educational Computing Research
Baywood Publishing Co., Inc.
120 Marine Street
P.O. Box D
Farmingdale, NY 11735

Journal of Medical Systems
Plenum Press
233 Spring Street
New York, NY 10013

M.D. Computing
Springer-Verlag New York, Inc.
175 Fifth Avenue
New York, NY 10010

Medical Computer Journal
Medical Computer Journal
42 East High Street E
Hampton, CT 06424

Medicine and Computer
American Association for Medical Systems and Informatics
470 Mamoaroneck Avenue
White Plains, NY 10605

Methods of Information in Medicine
Official Journal of the European Federation for Medical Information (EFMI)
(Pub. by F.K. Schattauer Verlag: Stuttgart and New York)

Micro MD Journal
Micro MD Publishers
P.O. Box 2500
Chesapeake, VA 23320

Physicians and Computers
Physicians and Computers, Inc.
P.O. Box 491
Lake Bluff, IL 60044

Sigbio Newsletter
Special Interest Group on Biomedical Computing
1133 Avenue of the Americas
New York, NY 10036

Software in Healthcare
Software in Healthcare Publishing
323$^{1}/_{2}$ Richmond Street
El Segundo, CA 90245

APPENDIX III

JOURNALS AND MAGAZINES REVIEWING COMPUTER HARDWARE/SOFTWARE

GENERAL COMPUTERS

Canadian Datasystems
1111 Melville Street, Suite 600
Vancouver, B.C., Canada V6E 3V6

Communication Systems
Lakeview Publications, Inc.
1200 Aerowood Drive, Unit 28
Mississauga, Ontario, Canada L4W 2S7

Computer
10662 Los Vaqueros Circle
Los Alamitos, CA 90720

Computer Decisions
P.O. Box 1417
Riverton, NJ 08077

Computer Design
Advanced Technology Group
119 Russell Street
Littleton, MA 01460

Computer Technology Review
West World Productions, Inc.
924 Westwood Boulevard, Suite 650
Los Angeles, CA 90024

Datamation
875 Third Avenue
New York, NY 10022

Electronic Products and Technology
1200 Aerowood Drive, Unit 28
Mississauga, Ontario, Canada L4W 2S7

Electronics
McGraw-Hill Bldg.
1221 Avenue of the Americas
New York, NY 10020

Infosystems
Hitchcock Bldg.
Wheaton, IL 60188

Mini-Micro Systems
270 St. Paul Street
Denver, CO 80206

MICROCOMPUTERS

Business Computing
Computer Age, Ltd.
4 Valentine Place
London, SE1, England

Byte
70 Main Street
Peterborough, NH 03458

Compute
P.O. Box 5406
Greensboro, NC 27403

Computers and Programming
380 Lexington Avenue
New York, NY 10017

Computing Today
145 Charing Cross Road
London WC2H 0EE, England

Creative Computing
39 East Hanover Avenue
Morris Plains, NJ 07950

Dr. Dobb's Journal
P.O. Box E
Menlo Park, CA 94025

Interface Age
P.O. Box 1234
Cerritos, CA 90701

Microcomputing
Micron Distributing
409 Queen Street, W.
Toronto, Ontario, Canada M5V 2A5

onComputing
onComputing Inc.
70 Main Street
Peterborough, NH 03458

Practical Computing
IPC Electrical Electronic Press, Ltd.
Quadrant House, The Quadrant
Sutton, Surrey SM25AS, England

Recreational Computing
People's Computer Co.
1263 El Camino Real, Box E
Menlo Park, CA 94025

Which Computer?
30-31 Islington Green
London N1, England

GENERAL SCIENCE MAGAZINES

Discover
Time-Life Bldg.
541 North Fairbanks Court
Chicago, IL 60611

High Technology
38 Commercial Wharf
Boston, MA 02110

Newscientist
Dee Knapp, IPC Magazines, Ltd.
205 East 42nd Street
New York, NY 10017

Popular Science
380 Madison Avenue
New York, NY 10017

Science 84
1515 Massachusetts Avenue, N.W.
Washington, D.C. 20005

Science Digest
224 West 57th Street
New York, NY 10019

Technology Illustrated
342 Madison Avenue, Suite 1224
New York, NY 10173

ELECTRONICS

Electronics Today
Unit 6, 25 Overlea Boulevard
Toronto, Ontario, Canada M4H 1B1

Elementary Electronics
380 Lexington Avenue
New York, NY 10017

Popular Electronics
P.O. Box 2774
Boulder, CO 80302

Practical Electronics
Westover House, Quay Road
Poole, Dorset BH15 1JG, England

Radio-Electronics
200 Park Avenue, S.
New York, NY 10003

Science & Electronics
380 Lexington Avenue
New York, NY 10017

Wireless World
Quadrant House, The Quadrant
Sutton, Surrey SM2 5AS, England

INDEX

A

Acceptance test procedure
  in functional specification, 181
  for new hardware, 52
Access, scheduled, description of, 65
Account number as system security, 162
Accounts receivable, systems for, 171
ACM; see Association for Computing Machinery
Acoustic coupler
  cost of, 38
  function of, 38-39
  for transmission of ECG, 38
  transmission rate of, 38
Acquisition, terms of, and functional specification, 181
Acquisition period of health care–computing system, 186-187
Address, definition of, 14
Administrative computing
  director of, 199
  versus patient-care and medical research computing, 196-197, 198
  responsibility of department of, 199
  role of user in, 201
Admitting/discharge/transfer systems as turnkey systems, 217
Alarm systems, limitations of, 104-105
ALGOL
  application of, 76
  as high-level programming language, 75-76
Algorithms
  definition of, 59
  encryption, of National Bureau of Standards, 152-153
Amdahl manufacturer, 52
American Medical Association, health care–computing consultation group, 95
Amortization period for computer systems, 164
Analog-to-digital converter
  as input device, 138
  and real-time systems, 78
Analysis
  cost-benefit; see Cost-benefit analysis
  economic, in proposal for health care–computing system, 224
Analysts, systems, definition of, 60
APL
  as interpreter language, 77
  as very high-level language, 80
Appendices in proposal for health care–computing system, 225
Application, real-time, definition of, 75
Applications packages, 73-81
  use for, 79
Applications programs, 79-80; see also Programs
  definition of, 64
  function of, 8
  software maintenance for, 166
Applications software; see also Applications programs
  and copyright, 180

Applications software—cont'd
  definition of, 8, 164-165
  in functional specification, 180
Applying for funds in health care computing, 220-221
Appraisal of system section of proposal for health care–computing system, 224-225
Arithmetic logic unit, definition of, 7, 10
Arpanet as digital communication network, 39
Array processors and minicomputers, 28
Arrhythmias and control software, 233
Artificial heart, future of, 232-233
Artificial intelligence research
  for computer language, 78
  and health care, 104
  LISP as interpreter in, 78
Artificial limbs, "intelligent," future of, 232
Assemblers
  definition of, 59
  description of, 58-59
  function of, 74-75
  in language hierarchy, 80
  macro, 74-75
  programming in, 75
Assembly languages; see Assemblers
Association for Computing Machinery, publications of, 211
Async; see Asynchronous communications
Asynchronous communications, description of, 34-36
ATP; see Acceptance test procedure
Attitudes towards computers, future of, 234-235
Automation
  in health care environment, 193
  of nonsystem, 93-94
  organizing for, 191-202
  in health care–computing systems, 113

B

Background in multitasking system, 70
Backup
  definition of, 71
  "hot," 150
  procedures for
    automatic, 92-93
    categories of, 92
  as protective measure, 150-151
Bar code printers, use for, 23
Bar code readers, 18, 19
  and voice output synthesizers, 23
Base 2 system, 11-13
Base 10 system, 11-13
BASIC
  application of, 76
  cost of, 81
  as high-level programming language, 75-76
  for microcomputers, 77
Batch, definition of, 65
Batch processing
  description of, 65, 66
  multistream, 65, 66

279

280 Index

Baud, use of term, 36
Benefit, definition of, in health care computing, 158
Benefit/cost ratio, 159-160
   for health care computing, 172
   unit of time in, 162
Binary digit, definition of, 11
Binary system, 12-13
   definition of, 11
Bits
   versus bytes in computer advertising, 49
   definition of, 10-11
   start, 35-36
   stop, 35-36
Blocks, definition of, 15
Books in health care computing, 211
Brain augmentation as role of computer, 230
Budgeting for patient care and medical research, 197
Buffer, definition of, 15
Bugs
   definition of, 71
   in new hardware, 50
   and software development, 129-130
Bundled
   as cost of software, 165
   definition of, 81
Bus network structure, 40
   description of, 41
Bytes
   versus bits in computer advertising, 49
   definition of, 10-11
   as measure of memory size, 14

C

Cable
   dedicated, 38
   TV, for data transmission, 40
Cache memories, definition of, 29
Calculation of present value, formula for, 160
Calculators, 228
   read only memory in, 58
Canada
   cost of hardware in, 49
   financial constraints of hospitals in, 205
Canadian Organization for the Advancement of Computers in Health, 211
Card readers, function of, 15, 17
Cardiac pacemaker registration system, 229
Cards, punched
   cost of, 167
   for inputting data, 15-17
Cartridges, disk, definition of, 25
Cath lab data acquisition systems as turnkey systems, 217
Cathode ray tube, function of, 21-22
Central processing unit, 10-13
   capabilities of, 10
   definition of, 7, 10
   and location of peripheral devices, 34
   and processor utilization, 65
Centralized approach to health care computing, 195-196
Channel
   definition of, 29
   grades of, 38
Character printer, 20
Checkup, automated, future of, 234
Chip
   definition of, 10
   in microprocessors, 27

Clock, real-time, definition of, 69
COACH; see Canadian Organization for the Advancement of Computers in Health Care
COBOL
   application of, 76
   cost of, for minicomputers, 81
   as high-level programming language, 75-76
   for business, 204
Code
   error, and human engineering, 140
   mnemonic, definition of, 59
   object, definition of, 76
   source; see Source code
Coding
   as phase of software development, 124-125, 128
   responsibility for, 90-91
Collection of money in health care computing, 170-171
COM; see Computer output microfilm devices
Committee
   computer advisory, role of, in health care computing, 200-201
   research user's, 201
   role of, in health care computing, 188
Communications, 30-43
   consultants for communications systems, 43
   design versus reality in, 105
   gap between health care and computer science, 1-2
   long-distance, alternatives for, 42
   polled, 41-42
Compatible, plug-to-plug, 51
Compilers, 76-77
   definition of, 8, 76
   optimizing, function of, 77
Computer advisory committee, role of, in health care computing, 200-201
Computer-assisted diagnosis, 171
Computer-based data, protective measures for, 150-153
Computer center in health care institutions, advantages of, 195
Computer operators, role of, 84
Computer output microfilm devices, use for, 22
Computer personnel; see Personnel
Computer products in proposal for health care–computing system, 223; see also Hardware; Software
Computer science
   as academic study, 204
   background in, for health care–computing specialist, 206
Computer scientist, senior, cost of, 61
Computer systems, 3-8; see also Computers
   alternative types of, 86-87
   and augmentation of human resources, 228-229
   and backup procedures, 92-93
   costs of, 120
   and savings in, 163
   creativity and, 107
   defenses of, 151-153
   definition of, 4
   development of new
      and functional specifications, 175
      successful, 84-85
   expansion of, need for, 178
   expenses of, 192
   failure of, 4, 5, 218
   financial losses from, 192-193
   in health care computing; see Health care computing

Computer systems—cont'd
  human factor in, 105-106
  impact of, 93-95, 193-194
  implementation of, 92-93
  inappropriate, in health care computing, 230-232
  leasing of, 164
  monitoring progress in, 93-95
  rental of, 164
  resistance to change in, 53-54
  room for, cost of, 168
  and saving funds, 94, 163
  security for, 30, 152
  in situ, 83-95
  success or failure of, 4, 5
  unreliable, 141
Computerizing people, 142
Computers; see also Computer systems
  communications in, 30-43
  definition of, 7
  digital, and human beings, 136
  functions of, 142-144
  future of, 30-31, 227-235
  heat generated by, 30
  large, 26-30
  mass production of, 27
  medium, 26-30
  obsolescence in, 50, 52-53
  power supply requirements of, 30
  self-programming, nonexistence of, 62
  size of chassis of, 216
  small, 26-30
  speed of, 10
  warnings about, 52
Computing
  administrative; see Administrative computing
  conspicuous, 113-114, 215-218
  consumer education in, 216-218
  distributed, for 100% availability, 93
  health care; see Health care computing
  hospital service, support for, 199
  medical research; see Medical research computing
  patient-care, 196-198
  politics of, 195-197
Conceptual security, 153
Conferences for health care computing, 211-212
Conflicts in health care computing, avoidance of, 197-202
Conspicuous computing, 113-114, 215-218
Consultants
  communications, for communications systems, 43
  data processing, role of, 90
  management, role of, 90
Consumer education
  in computing, 216-218
  and health care computing, 113-114
Continuing education in health care computing, 210-212
Contracts, 173-182
  and functional specifications, 86-87, 177
  and health care computing, 112
  maintenance; see Maintenance contract
Control unit, definition of, 7, 10
Converter, analog-to-digital, 78, 138
Cooperative studies, automation of, 234
Copyright
  and applications software, 180
  and software package, 80
    and modifications, 166

Cost, definition of
  in cost-benefit analysis, 158
  in cost-effectiveness, 160
Cost benefit, unit of time in, 162
Cost-benefit analysis
  definition of, 158
  in health care computing, 158-160
Cost-benefit justification in proposal for health care–computing system, 224
Cost-effectiveness
  and health care computing, 160-162, 172
  in proposal for health care–computing system, 224
  unit of time in, 162
Cost justification
  definition of, 158
  in health care computing, 172
Coupler, acoustic; see Acoustic coupler
Courses, supplementary, in health care computing, 209-210
CP/M as operating system, 64
CPU; see Central processing unit
Creativity and computer systems, 107
Credit, tax, for capital equipment, 49, 171
Critical analysis and comparison in proposal for health care–computing system, 223
CRT; see Cathode ray tube
CT scanner
  and application of computer, 62
  computer in, 217
  as health care automation, 196-197

D

DAA; see Data access arrangement
Data
  clinical, 99
  collection of
    design of printer forms for, 139
    and possibility of errors, 102
  computer-based, threats to security of, 147-153
  encrypting of, for security, 152-153
  inputting of; see Input process
  retrieval of, 99
  storage of, in functional specification, 86
Data access arrangement, definition of, 43
Data bus, 40, 41
Data definition language, function of, 78
Data-entry clerks, role of, 84, 91
Data-entry software package, description of, 100-101
Data management language
  cost of, 81
  definition of, 78
Data processing
  consultants for, role of, 90
  control of, in organization, 195
  in functional specification, 86
  types of, in health care computing, 194-195
  vice-president of, role of, 91, 194-195
Database
  management of, and signal processing, 201-202
  nonestablishment of, 153
  on-line literature, 100
Datamation, 211, 212
DATAPAC as digital communications network, 39
Dataset; see also Modems
  function of, 39
  limited distance, use for, 39
dBASE II, cost of, 81

DDD network; *see* Direct distance dialing network
DDL; *see* Data definition language
Debugging
   and interpreter, 78
   as phase of software development, 128-130
   of program, definition of, 61
Decentralized approach to health care computing, 195-196, 201
Decimal system, 11-13
Dedicated cable, definition of, 38
Dedicated wiring, definition of, 38
Degree programs in health care information sciences, 208-209
Demultiplexing systems, function of, 39
Density of floppy disks, 25
Design phase of software development, 124, 126-128
Development/acquisition period of health care–computing system, 186-187
Development staff, 90-91
Device independence, definition of, 71
Devices
   input; *see* Input devices
   output; *see* Output devices
   peripheral; *see* Peripheral devices
   secondary memory, definition of, 7, 23
   storage, 7, 23-26
Diagnosis and use of computer, 230-231
Dialog as on-line literature database, 100
Digit, binary, definition of, 11
Digital computers and human beings, 136
Direct distance dialing network, 38
Director of research computing, role of, 199-200
Discounts for hardware, 171
Dishonesty as threat to security of computer-based data, 148
Disk cartridges, definition of, 25
Disk drives, 26
Disk packs, 25, 26
   cost of, 167-168
Disk platter, 25
Diskette, definition of, 25; *see also* Floppy disks
Disks
   floppy; *see* Floppy disks
   hard, 25
   laser; *see* Laser disks
   optical; *see* Optical disks
   storage capacity of, 25
   types of, 24-25
Distributed computing for 100% availability, 93
Distributed processing, 41
DML; *see* Data management language
Documentation
   and design of software, 127-128
   elements in, 85
   and functional specification, 180
   levels of, 128
Documentation writer, role of, 91
Do-it-yourself approach to hardware maintenance, 165-166
Do-it-yourself systems, 87-88
Dot matrix printer
   definition of, 20-21
   quality of print with, 140
Down, definition of, 51
Down-time, cost of, 141
Drives
   disk, 26
   tape, function of, 23
Duke University and degree in health care information science, 209
Dumb terminals, definition of, 15

E

Economic analysis in proposal for health care–computing system, 224
Economics
   and feasibility study, 185
   and health care computing, 112, 157-172
Economy of scale, explanation of, 195
Education, consumer; *see* Consumer education
Educational issues in health care computing, 113-114
Effectiveness, definition of, in cost-effectiveness, 160-161
Electrical modifications of computer room, 168
Electromagnetic waveguides, function of, 39-40
Employer-employee relationship in health care institutions, 205
Encryption
   algorithm of National Bureau of Standards, 152-153
   of data for security, 152-153
Engineering
   human; *see* Human engineering
   software; *see* Software engineering
Environment and data entry, 137
Environmental costs in health care computing, 168
Equipment; *see* Hardware
Ergonomics; *see* Human engineering
Error code and human engineering, 140
Errors
   computer, detection of, 102, 104
   of input and programming, 139
   as threats to security of computer-based data, 148
Event-driven operating systems, 68-70
"Evolutionary pressures" and computer systems, 5-6
Executive summary of proposal for health care–computing system, 221
External specification of functional specification, 178-179

F

Fail-soft procedures, 92-93
Failure of health care–computing system, example of, 118-121
FDA and regulation of health care–computing software, 132
Feasibility study of health care–computing application, 184-185
Fibers, optical, function of, 40
Financing in health care environment, 205
Fire extinguishers and computer systems, 155
Fire hazards to computer system, 149, 151, 153
Fire protection as protective measure, 151
Firmware, definition of, 58
Floor space, methods of calculation of cost of, 168
Floppy disks
   costs of, 168
   density of, 25
   manageability of, 25
   sizes of, 25
   storage capacity of, 25
Flowcharting, obsolescence of, 61
Foreground in multitasking system, 70
Forms
   OMR, cost of, 167
   printed, for data collection, design of, 139
FORTRAN
   acronym, 76

FORTRAN—cont'd
  application of, 76
  as high-level programming language, 75-76
  variations in, 77
Fourier processors and minicomputers, 28
Full duplex mode, description of, 37
Fully connected network structure, 40, 41
Function-related programming languages, 74
Functional specifications, 173-182
  and contracts, 86-87, 177
  definition of, 46, 174
  elements in, 85-86
  format of, 177-182
  and health care computing, 112, 181-182
  in proposals for health care–computing systems, 221, 222
  purpose of, 174-177
Funding
  applying for, in health care computing, 220-221
  of health care computing, 219-226

G

General purpose systems and health care computing, 218
Generic reports, use for, 103
Georgia Institute of Technology and degree in health care information science, 209
"Gold standard" as process of analyzing cost-effectiveness, 162
Groking, definition of, 60
Guaranteed response time to service call in maintenance contract, 51
Guidance to system developers as purpose of functional specification, 175-177

H

Half duplex mode, description of, 37
Handprint identifying machines as systems security, 152
Hard disks, description of, 25
Hard-wired, definition of, 38
Hard-wired programming, 57-58
Hardware, 9-31, 45-54
  availability of, 51
  cost of, 49
    in health care–computing system, 163-164
    trend in, 5-6
  decision to acquire, 192
  definition of, 4
  discounts for, 171
  in functional specification, 179-181
  future of, 232-233
  leasing of, 48, 164
  life expectancy of, 164
  maintenance of; see Hardware maintenance
  modification of, 47
  new versus tested, 50
  redundant, need for, 93
  rental of, 48-49
  selection of, 46-47, 50
  shipment of, 52
  supplier for, 49-52
  used, 48
  warranty on, 51
Hardware maintenance
  in health care–computing systems, 165-166
  and supplier, 88
  types of, 165-166
Hardware specification
  definition of, 46

Hardware specification—cont'd
  items in, 46-47
Header characters, function of, 36
Health care
  background in, for health care–computing specialist, 206-207
  growth of field and use of computer, 231
Health care computing
  administrative computing versus patient-care and medical research computing, 196-197
  avoidance of conflicts in, 197-202
  centralized versus decentralized approach to, 195-196
  collection of money in, 170-171
  and consumer education, 113-114
  costs in, 162-169
    definition of, 158
    environmental, 168
    versus savings, 171-172
    of system, 120
  discounts for hardware in, 171
  economics of, 157-172
  education in, 113, 208-212
  factors in making commitment to computer technology, 192-193
  failure of system in, 118-121, 218
  and FDA regulation, 132
  feasibility study for, 184-185
  and functional specifications, 174-177, 181-182
  funding of, 110, 219-226
  future of, 114, 227-235
  inappropriate use of computer in, 230-232
  increasing productivity in, 170
  and inflation, 169
  introduction of system in, 142, 150-153
  issues in, 109-115
  limitations of, 106, 132-133
  management of projects in, 183-189
  manager in; see Manager, health care–computing
  managing systems development in, 113
  organizing for automation in, 113
  overlapping spheres of, 194
  and privacy and security, 111-112, 150-156
  proposal for system for, 185-186, 221-226
  realities in, 201-202
  reducing staff turnover in, 170
  reliability of, 141
  savings in, 169-171
  separation of departments of, 199
  and software engineering, 110-111, 132
  specialist journals in, 210
  specialists in; see Specialists in health care computing
  and turnkey systems, 187-188
  types of data processing in, 194-195
  use for computer in, 228-230
Health care–computing specialists; see Specialists in health care computing
Health care data, security of computer-based, 147-148
Health care environment
  computing needs in, 80-81
  financing in, 205
Health care providers, robot, as inappropriate use of computer, 230-231
Health records; see Medical records
Heat and computers, 30
HELP feature, 138
Hierarchical input, process, and output as system of software development, 127

Hierarchy of programming languages, 80-81
High capacity electromagnetic waveguides, function of, 39-40
High-level languages, 59, 75-79
   extension of, 78-79
   in language hierarchy, 80
   and programmers, 81
   in software specifications, 85
HIPO; see Hierarchical input, process, and output
HMRI as hospital-discharge summary abstraction system, 101-103
Hospital business computing versus patient-care computing, 198
Hospital-discharge summary abstraction systems, 101-103
Hospital service computing, support for, 199
Hospitals, computing needs of, 204-205
"Hot" backup, 150
Hot line for software maintenance, 88
House, systems, as computer system supplier, 88
Human engineering, 135-144
   definition of, 111
   function of, 136-137
   and health care computing, 111
   and input devices, 137-139
   and output process, 139-140
   and privacy and security, 140-141
   of programs, 60
   and reliability, 141
Human factor in computer systems, 105-106
Human interaction and continuing education in health care computing, 212
Humanizing of technology, 136-141
Hunter College (NY) and degree in health care information science, 209

I

IBM units, compatibility of microcomputers with, 52
ICs; see Integrated circuits
IEEE; see Institute of Electrical and Electronics Engineers
Impact printer, 20
Implants, computer-controlled, future of, 232-233
Independence, device, definition of, 71
Index
   of data, 99
   of literature, automation of, 99-100
Inflation and cost of health care computing, 169
Information science, health care, degree programs in, 208-209
Ink-jet printers, 21
Input devices, 14-19
   definition of, 7
   and human engineering, 137-139
Input/output, definition of, 67
Input process, 137-139
   errors in, 100
   limitations of, 99-103
Institute of Electrical and Electronics Engineers, publications of, 211
Instruction set
   definition of, 10, 56
   of microcomputers, 57
Instructions, definition of, 10
Integrated circuits in microprocessors, 27
Integrator, system, function of, 47-48
"Intelligent" body parts, future of, 232-233
Intelligent terminals, description of, 28-29

Interface, parallel, definition of, 34
Internal memory, 11, 14
   of advanced operating systems, 72
   definition of, 7
   measurement of, 14
Interpreters, 77-78
   of computer installation, 186-187
   definition of, 8
   function of, 77
Introduction
   to functional specification, 177-178
   to problem in proposal for health care–computing system, 221, 222
Investment tax credit
   for capital equipment, 49
   for computer equipment, 171
I/O; , see Input/output
I/O bound, definition of, 68

J

Job, definition of, 66
Journaling as backup procedure, 92
Journals and health care computing, 210, 211
Justification, cost, definition of, 158

K

1K, definition of, 14
Keyboard
   as input device, 14-15
   with special key arrangements, 137
Keypad
   definition of, 14
   specialized, 137
Keypunch machine, function of, 15, 17
Kilobyte, definition of, 14

L

Languages, programming, 73-81
   assembler; see Assembler
   compilers, 76-77
   cost of, 81
   data definition, function of, 78
   data management; see Data management language
   definition of, 8
   function-related, 74
   in functional specification, 179
   future of, 74
   hierarchy of, 80-81
   high-level; see High-level languages
   interpreters, 77-78
   machine, 57, 80
      programming in, 58
   and modification of system, 74
   and productivity of programmers, 81, 126
   query, function of, 78
   standards for, 77
   variations in, 77
   very high-level, 80-81
LANs; see Local area networks
Large computers, 26-30
Laser disks
   description of, 26
   future of, 233
   storage capacity of, 26
Laser printers, 21
LDDS; see Limited distance dataset
Lease
   definition of, 48

Lease—cont'd
    for hardware, 48, 164
        cost of, 48, 163
    of software, cost of, 165
Legal tender in computer purchase, 50-51
Letter-quality printers, cost of, 140
Light pen as input device, 18
Limited distance dataset, use for, 39
LINC processor as prototype minicomputer, 28
Line printer, 20
LISP as interpreter language, 78
Literature index, automation of, 99-100
Local area networks for data transmission, 40
Log, transaction
    as backup procedure, 92, 150
    definition of, 71
    as protective measure, 150-151
    as security, 152
Logic flow in structured programming, 127
Long-distance communications, alternatives for, 42

M

Machine language; see Languages, programming, machine
Machine language program, definition of, 10
Machines, von Neumann, 58
Macro
    definition of, 75
    function of, 75
Macro assembler, 74-75
Magnetic recording devices, 24
Magnetic tapes
    cost of, 168
    format of, 24
    as storage medium, 23-24
Mainframes, definition of, 29; see also Maxicomputers
Maintenance
    hardware; see Hardware maintenance
    of programming language, 81
    for rented equipment, 48-49
    of software; see Software maintenance
    of system and functional specification, 181
Maintenance contract
    considerations in, 166
    cost of, 51
    for hardware
        leased, 48
        renewal of, 165
        used, 48
        usual terms of, 165
    items in, 51
    for software, 92
        cost of, 166
        and debugging, 71
Management
    of health care–computing projects, 183-189
    divisions of, 199
    project, of software development, 131
    role of, in avoiding conflicts in health care computing, 197-200
    of systems development in health care computing, 113
Management augmentation as role of computer, 229-230
Management consultants, role of, 90
Manager
    health care–computing
        attributes of, 184
        importance of, 188-189
        roles of, 185-187

Manager—cont'd
    of health care–computing center and politics of computing, 196
    project, role of, 90
Manual procedures and installation of computer system, 92
Manuals, systems and users', in functional specification, 180; see also Documentation
Mass storage devices, definition of, 23
Maxicomputers, capabilities of, 29
Mean time between failures of modems, 43
Mean time to repair telephone company devices, 43
Medical records
    abstracting of, 101-103
    cradle-to-grave, 233
    as implant, 233
    and privacy, 146
    security of, 147-148
Medical research computing
    versus administrative computing, 196-197
    future of, 227-235
    requirements in, 198
    and role of user, 201
Medical Research Council–Canada as funding source, 220
Medinfo International Conference, 211
Medium computers, 26-30
Medline as on-line literature database, 100
Megabyte, definition of, 25
Memories
    cache, definition of, 29
    computer, unreality of, 98-99
    internal; see Internal memory
Memory devices
    pseudorandom-access, 25
    secondary, 7, 23
Meta stepwise refinement as system of software development, 127
Microcomputer systems
    for accounts receivable in physician's office, 171
    BASIC as language for, 77
    cost of, 81
    versus computer centers, 195
    cost of, 28, 47
        including programming languages, 81
    electrical modifications for, 168
    instruction set of, 57
    as terminals, 28-29
Microphone as input device, 19
Microprocessors
    application of, to health care, 27-28
    development of, 27
Microwave facilities for data transmission, 39
Midicomputers, definition of, 29
Miniaturization in hardware, 232-233
Minicomputer system
    availability of, 28
    capabilities of, 28
    cost of, 28
    extension of, 28-29
Mnemonic code, definition of, 59
Modems
    cost of, 39, 42-43
    function of, 39
    security for, 152
    transmission rate of, 39

Modularization
  definition of, 27
  trend towards, 27
Modulator/demodulator; see Modems
Monitoring system
  computerized, limitations of, 104-105
  as turnkey system, 217
Morbidity as measure of cost-effectiveness, 161
Mouse, function of, 18, 137-138
MP/M as operating system, 64
MRC; see Medical Research Council-Canada
MS DOS as operating system, 64
MTBF; see Mean time between failures
MTTR; see Mean time to repair
Multiplexers, function of, 39
Multipoint network structure, 40
  description of, 41
Multiprogramming system, definition of, 69
Multistream batch system, description of, 65, 66
Multitasking operating system
  definition of, 69
  limitations of, 70
MUMPS
  as interpreter language, 77-78
  as very high-level language, 80

N

National Bureau of Standards, encryption algorithm of, 152-153
National Institutes of Health as funding source, 220
National Library of Medicine as funding source, 220
Natural disasters as threats to computer-based data, 149
NBS; see National Bureau of Standards
Networks, 40-41
  basic structure of, 40
  future of, 105
  local area, 40
NIH; see National Institutes of Health
Node in network, 41
NOMAD, use of, 78-79
"Number crunching," definition of, 28

O

Object code, definition of, 76
Object program, 76
Obsolescence
  in computers, 50, 52-53
  of flowcharting, 61
Obsolete methods, support of, as inappropriate use of computer, 231
OCR input devices, 138
OCR readers, function of, 18
OEM; see Original equipment manufacturer
Off-line, definition of, 23
Office, physician's
  accounts receivable systems, 171
  turnkey system for, 87
OMR (optical mark recognition) cards, 17-18
OMR form, 17-18
  cost of, 167
OMR input devices, 138
OMR reader, 17-18
Operands, definition of, 10
Operating systems, 63-72
  categories of, 64
  definition of, 8, 64
  event-driven, 68-70

Operating systems—cont'd
  functions of, 70-71
  multitasking; see Multitasking operating system
  problems with, 71
  and programming language, 81
  real-time, description of, 69-70
  time-driven, 67-68
Operational detail section in proposal for health care-computing system, 224
Operational procedures as security, 153
Operational staff, 91-92
Operators, computer, role of, 84, 91
Optical disks; see also Laser disks
  description of, 26
  future of, 233
  storage capacity of, 26
Optical fibers, function of, 40
Optimizing compilers, function of, 77
Oracle, cost of, 81
Organizing for automation, 113, 191-202
Original equipment manufacturer as supplier of computer system, 88
Output, 76
  format of, 103
  human versus computer, 136
  limitations of, 103-104
  mistrust of, 132-133
Output devices, 19-23
  definition of, 7, 19
Output process and human engineering, 139-140
Overhead, definition of, 70
Overseer of computer installation, 186

P

Pacemakers
  "intelligent," future of, 232
  registration system for, 229
Packages
  applications, 73-81
  software; see Software packages
Packs, disk, 25, 26
Paper
  as fire hazard, 149, 151, 153
  perforated, fanfold, cost of, 167
Parallel interface, definition of, 34
Parallelism, definition of, 29
Pascal as high-level programming language, 75-76
PAS/QAM as hospital-discharge summary abstraction system, 101-103
Passwords, selection of, and system security, 152
Patchboards, function of, 57
Patches, definition of, 71
Patient-care computing
  versus administrative computing, 196-198
  versus medical research computing, 197
Patients, interaction with, by computer, 230-231
Payback and success of computer system, 142
Peer review
  and proposal for health care-computing system, 185-186
  as purpose of functional specification, 174-175
Pen-plotters, function of, 22
Per-call basis of hardware maintenance, 165
Peripheral devices; see also Input devices; Output devices
  definition of, 7
  makeup of, 7-8

Personnel; *see also* Staff
    computer, 89-92
        costs of, in health care computing, 167
    and new computer system, 94
    reducing costs of, in health care computing, 169
    and system design, 84
Personnel augmentation as role of computer, 228-229
Physical security as protective measure, 151
Physician as project manager, 90
Physician's office; *see* Office, physician's
Pilot project as assessment of larger project, 172
Plan in proposal for health care–computing system, 223-224
Platter disk, 25
Plotters, function of, 21-22
Plug-to-plug compatible, definition of, 51
Point-to-point network structure, 40
Politics of computing, 195-197
Polled communications, description of, 41-42
Polling
    advantages of, 42
    definition of, 41
Portable terminals, requirements for, 99
Power supply requirements and computers, 30
Present value calculation, formula for, 160
Previous work section of proposal for health care–computing system, 222-223
Print, quality of, from computers, 140
Printed forms for data collection, design of, 139
Printer-plotters, function of, 22
Printers
    bar code, 23
    character, 20
    dot matrix, 20-21, 140
    impact, 20
    ink-jet, 21
    laser, 21
    letter-quality, cost of, 140
    line, 20
Privacy, 145-156
    factors in, 146
    and health care computing, 111-112, 146
    and human engineering, 140-141
    of patient and research protocol, 154
Problems with operating system, 71
Procedures, operational, as security, 153
Processing
    batch, 65, 66
    data; *see* Data processing
    distributed, 41
    multistream batch, 65, 66
Processor utilization
    definition of, 65
    in single-task computers, 65
Processors; *see also* Central processing unit
    array, and minicomputers, 28
    definition of, 7, 10
    Fourier, and minicomputers, 28
    LINC, 28
Product line and functional specification, 182
Productivity
    and computer system, 229
    increase in, in health care computing, 170
    of new staff person, 170
    of programmers, 81, 125-126
Program documentation; *see* Documentation
Programmer/analysts and software development, 90
Programmer team concept and system development, 127

Programmers
    cost of, 61
    definition of, 60
    as operators, 91
    personality of, and program, 136-137
    productivity of, 125-126
        and use of program language, 81, 126
    role of, 84
    skills of, 121
    and software development, 90-91
Programming
    in assembler language, 75
    chicken house, 124
    and data-entry errors, 139
    errors in, and software testing, 128-130
    limitations of process in, 125
    necessity for, 61-62
    process of, 60-61
    structured, 126-127
        principles of, 60
Programming languages; *see* Languages, programming
Programs
    applications; *see* Applications programs
    definition of, 10, 56, 79
    description of, 56-57
    hard-wired, 57-58
    human engineering of, 60
    machine language, 10
    object, 76
    for one-time use, 61
    routines of, 75
    stored, 58
    source, 76
    utilities, definition of, 71
    writing of, definition of, 10
Project
    pilot, as assessment of larger project, 172
    management of
        and health care computing, 188-189
        of software development, 131
Project manager, role of, 90
Prompting, definition of, 138
Proposal for health care–computing system, 185-186, 221-226
Protective measures for computer-based data, 150-153
Protocol management and computer systems, 230
Pseudorandom-access memory devices, disks as, 25
Punched cards, 15-17, 167

Q

Quality control of hospitalization data, 101-103
Quality control officer of computer installation, 187
Query languages, function of, 78
Queue in time-share system, 67
Quotation for hardware, 47-48

R

Radiology reporting system as turnkey system, 217
RAM; *see* Random access memory
RAMIS, use of, 78-79
Random access memory, definition of, 23
Rate, transmission; *see* Transmission rate
Ratio, benefit/cost; *see* Benefit/cost ratio
Read only memory in calculators, 58
Readers
    bar code; *see* Bar code readers
    card, 15, 17
    OMR, 17-18

Real-time applications, definition of, 75
Real-time clock, definition of, 69
Real-time operating system
  and analog-to-digital conversion, 78
  description of, 69-70
Records
  health; *see* Medical records
  medical; *see* Medical records
Reels, tape, storage capacity of, 23
Registers, definition of, 10
Reliability and human engineering, 141
Remote job entry, definition of, 42
Rental
  of computer system, 164
  of hardware, 48-49
Reports, generic, use for, 103
Request for tender in computer purchases, 50-51
Research
  artificial intelligence; *see* Artificial intelligence research
  medical, and hospital administration, 196
Research computing
  administration for, 199
  director of, 199-200
  support for, 199
Research protocols and patient privacy, 154
Resistance to change in computer system, 53-54
Resources, description of, 64
RFT; *see* Request for tender
Ribbons for printers, cost of, 167
Ring network structure, 40
  advantages of, 41
RJE; *see* Remote job entry
Robot health care providers as inappropriate use of computers, 230-231
ROM; *see* Read only memory
Routines of program, definition of, 75
RPG as high-level programming language, 75-76

S

SAS applications package, 79
Satellites for data transmission, 39
Savings in health care computing, 169-171
Scale, economy of, explanation of, 195
SCAMC; *see* Symposium on Computer Applications in Medical Care
Scanner, CT; *see* CT scanner
Schedule
  and functional specification, 180
  in proposal for health care–computing system, 224
Scheduled access, description of, 65
Science, computer, as academic study, 204
Scrambling of data for security, 152-153
Screens, touch, function of, 18
Secondary memory devices, definition of, 7, 23
Security, 145-146
  breaches of, 153-156
  of computer-based data, threats to, 148-153
  for computers, 30
  conceptual, 153
  definition of, 71
  and health care computing, 111-112, 147-148
  and human engineering, 140-141
  physical, as protective measure, 151
Security capability, definition of, 71
Selection in proposal for health care–computing system, 223-224

Self-aggrandizement as inappropriate use of computer, 231
Semiconductor chip, definition of, 10
Serial mode, definition of, 35
Service call, guaranteed response time to, 51
Set, instruction; *see* Instruction set
Signal processing and database management, 201-202
"Silly money," rental payments as, 164
Small computers, 26-30
Smart terminal, definition of, 15
Smoking
  in computer rooms and near magnetic media, 151
  and damage to computer, 149
SNOBOL as high-level programming language, 75-76
Software, 55-62
  applications; *see* Applications software
  bundled, 81, 165
  categories of, 8, 64, 164-165
  copyright of, and possibility of modifications, 166, 180
  cost of
    development of, 61, 124, 192
    in health care–computing system, 164-165
    trend in, 5-6
  definition of, 4
  design phase of development of, 126-128
  development of, and maintenance, 88
  engineering; *see* Software engineering
  in functional specification, 179, 180
  future of, 233-234
  limitations of, 104-105
  maintenance of; *see* Software maintenance
  modification of, 62
    and copyright, 166
  phases in creating, 124
  specification of, 85
  systems; *see* Systems software
  testing of, levels of, 130
  transportability of, 77
  unbundled, 81, 165
Software engineering, 61, 123-133
  definition of, 124
  discipline of, 126
  and health care computing, 110-111, 132
  limitations of, 131-133
Software maintenance, 88
  for applications programs, 166
  contract for, 92
  and debugging, 71
  cost of, 93, 131, 166
  definition of, 61
  and functional specification, 181
  in health care computing, 166
  as phase of development, 125
  as process, 130-131
Software packages
  advantages of, 79
  data-entry, 100-101
  definition of, 8
  disadvantages of, 79-80
Source as on-line literature database, 100
Source code
  definition of, 76
  and software specifications, 85
Source program, 76
Specialist journals for health care computing, 210

Specialists in health care computing
  skills of, 205-208
  training of, 113, 203-214
Specifications
  functional; *see* Functional specifications
  hardware, definition of, 46
  of software, 85
SPSS applications package, 79
Staff
  cost of, in health care computing, 167
  development of, 90
  operational, 91-92
  reduction of turnover of, in health care computing, 170
Stanford University and degree program in health care information science, 208, 209
Star network structure, 40
  description of, 41
Start bits, 35-36
Start/stop transmission, 34
Starter system, growth of, 192
Statistics software package and errors, 129
Stop bits, 35-36
Storage
  of data in functional specification, 86
  expansion of, 71
Storage devices, 23-26
  definition of, 7
  mass, 23
Stored program, 58
Structured programming
  principles of, 60
  of software development, 126-127
Structured walk-through and software development, 127
Students of health care computing, 212-213
Sublanguages, purpose of, 78
Summary of proposal for health care–computing system, 221
Supercomputers, cost of, 29-30
Supplementary courses in health care computing, 209-210
Suppliers
  and contract, 86
  for hardware, 49-52
  selection of, 88-89
Supplies
  cost of, in health care computing, 167-168
  saving of, in health care computing, 170
Swapping as time-sharing system, 67, 68
Symposia for health care computing, 211-212
Symposium on Computer Applications in Medical Care, 211
Synchronous communications, 36-37
Synthesizers, voice output, 22-23
System integrator, function of, 47-48
Systems
  admitting/discharge/transfer, 217
  alarm, 104-105
  base 2, 11-13
  base 10, 11-13
  binary, 11-13
  computer; *see* Computer systems
  decimal, 11
  definition of, 4
  do-it-yourself, 87-88
  event-driven operating, 68-70
  hospital-discharge summary abstraction, 101-103
  multiprogramming, definition of, 69

Systems—cont'd
  multitasking, definition of, 69
  operating; *see* Operating systems
  turnkey; *see* Turnkey systems
  upward compatible, description of, 50
Systems analysts
  definition of, 60
  role of, 84
  and software development, 90
Systems developer
  and functional specification, 175-177
  management of, in health care computing, 113
Systems documentation, function of, 128
Systems house as computer system supplier, 88
Systems software, definition of, 8, 164

T

Tape device, function of, 23
Tape reels, storage capacity of, 23
Tapes, magnetic; *see* Magnetic tapes
Task, definition of, 69
Tax credit for capital equipment, 49, 171
Taxonorics, description of, 100
Technical journals and health care computing, 211
Technological imperative
  and computer systems, 5
  definition of, 216
Technology
  definition of, 216
  humanizing of, 136-141
  limitations of, 97-108
Temperature, pulse, respiration chart, 104
Tender, legal, in computer purchase, 50-51
Terminal
  definition of, 15
  dumb, definition of, 15
  hard copy, 16
  intelligent, description of, 28-29
  portable, requirements for, 99
  smart, definition of, 15
Test results, clinical, definition of effectiveness of, 162
Testing
  as phase of software development, 125, 128-130
  of program
    definition of, 61
    levels of, 130
  of system in functional specification, 181
Tests, clinical, and use of computer systems, 171
Threats to security of computer-based data, 148-153
Throughput, definition of, 29, 46, 65
Time
  down-, cost of, 141
  turnaround, 86
Time-driven operating systems, 67-68
Time-sharing
  as alternative to hardware purchase, 49
  and asynchronous communication, 36
  description of, 68
  types of, 67
Toll-free number for software maintenance, 88
Top-down development of software design, 126-127
Touch screens, function of, 18
TPR chart; *see* Temperature, pulse, respiration chart
Tracks of disk, 25
Training of health care–computing specialists, 113, 203-214

106797

```
362.1028  Covvey, H.
C873c     Dominic.

          Concepts and
            issues in health
            care computing
```

$28.95

DATE			

© THE BAKER & TAYLOR CO.